OUR "REGULAR" READERS RAVE!

"**I** received some money for my birthday a few years back and I picked up a *Bathroom Reader* at a local bookstore. My life hasn't been the same since! I *NEVER* make a trip to the john without my beloved book."

—*Michael S. (Pennsylvania)*

"Your books are the sources of many conversations, deep thoughts, and of course, many late appointments from sitting in the bathroom too long."

—*John S. (Ontario)*

"I'm a card-carrying member of both the Bathroom Readers Institute and the Society of Professional Journalists. It would be a lie if I were to say I was familiar with your work "only in passing." The researchers at the BRI need to know that their tireless investigations into the very frontiers of completely useless knowledge are not going unappreciated."

—*James W. (Mississippi)*

"I've been a fan since I was ten. Since I could read, I've read in the bathroom. There would always be about 20 books in there, but this always upset my mom: 'Alex, these books are getting ruined.' Finally I found the *Bathroom Reader* and she said I could have it if it was the *only* book I would keep in there.

I now have 5 (it would be 6, but one fell in the tub while reading). I hung it on the shower rod to dry but mold grew instead, and Mom made me throw it out saying it was a health hazard.

I'm glad I found the *Bathroom Readers*."

—*A Faithful Reader, Alex (Texas)*

"I just wanted to let you know how much I love *Uncle John's Bathroom Readers!* My mom says she wishes she had saved the money that she spent sending me to college, since I quote the *Readers* more than anything I learned in school! I refer to them as 'the source of all knowledge and wisdom.' I even enjoyed re-reading some of them when I was in labor with each of my two kids."

—*Leslie C. (Minnesota)*

"As a trivia buff cursed with a short attention span, your books are tailor-made for me. You keep writing 'em, I'll keep buying 'em. And recommending them to my friends."

—*Deborah W. (Colorado)*

"I've spent many hours on the throne laughing, crying, and just stunned in awe while reading yours books. They are filled with so much knowledge I thought my head was going to explode. I even got stuck on the toilet once for staying there so long reading, I needed the fire department to help me out. (I have the police report on that, too.)"

—*Doug L. (New York)*

"I picked up *Uncle John's Absolutely Absorbing Bathroom Reader* from a U.S. bookstore. It's now my bible, my encyclopedia, and my claim to fame. It's a most satisfying feeling, you know, to have an edge."

—*Shani G. (Pakistan)*

"Without your books, I'd be unable to supply my friends and family with random information at the best of times. For example, while taking a presentation skills class yesterday, I wowed the presenter with the fact about how Abe Lincoln's high, squeaky voice helped his campaign speeches travel further through the crowds. Thanks again, BRI."

—*Ephraim F. (New Mexico)*

Uncle John's
ALL-PURPOSE
EXTRA
STRENGTH
BATHROOM
READER®

The Bathroom Readers' Institute

Bathroom Readers' Press
Ashland, Oregon

UNCLE JOHN'S
ALL-PURPOSE EXTRA STRENGTH
BATHROOM READER®

For information, write The Bathroom Readers' Institute, P.O. Box 1117, Ashland, OR 97520
www.bathroomreader.com

Cover design by Michael Brunsfeld, San Rafael, CA (*brunsfeldo@comcast.com*)

BRI "technician" on back cover: Larry Kelp

Uncle John's All-Purpose Extra Strength Bathroom Reader®
by The Bathroom Readers' Institute

ISBN: 1-57145-494-2

Library of Congress Catalog Card Number: 00-091923

Printed in the United States of America

Seventh printing: 2003

17 16 15 14 13 12 11 10 9 8

* * * * *

THANK YOU!

The Bathroom Readers' Institute sincerely thanks the people whose advice and assistance made this book possible.

John Javna
Gordon Javna
John Dollison
Jennifer
Jeff Altemus
Jay Newman
Jennifer Strange
John Darling
Jeff Cheek
Selene Foster
Erin Keenan
Antares Multimedia
Michael Brunsfeld
Jonathan Lee F.
Sharilyn Hovind
Claudia Bauer
Dee & Kellar
Liz Stahlman
Ask Janis Editorial
Greg Younger
Eric Stahlman
Taylor Clark
Lori Larson

Mike Nicita
Allen Orso
Elizabeth McNulty
JoAnn Padgett
Bobby Wong
Mana Monzavi
Margaret Faherty
Alisa Judge
The AMS/APG staff
Kim Weimer
Paul Stanley
Lonnie Kirk
Randy Apa
Barb Porshe
Debra Gates
Paula Leith
Uncle Edgester
Mustard Press
Beanery/Evos/Blue Mtn.
Thomas Crapper
Marley & Catie Pratt
Jesse & Sophie, *B.R.I.T.*
Hi to Emily and Molly!

*　　*　　*

Muppet creator Jim Henson created Kermit
the Frog by cutting up his mother's coat.

CONTENTS

NOTE

Because the BRI understands your reading needs, we've divided the contents by length as well as subject.

Short—a quick read

Medium—2 to 3 pages

Long—for those extended visits, when something a little more involved is required

*Extended—for those leg-numbing experiences

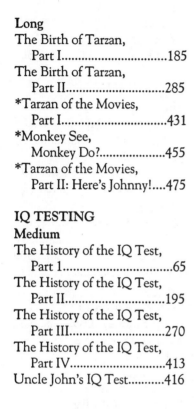

OOPS!

"British education officials were red-faced Friday after having to
scrap 48,000 literacy posters sent to teachers with two glaring
spelling mistakes. It shouldn't have happened. The Department
of Education failed to notice that 'vocabulary' was misspelled 'vo-
cabluary' and that pupils were being urged to learn about writing
'though' their own work instead of 'through' it. The posters have
been reprinted and sent to schools with letters blaming the blunder
on [the proofreaders]."

—Reuters

MADERA, CA—"A sheriff's SWAT team surrounded a house for
seven hours because the sound of a blown tire nearby made a police
officer believe he had been fired on from inside."

—News of the Weird

INTRODUCTION

A t last we made it to the front page. Do you read the introduction first?...or do you read it last? If you do read it last, that makes sense, because we write it last. In fact, we should probably call it the "Outroduction."

Here at the BRI we work late into the night, every night, for weeks before deadline, drinking gallons of organic coffee (Jeff prefers a French roast) so we can stay awake shuffling pages, re-writing, re-editing...and then...VOILA! Our new favorite book is ready to go to press.

Then we write the introduction.

Why wait? Well, we don't really know what important bits of information we need to pass on until we get to the end of the book. For example, now we can tell you...

• This is our 13th edition, so we've included a few extra pieces about superstitions, lucky numbers, and...triskaidekaphobia. And believe it or not, the book actually goes to print on Friday the 13th (We're not kidding—October 13, 2000). Hmm. Watch out.

• Another thing. The other day, as J.D. (our senior writer) was putting the finishing touches on his great history of Tarzan, we realized that this book contains quite a few pieces about monkeys and chimpanzees. And then Jennifer noticed that all of our inter-office communications referred to the new book, *All-Purpose Extra Strength,* by its acronym: A.P.E.S. Get it? Well, we all thought it was pretty spooky.

And finally...

Last week one of our new staffers took a phone call from a reader who wanted to tell us about a mistake he said we made several years ago. We quoted author Mario Puzo saying that he had invented the term "godfather." But the caller was sure we were wrong—he'd just seen the *real* story on TV. Turns out, in an old newsreel, a mobster testifying before Congress used the term first.

Our rookie was amazed. He couldn't believe how loyal and dedicated our readers are to the BRI mission. And now that we mention it, he's right—it *is* incredible. Every year we get tons of letters of thanks, praise, ideas, suggestions, and (we don't mind them) corrections. And, amazingly, every year our ranks get bigger.

So, now it's our turn. Thank you, loyal readers, for being part of our BRI family. We're glad you like what we do, because we like doing it.

Is that our mission? Well, it's one of them. Another one is to remind you that...

It's a weird world out there, so keep on flushin'.

And, as always,

Go with the flow.

—Uncle John and the BRI staff

P.S. If you're looking for the long-promised "History of the Bra," we're sorry to let you down. It's not ready yet. Yes, we've been promising it for years, but we *swear* it'll be ready...next year.

YOU'RE MY INSPIRATION

*It's fascinating to find out the inspirations
behind cultural milestones like these.*

POPEYE. A real Popeye? Apparently so. E. C. Segar's character was based on a beady-eyed, pipe-smoking, wiry old barroom brawler named Frank "Rocky" Feigle—a legend in Segar's hometown of Chester, Illinois, around 1915. Like Popeye, Feigle was reputed never to have lost a fight. But he was no sailor; he earned his drinking money by sweeping out the local saloon.

Note: There was a real Olive Oyl, too: Dora Paskel, a shopkeeper in Chester. She was tall and skinny, wore her hair in a bun, and even wore tall, button-up shoes.

ROCKY. In March 1975 Chuck Wepner fought Muhammed Ali for the heavyweight boxing title. Wepner, a second-rate fighter from Bayonne, New Jersey, was considered a joke. Ali didn't even bother training full-time for the match. But to everyone's surprise, Wepner lasted 15 rounds with the champ, and even knocked him down. Sly Stallone saw the fight on TV, and was inspired to write his Oscar-winning screenplay about Rocky Balboa.

STAGE NAMES
• Nicolas Coppola "always loved the comic book character, Luke Cage, Power Man." So he changed his name to Nicolas Cage.
• Roy Scherer got his stage name by combining two geographical spots: the Rock of Gibraltar and the Hudson River: Rock Hudson.

THE SHINING. Inspired by John Lennon...or at least the term was. Stephen King came up with the idea of the "shining" as a description of psychic power after hearing Lennon's tune "Instant Karma." King recalls: "The refrain went, 'We all shine on.' I really liked that, and used it. The [book's] name was originally *The Shine*, but somebody said, 'You can't use that because it's a pejorative word for Black'....So it became *The Shining*."

Today as many people live in the U.S. (270 million) as lived in the entire world in 1000 A.D.

COURT TRANSQUIPS

We're back with one of our regular features. Do court transcripts make good bathroom reading? Check out these real-life quotes. They're things people actually said in court, recorded word for word.

Lawyer: "Okay, we've talked at length about how the accident happened, is there anything we haven't covered that you can think of, anything in your mind that you're thinking about how the accident happened that I haven't asked you and you're thinking 'he hasn't asked me that' and 'I'm not going to tell him because he hasn't asked me,' is there anything?"
Witness: "Have you lost your mind?"

Q: "Mr. Slatery, you went on a rather elaborate honeymoon, didn't you?"
A: "I went to Europe, sir."
Q: "And you took your new wife?"

Q: "Doctor, as a result of your examination of the plaintiff, is the young lady pregnant?"
A: "The young lady is pregnant, but not as a result of my examination."

Q: "Why do you handle the family finances?"
A: "Because my mom and sister ain't that bright."

Q: "Is there a difference between a reconditioned and rebuilt piece of equipment in your mind, if you have one?"

Q: "How far apart were the vehicles at the time of the collision?"

Q: "Are you being selective about what you remember and what you don't remember as to the details of your previous record?"
A: "I don't remember."

Q: "Now doctor, isn't it true that when a person dies in his sleep, he doesn't know about it until the next morning?"

Q: "She had three children, right?"
A: "Yes."
Q: "How many were boys?"
A: "None."
Q: "Were there any girls?"

Defendant: "You know, I hate coming out here at seven in the morning and sitting downstairs with a bunch of criminals."
Judge: "I have to do the same thing every day."
Defendant: "Yeah, but you don't have to sit down in a holding tank with 'em."
Judge: "Every day I come in and I meet the dregs of society, and then I have to meet their clients."

Q: "The youngest son, the twenty-year old, how old is he?"

ORIGINS

Once again, the BRI asks—and answers—the
question: where did all this stuff come from?

GRANOLA

In the 1860s a "fanatical vegetarian hydrotherapist" named Dr. James Caleb Jackson created a breakfast food consisting of twice-baked whole wheat graham dough, crumbled into pebble-sized clusters. He named his creation Granula...and attracted the attention of Dr. John Harvey Kellogg. Years away from inventing corn flakes, Kellogg was looking for something to serve for breakfast at his Battle Creek, Michigan sanitarium besides crackers and dry toast. Dr. Kellogg made his own crumbly cereal using a baked mixture of wheat flour, cornmeal, and oatmeal...and like Dr. Jackson, he called his new food Granula. Jackson sued. Kellogg lost—and changed the spelling of his cereal to *Granola*.

BUTTON-DOWN SHIRTS

In the 1920s it became fashionable for wealthy vacationers on the French Riviera to wear "polo shirts"—lightweight knit shirts with collars adapted by polo players from a shirt worn by Basque fishermen. The polo players added button-down collar points so that collars wouldn't fly up in their faces during a hard gallop...and at the turn of the century a New York haberdasher named John Brooks saw the shirts in England. He sent some home to his family business—Brooks Brothers—which incorporated the collar into a line of dress shirts.

NEWSPAPERS

The first medium used to spread news and information is believed to be the *Acta Diurna* ("Daily Events"), founded by Julius Caesar in 59 B.C. Posted in prominent areas and gathering places all over Rome, the daily paper contained news items as well as birth, death, and marriage announcements, updates on criminal trials and executions...and even news of sporting and theatrical events.

PARACHUTES

The trouble with inventing parachutes is that if you test them yourself, you only have one chance to get it right. Andre-Jacques Garnerin became the first person to invent a *successful* parachute in 1797, when he took a hot-air balloon up to 3,000 feet and then floated back to earth in a basket tethered to a parachute similar to a large umbrella.

TRAFFIC LIGHTS

The world's first blinking green-and-red traffic light is believed to be the one erected on the corner of George and Bridge Streets in London, near Parliament. The manually-operated signal featured a red gaslight for "stop" and a green light for "caution." The sign was operated by a constable standing watch for members of Parliament who wanted to cross the busy street.

The first American traffic light was installed at Euclid Avenue and 105th St. in Cleveland, Ohio on August 4, 1904. It had red and green lights, and a warning buzzer to let motorists know when the light was about to change. Why *red* and *green* lights? They're believed to be descended from the practice of hanging red lights on trains that weren't moving.

CHOPSTICKS

"According to one theory of their origin, food was cooked in large pots, which held the heat long after everything was ready to be eaten. Hungry people burned their fingers reaching into the pot, so they sought alternatives, and grasping the morsels with a pair of sticks protected the fingers. Another version credits Confucius with advising against the use of knives at the table, since they would remind the diners of the kitchen and the slaughterhouse, places the 'honorable and upright man keeps well away from.'"

—*The Evolution of Useful Things*, by Henry Petroski

*   *   *

"It may be the cock that crows, but it's the hen that lays the egg."

—*Margaret Thatcher*

OOPS!

Everyone is amused by tales of outrageous blunders—probably because it's comforting to know that someone's screwing up even worse than we are. So go ahead and feel superior for a few minutes.

A FINE BOUQUET?

"Wine merchant William Sokolin had paid $300,000 for a 1787 bottle of Châteaux Margaux once owned by Thomas Jefferson. He presented it before a group of 300 wine collectors at Manhattan's Four Seasons restaurant in 1989, hoping that one of them might offer $519,000 for it. Before bidders could get out their checkbooks, he dropped the bottle and broke it."

—*Oops!*, **by Smith and Decter**

WHAT A CLOWN

"On its July 30 'Family Fun' page, the *Kansas City Star* ran a blurb on National Clown Week. Accompanying the text, naturally enough, was a photo of a clown. But the editor selecting the file photo neglected to look at the flip side, which would have revealed that the clown in question was John Wayne Gacy, a Chicago serial killer (and onetime clown) executed five years ago for killing 33 boys and young men. The *Star* apologized the next day in an editor's note."

—*Brill's Content*

1-900-JACK-ASS

"Harold Reinke in Troy, New York, called a European 900 sex line that charged $9.95 per minute. There was only one problem—Reinke was drunk and fell asleep. He woke up hours later still connected. The bill? $7,164."

—*Bizarre News*

COULD WE DROP THE DROP?

"The Joseph A. Bank Clothiers, Inc., of Atlanta, Georgia, requested that the word 'Inc.' be dropped from its listing in the 1982 telephone directory yellow pages. As a result, the store was listed as 'Drop Inc.'"

—*Atlanta Constitution*

Among his other hobbies, ex-Beatle Ringo Starr likes to design furniture.

SINCERELY YOURS...

"The Clinton Legal Expense Trust, set up to defray President Clinton's legal expenses, sent fundraising letters to names on a Democratic mailing list. Apparently no one screened them—one went to Bernard Lewinsky, Monica's father. His written response: 'You must be morons to send me this letter!'"

—*Time* magazine

NOT JUST ANY MAN

"At a White House reception for the nation's mayors, President Ronald Reagan went up to a black man, shook his hand and said, 'How are you, Mr. Mayor? I'm glad to see you. How are things in your city?' The man Reagan didn't recognize was Samuel Pierce, the Secretary of Housing and Urban Development, who regularly attended Cabinet meetings at which Reagan was present."

—*Oops!,* by Smith and Decter

WEEKNIGHT AT BERNIE'S?

"Last October, Ian Clifton of Sheffield, England, slumped over in a pub after consuming 11 pints of lager and untold amounts of bathtub punch. Pub regulars [who assumed he had passed out] shaved off his hair and took pictures of him posed with an inflatable doll. Actually, Clifton had died of acute alcoholic poisoning. By the time [his mates realized their mistake] and called paramedics, Clifton had been dead for about an hour."

—*Bizarre News*

SUB-CONTRACT

"To make a few extra bucks, Canada sold two old navy destroyers, the *Kootenay* and the *Restigouche,* to Richard Crawford of Florida. However, they inadvertently transformed him into a military power because they forgot to remove a 10-foot-tall, eight-barreled anti-submarine launcher from one of the ships. Embarrassed Defense Department officials announced that Crawford wouldn't be allowed to leave Canadian waters until he turned in his guns."

—*In These Times*

WAS IT MURDER...
OR SUICIDE?

Uncle John was going through some old files recently and found this article from Fire and Rescue *magazine. It was sent to us back in 1996 by Mica Calfee of Duncanville, Texas. We don't know how it got misplaced, but better late than never. (Your free book is on its way, Mica.) This story is so amazing that it's hard to believe.*
It's repeated in the film Magnolia.

A BIZARRE DEATH

At the 1995 annual awards dinner given by the American Association for Forensic Science, AAFS president Don Harper Mills astounded his audience in San Diego with the legal complications of a bizarre death. Here is the story:

"On 23rd March, 1994, the medical examiner viewed the body of Ronald Opus and concluded that he died from a shotgun wound to the head. The deceased had jumped from the top of a 10-story building intending to commit suicide (he left a note indicating his despondency). As he fell past the ninth floor, his fall was interrupted by a shotgun blast through a window, which killed him instantly.

"Neither the shooter nor the deceased was aware that a safety net had been erected at the eighth floor level to protect some window washers and that Opus would not have been able to complete his suicide because of this."

A HOMICIDE?

"Ordinarily," Dr. Mills continued, "a person who sets out to commit suicide ultimately succeeds, even though the mechanism might not be what he intended. That Opus was shot on the way to certain death nine stories below probably would not have changed his mode of death from suicide to homicide. But the fact that his suicidal intent would not have been successful caused the medical examiner to feel that he had a homicide on his hands.

"The room on the ninth floor (where the shotgun blast came from) was occupied by an elderly man and his wife. They were arguing and he was threatening her with the shotgun. He was so upset that, when he pulled the trigger, he completely missed his wife and pellets went through the window striking Opus. When one intends to kill subject A but kills subject B in the attempt, one is guilty of the murder of subject B."

AN ACCIDENT?

"When confronted with this charge, the old man and his wife were both adamant that neither knew that the shotgun was loaded. The old man said it was his long-standing habit to threaten his wife with the unloaded shotgun. He had no intention of murdering her—therefore, the killing of Opus appeared to be an accident. That is, the gun had been accidentally loaded.

"The continuing investigation turned up a witness who saw the old couple's son loading the shotgun approximately six weeks prior to the fatal incident. It transpired that the old lady had cut off her son's financial support, and the son, knowing the propensity of his father to use the shotgun threateningly, had loaded the gun with the expectation that his father would shoot his mother.

"The case now becomes one of murder on the part of the son for the death of Ronald Opus."

ALL OF THE ABOVE

"There was an exquisite twist. Further investigation revealed that the son, one Ronald Opus, had become increasingly despondent over the failure of his attempt to engineer his mother's murder. This led him to jump off the 10-story building on March 23rd, only to be killed by a shotgun blast through a ninth-story window.

"The medical examiner closed the case as a suicide."

*   *   *

A BRI "FAVORITE ROLE MODEL"

Role Model: Barbara De Angelis, bestselling author of *Making Love Work, Are You the One For Me?*, and others.

Setting An Example: She's been married five times. (Once, ironically, to another relationship guru—John "Venus-Mars" Gray)

Actually, the article above is an urban legend. But this is exactly how they're spread, isn't it?

THE CLASSIFIEDS

Have you ever been in a place where all you can find to read in the bathroom is an old newspaper? Try flipping to the classifieds and look for unintentionally goofy ads and notices like these. (Then send them to us!)

FOR SALE

Mixing bowl set designed to please a cook with round bottom for efficient beating.

Snow blower for sale...only used on snowy days.

Great Dames for sale.

Four-poster bed, 101 years old. Perfect for antique lover.

Free puppies...part German Shepherd, part dog.

'83 Toyota hunchback—$2,000.

Free puppies: Half cocker spaniel, half sneaky neighbor's dog.

Free Yorkshire Terrier: Eight years old. Unpleasant little dog.

Full-sized mattress, 20 yr. warranty. Like new. Slight urine smell.

Nordic Track: $300. Hardly used. Call Chubbie.

WANTED

Mother's helper—peasant working conditions.

Attractive Girl Needed. Exciting interesting work. Lucrative. Nudity required.

Wanted: Unmarried girls to pick fresh fruit and produce at night.

Girl wanted to assist magician in cutting-off-head illusion. Blue Cross and salary.

MISCELLANEOUS

Notice: To person or persons who took the large pumpkin on Highway 87 near Southridge Storage. Please return the pumpkin and be checked. Pumpkin may be radioactive. All other plants in vicinity are dead.

Open house: Body shapers, toning salon. Free coffee and donuts.

Publicize your business absolutely free! Send $6.

Found: Dirty white dog... looks like a rat...been out awhile...better be reward.

Lost: Small apricot poodle. Reward. Neutered. Like one of the family.

Get a Little John: The traveling urinal holds 2 1/2 bottles of beer.

Twice as many people live in Shanghai, China as in New York City.

WORD ORIGINS

Ever wonder where words come from?
Here are some interesting stories.

BOOTLEGGER

Meaning: Someone illegally distributing alcohol

Origin: "In the 19th century, bootleggers actually carried illicit merchandise in the legs of high boots when making deliveries. The term was well-known and since their most common commodity was liquor, it gradually became applied exclusively to distributors of illegal booze." (From *Dictionary of Word and Phrase Origins*, by William and Mary Morris)

SHREWD

Meaning: Clever, cunning

Origin: "Probably derives from the mouselike shrew, which will fight for the smallest morsel...and finish the meal by eating its defeated foe. Original meaning: 'wicked, dangerous, ugly.' By the 16th century, it had its current meaning." (From *Take My Words*, by Howard Richler)

PLAYING HOOKY

Meaning: Skipping school

Origin: "First appeared in the late 1840s. It probably comes from the Dutch *hoekje*, a name for the game of hide and seek. The derivation is obviously one of skipping school to play games." (From *Etymologically Speaking*, by Steven Morgan Friedman)

CADDIE

Meaning: A person hired to carry a golfer's clubs

Origin: "From the French word *cadet*, for 'younger son.' In noble families the second son inherited neither title nor fortune and consequently often joined the army. The word *cadet* retained this military meaning, but acquired the connotation of someone who hung around waiting to be called on to do errands. This kind of cadet was abbreviated to caddie." (From *Fighting Words*, by Christine Ammer)

Marilyn Monroe's dog was named Maf. It was a gift from Frank Sinatra.

FAMOUS FOR 15 MINUTES

Here it is—our feature based on Andy Warhol's prophetic remark that "in the future, everyone will be famous for 15 minutes." Here's how a few folks have used up their allotted quarter-hour.

THE STAR: Tony Wilson, 29, a British light heavyweight boxer in the late 1980s

THE HEADLINE: *Boxer Wins Bout…With Help From Mom*

WHAT HAPPENED: In September 1989, Wilson fought a bout with Steve McCarthy. Wilson was losing: In the middle of the third round, McCarthy landed a punch that sent Wilson to the canvas for an eight count and then pinned him against the ropes as soon as he got up.

That was all Wilson's 62-year-old mother could take. Somehow she managed to jump over rows of spectators, get past security guards, and climb into the ring. She removed her high-heeled shoe and began clubbing McCarthy on the head with it, opening a wound in his scalp. The referee stopped the fight for a few minutes, then ordered McCarthy and Wilson to resume fighting. McCarthy, bleeding profusely from his head, refused…and the referee disqualified him. He awarded the match to Wilson.

THE AFTERMATH: Newspapers all over the world ran the story the following day, turning Wilson from a promising fighter into a laughingstock—the first boxer in the history of the sport to win a match with help from his mother. He barred her from attending any more of his fights, but it was too late; his career was already on the ropes.

THE STAR: Daron Malmborg, a Utah motorist

THE HEADLINE: *Vanity Plate Injures Utah's Vanity*

WHAT HAPPENED: In 1999, it was disclosed that Salt Lake City officials had given cash and other gifts to members of the International Olympic Committee, trying to secure the 2002 Olympics for their city. Outraged, Malmborg ordered commemorative "Olympics"

license plates for his car…and customized the tag number to read SCNDL.

Malmborg had the special plates for 11 months when he received a letter from the Department of Motor Vehicles ordering him to give them back. Malmborg's lawyer—license plate "ISUE4U"—referred him to the American Civil Liberties Union, which took the case public.

THE AFTERMATH: The Associated Press picked up on the story, and it became fodder for TV and radio talk show hosts all over the country. Ultimately, the state backed down and let Malmborg keep his plates. According to press reports, "SCNDL was Malmborg's second choice for the plate. His first—'BRIBE'— was turned down because someone else already had it."

THE STAR: "Miracle" Morris Lieberman, a furniture salesman from Queens, New York who was addicted to being "famous for 15 seconds."

THE HEADLINE: *Salesman Sneaks His Way Into High Society*

WHAT HAPPENED: In 1928, 16-year-old Morris picked up his unusual hobby by accident. He went to a political rally for presidential candidate Al Smith, saw an empty seat in the front row next to Smith's family, and sat in it. When Smith's entourage left the rally, Lieberman followed close behind—so close, in fact, that the following morning a photograph of Smith and Lieberman together appeared on the front page of at least two newspapers.

Lieberman was hooked. He began crashing parties in his spare time and getting photographed with presidents, royalty, and movie stars.

"I could look up at Adlai Stevenson, Eleanor Roosevelt, the Duke of Windsor arriving at a tribute diner," a *New York Post* columnist wrote in 1974, "and there would be Miracle Morris chatting intimately with them as though he was reception chairman."

THE AFTERMATH: In the late 1970s, Lieberman hung up his tuxedo and retired to Florida…and that's when he became famous. He proudly told reporters that in his 50 years of gatecrashing, he was never once asked to leave…and he was never once accompanied by his wife, Fay, who refused to go anyplace she wasn't invited. "It was his thing," she explains. "He didn't smoke, drink, or fool around. He liked being around important people."

THE STAR: Rollin Stewart, a.k.a. Rainbow Man
THE HEADLINE: *Clown-Wigged Crusader Says: John 3:16!*

WHAT HAPPENED: During a 1976 trip to Mardi Gras, Stewart had a vision. It told him to take a sign that read "John 3:16" (a passage in the *Bible*) to nationally televised sporting events and wave it for the television cameras while wearing a rainbow-colored clown wig.

"I wanted to go into show business," he explained a few years later, "and I got this idea for a character who could be a people pleaser. My ultimate goal was to be an actor and spend an occasional day shooting a commercial, then sit back and collect the residual checks."

Stewart never made much money off of his clown-wig crusade for Christ, but by 1980, the year he gave up the sign, he'd become one of the most recognized figures in the sports world, even if nobody knew who he was.

AFTERMATH: Stewart couldn't bear to be out of the limelight. He blew an air horn on the 16th green of the 1991 Masters Tournament, set off some stink bombs in Robert Schuller's Crystal Cathedral during a service, and then did it again during the title fight between Evander Holyfield and George Foreman. His final "stunt" (so far) was in 1992, when, brandishing a .45-caliber assault rifle, he barricaded himself in a hotel room near the L.A. International Airport and threatened to shoot down arriving jumbo jets "if he wasn't given three hours of network television prime time to offer his views of world politics, the weather situation, and the Second Coming of Jesus." The seige ended when a SWAT team broke down the door and took him into custody. Today Stewart is serving three concurrent life sentences in the California prison system.

*　　*　　*

"If you can't beat them, arrange to have them beaten."
—*George Carlin*

Longest Main Street in the U.S.: The one in Island Park, Idaho. It's more than 33 miles long.

D'OH!

Words of wisdom from Homer Simpson,
America's most popular animated father.

"Kids, you tried your best and you failed miserably. The lesson is, never try."

"If you really want something in this life, you have to work for it. Now quiet! They're about to announce the lottery numbers."

"TV respects me. It laughs with me, not at me!"

"Old people don't need companionship. They need to be isolated and studied so it can be determined what nutrients they have that might be extracted for our personal use."

"If the Bible has taught us nothing else—and it hasn't—it's that girls should stick to girls' sports, such as hot-oil wrestling, foxy boxing, and such-and-such."

"Weaseling out of things is important to learn. It's what separates us from the animals! Except the weasel."

"Kill my boss?! Do I dare live out the American dream?"

"The whole reason we have elected officials is so we don't have to think all the time. Just like that rain forest scare a few years back: our officials saw there was a problem and they fixed it...didn't they?"

"Son, when you participate in sporting events, it's not whether you win or lose, it's how drunk you get."

"Facts are meaningless. You could use facts to prove anything that's even remotely true!"

"English? Who needs that? I'm never going to England!"

"A woman is like a beer. They look good, they smell good, and you'd step over your own mother just to get one!"

"Crying isn't going to bring the dog back...unless your tears smell like dog food."

"Cartoons don't have any deep meaning. They're just stupid drawings that give you a cheap laugh."

Scientists say: There are more creatures in your mouth than there are humans on earth.

CLASSIC (B)AD CAMPAIGNS

Every year, we feature stories of ad campaigns or promotions that backfired. There seems to be an endless supply—which leads us to believe either that Murphy's Law is alive and well (see page 46) or there are an awful lot of clueless marketing people. What do you think?

SKY HIGH

Brilliant Marketing Idea: In 1999 the Healthy Choice diet food line offered 1,000 frequent flier miles to anyone who sent in 10 proof-of-purchase seals from *any* of their products.

Oops: The company made the classic blunder of awarding a prize worth more than the item being sold. David Philips of Davis, California, figured that out. When he saw the proof-of-purchase seals on Healthy Choice's 25¢ pudding cups, "I quickly realized that for 25¢, I was getting 100 free miles," he says. So Philips bought $3,140 worth of the diet pudding cups (which he donated to food banks), and earned 1.25 million frequent flier miles, good for $25,000 worth of airline flights. The promotion was discontinued.

I'M NOT A DRINKER, BUT I PLAY ONE ON TV

Brilliant Marketing Idea: Hire superstar musician Eric Clapton to be a part of Anheuser-Busch's "The Night Belongs to Michelob" advertising campaign.

Oops: Clapton was an alcoholic. Shortly after the ad was filmed, the guitarist checked himself into an drug rehab clinic...and was actually in treatment in Minnesota when the ad premiered on TV. The first time he saw it, he says, "I was in a room full of alcoholics, myself being one of them, and everybody went, 'Is that *you?*'" Anheuser-Busch quickly pulled the ad.

HEIL HEATER

Brilliant Marketing Idea: In 1999 the Taiwanese trading company K. E. and Kingstone ran a promotion for German heaters, using the light-hearted slogan, "Declare War on the Cold Front!"

U.S. law requires that Yankee bean soup be served in the Congressional dining room at all times.

Oops: The war they had in mind was World War II. According to news reports, "The company's posters had a smiling caricature of Adolf Hitler in a khaki uniform and black jackboots, his right arm raised high in a salute." Faced with a storm of protest, the company's shell-shocked marketing manager explained that he hadn't intended to show support for Hitler—only to show that the heaters were made in Germany. "We thought it was just a comic picture," he said.

OFF WITH HIS...

Brilliant Marketing Idea: Court TV scheduled a series of specials on Super Bowl Sunday, hoping to attract women uninterested in the game.

Oops: Every single one of the specials turned out to be a story about a woman who attacked her husband—starting with the trial of Lorena Bobbitt, accused of cutting off her husband's genitals. To make things worse, the network advertised the shows with a commercial depicting a disgruntled wife reaching for a knife to get revenge on a football-obsessed husband. The weekend before the Super Bowl, they issued a public apology.

CRASH COURSE

Brilliant Marketing Idea: Show a celebrity endorsing South Korea's Kia automobile.

Oops: The celebrity was Princess Diana, who was dead...and the company's TV ad re-created the car crash that killed her. London media reported that the commercial showed a "Diana lookalike in a Kia being chased through the streets by paparazzi...then emerging from the wreck unhurt and giving the camera a knowing wink." Kia withdrew the ad.

*　　*　　*

IT'S A WEIRD, WEIRD WORLD

"Alaskan authorities have been hunting a gunman who has held up 21 people and forced them to whistle, 'Hail, Hail, the Gang's All Here.' He has never hurt anyone or stolen any property."

—*Portland Oregonian*

Beavers' teeth are so sharp that Native Americans once used them as knife blades.

"SPECIAL" EVENTS FOR TOURISTS

We're always on the lookout for bizarre tourist attractions…and these events—which attract tens of thousands of people every year—definitely qualify.

THE BUG BOWL

Location: Purdue University, West Lafayette, Indiana

Background: In 1990, a Purdue professor named Tom Turpin organized a cockroach race on campus to attract students to the field of entomology (the study of insects). Like roach problems, the Bug Bowl grew; today the Bug Bowl draws more than 12,000 people a year. But now there's a new attraction—tourists come not only to look at bugs, but to *eat* them.

Don't Miss: The exotic menu. Items include: mealworm chow mein; caterpillar crunch (a trail mix made with waxworms); chocolate chirpy chip cookies, which contain crickets; and basic bug quiche, made with sauteed bee larvae "or crickets, depending on your mood." There's also a cricket-spitting contest.

THE WORLD'S LARGEST RATTLESNAKE ROUNDUP

Location: Sweetwater, Texas

Background: Started in 1958, it takes place on the second full weekend of March. Inspired by area farmers and ranchers trying to get rid of the rattlers "that were plaguing them and their livestock." About 30,000 people show up each year to hunt and eat rattlesnakes. As of 1996, an astounding 231,636 pounds of western diamondback rattlesnake had been collected.

Don't Miss: The Rattlesnake Review Parade, the Miss Snake Charmer Queen Contest, rattlesnake dances, a snake-handling demonstration, instructions on snake-milking techniques, and of course, guided snake hunts. After the snakes are gutted and eaten, "the severed heads are adorned with blue wigs and Dallas Cowboys helmets."

THE REDNECK GAMES

Location: East Dublin, Georgia

Background: The only rules for tourists: If you don't like rednecks, stay home. "Some folks would prefer we didn't have this celebration of being a redneck," says East Dublin mayor George Goruto, "but they don't have to come down here. I mean, man, I wouldn't go to an opera!"

Don't Miss: The Mudpit Belly Flop, the Hubcap Hurl, Bobbing for Pigs' Feet, and the Armpit Serenade—a talent competition in which "pimply-faced prepubescents stick one hand up their T-shirts, flap the other arm and perform flatulent renditions of classics like 'Old MacDonald' and 'Green Acres.'" First prize: "a crumpled can of Bud."

THE MOSQUITO COOKOFF

Location: Crowley's Ridge State Park, Arkansas

Background: If the Bug Bowl whets your appetite, here's the next event to put on your itinerary. It's part of the annual World Championship Mosquito Cooking Contest. Participants try to top one another with recipes containing mosquitos. (Cooking the bugs for at least 30 minutes makes the mosquitos safe to eat.) "I'd also suggest using dry mosquitos," says park superintendent Larry Clifford, "so you don't get the gummy quality to it."

Don't Miss: The mosquito meat pie, mosquito supreme pizza, and mosquito paté.

AND DON'T FORGET...

• **The Annual Casket Race,** Goodwater, Alabama. "Pallbearers manhandle a coffin over an obstacle course, including a pile of sawdust and a mud-pit....The 'corpse' within must carry a cup of water through the course, not spilling one drop."

• **The National Hollerin' Contest,** Spivey's Corner, North Carolina. "Traces its origin to the tradition of local farmers yodeling hello to each other in the morning."

• **The International Worm Fiddling Contest,** Caryville, Florida. The challenge: "Drive a stake into the ground to entice worms to come up" and check out what's happening.

The planet Mercury is 800° F. at its equator, but has ice at its North and South Poles.

IT'S SERENDIPITY

The word "serendipity" means "making happy and unexpected discoveries by accident." The more we study the details of history—scientific, pop, political...or any kind at all—the more we realize just how many things that impact our lives are basically accidents. For example...

THE FIRST SYNTHETIC FIBER

In 1854 a devastating silkworm epidemic struck the silk industry in France, wiping it out, and in 1865 the renowned French scientist Louis Pasteur was asked to study the disease. One of his assistants, a young chemist named Hilaire de Chardonnet, became convinced that France needed some kind of artificial substitute for silk. Unfortunately, he had no idea how to find one.

In 1878 Chardonnet was working in a darkroom with some photographic plates when he knocked over a bottle of a photographic chemical called *collodion* (cellulose nitrate). He didn't bother to clean it up right away, and by the time he got around to it, much of the spill had evaporated. What was left? A sticky mess that produced "long, thin strands of fiber" as he wiped it up. The strands reminded him so much of silk fibers that he spent the next six years experimenting with the substance. Finally he invented what he called "artificial silk." In 1924 the name was changed to Rayon. It was the first commercially viable synthetic fiber, and paved the way for the entire synthetics industry.

THE FIRST ARTIFICIAL SWEETENER

In 1879 Constantin Fahlberg, a chemist at Johns Hopkins Universtiy, put in a long day at the lab. Then he washed up and went home for dinner. As he sat at the dinner table, Fahlberg noticed that the bread was surprisingly sweet. Then he realized that it wasn't the bread at all—it was something on his hands...and even his arms. He went back to the lab and tasted every beaker and basin he'd worked with that day (chemists weren't as cautious about poisoning themselves then). He finally found the source of the sweetness—a chemical called *ortho-sulfobenzoic acid imide*, which is 200-700 times as sweet as granulated sugar. Fahlberg patented the substance—the world's first artificial sweetener—in 1885 under the name saccharin, from *saccharum*, the Latin word for sugar.

A FEW POP ICONS

A Classic Movie: When Frank Capra's *It's a Wonderful Life* was released in 1946, it was dismissed by critics as sappy and sentimental; by the 1950s it was largely forgotten. In the mid-1970s the movie's copyright lapsed and nobody remembered—or bothered—to renew it. That made the film "public domain"—i.e., legally, TV stations could broadcast it for free. That's why so many stations started showing it every holiday season...which is what turned it into the "Christmastime classic" it is today.

A Popular Radio Show: In 1977 the Program Director at Boston's public radio station WBUR invited five Boston-area mechanics to sit on a panel for a call-in talk show about cars. Two of the mechanics he asked were brothers Tom and Ray Magliozzi, owners of the Good News Garage in Cambridge, Massachusetts. Ray was busy, but Tom accepted the offer...and turned out to be the *only* person who showed up. He answered callers' questions so well that he was asked to return the next week. The week after that, he brought Ray along—and they've been doing "Car Talk" together (as Click and Clack The Tappet Brothers) ever since.

A Movie Star: In 1983, Martha Coolidge, director of a film called *Valley Girl*, was angry with the casting director, who kept auditioning "pretty boys" for the lead role. So Coolidge went to the reject pile, pulled the first photo off the top, held it up and said. "Bring me someone like this." The picture was of Nicolas Cage, and he got the part. It was his first lead role.

...AND EVEN WORLD WAR II

"Private Henry Tandey had the man in his rifle sights at point-blank range. It was September 28, 1918, on the French battlefield of Marcoing...and Tandey's courage in battle that day would earn the young soldier [a medal]. Yet when Private Tandey realized the German corporal he was aiming for was already wounded, he couldn't bring himself to pull the trigger. Only years later did he realize that the object of his mercy was none other than Adolf Hitler." (*Bizarre* magazine)

Good news! A Karaoke singing of "We Are the World" burns 20.7 calories.

WISE WOMEN

Some thoughtful observations from members of the stronger sex.

"If the world were a logical place, men would ride side saddle."
—*Rita Mae Brown*

"Creative minds have always been known to survive any kind of bad training."
—*Anna Freud*

"Blessed is the man who, having nothing to say, abstains from giving worthy evidence of the fact."
—*George Eliot*

"If you just set out to be liked, you would be prepared to compromise on anything at any time, and you would achieve nothing."
—*Margaret Thatcher*

"If you don't risk anything, you risk even more."
—*Erica Jong*

"How wonderful it is that nobody need wait a single moment before starting to improve the world."
—*Anne Frank*

"It is not true that life is one damn thing after another. It's one damn thing over and over."
—*Edna St. Vincent Millay*

"The heresy of one age becomes the orthodoxy of the next."
—*Helen Keller*

"Regret is an appalling waste of energy; you can't build on it; it is only good for wallowing in."
—*Katherine Mansfield*

"In the face of an obstacle which is impossible to overcome, stubbornness is stupid."
—*Simone de Beauvoir*

"Spend the afternoon. You can't take it with you."
—*Annie Dillard*

"You can be up to your boobies in white satin, with gardenias in your hair and no sugarcane for miles, but you can still be working on a plantation."
—*Billie Holiday*

"You take your life in your own hands, and what happens? A terrible thing: no one to blame."
—*Erica Jong*

"Just remember, we're all in this alone."
—*Lily Tomlin*

Left to its own devices, 1 ton of iron can turn into 3 tons of rust.

FLUBBED HEADLINES

*These are 100% honest-to-goodness headlines. Can
you figure out what they were trying to say?*

*Lebanon Will Try
Bombing Suspects*

**Officials Warn Clams,
Oysters Can Carry Virus**

Man Shoots Neighbor
with Machete

STRIPPER RESENTS
EXPOSURE

*Multiple-Personality Rapist
Sentenced to Two Life Terms*

Iran Claims Success in Its
Attack on Iran

RETIRED PRIEST TO
MARRY SPRINGSTEEN

**Defendant's Speech Ends
in Long Sentence**

*Old School Pillars Are
Replaced by Alumni*

**19 Feet Broken in
Pole Vault**

Kicking Baby Considered
to Be Healthy

*Henshaw Offers Rare
Opportunity to Goose Hunters*

TERMINAL SMOG
NOT LETHAL

**Cause of Aids Found—
Scientists**

Police Kill Man
with TV Tuner

**Milk Drinkers Are
Turning to Powder**

*Bible Church's Focus
Is the Bible*

TWO CONVICTS EVADE
NOOSE, JURY HUNG

Stiff Opposition Expected to
Casketless Funeral Plan

**Council to Examine
Impotant Problems**

LITERARCY WEEK
OBSERVED

*Prosecutor Releases Probe
into Undersheriff*

Queen Mary Having
Bottom Scraped

LARGE CHURCH
PLANS COLLAPSE

***Potential Witness to
Murder Drunk***

BRITAIN INCHES GRUDGINGLY
TOWARDS METRIC SYSTEM

NJ JUDGE TO RULE
ON NUDE BEACH

Official: Only rain will cure
drought

When pronounced correctly, Chinese surnames never have more than one syllable.

REEL LIFE

They say art imitates life, but sometimes the facts get screwed up. And in Hollywood, truth inevitably takes a back seat to drama. Here are a few examples.

THE BRIDGE ON THE RIVER KWAI (1957, *Alec Guinness, William Holden, Sessue Hayakawa*)

The movie plot: British POWs in WWII Burma are forced to build a railway bridge for their cruel Japanese captors. Using superior British know-how, they succeed. British commander, Col. Nicholson takes such pride in the construction that at first he defends it against saboteurs, but then comes to his senses and blows it up himself.

The real story: The POWs actually built two bridges. And they used Japanese know-how, not British. The Japanese weren't all cruel. In fact, the real British commander, Lt. Col. Toosey, testified on behalf of Japanese commander Major Saito at his war crimes trial, saving him from a death sentence. The bridges were destroyed two years later, by the RAF, not saboteurs.

THE ENGLISH PATIENT (1996, *Ralph Fiennes, Kristin Scott Thomas, Juliette Binoche*)

The movie plot: French-Canadian nurse cares for dashing Count Laszlo Almasy (Ralph Fiennes), a burn victim, in a Tuscan villa at the end of WWII. Using flashbacks, the film recounts Almasy's illicit love affair with a friend's wife (Kristin Scott Thomas), his devotion to her and her tragic death. As he lays dying, his last thoughts are of her.

The real story: The real Count Almasy was a puny man with bad teeth. He was gay. He was in love with a German Army officer. He wasn't burned and did not die at the end of WWII. Actually, after the war, he worked as a Soviet spy.

THE STING (1973, *Robert Redford, Paul Newman, Robert Shaw*)

The movie plot: Two con artists, Gondorf (Newman) and Hooker (Redford) set up an elaborate betting parlor scam on an Irish racketeer to avenge the murder of a fellow grifter. The sting works and the lovable con-men get away with it.

The real story: There really was a Gondorf (but no Hooker). He and his brother really did work this scam. But they did it for money, not for justice. The real "sting" was pulled on an Englishman in 1914 who was cheated out of $10,000. He went to the real police and Gondorf went to a real prison.

SATURDAY NIGHT FEVER (1977, *John Travolta, Karen Lynn Gorney*)

The movie plot: Bored with his day-to-day life, Tony Manero, a Brooklyn teenager (played by John Travolta) becomes the local Disco king.

The real story: The movie was based on an article in *New York* magazine by writer Nik Cohn, who supposedly met, and interviewed the real Tony Manero. But it turned out to be a lie—there was no real Tony Manero. In 1997 Cohn admitted he had made the character up.

RAIDERS OF THE LOST ARK (1981, *Harrison Ford, Karen Allen, John Rhys-Davies*)

The movie plot: Swash-buckling, whip-wielding archeologist Indiana Jones battles the Nazis to locate the mythical Ark of the Covenant, which contains the original Ten Commandments. Good triumphs over evil, and Indie returns to his job as college professor awaiting his next adventure.

The real story: Jones' character is based on the 18th century inventor (and circus performer)-turned-archeologist, Giovanni Belzoni, who discovered several lost tombs in Egypt's Valley of the Kings. He battled French Egyptologists, not Nazis. And he didn't live happily ever after—he died from dysentery at the age of 55 while searching for the lost city of Timbuktu.

*   *   *

IT'S A WEIRD, WEIRD WORLD

"One hundred and twenty men named Henry attacked each other during a "My Name is Henry" convention in Sydney, Australia. The melee was set off when one Henry accused another of not being a Henry at all but an Angus, provoking an instant fistfight."

—*Bizarre* magazine

PRESIDENTIAL QUIZ

*Some presidential deeds are well-known; others are more obscure. But
nothing's too obscure for the BRI. So in that spirit, Uncle John and Leland
Gregory III, author of* Presidential Indiscretions, *have put together this
multiple-choice quiz to test your knowledge of presidential footnotes.*

1. Which president, when asked what he would do after leaving
office, responded: "There's nothing left [to do] but get drunk."
a) Franklin Pierce (1853–1857)
b) Andrew Johnson (1865–1869)
c) Lyndon Baines Johnson (1963–1969)

2. The first (and maybe only) president to give a dog a presidential
pardon was…
a) Abraham Lincoln (1860–1865)
b) Warren G. Harding (1921–1923)
c) Ronald Reagan (1981–1989)

3. Referring to ex-presidents Gerald Ford, Jimmy Carter, and Richard Nixon, who were standing together, Bob Dole once said:
a) "Think of it—we survived disco music *and* those guys in the
seventies!"
b) "That's a decade I'd like to forget."
c) "There they are—See No Evil, Hear No Evil, and Evil."

4. Which president once confessed to murdering his own
grandmother?
a) Grover Cleveland (1885–1889 and 1893–1897)
b) Franklin D. Roosevelt (1933–1945)
c) Bill Clinton (1993–2001)

5. To help persuade the North Vietnamese to give up Communism
in 1972, the United States dropped "Democracy kits" over North
Vietnam. Among other things, each kit included…
a) A tape-recorded message from President Richard Nixon.
b) A pen-and-pencil set decorated with the presidential seal and
President Nixon's autograph.
c) A photo of the Washington Redskins football team.

"Kryptonite" made its first appearance on the Superman radio show…not in the comic book.

6. Which president once had his credit card number stolen by a crook who apparently didn't recognize his name?
a) Gerald Ford (1974–1977)
b) Jimmy Carter (1977–1981)
c) George Bush (1989–1993)

7. Against odds of 125,000 to 1, a president survived two assassination attempts within minutes of each other. Who was it?
a) Andrew Jackson (1829–1837)
b) Abraham Lincoln (1860–1865)
c) Gerald Ford (1974–1977)

8. Which president had a fear of being buried alive?
a) George Washington (1789–1797)
b) Theodore Roosevelt (1901–1909)
c) Harry Truman (1945–1953)

9. Which president once boxed with a heavyweight champion?
a) Theodore Roosevelt (1901–1909)
b) Harry Truman (1945–1953)
c) Ronald Reagan (1981–1989)

10. Who was the first president to write a screenplay…and have it rejected?
a) Franklin D. Roosevelt (1933–1945)
b) Gerald Ford (1974–1977)
c) Ronald Reagan (1981–1989)

11. Which president, traveling in Air Force One, was once unable to land because two dogs were mating on the runway?
a) Dwight D. Eisenhower (1953–1961)
b) John F. Kennedy (1961–1963)
c) Ronald Reagan (1981–1989)

12. Which president has reportedly been seen (by reliable sources—not the *Weekly World News*) haunting the White House ?
a) George Washington (1789–1797)
b) Abraham Lincoln (1860–1865)
c) John F. Kennedy (1961–1963)

Answers on page 489.

Got any sunscreen? One fourth of the land on Earth is classified as desert.

WEIRD GAME SHOWS

It's a unique TV art form. You get to answer stupid questions, perform idiotic stunts and humiliate yourself in front of millions of people for cash and prizes. Here are some of the strangest TV game shows ever.

Who Pays? (U.S.) Hosted by Mike Wallace. A Hollywood domestic servant—gardener, valet, or chauffeur—is brought out on stage, and contestants try to guess which celebrity they work for.

Clash (Canada) Teams of "people with a common experience" compete by performing physical tests like "egg-beating." Typical contestants: "People who have been punched in the face" vs. "People who have been kicked in the butt," or "Acne sufferers" vs. "Hemorrhoid sufferers."

Comeback Story (U.S.) "A talent contest designed to give a humiliating second chance to has-been celebrities....The audience decreed their fate via applause meter."

Let's See (U.S.) Sponsored by the Atlantic City Chamber of Commerce. The host "asked contestants questions about the wonderful things they had seen in Atlantic City....The show lasted a month."

With This Ring (U.S.) "Engaged couples submit themselves to the inspection of a panel of marriage counselors." Couples who are rated acceptable win a free honeymoon.

Wheel of Fortune (China) "Evidently some wires got crossed somewhere along the line, as the Chinese version features small boys strapped to the wheel, trying to win prizes."

Monopoly (U.S.) "The game show uses a midget—dressed in a top hat and tails—to move tokens around a giant board."

Trump Card (U.S.) Named after Donald Trump... but hosted by Jimmy Cefallo. "Trump, in fact, will not have a great deal to do with his namesake show. He'll make occasional appearances and star in TV commercials promoting it. When a contestant wins a big cash award, Trump will be on hand to pass over the check."

Shirley Temple made $300,000 in 1938...but her allowance was only $4.25 a week.

WERE YOU RAISED IN A BARN?

*Tell the truth—how are your manners? Maybe you need
some help from these old etiquette books. You may
not believe it, but we really didn't make them up.*

"Although asparagus may be taken in the fingers, don't take a long drooping stalk, hold it up in the air, and catch the end of it in your mouth like a fish."
—*Etiquette* (1922)

"Do not move back and forth on your chair. Whoever does that gives the impression of constantly farting or trying to fart."
—*On Civility in Children* (1530)

"If a dish is distasteful to you, decline it, but make no remarks about it. It is sickening and disgusting to explain at a table how one article makes you sick, or why some other dish has become distasteful to you. I have seen a well-dressed tempting dish go from a table untouched, because one of the company told a most disgusting anecdote about finding vermin served in a similar dish."
—*Martine's Handbook of Etiquette* (1866)

"It is not the correct thing to put the spoon or fork so far into the mouth that the bystanders are doubtful of its return to the light."
—*The Correct Thing in Good Society* (1902)

"No decent person laughs at a funeral."
—*The Bazar Book of Decorum* (1870)

"When you have blown your nose, you should not open your handkerchief and inspect it, as though pearls or rubies had dropped out of your skull. Such behavior is nauseating and is more likely to lose us the affection of those who love us than to win us the favor of others."
—*The Book of Manners* (1958)

"Never put your cold, clammy hands on a person, saying, 'Did you ever know anyone to have such cold hands as mine?'"
—*Manners for Millions* (1932)

The "Pretend Cafe" in Tel Aviv served empty plates. (They've since closed down.)

"It is unmannerly to fall asleep, as many people do, whilst the company is engaged in conversation. Their conduct shows that they have little respect for their friends and care nothing either for them or their talk. Besides, they are generally obliged to doze in an uncomfortable position, and this nearly always causes them to make unpleasant noises and gestures in their sleep. Often enough they begin to sweat and dribble at the mouth."
—*The Book of Manners* (1958)

"Peevish temper, cross and frowning faces, and uncomely looks have sometimes been cured in France by sending the child into an octagonal boudoir lined with looking glasses, where, whichever way it turned, it would see the reflection of its own unpleasant features, and be constrained, out of self-respect, to assume a more amiable disposition."
—*Good Behavior* (1876)

"If you ask the waiter for anything, you will be careful to speak to him gently in the tone of request, and not of command. To speak to a waiter in a driving manner will create, among well-bred people, the suspicion that you were sometime a servant yourself, and are putting on airs at the thought of your promotion."
—*The Perfect Gentleman* (1860)

"It is bad manners, when you see something to nauseate you by the roadside, as sometimes happens, to turn to your companions and point it out to them. Still less should you offer any evil smelling object for others to sniff, as some people do, insisting upon holding it up to their noses and asking them to smell how horrible it is."
—*The Book of Manners* (1958)

"When not practicable for individuals to occupy separate beds, the persons should be of about the same age, and in good health. Numerous cases have occurred where healthy, robust children have 'dwindled away' and died within a few months, from sleeping with old people."
—*The People's Common Sense Medical Adviser* (1876)

"Applause is out of order at any religious service."
—*Your Best Foot Forward* (1955)

It's against French law to reveal the true identity of a member of the French Foreign Legion.

A 'TOON IS BORN

*TV cartoons used to be tame and bland. But now, with cable,
there's a whole new breed of 'toons. Here are the stories
of how a couple of new cable-classics were created.*

RUGRATS
Background: Arlene Klasky and her husband, Gabor Csupo, owned the studio that animated *The Simpsons* in the late 1980s. One afternoon in 1989, Klasky was at home trying to plan for a meeting the following day with Nickelodeon. The kids' cable channel was looking for new Sunday morning programming, but Klasky and Csupo didn't have any viable ideas.

Inspiration: As Klasky sat watching her three-year-old and 15-month-old playing with each other, the idea suddenly came to her: create a cartoon that explored childhood from a toddler's point of view. She called Csupo and their creative director, Paul Germain, and the trio fleshed out the "Rugrats" concept that night.

"People kept telling me, 'Everybody's done babies already,'" recalls the exec who bought the show, "but this was perfect." The first six-minute *Rugrats* test cartoon featured a big-headed, pigeon-toed baby (inspired by Klasky's son Jarett) "staring up at a toilet as though it were the monolith from *2001: A Space Odyssey*."

On the Air: Rugrats premiered in August 1991. It ran for four years on Sunday morning, then Nickelodeon stopped buying new episodes. Ironically, that's when the show became a hit. Nickelodeon began airing reruns twice a day on weekdays, and kids finally discovered it. Today, according to surveys, the *Rugrats* characters are more recognizable to small children than even Mickey Mouse and Bugs Bunny.

SOUTH PARK

Background: In 1994, a Fox executive named Brian Graden saw a film called *Cannibal: The Musical*, created by Trey Parker and Matt Stone, two University of Colorado film students. Graden was impressed and tried to develop a few show ideas for Fox with the pair. But nobody at the network was interested either in *Cannibal*,

---

Short-sighted: Nobody remembers who invented eyeglasses.

or in "Conifer," a show based on kids Parker had grown up with in Conifer, Colorado.

Inspiration: In the meantime, Graden hired Parker and Stone to make him an animated video Christmas card—partly out of admiration for their talents…but also to help them pay their rent. He gave them $2,000. Rather than burn the money on sophisticated animation, the pair spent $750 animating construction paper cutouts and pocketed the difference. Result: A five-minute cartoon called "The Spirit of Christmas," in which Jesus and Santa Claus curse each other out and battle to see who has the biggest claim on the holiday.

"I was supposed to send it to 500 people on my executive kiss-a— list," Graden says. "Then I saw it, and thought, OK, this is the funniest thing I've ever seen, but I can't send it to studio heads. So I sent it to about 40 friends, most of them not even in the business." Graden's friends passed it on to their friends, and so on, and from there the video was distributed to tens of thousands of people over the Internet, generating such a buzz in Hollywood that people who'd earlier turned down Parker and Stone's work took a second look.

On the Air: Comedy Central eventually bought "Conifer" …but by then the name of the show had changed. "'Conifer' just wasn't a great name for a show," Parker explains, "so we named it after the town of South Park," a real town about an hour away from Conifer. Why South Park? "Because," says Parker, "that was where all the weird stuff was happening."

It aired for the first time on August 13, 1997. Thirteen episodes later, *South Park* had become the highest-rated series in Comedy Central's history; it has gone on to become the top-rated series on cable, seen by five million people every week.

*   *   *

WEIRD CLAIM TO FAME

"In 1973, Amar Bharti of India raised his right arm—and has kept it there ever since. This 26-year-and-counting endeavor supposedly shows respect for the Hindu god Shiva." (*Stuff* magazine)

Pound for pound, oysters have 20 times as much cholesterol as eggs.

THE REAL STORY OF MURPHY'S LAW

The amazing thing about Murphy's Law is that it's true. In other words, whatever can go wrong, actually will go wrong. Scientific experiments have proven it. For example, if we weren't careful, this paragraph might get printed backwards. Boy, wouldn't that be embarrassing. Well...it could happen. Here's why.

HISTORY

The sentiment expressed in Murphy's Law, "Anything that can go wrong, will go wrong," has probably been around as long as there have been things to go wrong. In 1786, for example, Scottish poet Robert Burns wrote, "The best laid schemes o' mice an men gang aft a-gley [are prone to go awry]."

But the official Murphy's Law is much more recent. In fact, it's barely 50 years old.

HOT SEAT

In 1949, the U.S. Air Force conducted a series of tests on the effect of rapid deceleration on pilots, so they could get a better understanding of how much force people's bodies can tolerate in a plane crash. The tests, part of what was known as Project MX981, consisted of strapping volunteers into a rocket-propelled sled, accelerating the sled, and then slamming on the brakes—bringing the sled to a very abrupt stop. The volunteers wore a special harness fitted with 16 sensors that measured the acceleration, or G-forces, on different parts of their body.

The harness was the invention of an Air Force captain named Edward A. Murphy...but the 16 individual sensors were installed by someone else.

BRAKE DOWN

On the day of the fateful test, a volunteer named John Paul Stapp was strapped into the sled and the rockets were fired. The test went off as expected—the sled accelerated to a high speed and then

Count them yourself: One speck of dust contains a quadrillion atoms.

abruptly braked to a stop, subjecting his body to such enormous forces that, according to one account, when he stumbled off the sled, his eyes were bloodshot and his nose was bleeding. Stapp's body is believed to have endured forces equivalent to 40 Gs, or 40 times the force of gravity. But no one will ever know for sure, because all 16 of the sensors failed, each one giving a zero reading for the test.

When Murphy examined the harness to see what had gone wrong, he discovered that the technician who had installed the sensors had wired every single one of them backward. Because of a simple human error, Stapp's life had been put at risk in vain.

There are varying accounts of what Murphy said next—he may have cursed out the technician responsible for the mistake, saying "If there is any way to do it wrong, he'll find it." Whatever he said originally, at a press conference a few days later Stapp quoted him as having said, "If there are two or more ways to do something and one of those results in a catastrophe, then someone will do it that way."

Within months, this expression became known throughout the aerospace industry as "Murphy's Law."

FIRST VICTIM

This first version of Murphy's Law might never have become known beyond the participants of Project MX981 had it not been a very sound design and engineering principle. The sensors in Murphy's harness failed not just because they had been installed backward, but also because they were *capable* of being installed backward. Had they been designed so they could only be installed one way—the correct way—they would never have failed in the first place.

A few days later, Murphy himself redesigned the sensors so that they could only be installed one way, and the problem never came up again. (Murphy's Law is why two-pronged electrical plugs are now designed with one prong slightly larger than the other—so they can only be plugged in the proper way.)

Murphy's Law became a popular principle throughout the aerospace industry, and from there it spread to the rest of the world. But as it spread it also evolved into the popular, more pessimistic form, "If anything can go wrong, it will go wrong."

Polished, not stirred: before he became an actor, Sean Connery had a job polishing coffins.

THE SCIENCE OF MURPHY'S LAW

Since 1949, any number of permutations of Murphy's Law have arisen, dealing with subjects as diverse as missing socks and buttered bread falling to the floor. As the BRI's own research has shown us, some of these laws are grounded in very solid science:

• **Murphy's Law of Buttered Bread:** "A dropped piece of bread will always land butter side down."

Scientific analysis: The behavior of a piece of bread dropped from table height is fairly predictable: As it falls to the ground it is more likely than not to rotate on its axis; and the distance to the ground is not sufficient for the bread to rotate the full 360 degrees needed for it to land face up. So more often than not, it will land face down.

• **Murphy's Law of Lines:** "The line next to you will move more quickly than the one you're in." (Also works with a line of traffic.)

Scientific analysis: On average, all the lanes of traffic, or lines at a K-Mart, move at roughly the same rate. That means that if there's a checkout line on either side of you, there's a two in three chance that one of them will move faster than the one you're in.

• **Murphy's Law of Socks:** "If you lose a sock, it's always from a complete pair."

Scientific analysis: Start with a drawer containing 10 complete pairs of socks, for a total of 20 socks. Now lose one sock, creating one incomplete pair. The drawer now contains 19 socks, 18 of which belong to a complete pair.

Now lose a second sock. If all of the remaining socks have the same odds of being lost, there's only 1 chance out of 18 that this lost sock is the mate of the first one that was lost. That means there's a 94.4% chance that it's from one of the complete pairs.

• **Murphy's Law of Maps:** "The place you're looking for on the map will be located at the most inconvenient place on the map, such as an edge, a corner, or near a fold."

Scientific analysis: If you measure out an inch or so from each edge of the map and from each fold, and then calculate the total area of these portions of the map, they'll account for more than half the total area of the map. So if you pick a point at random, there's a better than 50% chance that it will be in an inconvenient-to-read part of the map.

ZAPPA'S LAW & OTHER FACTS OF LIFE

You know Murphy's Law: "If someting can go wrong, it will." Here are some other immutable laws of the universe to consider.

Zappa's Law: "There are two things on Earth that are universal: hydrogen and stupidity."

The Murphy Philosophy: "Smile. Tomorrow will be worse."

Baruch's Observation: "If all you have is a hammer, everything looks like a nail."

Lowe's Law: "Success always occurs in private, and failure in full public view."

Todd's Law: "All things being equal, you lose."

Thompson's Theorem: "When the going gets weird, the weird turn pro."

Vac's Conundrum: "When you dial a wrong number, you never get a busy signal."

The Golden Rule of Arts and Sciences: "Whoever has the gold makes the rules."

The Unspeakable Law: "As soon as you mention something...
• if it's good, it goes away.
• if it's bad, it happens."

Green's Law of Debate: "Anything is possible if you don't know what you're talking about."

Hecht's Law: "There is no time like the present to procrastinate."

Sdeyries's Dilemma: "If you hit two keys on the typewriter, the one you don't want hits the paper."

The Queue Principle: "The longer you wait in line, the greater the likelihood that you are standing in the wrong line."

Johnson's Law: "If you miss one issue of any magazine, it will be the issue that contained the article, story or installment you were most anxious to read."

Issawi's Law of Progress: "A shortcut is the longest distance between two points."

Ginsberg's Theorem:
"1. You can't win.
2. You can't break even.
3. You can't even quit the game."

Q. Which city has the lowest divorce rate on earth? A. Vatican City (0.00 per 1,000 residents)

Perkins's Postulate: "The bigger they are, the harder they hit."

Johnson and Laird's Law: "A toothache tends to start on Saturday night."

The Salary Axiom: "The pay raise is just large enough to increase your taxes and just small enough to have no effect on your take-home pay."

Hutchin's Law: "You can't out-talk a man who knows what he's talking about."

Wellington's Law of Command: "The cream rises to the top. So does the scum."

Todd's Two Political Principles:
"1. No matter what they're telling you, they're not telling you the whole truth.
2. No matter what they're talking about, they're talking about money."

Kirby's Comment on Committees: "A committee is the only life form with 12 stomachs and no brain."

Harrison's Postulate: "For every action, there is an equal and opposite criticism."

Murphy's Paradox: "Doing it the hard way is always easier.

*　　*　　*

WORD ORIGINS

BUTTERFLY
Meaning: An insect
Origin: "The most generally accepted theory of how this insect got its name is a once-held notion that if you leave butter or milk uncovered in a kitchen, butterflies will land on it...and eat it. Another possibility is that the word is a reference to the color of the insects' excrement." (From *Dictionary of Word Origins*, by John Ayto)

GENUINE
Meaning: Real, not fake
Origin: "Originally meant 'placed on the knees.' In Ancient Rome, a father legally claimed his new child by sitting in front of his family and placing his child on his knee." (From *Etymologically Speaking*, by Steven Morgan Friedman)

A squirrel can fall as much as 600 feet to the ground without injuring itself.

THE MINIATURE GOLF CRAZE

Most of us have played this "sport" at least once, but today we can't imagine how popular it was in the late 1920s. Here's the story of one of the most popular American fads of all time.

LILLIPUTIAN LINKS

It all started in 1927 at a hotel perched on Tennessee's Lookout Mountain, the picturesque site of a major Civil War battle. The owner, Garnet Carter, wanted to find a way to promote his resort and golf course. He decided to build a new golf course that anyone could play—a cheap version of the tiny courses which used to appear in front of English Inns. The hazards on the course—tree roots, sand traps, and water hazards—were arranged so that even the most pathetic golfer could handle them. His plan worked so well that the mini-links soon eclipsed the resort's other attractions, and he had to charge a "greens fee" to keep the massive crowds down.

BOOM

Carter was an astute businessman—he immediately recognized the potential profits in miniature golf. So he founded the Fairyland Manufacturing Company and began constructing "Tom Thumb" courses all over Tennessee, and eventually, the entire South.

In the fall of 1929, the pygmy links invaded California and New York, and then the rest of the nation. For only $2,000, Carter's company would lay down a course that would be operational in less than a week, and they proved so popular (and profitable) that many courses would earn back their initial investment in only a few days. The game was the first of many recreational fads of the Great Depression, successful mainly because it was so inexpensive to play.

Within a year, you could find mini golf courses everywhere— from highway filling stations to vacant city lots. And by the mid-1930s, 20 million Americans were regular players. On any given night, there were close to four million people flooding over 40,000

---

courses nationwide. People joked that the only industry still hiring during the Depression was miniature golf, which in 1930 employed 200,000 workers and generated profits of over $225 million in a single year.

Not only that, the fad helped bolster the flagging Depression-era cotton and steel industries. How? Crushed cotton seed hulls were used as a surfacing material for the greens and steel pipes were used for trick shots and hazards.

IT'S A SIN

Even a pastime as harmless as miniature golf was not without controversy. The courses were banned within 50 feet of churches, hospitals, and public schools, and the nongolfing element of the population complained nightly that the late night revelry of reckless young golfers—who would spike their sodas with bootleg liquor—disturbed their sleep. The game also sparked a debate between physicians and pastors. Doctors liked it—miniature golf took young folks out of stuffy movie theaters at night and put them in the fresh outdoor air for some healthy activity. But church officials claimed that playing on the Sabbath—the most popular day for recreation—was a sin. Ironically, a few churches around the country saw a chance to help pay off their debts and went over to the dark side, encouraging one and all to come and play (but never on the Sabbath.)

BUST

In the end, too many entrepreneurs saw a cheap, profitable Tom Thumb course as their road out of financial hardship. The fatal combination of market saturation and dwindling interest in the game brought about its swift end. In 1931 *Miniature Golf Management*, a one-year-old publication, noted that every California course was in the red financially.

But its shrewd inventor survived the fall. In 1929, he had the foresight to sell out to a Pennsylvania pipe manufacturer and settle for royalties from future miniature courses. At the end of the tiny sport's three year heyday, he emerged unscathed. A half-century later, the game retains a small following in more than one sense of the word—it has been bequeathed to children.

Q & A:
ASK THE EXPERTS

Everyone's got a question or two they'd like answered—basic stuff, like "Why is the sky blue?" Here are a few of those questions, with answers from books by some of the nation's top trivia experts.

WRONG TURN

Q: *Why do so many earthworms come out on the sidewalk when it rains?*

A: "Most people assume that earthworms come to the surface during heavy rains to avoid drowning in their tunnels. In fact, worms can live totally submerged in water, so drowning isn't the problem. But the rainwater that filters down through the ground contains very little oxygen, so the real reason earthworms come to the surface is to breathe.

"Once above ground, earthworms are very sensitive to light, and even a brief exposure to the sun's rays can paralyze them. Unable to crawl back into their burrows, they eventually dry out and die on the sidewalk." (From *101 Questions & Answers About Backyard Wildlife*, by Ann Squire)

FUZZY LOGIC

Q: *Why are tennis balls fuzzy?*

A: "The fuzz is to slow the balls down. Tennis balls are made to exacting standards so players have a decent chance of hitting them. The fuzz makes the ball softer and less bouncy and increases wind resistance. In addition, the fuzz adds to a player's racket control because the strings hold onto the surface of the ball longer." (From *Just Curious, Jeeves*, by Jack Mingo and Erin Barrett)

ASLEEP AT THE WHEEL

Q: *You are driving in bumper-to-bumper traffic on the highway. Then, suddenly, inexplicably, traffic clears. What caused the jam? What caused the traffic to clear?*

A: "It's the shock-wave effect. Highway drivers operate best at speeds of 35 mph and higher. When highway traffic volume nears its capacity, some stragglers begin driving under 35 mph and a traffic jam is born.

"Slower speeds, theoretically, should increase control and maneuverability, but drivers grow fearful as their pace declines. The shock-wave effect occurs because drivers look for the reason they had to slow down in the first place: they overreact to any stimuli, particularly the brake lights of cars ahead of them. A few drivers at 25 mph can set off a shock-wave effect for miles behind them and create bumper-to-bumper traffic without any ostensible reason.

"Why do these traffic jams suddenly disappear? Usually, it's because there is enough breathing room ahead to prompt even slow-poke victims of the shock-wave effect to risk peeling away at 35 mph or more." (From *Imponderables*, by David Feldman)

CAPTAIN'S LOG, SUPPLEMENTAL

Q: *"Star Trek" episodes often refer to the "star date." What exactly is a star date?*

A: "Who knows? Star dates were among hundreds of unexplained space terms invented by 'Star Trek' scriptwriters.

"The dates in the original show (1966–1969) were of the form 0000.0 and were assigned pretty much at random, the producers merely keeping a list to avoid duplication. Eventually it was agreed that the units were roughly equivalent to Earth days and decimals were tenths thereof. For 'Star Trek: The Next Generation,' one production staffer was actually 'keeper of the star dates'...but everybody is still pretty vague on what the numbers mean." (From *Return of the Straight Dope*, by Cecil Adams)

SWEET SCIENCE

Q: *Why can I melt sugar, but not salt?*

A: "Who says you can't melt salt? Any solid will melt if the temperature is high enough. Lava is molten rock, isn't it? If you want to melt salt, all you have to do is turn your oven up to 1474° F. Sugar, being made from a living thing, is an 'organic' compound and melts at a much lower temperature—365° F. Salt, being a mineral, is inorganic. Inorganic compounds require more energy (in this case, heat) to break apart." (From *What Einstein Didn't Know*, by Robert L. Wolke)

HOW TO DRIVE PEOPLE NUTS

Bored? Here's a thought: Why not drive the people around you absolutely insane? How, you ask? This is adapted from a Maxim magazine article by our good friend Uncle Edgester.

Call an addiction hot line and explain that you're hooked on phonics.

Go to the airport wearing a suit of armor and try walking through the metal detector.

Wash out a gas can, punch a hole in it, then fill it with water and carry it down a busy lunch-hour sidewalk while smoking the biggest cigar you can find.

Call the Q-Tips 800 number and say that one of the cotton swab parts just came off in your ear. When they reply, keep shouting, "What? What? What did you say?"

Go to the polar bear enclosure at the zoo and shout, "C'mon Larry, enough's enough! Take off that costume and come back to the office!"

Fill an inflate-a-date with helium and release it at rush hour on a windy day. Chase it down the street, yelling, "Come back here, you tramp!"

Call National Acme Co. Ask if they have any products you could use to kill a roadrunner.

Rush yourself to the ER and explain to the night nurse that you were resting on your leg for a long time and now it feels like pins and needles. Ask if they'll have to amputate.

In the middle of the night, noisily bury a fully dressed mannequin in your backyard. Arrange lawn furniture on the fresh mound and sit down in it quickly when the police arrive.

Get a video camera and microphone and chase a local TV news crew around. Interrupt on-the-scene shots by shouting questions like "Where have all the cowboys gone?"

Ask strangers if they have change for a nickel.

In the bathroom at work, utter loud, pain-wracked screams, then emerge holding a large hen's egg.

What's a *singulthus*? A hiccup.

RANDOM ORIGINS

Once again, the B.R.I. asks—and answers—the
question: where did all this stuff come from?

T HE TELEPHONE BOOTH
Alexander Graham Bell invented the telephone, but it was
his assistant, Thomas Watson ("Come here, Mr. Watson"),
who invented the phone booth. The reason: His landlady complained that he made too much noise shouting into the phone during his calls. Watson remedied the situation by throwing blankets
over some furniture and climbing underneath whenever he needed
to make a call; by 1883 he'd upgraded to an enclosed wooden
booth with a domed top, screened windows, a writing desk, and
even a ventilator.

THE SLOT MACHINE

Other types of gambling machines date back as far as the 1890s, but
the first one to really catch on was a vending machine for chewing
gum introduced by the Mills Novelty Company in 1910. Their machine dispensed three flavors of gum—cherry, orange, and plum—
depending on which fruits appeared on three randomly spinning
wheels. If three bars reading "1910 Fruit Gum" appeared in a row,
the machine gave *extra* gum; if a lemon appeared, it gave no gum at
all (which is why "lemon" came to mean something unsatisfactory
or defective.) You can't get gum in a slot machine anymore—the
1910 Fruit Gum machine was so popular that the company converted them to cash payouts—but the same fruit symbols are still
used in slot machines today.

THE CINEMA MULTIPLEX

Invented by accident by theater owner Stan Durwood in 1963,
when he tried to open a large theater in a Kansas City, Missouri
shopping mall. The mall's developer told Durwood that the support
columns in the building could *not* be removed to build a single
large theater...so Durwood built two smaller theaters instead. He
showed the same movie on both screens—until it dawned on him
that he'd sell more tickets if he showed two different films. It was a
huge success; the national attention he got spurred a "multiplex
boom" in other cities.

A FOOD IS BORN

The origin of some famous foods (and drinks), from the book Rare Bits, *by Patricia Bunning Stevens.*

SCREWDRIVERS. Created in the early 1950s by American engineers working in the Middle East oil fields, who surreptitiously added vodka to small cans of orange juice. Where did the name come from? They stirred the mixture with their screwdrivers.

KAISER ROLLS. Over 20 million immigrants came to the United States in the half century following the Civil War. Each group brought the foods of its homeland, including breads and rolls. The Kaiser roll was created in Vienna and brought to America by Austrian bakers. It takes its name from the German *Kaiser* (from the Latin *Caesar*), "emperor," and refers to the appearance of the roll...which does indeed resemble the high, ornate, velvet-filled crowns of 19th-century monarchs.

MARSHMALLOWS. Named after an edible plant, the marsh mallow, a close relative of the hollyhock. Why? A jellylike gum can be extracted from roots. It was first used as a folk medicine and as an ingredient in cough syrups. Later, confectioners used it as a firming agent in soft, puffy "marshmallow candies." What does it taste like? You'll probably never know. Today, gum arabic or gelatin is used—so there's no marsh mallow in marshmallows.

BLOODY MARYS. Created in the 1920s at Harry's New York Bar in Paris. Vodka, newly arrived in the West from Russia and Eastern Europe, inspired a French bartender by the name of Fernand "Pete" Petiot to concoct a blend of tomato juice, vodka, and seasonings. American entertainer Roy Barton christened the drink "Bucket of Blood" after a nightclub in Chicago.

Petiot left Paris in 1933 to work at the St. Regis Hotel in New York City and brought the drink with him. At first it was popular as the less offensive "Red Snapper." But it eventually became known as a "Bloody Mary." The Bloody Mary from whom the

---

The typical violin contains more than 70 separate pieces of wood.

drink got its name was, of course, Mary Tudor, the English queen remembered for her bloody persecutions of the Protestants.

BOSTON BAKED BEANS. In the 1600s, the Puritan Sabbath was strict and stern. Beginning at sundown on Saturday, no work was allowed except tasks that couldn't possibly be avoided. Food could be served, but not actually prepared. Faced with these restrictions, Puritan women devised dishes that could be made well in advance and held for the Sabbath meals. The most popular was baked beans. The big pot of beans set at the side of the fireplace could be prepared early Saturday morning, used for supper Saturday night, dished up again for Sunday breakfast, and even finished for Sunday dinner. Long after the Sabbath rules had been moderated, the tradition of baked beans and brown bread on Saturday night remained, earning Boston the nickname "Bean Town."

WELSH RABBIT (RAREBIT). The English, Scots, and Welsh do not always get along as well as most Americans might presume. The English traditionally scorned the Welsh as poor and not always trustworthy. When a new dish of melted cheese on toast was devised in the 18th century, it was jokingly called a *Welsh Rabbit*, meaning that a Welshman, too poor to have meat, would call his cheese a rabbit. The alternate spelling, Welsh Rarebit, developed later.

THOUSAND ISLAND DRESSING. Although it's now found in fast food joints across North America, this dressing was considered gourmet food when it was introduced at two posh restaurants—one in New York, one in Chicago—during the 1920s.

Both cities claim credit for it, but it actually originated in Canada, where it was bottled and sold by grocers. It happened that two restauranteurs—George C. Boldt, of the Waldorf-Astoria in New York and Chef Theodore Reums of the Blackstone Hotel in Chicago—spent summers in the Thousand Islands area along the St. Lawrence River. Each discovered the new dressing there and introduced it in his city. The name recalls the Thousand Islands where it was found, as well as the dressing's numerous bits and pieces.

MADE IN SWITZERLAND

If you've ever owned a Swiss Army knife, chances are you've asked yourself these two questions: Is there a Swiss army? And if so, do they really use these knives? The short answer is yes...and yes. The long answer is...

BACKGROUND. In 1891 Karl Elsner, owner of a company that made surgical instruments, got a rude shock—he found out that the pocket knives used by the Swiss Army were made in Germany. Outraged, he founded the Association of Swiss Master Cutlers. Their purpose: Swiss knives for Swiss soldiers.

Elsner designed a wood-handled knife that also contained a screwdriver, a punch, and a can-opener. He called it "the Soldier's Knife," and sold it to the Swiss Army.

But Elsner wasn't done yet—he also wanted to develop a better knife for officers. It took five years, but he finally found a way to put blades on both sides of the handle, using the same spring to hold them in place—something no one had done before. This made it possible to put roughly twice as many features on the knife. Elsner replaced the wood handle with red fiber (which lasted longer), then added a second blade and a corkscrew.

CHANGES. Elsner had the market all to himself until 1908. Then a preacher named Theordore Wenger, from the French-speaking region of the country, started selling a similar product. The Swiss government, sensitive to regional favoritism, started buying half their pocket knives from him...and they still do. Today, the two companies are rivals. Elsner's company, Victorinox (after his mother, Victoria) calls its knife the "original" Swiss Army Knife. The Wenger Company calls its knife the "genuine" Swiss Army Knife. Each is allowed to put the Swiss White Cross on its knife—but no other company is.

Swiss Army knives became popular in the United States after World War II; returning G.I.'s brought them home by the thousands. Today, the U.S. is the world's largest market for them. And ironically, Victorinox, founded to prevent the Swiss Army from buying German pocket knives, is now the official supplier of pocket knives to the German Army.

Why does NASA send small animals into space? Among other things, to see if they throw up.

HOW TO AVOID GETTING HIRED

Your resumé is a carefully-crafted chronicle of what you've achieved...
and how indispensable you'll be to prospective employers. That's
what it's supposed to be, anyway. This list of real-life resume
bloopers appeared in Fortune *magazine.*

"I demand a salary commiserate with my extensive experience."

"I have lurnt Word Perfect 6.0, computor and spreadsheat progroms."

"Received a plague for Salesperson of the Year."

"Reason for leaving last job: maturity leave."

"Wholly responsible for two failed financial institutions."

"Failed bar exam with relatively high grades."

"Let's meet, so you can 'ooh' and 'aah' over my experience."

"You will want me to be Head Honcho in no time."

"Marital status: single. Unmarried. Unengaged. Uninvolved. No commitments."

"Reason for leaving last job: They insisted that all employees get to work by 8:45 every morning. Could not work under those conditions."

"Note: Please don't misconstrue my 14 jobs as 'job-hopping.' I have never quit a job."

"I am loyal to my employer at all costs....Please feel free to respond to my resume on my office voice mail."

"I procrastinate, especially when the task is unpleasant."

"As indicted, I have over five years of analyzing investments."

"Personal interests: donating blood. Fourteen gallons so far."

"Instrumental in ruining entire operation for a Midwest chain store."

"The company made me a scapegoat, just like my three previous employers."

"Finished eighth in my class of ten."

"References: None. I've left a path of destruction behind me."

"It's best for employers that I not work with people."

STRANGE LAWSUITS

These days, it seems that people will sue each other over practically anything. Here are a few real-life examples of unusual legal battles.

THE PLAINTIFF: Rene Joly, 34

THE DEFENDANT: Canadian Defense Minister Art Eggleton, Citibank, and several drug-store chains

THE LAWSUIT: In 1999 Joly filed suit claiming that the defendants were trying to murder him because he is a Martian.

THE VERDICT: Case dismissed. The judge ruled that since Joly said he isn't human, he "has no status before the courts."

THE PLAINTIFF: Gerald Overstreet

THE DEFENDANT: Gibson's Discount Store

THE LAWSUIT: In 1979, Overstreet, of Del Rio, Texas, was shopping at Gibson's. He reached for a jar of jelly...and a rattlesnake bit him. He sued for negligence.

THE VERDICT: Overstreet lost. According to a report by Donald Sobol, the court ruled "that a store's duty to protect its customers from wild animals does not begin until the store knows the animal is there."

THE PLAINTIFF: Joel R. Bander, a lawyer and Deadhead

THE DEFENDANT: Malek H. Shraibati, a lawyer who rented office space from Bander

THE LAWSUIT: Grateful Dead leader Jerry Garcia died on August 9, 1995. Bander's suit claimed that shortly after he heard the news of Garcia's passing, he spotted a cardboard tombstone on Shraibati's shelf. It read: "R.I.P./Jerry Garcia (a few too many parties perhaps?)" Bander was already upset...and that was the last straw. He sued, contending that Shraibati "should have known how such a joke would impact him." He claimed to have suffered "humiliation, mental anguish, and emotional and physical distress" after seeing the sign.

THE VERDICT: Unknown.

A female flea can drink 15 times her weight in blood a day.

THE PLAINTIFF: Mrs. Margaret Taylor

THE DEFENDANT: Randle & Sons Funeral Home, St. Louis, Missouri

THE LAWSUIT: The casket for William Taylor's 1997 funeral was closed until after the pastor finished his eulogy. Then it was opened...and people yelled "That's not Willie, you got the wrong man!" Mrs. Taylor called the police to keep the funeral home "from literally burying their mistake," and the body was taken to the morgue. It was identified as Frederick Ware—whose own funeral had passed without anyone noticing he wasn't really there. Taylor's body was finally located, but Mrs. Taylor was enraged. She sued for $2.2 million for emotional distress and "fear of not knowing the whereabouts of her husband's body for more than one week."

THE VERDICT: Unknown.

THE PLAINTIFF: Cleanthi Peters

THE DEFENDANT: Universal Studios

THE LAWSUIT: In 1998 Peters visited the Halloween Haunted House at Universal Studios in Orlando, Florida. She expected to be scared—but a costumed guy chasing her with a chain saw was too scary. She sued for $15,000 for unspecified physical injuries, "extreme fear, emotional distress and mental anguish."

THE VERDICT: Unknown.

THE PLAINTIFF: Joan Hemmer

THE DEFENDANT: Ronald Winters, owner of a chimpanzee named Mr. Jiggs

THE LAWSUIT: Hemmer was eating at a restaurant in Freehold, New Jersey when she looked up and saw Mr. Jiggs walk in—dressed in a Boy Scout uniform. She freaked out and bumped into a wall, injuring her shoulder. So she sued. Winters told the jury that Mr. Jiggs was no danger to anyone: he was thoroughly domesticated, lived in a house, could even feed himself...and besides, he was actually on his way to a Boy Scout party in the restaurant.

THE VERDICT: "The jury sided with Mr. Jiggs."

KOKO THE TALKING APE

What if gorillas could talk? According to some experts, this one—perhaps the most famous gorilla in the world—can.

B ACKGROUND
In July 1972, a researcher named Penny Patterson obtained permisson from the San Francisco Zoo to begin an amazing experiment: She wanted to try to teach American Sign Language (ASL) to one of their gorillas, a baby named Koko. Patterson taught Koko by first modeling symbols for the gorilla to imitate and then taking Koko's hands and shaping them to form ASL symbols.

More than 25 years have passed since Koko learned her first symbol. Patterson estimates that the gorilla knows about 1,000 symbols, has a vocabulary of 500 symbols that she uses regularly in sentences and understands about 2,000 words of spoken English. She can also carry on conversations, by responding in sign language to questions asked in spoken English. She can even read a few printed words, including her own name.

Expanding the Experiment

A three-year-old gorilla named Michael was added to the project in 1976. Though he was introduced to sign language late, he managed to acquire a vocabulary of 400 signs before he died suddenly from heart disease in April 2000.

Dr. Patterson hopes to breed Koko with another gorilla, Ndume, who was added to the program in 1991, and then to study whether Koko passes on her language skills to her offspring. But so far, Koko and Ndume have not bred.

LANGUAGE

How does it work? According to The Gorilla Foundation, gorillas use sign language in much the same way as human beings:

• Gorillas express emphasis by "modulating" their signing—signing more rapidly, using more space to make the gesture, and exaggerating their facial expressions. When Koko wants to express that she's thirsty, for example, she signs from the top of her head to her throat. When she's *very* thirsty, she signs from the top of her head all the way down to her stomach.

• Gorillas can communicate numbers by repeating symbols. When Koko sees one bird, she signs "bird." When she sees two, she signs "bird bird."

• Koko remembers past events in her life and can "talk" about them. She understands and can properly use time-related words such as *before*, *after*, *later*, and *yesterday*.

• She can talk about her feelings, using words like *happy*, *sad*, *afraid*, *enjoy*, *eager*, *frustrate*, *mad*, and *love*. She expresses grief when she loses a friend—such as when her favorite kitten was hit by a car and when Michael died—and becomes fidgety when asked to discuss their death or contemplate her own.

• Koko tells jokes and also laughs at jokes told by others. In one incident, for example, Koko pointed to a white towel and signed, "That red." The researcher corrected her, saying it was white, but Koko repeatedly insisted it was red. Then she reached over to where she was pointing, picked up a piece of red lint and, grinning, signed again, "That red."

• Koko and Michael taught each other symbols and they sign more slowly and with repetition when signing with humans who are not very experienced signers. Koko has even been observed molding her dolls' hands into signs.

CONVERSATIONS WITH KOKO

Does Koko really speak? Some scientists say no. We say, "What do you expect? Shakespeare? She's a gorilla." You be the judge. Here are some actual conversations:

"What do gorillas like to do most?"
   "Gorilla love eat good."

"What makes you happy?"
   "Gorilla tree."

"What do gorillas do when it's dark?"
   "Gorilla listen, sleep."

"What makes you angry?"
   "Work."

"How did you sleep last night?"
   "Floor blanket." (Koko sleeps on the floor with blankets.)

"How do you like your blankets to feel?"
   "Hot Koko-love."

It took da Vinci about five years to paint the Mona Lisa. (He took a lot of breaks.)

THE HISTORY OF
THE IQ TEST, PART I

Do you think IQ tests really measure intelligence?
Don't answer now—wait until you read this dark,
strange history. Then see what you think.

ORIGIN
In 1904, the minister of public instruction in Paris became concerned that mentally retarded children in the French capital were not receiving an adequate education. He also feared that teachers were dumping disruptive children into retarded classes—not because they were retarded, but because they were distracting other children.

The minister appointed a commission to study the problem and then hired Alfred Binet, head of the Sorbonne's psychology laboratory. Binet's mission was to come up with some kind of intelligence test that could be used to identify which children had learning problems severe enough to justify placing them in special schools.

PULL MY FINGER

Binet was not the first person to take on the job of creating a test to measure people's intelligence. In 1884, Sir Francis Galton, a cousin of Charles Darwin and father of the eugenics movement—which advocated the use of "selective breeding" techniques to improve the human race (Note: see "The Birth of Tarzan, Part I," page 185)—opened the Anthropometric Laboratory at the South Kensington Museum in London. There, for a small fee, he would administer his own version of an intelligence test.

Like most scientists of his day, Galton reasoned that since all knowledge of the surrounding world is transmitted to the brain through sight, sound, and the other senses, the people with the most acute senses would also have the most developed minds. So he devised a number of "Galtonian tasks" that measured the senses. One measured the listener's ability to hear high-pitched sounds; another measured sensitivity to subtle differences in color of pieces of dyed wool. There was also a test that measured how accurately a person

---

Q. Take a century and divide it into fifty million parts—what do you get? A. About a minute.

could approximate the weights of different objects. In the six years that Galton's laboratory was open, he tested 9,337 people. While that isn't a large sample by modern IQ test standards, historians consider Galton's research to be the first large-scale attempt to measure human intelligence in history.

THE OLD COLLEGE TRY

One of Galton's students was an American named James Cattell. When Cattell returned to the United States, he brought Galton's test with him and used it to test the intelligence of students entering the University of Pennsylvania and Columbia University. Then he tracked the students' grades to see if the test results related in any way to academic performance. He wanted to find out whether the Galtonian tasks really did measure intelligence.

But it turned out there was no correlation—for that matter, the individual Galtonian tasks weren't even good at predicting a person's ability to perform other Galtonian tasks. This led Cattell to the conclusion that Galton's sensory tests were of no use in measuring intelligence...and they soon fell out of favor.

A NEW APPROACH

Binet's attempts to measure intelligence a few years later were no more successful than Galton's. "I began with the idea, impressed upon me by the studies of so many scientists, that intellectual superiority is tied to superiority of cerebral volume," he wrote. So the first thing he tried was measuring children's skulls. The smartest kids must have the largest heads because they contain the biggest brains...or so the logic went.

The logic was wrong. Binet found virtually no difference in skull size between good and poor students. So he began looking for some other way to measure intelligence. He tried studying the shapes of childrens' ears, reading their palms, and even testing their ability to perform Galtonian tasks. Nothing worked. Finally, he decided to test more sophisticated skills such as judgment, comprehension, reasoning, memory, academic aptitude, and how quickly kids could absorb new information and concepts.

HOW OLD ARE YOU?

Binet and a colleague, Theodore Simon, studied the abilities of "normal" schoolchildren and institutionalized retarded children. They compiled a long list of intellectual tasks, or "stunts," for the children to perform, starting with very simple ones and increasing them in complexity. After three more years of testing children, they were able to group the stunts by age level. Normal three-year-olds, for example, should be able to point to their eyes, nose, and mouth; and normal four-year-olds should be able to repeat three digits in the same order as the person giving the test had recited them.

Once Binet and Simon had the questions sorted according to age, they were able to measure what they called the "mental age" of the children they tested. The examiner began by asking questions that corresponded to the child's chronological age or slightly younger, and then progressed to more complicated questions to see how high the child could go before they could no longer answer questions correctly. If an 8-year-old could answer questions at the 10-year-old level, they were said to have a "mental age" of 10. Likewise, if a 13-year-old was only able to answer at the 11-year-old level, they had a mental age of 11.

HELPING HAND

The Binet-Simon tests didn't attempt to distinguish between children whose low scores were caused by external factors (such as poor education) and those whose scores were caused by learning disabilities. All the tests did was measure how much children "knew," so those who didn't know very much—for whatever reason—could receive the special attention they needed and reach their full intellectual potential.

Binet vehemently objected to the notion that a person's intelligence is predetermined. In his writings he lashed out at "some recent philosophers," as he called them, "who appear to have given their moral support to the deplorable verdict that the intelligence of an individual is a fixed quantity....We must protest and react against this brutal pessimism."

"With this orientation," Leon J. Kamin writes in *The Politics of IQ*, "it is perhaps as well that Binet died in 1911, before witnessing the uses to which his test was speedily put in the United States."

For Part II of The History of the I.Q. Test, see Page 195.

UNCLE JOHN'S STALL OF FAME

*You'd be amazed at the number of newspaper articles BRI
members send in about the creative ways people get involved
with bathrooms, toilets, toilet paper, etc. So we've
created Uncle John's "Stall of Fame."*

Honoree: David Garza of Henrietta, Texas
Notable Achievement: Owns "The Toilet of Mystery"
True Story: Between 1991 and 1993, Garza fished more
than 75 Papermate ballpoint pens out of his toilet—sometimes as
many as 5 pens a day—and still has no idea how they got there. It
has made him into a local celebrity. "Everywhere I go people say to
me, 'Hey, have you got a pen?'"

Honoree: Ann Landers
Notable Achievement: Demonstrated how passionate people are
about even the most trivial bathroom issues
True Story: In the mid-1980s, Landers innocently printed a letter
raising the issue of whether toilet paper should come off the top or
the bottom of the roll, in her advice column. A flood of letters en-
sued. In fact, Landers revealed in 1986 that, "in 31 years, this question has been the most controversial" of all the issues ever raised in
the column. Her own conclusion: The paper should come over the
top. Why? "Fine quality toilet paper has designs that are right side
up," she explained.

Honorees: Paul and Virginia Alee of Boulder, Colorado
Notable Achievement: Solved—once and for all—the "top or
bottom" toilet paper issue (see above)
True Story: The couple couldn't agree. So, "when we built our
house," they told the *Rocky Mountain News*, "we had the builder put
two dispensers in each bathroom, with one unrolling in one direction, and the other rolling in the other direction. The builder told
us he got more contracts as a result of showing our home to the public than any other 'show home' they'd ever put on display."

One reason why Fidel Castro grew a beard: The U.S. embargo cut off his razorblade supply.

Honoree: A Halifax bar called "Number 15"
Notable Achievement: The only pub in England built in a public restroom
True Story: Halifax is considered the pub capital of Britain. According to news reports, there are more pubs per household than anywhere in the country. "The local paper, the *Evening Courier*, even boasts its own Pub Correspondent." The demand for pubs is so strong that when an underground public lavatory became available, someone bought it and converted it into a pub called W.C.'s. When it was recently sold, the name was changed to Number 15. (*Ed. note:* Why not Number 2?)

Honoree: Edmond Rostand (1868–1918)
Notable Achievement: Author of the most famous play ever written in a bathroom
True Story: Rostand didn't like to be rude to his friends, but didn't like to be interrupted when he was working either. Rather than risk having to turn away any friends who might drop by to visit, "he took refuge in his bathtub and wrote there all day." His biggest bathroom success: *Cyrano de Bergerac*.

Honoree: Yang Zhu, a young mother in China
Notable Achievement: Gave birth in a train bathroom…and lost the baby down the toilet (she got it back).
True Story: Yang Zhu was nine months pregnant and headed home by train on May 4, 1999, when she began to suffer stomach pains. Her husband took her to the washroom where, "to her great surprise," she gave birth to her first child into the toilet "as soon as she squatted down.…The panic-stricken and screaming Yang ripped off the umbilical cord with her hands, and the baby immediately slipped down through the toilet and fell onto the rails."

Three security guards spotted the baby, covered in blood and lying in the middle of the tracks, but before they could reach him, another train sped by right over him. Miraculously, he only had slight bruises and a small cut on his head that needed three stitches.

The Arctic tern flies as far as 10,500 miles when it migrates.

EXECUTIVE DECISIONS

They may be in positions of responsibility…they may be captains of industry…they may be among the world's most successful business people. But that doesn't mean they can't make really dumb decisions, just like the rest of us. Here are some classics.

SHOULD WE SIGN THEM UP?

Mike Smith and Dick Rowe, executives in charge of evaluating new talent for the London office of Decca Records.

Background: On December 13, 1961, Mike Smith traveled to Liverpool to watch a local rock 'n' roll band perform. He decided they had talent, and invited them to an audition on New Year's Day 1962. The group made the trip to London and spent two hours playing 15 different songs at the Decca studios. Then they went home and waited for an answer.

They waited for weeks.

Decision: Finally, Rowe told the band's manager that the label wasn't interested, because they sounded too much like a popular group called The Shadows. In one of the most famous of all rejection lines, he said: "Not to mince words, Mr. Epstein, but we don't like your boys' sound. Groups are out; four-piece groups with guitars particularly are finished."

Impact: The group was The Beatles, of course. They eventually signed with EMI Records, started a trend back to guitar bands, and ultimately became the most popular band of all time. Ironically, "Within two years, EMI's production facilities became so stretched that Decca helped them out in a reciprocal arrangement, to cope with the unprecedented demand for Beatles records."

SHOULD WE LET THAT DIRECTOR USE OUR CANDY IN HIS FILM?

John and Forrest Mars, Jr., owners of Mars Inc., makers of M&M's

Background: In 1981, Universal Studios called Mars and asked for permission to use M&M's in a new film they were making.

Thyme for a checkup? According to food researchers, thyme helps prevent tooth decay.

This was (and is) a fairly common practice. Product placement deals provide filmmakers with some extra cash or promotion opportunities. In this case, the director was looking for a cross-promotion. He'd use the M&M's, and Mars could help promote the movie.

Decision: The Mars brothers said "No."

Impact: The film was *E.T. The Extra-Terrestrial*, directed by Stephen Spielberg. The M&M's were needed for a crucial scene: Elliot, the little boy who befriends the alien, uses candies to lure E.T. into his house.

Instead, Universal Studios went to Hersheys and cut a deal to use a new product called Reese's Pieces. Initial sales of Reese's Pieces had been light. But when *E.T.* became a top-grossing film—generating tremendous publicity for "E.T.'s favorite candy"—sales exploded. They tripled within two weeks and continued climbing for months afterward. "It was the biggest marketing coup in history," says Jack Dowd, the Hershey's executive who approved the movie tie-in. "We got immediate recognition for our product. We would normally have had to pay 15 or 20 million bucks for it."

HOW DO WE COME UP WITH SOME QUICK CASH?

Executives of 20th Century Fox's TV division (pre-Murdoch)

Background: No one at Fox expected much from M*A*S*H when it debuted on TV in 1972. Execs simply wanted to make a cheap series by using the M*A*S*H movie set again—so it was a surprise when it became Fox's only hit show. Three years later, the company was hard up for cash. When the M*A*S*H ratings started to slip after two of its stars left, Fox execs panicked.

Decision: They decided to raise cash by selling the syndication rights to the first seven seasons of M*A*S*H on a futures basis: local TV stations could pay in 1975 for shows they couldn't broadcast until October 1979—four years away. Fox made no guarantees that the show would still be popular; the $13,000 per episode was non-refundable. But enough local stations took the deal so that Fox made $25 million. They celebrated...

Impact: ...but prematurely. When M*A*S*H finally aired in syndication in 1979, it was still popular (in fact, it ranked #3 that year). It became one of the most successful syndicated shows ever, second only to "I Love Lucy." Each of the original 168 episodes grossed over $1 million for local TV stations; Fox got nothing.

THEY WENT THATAWAY

Malcolm Forbes wrote a fascinating book abut the deaths of famous people. Here are some of the weirdest stories he found, along with some from the BRI's own files.

STEPHEN FOSTER

Claim to Fame: 19th-century American songwriter; composer of "Oh! Suzanna," "Camptown Races," and "Swanee River"

How He Died: Broke.

Postmortem: Foster was a reckless spender who apparently never realized the value of his songs. In 1848, for example, he sold the rights to the classic "Oh! Suzanna" for $100.

In 1857, Foster was so desperate for cash that he sold the rights to *all* the songs he'd written for $1,900. Three years later, Foster left his wife and moved to a rundown rooming house in New York City. Sinking into alcoholism, tubercular and broke, he cranked out 105 songs over the next three years—most of them mediocre.

On the morning of January 13, 1864, Foster awoke with a fever and fell onto his porcelain washbasin while washing himself. The basin shattered, and one of the sharp pieces gouged deeply into his neck. He died, anonymous and alone, three days later. His body was sent to a morgue for "John Doe" corpses, where it remained until friends realized what had happened and came to claim the body.

Ironically, his last song, "Beautiful Dreamer," written only a few days earler, became one of his greatest hits.

CASEY JONES

Claim to Fame: Legendary railroad man and inspiration for the popular folk song

How He Died: In a trainwreck, just like the song says.

Postmortem: On the night of April 29, 1900, Jones pulled into Memphis aboard the *Cannonball Express*, one of the fastest trains of the Illinois Central. It should have been his last stop, but Jones was working a double shift.

---

20 million bats live in Texas's Bracken Cave. They eat 100 tons of insects every night.

The *Cannonball* was more than an hour late. Casey decided to make up for lost time by pushing the passenger train to over 100 mph on the 50-mph route to Canton, Mississippi. Fifteen minutes outside of Canton, Jones was only two minutes behind schedule.

But he was tired, and as he roared down the tracks that foggy night, Jones missed a flagman's signal—a freight train was stopped on the tracks ahead. By the time he saw the red tail lights on the caboose, it was too late. Jones pulled the air brakes, slammed the train into reverse, and, as the ballad says, blew the whistle just before he crashed.

The engine was destroyed and Jones was killed—an iron bolt pierced his neck—but no one else was...and none of the *Cannonball*'s passenger cars were even damaged. Less than a week later, a railroad worker named Wallace Saunders started singing about the crash. The song spread from one worker to another, and people added new stanzas. It was published in 1909 and became a huge hit on the vaudeville circuit.

MERIWETHER LEWIS

Claim to Fame: 18th century explorer who, together with William Clark, led the first overland expedition to the Pacific Northwest

How He Died: Was it suicide...or murder?

Postmortem: Lewis was better at exploring than he was at politics. President Thomas Jefferson appointed him governor of the upper Louisiana Territory in 1807, but dealing with corrupt officials, settlers, and Indian tribes took its toll on Lewis. He became increasingly troubled by the pressures of his office. In September 1809, Lewis traveled to Washington to deal with some unreimbursed expenses that had left him in debt. On the return leg of the journey, he had a nervous breakdown, and spent the next few weeks recovering at Fort Pickering. Then he set out for Nashville along the trail called the Natchez Trace. On October 10, Lewis and two servants stopped for the night at a cabin owned by Mrs. Robert Grinder. According to Mrs. Grinder, Lewis appeared to be very troubled, pacing back and forth late into the night, mumbling about his problems and occasionally screaming out loud.

That night, Mrs. Grinder heard a gunshot coming from Lewis's cabin, then a thud, then Lewis shouting, 'Oh, Lord!', and then another shot. Lewis staggered from his cabin to Mrs. Grinder's and pounded on the door, shouting to be let in.

Terrified, Mrs. Grinder refused to open the door. The following morning, she and Lewis's servants found Lewis in his bed, dying from bullet wounds in the chest and head. He died a short time later.

Did he commit suicide or was he murdered? Lewis had $200 with him when he left Fort Pickering, but only 25¢ was found on his body after he died...which led to speculation that Lewis was killed by Indians, by his servants (who were underpaid), by highway robbers who plagued the Natchez Trace, or even by Mrs. Grinder. What really happened? No one will ever know.

RANDOM LISTS

TEN INTERNATIONAL WORDS FOR "FART"

1. Afrikaans—*maagwind*
2. Israeli—*nuhfeechah*
3. Japanese—*he*
4. Cantonese/ Chinese—*fang*
5. German—*furz*
6. Bantu—*lu-suzi*
7. Hindu—*pud*
8. Polish—*pierdzenic*
9. Italian—*peto*
10. Russian—*perdun*

6 EVERYDAY LIES FROM THE BOOK OF LIES

1. "I'll just be a minute."
2. "Let's get together for lunch. I'll give you a call."
3. "Everything's fixed."
4. "The check is in the mail."
5. "I'll return your book as soon as I finish reading it."
6. "The doctor will be with you shortly."

3 MOST PRIZED AUTOGRAPHS OF ALL TIME

1. Shakespeare (only six known to exist)
2. Christopher Columbus (eight exist)
3. Julius Caesar (none known to exist)

FIRST 7 ROCK RECORDS TO WIN GOLD DISCS

1. "Hard Headed Woman," Elvis Presley (1958)
2. *Pat's Greatest Hits*, Pat Boone (1960)
3. *Elvis*, Elvis Presley (1960)
4. *Elvis' Golden Records*, Elvis Presley (1961)
5. *Encore—Golden Hits*, The Platters (1961)
6. *Blue Hawaii*, Elvis Presley (1961)
7. "Can't Help Falling in Love," Elvis Presley (1962)

If you're an "average" U.S. male, you'll spend 2,965 hours shaving in your lifetime.

NOT WHAT THEY SEEM TO BE

We take an awful lot of things for granted, based on image. But things (and people) aren't always what we think they are. Here are some examples.

BEATRIX POTTER

Image: A sentimental, animal-loving author who named her Peter Rabbit children's stories after her own pet rabbit, Peter.

Actually: Well, she did love animals, but she wasn't sentimental about them. Potter also wrote—in her diaries—about killing, boiling, and dissecting rabbits so she could study their organs.

FREDERIC REMINGTON

Image: Perhaps more than the work of any other artist, Frederic Remington's vivid, action-packed sculptures, paintings, and illustrations of the Old West have defined the look and feel of American cowboys and Indians and the world in which they lived.

Actually: Remington's works "were in fact largely studio creations based on a lively imagination," Bill Bryson writes in *Made in America.*

> He never saw any real cowboys in action. For one thing, he was much too fat to get on a horse, much less ride it into the midst of Indian battles. Even more crucially, by the time he made his first trip to the West, the age of the cowboy was all but over.

PAUL CÉZANNE

Image: A Post-Impresssionist painter known for his "attachment to nature," which manifested itself in his landscapes and still lifes. His paintings of fruit in a bowl are among the most famous still lifes ever produced.

Actually: Many of Cézanne's still lifes were much more *still* than *life*: It took him so long to paint a bowl of fruit that the fruit often rotted before he could finish. So he used wax fruit.

Patriotic state: More U.S. flags are manufactured in New Jersey than in any other state.

BELA LUGOSI

Image: Lugosi's groundbreaking role as the bloodthirsty Count Dracula in the early 1930s helped establish him as Hollywood's leading horror star.

Actually: Lugosi wasn't quite as bloodthirsty as he looked: According to one biographer, "he became sick and fainted at the sight of his own blood."

ROBERT E. LEE & ULYSSES S. GRANT

Image: Grant, who commanded the Union Army, was against slavery; Lee, who commanded the Confederate Army, was for it.

Actually: According to David Wallechinsky in *Significa*, both were slave-owners—"and the Southern general, Lee, freed his slaves *before* the Northern general, Grant, freed his." When Grant married his wife, Julia, she had four slaves, and although he freed his own slave in 1849, Julia's "slaves were not freed until the end of the Civil War. Mrs. Grant was an apologist for slavery all her life, and her husband stood up to her."

On the other hand, Robert E. Lee once wrote: "Slavery as an institution is a moral and political evil." In the late 1840s, Lee reportedly freed his four slaves. And he released his wife's slaves, whom he had inherited from his father-in-law, in 1863—two years before those owned by Julia Grant gained their freedom.

NEWSREEL FOOTAGE

Image: In the early black-and-white newsreel days of broadcast journalism, covering traffic accidents was as common a practice as it is today; yet somehow, the footage somehow seemed even gorier.

Actually: "Newsreel camera crews would sometimes pour several gallons of water on the roadway before filming. In black-and-white film, the water looked like blood." (*If No News, Send Rumors*, by Stephen Bates)

FOSTER'S LAGER

Image: Sold under the slogan "Australian for beer," Foster's Lager has become one of the most easily identifiable Australian imports.

Actually: The Foster's Lager sold in the U.S. is imported, but not from Australia—it's brewed in Canada.

UNCLE JOHN'S LIST OF SEVENS

Do you believe in magic numbers? Some people believe the
number seven has mystic significance. We don't...but
we put this list on page 77 just in case we're wrong.

7 Wonders of the Ancient World
Great Pyramid of
Cheops at Giza,
Hanging Gardens of
Babylon,
Statue of Zeus at
Olympia,
Temple of Artemis
at Ephesus,
Mausoleum at
Halicarnassus,
Colossus of Rhodes,
Pharos (Lighthouse)
of Alexandria

7 Liberal Arts
Grammar, Rhetoric,
Logic, Arithmetic,
Geometry, Music,
Astronomy

7 Deadly Sins
Pride, Envy, Wrath,
Sloth, Avarice,
Gluttony, Lust

7 Seas
Red, Adriatic, Black,
Caspian, Mediterra-
nean, Persian Gulf,
Indian Ocean

7 Days of the Week
Sun's day
Moon's day
Tiw's day
Woden's day
Thor's day
Frig's day
Saturn's day

7 Virtues
Faith, Hope, Charity,
Fortitude, Prudence,
Justice, Temperance

7 Sages of Greece
Solon of Athens
Pittacus of Mytilene
Bias of Priene
Cleobulus of Lindus
Periande of Corinth
Chilon of Sparta
Thales of Miletus

7 Japanese Gods of Happiness
Laughing Buddha
Watchman
God of longevity
God of scholarship
God of nutrition
God of fishing
Goddess of music

7 Hills of Rome
Palatine, Capitoline,
Quirinal, Viminal,
Esquiline, Caelian,
Aventine

7 Metals of Alchemy
Gold, Silver, Lead,
Quicksilver, Copper,
Iron, Tin

7 Muslim Heavens
Pure silver, Pure gold,
Pearl, White gold,
Silver, Ruby and gar-
net, Divine Light

7 Sisters (Pleaides)
Alcyone, Asterope,
Celaeno, Electra,
Maia, Merope,
Taygete

7 Ancient Rivers
Nile, Tigris, Oxua,
Euphrates, Indus,
Yaksart, Arax

7 Taxonomic Classifications
Kingdom, Phylum,
Class, Order, Family
Genus, Species

Shear madness: New Zealand sheep outnumber New Zealanders 13 to 1.

TURNER'S BROADCASTS

What does a billionaire think about success…money…and himself?
Ted Turner, the titan of TBS is only too happy to share his ruminations.

"Nuclear war would certainly set back cable."

"Life is like a B-grade movie. You don't want to leave in the middle of it, but you don't want to see it again."

"Being a billionaire or being a millionaire or being broke—and I've been all three at one time or another—it doesn't make that much difference."

"I would say that anything that is indecent and violent in TV is a crime against humanity and they should shoot the head man responsible."

"I don't really like television, if you want to know the honest truth. I think the more time you spend in conversation and playing bridge and playing golf and chatting with your children or reading a good book the better off you are. But since we have television with us—and since not everyone's going to read a book or converse with their children—I might as well be in it."

"People love money. It doesn't matter how much you've got, you want more."

"You've got to live like a poor person when you're getting started and save your money if you want to get rich. And then, once you get in the habit of saving it, you know, then it's hard to ever start spending again…and you get where you want to make more and more."

"If I give away a billion, I can still live pretty good on two, don't you think?"

"It's hard to find a house for more than $30 million or $40 million—even in Hollywood. And that's just 3% of a billion dollars."

"They're a little out of date. If you're only going to have 10 rules, I don't know if adultery should be one of them."
—*on the Ten Commandments*

"If only I had a little humility, I'd be perfect."

THE BIRTH OF THE SUBMARINE, PART I

Trivia question: In what American war was the submarine first used in battle? Answer: The American Revolution. (No, we're not kidding.) Here's Part I of the BRI's story of the submarine.

DIVE BOMBER

In 1774, a Yale University student named David Bushnell invented an underwater bomb to use against England's Royal Navy. Bushnell's plan: Sneak up beside the enemy ship, drill the hull, and attach the bomb. After activating a time-delayed detonator, you had 30 minutes before the bomb went off. But the bomb weighed over 150 pounds—too heavy for a swimmer to tow…and in wartime any approaching boat carrying a big bomb was sure to be fired on and sunk. Bushnell realized that a new kind of boat was needed to deliver his bomb: a "sub-marine," a ship that could travel unseen *under* the water. He set out to build one.

THE FIRST SUBMARINES

Bushnell was not the first to look for a way to travel beneath the waves. In the early 1500s, Leonardo da Vinci drew plans for a submersible boat made of goat skins stretched over a wooden frame. In 1620, Dutch inventor Cornelious Drebel actually built one. Drebel's boat was leather stretched over a wooden frame, and was powered by oars poked through waterproof flaps on both sides. Between 1620 and 1624, Drebel made several trips up the Thames River, as much as 15 feet below the surface.

But Bushnell was the first to build a sub designed to be used in battle. Bushnell's 1776 vessel was 7 1/2 feet long, 8 feet tall, and 4 feet wide, not much bigger than a barrel—barely large enough to hold one man and 30 minutes' worth of air. Made of iron, brass, and wood, it looked like "two gigantic tortoise shells joined together and stood on end," as Robert Burgess writes in *Ships Beneath the Sea*.

Hands On

The *American Turtle*, as it came to be known, weighed more than a ton but had no motor (it was 1776)—so the pilot had to move it with foot pedals and manual controls.

Opening a valve let water into a ballast tank and caused the submarine to sink; a foot-powered pump pushed the water out and enabled the *Turtle* to surface. Foot pedals connected to a propeller moved the vessel forward and backward; a hand crank connected to a second propeller moved it up and down. As if there weren't already enough to do, the pilot also had to use a hand rudder to steer and another hand crank to drill a hole in the enemy ship. A candle used too much precious air, so phosphorescent fungus was smeared on the instruments to make them glow in the dark.

George Washington was impressed enough by the effort to fund it. "Bushnell is a man of great mechanical powers," he wrote to Thomas Jefferson, "fertile in invention and a master of execution."

BOMBS AWAY!

In 1775, England and the American colonies went to war. And in September 1776, the *American Turtle* was sent into action against the 350 ships and 10,000 sailors of the Royal Navy massing along the Eastern seaboard. The *Turtle*'s first target: the HMS *Eagle*, anchored near Governor's Island. The *Eagle* was the 64-gun flagship of British admiral Earl Howe, who was in charge of the blockade of New York.

In the early morning hours, longboats towed the *Turtle* within a few hundred yards of the *Eagle*. The *Turtle* then submerged and traveled the rest of the way under its own power. The pilot, Ezra Lee, managed to make it underneath the *Eagle*, but when he tried to drill the hull, he missed and struck an impenetrable iron crossbar. Dawn was approaching and he was running out of air, so rather than risk another attempt, he decided to make a getaway. Too late—Lee was spotted by some British sailors, who gave chase in rowboats. Since he still had a bomb, Lee released it in the middle of New York Harbor, where it detonated and scared his pursuers away.

THAT SINKING FEELING

The attack had failed miserably, and so did the two that followed. British ships were not sunk, the blockade was not lifted, and the *Turtle* itself was captured by the British and destroyed. Bushnell's later attempts to sink British warships with floating mines also failed;

he never managed to sink a single British ship.

Perhaps because he was embarrassed by his failure, Bushnell disappeared from view around 1783. According to Alex Roland in *Underwater Warfare in the Age of Sail*, he relocated to Georgia, where he lived under the assumed name of Dr. David Bush. There, Bushnell "lived out his life as a teacher and a physician, and died in 1826, anonymous to all but a few close friends."

Want to immerse yourself in more of the story?
Turn to page 200 for Part II.

*   *   *

PRIMATE HALL OF FAME: BONZO

Background: In the 1951 film *Bedtime for Bonzo*, Bonzo the chimp (real name: Tamba) became the only animal star ever to share top billing with a future president of the U.S. The film was one of Reagan's few box office successes.

The Plot: Reagan plays a psychology professor whose father was a crook. To prove that environment, not heredity, is to blame, he borrows a chimp from the zoology department and raises it like a son. It backfires. When the chimp pilfers some jewelry, Reagan is accused of training it to steal. Reagan winds up in jail until Bonzo's blonde nurse (Diana Lynn) convinces the chimp to come clean. Bonzo returns the loot, Ronnie marries the nurse, and they all live happily ever after.

Tricks and Training: Reagan recalls: "The normal procedure called for the director, Fred de Cordova, to tell the trainer what he wanted from the chimp. But after a time Freddie was so captivated by Bonzo's acting that he'd forget and start to direct Bonzo as he did the human cast members. He'd say, 'No, Bonzo, in this scene you should…' Then he'd hit his head and cry, 'What the hell am I doing?'"

• Reagan made light of the experience, but it wasn't always safe. Once, on the set, Bonzo suddenly grabbed Reagan's necktie and almost strangled him with it.

Q. What do Bob Hope and Billy Joel have in common?   A. They were both once boxers.

"WE WANT MORE OF YOUR MONEY" DAY

You want to take a day off, but can't think of an excuse? No problem—there are hundreds of "holidays" to celebrate that you've probably never heard of. This article by Dana Canedy might even inspire you to create your own.

I T'S A HOLIDAY!
Banks did not shut their doors and the mail still arrived on May 18. For the record, though, it was "Don't Do Dishes Day." This "holiday" was not, as one might guess, dreamed up by two-career couples rebelling against domesticity; it was the creation of the makers of Dixie paper plates and Reynolds Wrap, two products that, as it happens, would sell very nicely if Americans turned their backs on the kitchen sink.

How to celebrate? Well, the sponsors envisioned a moment of silence in kitchens around the country as overworked Americans ignored their dishwashers and dined on paper and foil.

The goal, according to the Fort James Corporation, maker of Dixie products, and the Reynolds Metals Company, was to cut down on the time consumers spend scrubbing melted cheese and sticky pie filling off plates and pans, which the companies went to the trouble of estimating at 7,000 minutes a year.

"That is three full workweeks tackling dirty dishes," said Bill Schultz, a general manager at Fort James. "For most of us, that's more time than we spend on vacation each year. Our whole reason for being is to make washing dishes obsolete."

CHECK YOUR CALENDAR

That is a visionary goal, indeed, but even if it is never reached, the company will not complain. "Naturally, we want to sell product," Schultz acknowledged. So, Fort James teamed up with Reynolds Metals to promote the day with sweepstakes, national television advertising, and supermarket displays.

And the calendar is getting crowded. A growing number of companies that make and market everything from pain relievers to re-

---

Dogs are mentioned 14 times in the Bible. Cats aren't mentioned even once.

frigerators are creating "national days," ostensibly for consumers to reflect on weighty issues and trends. Others go for a week or even a full month, like "Toilet Tank Repair Month," in October, sponsored by Fluidmaster Inc., which makes toilet valves.

The beauty of this is that anyone can do it. If you have something to sell, just proclaim a special day—and hope someone listens. Authentic proclamations must come from the president or state or local elected officials, who generally deny requests to support events that are too obviously commercial. But that doesn't stop states from declaring events like "National Mule Appreciation Day" (observed in Tennessee) or companies and their trade groups from promoting official-*sounding* holidays.

HERE'S RELIEF!

And if the thought of adding more days to remember to your calendar is enough to give you a headache, don't fret. Now there is a "Migraine Recognition Day," designated by Bristol-Myers Squibb, the pharmaceutical company.

The day, which is observed on May 5, was scheduled just four months after the company received regulatory approval to market a new migraine formula of Excedrin, and Bristol-Myers says the event was created to educate the public about the differences between migraines and, say, stress or sinus headaches.

Some marketing experts scoff at this approach. "You've got to be kidding; I don't need a day of the year to tell me I have a headache," said Clive Chajet, of Chajet Consultancy, which advises corporations on brand-building strategies. "I would definitely discourage my clients from spending their money that way." The risk, as Mr. Chajet sees it, is that consumers may be turned off by such obvious selling strategies.

OUR DAY WILL COME

Tell that to Burger King, which early in 1998 was unapologetic in its use of a manufactured special day to drum up business. Looking for an edge in its long-running burger battle with McDonald's, the company introduced what it touted as a tastier french fry and proclaimed January 2 as national "Free Fryday." Then they gave away an estimated 15 million orders of fries as part of a $70 million advertising and marketing campaign.

Q. Which place has more judges—Los Angeles, or France?   A. Los Angeles.

Even marketers of goods that people give little thought to have found an angle to wrap a day around. The Whirlpool Corporation sponsors "National Clean Out Your Refrigerator Day" each November.

Whirlpool times its annual event to fall the week before Thanksgiving, when most people need extra space in their refrigerators anyway. On clean-out day, refrigerator technicians and nutritionists operate a toll-free information line to answer questions about defrosting and food mold. Whirlpool also has customer service representatives standing by to explain to callers the virtues of its latest appliances and to offer a list of stores that carry them.

"Nobody is trying to sell them anything," Carolyn Verweyst, manager of marketing communications for the company, said without a hint of irony.

Last year, Whirlpool recorded about 1,000 calls to its special line and hundreds of hits on its Web site. "We hope if and when they need a refrigerator, the first name that comes to mind will be the Whirlpool folks," she added.

THEY'RE ALL SPECIAL DAYS

Chajet, the brand consultant, says people have a hard enough time remembering their own anniversaries, let alone trying to keep track of who sponsored what corporate commemoration.

Even so, he predicted, "I can't help thinking that next we'll have a 'Viagra Day.'"

Trying to stand out from the clutter of advertising, marketers have created a calendar crowded with sponsors. Here are some examples:

Free Fryday—
Jan. 2
Sponsor: Burger King

Prune The Fat Month—
January
Sponsor: California Prune Board

Egg Salad Week
April 13-19
Sponsor: American Egg Board

Clean Out Your Refrigerator Day—
Nov. 18
Sponsor: Whirlpool

How would you know a *cherophobe* if you met one? They'd be "afraid of having fun."

HAPPY DONUT DAY!

Like to party? Well, here are some more special days, weeks, and even months that you can celebrate!

JANUARY: Bread Machine Baking Month (*Sponsor: Continental Mills*)

Jan. 1: Get a Life Day

Jan. 27: Thomas Crapper Day (*BRI Offices Closed*)

FEBRUARY: Return Shopping Carts to the Supermarket Month (*Sponsor: Illinois Food Retailers*)

Feb. 11: Be Electrific Day

Feb. 29: Gravity Observance Day (*Very Heavy*)

MARCH: National Sauce Month

Mar. 1: National Pig Day (*Oink!*)

Mar. 5: National Pancake Week (*Sponsor: Bisquick Baking Mix*)

Mar. 9: Panic Day

APRIL: Holy Humor Month

Apr. 14: Polkabration Weekend (*South Fallsburg, New York*)

Apr. 28: National Hairball Awareness Day

Apr. 30: Hairstylist Appreciation Day

MAY: National Salsa Month (*Sponsor: Pace Foods*)

...*and* National Egg Month (*Sponsor: The Egg Council*)

May 17: National Be a Millionaire Day

May 26: Morning Radio Wise Guy Day

JUNE: National Frozen Yogurt Month (*Sponsor: TCBY*)

...*and* National Accordian Awareness Month

June 2: Yell "Fudge" at the Cobras in North America Day

June 2–3: Donut Day (*Sponsor: The Salvation Army*)

June 8: World Pork Expo (*Sponsor: National Pork Producers Council*)

JULY: National Hot Dog Month

July 1–4: Spam Town USA Festival (Austin, Minnesota)

July 2–8: Be Nice to New Jersey Week

July 10–16: Nude Recreation Week

July 15: Cow Appreciation Day

July 18: National Baby Food Festival (Fremont, Michigan)

AUGUST: National Hypnosis Awareness Month

Aug. 5: National Mustard Day (*Sponsor: Mt. Horeb Mustard Museum*)

Q. How do you tell if an Amish man is married?   A. He has a beard.

Aug. 8: Sneak Some Zucchini onto Your Neighbors' Porch Night

Aug. 10–16: Elvis Week

SEPTEMBER: National Chicken Month (*Sponsor: The National Chicken Council*)

Sept. 6: Do It! Day (Fight Procrastination Day)

Sept. 10: Old Timers Day (Lisco, Nebraska)

Sept. 11: No News Is Good News Day

OCTOBER: National Toilet Tank Repair Month (*Sponsor: Fluidmaster, Inc.*)

Oct. 4: Ten-Four Day

Oct. 13: Skeptics' Day (Don't believe it)

Oct. 15: National Grouch Day

NOVEMBER: National Bone Marrow Awareness Month

Nov. 5: National Split Pea Soup Week (*Sponsor: Dry Pea and Lentil Council*)

Nov. 6: Shallow Persons Awareness Week

DECEMBER: Bingo's Birthday Month (*the game, not the dog*)

Dec. 5: Bathtub Party Day

Dec. 15: Underdog Day

Dec. 26: National Whiner's Day

* * *

BRI "FAVORITE ROLE MODELS"

Role Model: Patricia Downey, Nebraska's Mother of the Year
Setting an Example: In April 2000 "she surrendered her title after one of her sons accused her of nominating herself for the honor, and forging his signature on a letter of support. According to press reports, 'only five of Downey's seven sons actually supported her nomination.'"

Role Model: Koo-Koo the Klown
Setting an Example: In 1993 the Legal Aid Society of Santa Clara County filed charges against the man who portrayed Koo-Koo for nearly 30 years, entertaining children at parties, for routinely violating state law at an apartment complex he owned. Which law? According to the society, Koo-Koo "refused to rent to tenants with children."

How did the kerosene fungus get its name? It eats kerosene and lives in jet fuel tanks.

A TOY IS BORN

Here are the origins of some toys you may have played with.

THE ERECTOR SET

Inventor: A.C. Gilbert, an Olympic pole-vaulter who owned the Mysto Company, which sold magic tricks and magicians' equipment

Origin: The market for magic tricks was pretty narrow, and Gilbert was hoping to break into the toy business. But he couldn't think of a product. Then one day in 1911, while riding a commuter train to New York City, Gilbert saw some new power lines being strung from steel girders. It suddenly occurred to him that kids might enjoy building things out of miniaturized girders. So he went home, cut out prototype girders from cardboard, and gave them to a machinist to make out of steel. "When I saw the samples," Gilbert wrote in his autobiography, "I knew I had something."

Selling It: Gilbert brought the prototypes to the big toy fairs of the year, in Chicago and New York...and walked out with enough orders to keep his factory busy for a year. So Gilbert took a chance and the following year, he made the Erector Set the first major toy ever to be advertised nationally. It sold so well that overnight, the Gilbert Toy Company became one of America's largest toy manufacturers.

THE BABY ALIVE DOLL

Inventor: The Kenner Products Company

Origin: Baby dolls that wet themselves were nothing new in the early 1970s, and they were popular sellers. So in 1972 Kenner decided to take the concept to the next level with a doll called Baby Alive. When someone held a spoon or a bottle up to the doll's mouth, she took in the food...and after "a suitable interval," she pooped it back out again. The baby's "food" consisted of cherry, banana, and lime "food packets" that were actually colored gel. "And to answer the obvious question," writes Sydney Stern in *Toyland*, "yes, what went in red, yellow, or green came out red, yellow or green."

Selling It: At the time, Kenner was owned by food giant General

---

Australia has a robot that shears sheep; Japan has one that makes sushi.

Mills—which meant that Kenner president Bernie Loomis had to get approval from the Chairman of General Mills before he could put the doll into production. He nearly blew it, Stern writes:

> Unfortunately, he forgot to put a disposable diaper on the doll before feeding it, and it extruded poo-poo gel all over his boss's arm. "Who in the world would ever want such a messy thing," asked the disgruntled chairman. As it turned out, there were fast hordes of children eager to own a defecating dolly. Baby Alive was the number-one-selling doll in 1973, and Kenner went on to sell three million of them.

RISK

Inventor: Albert Lamorisse, a French filmmaker

Origin: In 1957, a year after winning an Academy Award for his (now-classic) film, *The Red Balloon*, Lamorisse created the game he called La Conquête du Monde (Conquest of the World).

Sales Tales: La Conquête du Monde was a big hit in France, prompting U.S. game maker Parker Brothers to snap up the rights to the American version. They immediately ran into a problem: many of the executives at Parker Brothers were veterans of World War II and the Korean War, and they were uncomfortable with the game's title. So Parker Brothers ordered their R&D department to come up with a less warlike name. No luck—nobody could think of a name until a salesperson happened to hand the Parker Brothers president a piece of paper with the letters R-I-S-K written on it. A divine inspiration? No. According to company lore, R-I-S-K were merely the first letters of the names of each of Parker Brothers president's four grandchildren.

Historical Footnote: Risk was banned in Germany for years...until the object of the German version was changed from "conquering the world" to "liberating the world."

*   *   *

Koosh balls were invented when Scott Stillinger, an engineer, was looking for a safe ball to play catch with his small children. Foam balls bounced out of their hands, and bean bags were too heavy. So he made a ball from more than 2,000 rubber strings, joined together at the center.

WORD ORIGINS

Here are some more interesting word origins.

THIRD DEGREE

Meaning: Intense, often brutal questioning, especially by police

Origin: "Dating to the 1890s in America, it has no connection with criminal law. The third degree is the highest degree in Freemasonry. Any Mason must undergo very difficult tests of proficiency before he qualifies for the third degree and it is probably from these 'tests' that the exhaustive questioning of criminals came to be called the third degree." (From *QPB Encyclopedia of Word and Phrase Origins*, by Robert Hendrickson)

HANGNAIL

Meaning: A small piece of torn skin at the base or sides of a fingernail

Origin: "Had nothing to do with a hanging nail—the original word was *angnail*. The *ang* referred to the pain it caused—as in ang/uish." (From *Take My Words*, by Howard Richler)

GYPSY

Meaning: A nomad, or a member of a nomadic tribe

Origin: "In the early 16th century members of a wandering race who called themselves Romany appeared in Britain. They were actually of Hindu origin, but the British believed that they came from Egypt, and called them *Egipcyans*. This soon became shortened to *Gipcyan*, and by the year 1600, to *Gipsy* or *Gypsey*." (From *Webster's Word Histories*)

SIEGE

Meaning: A prolonged battle or period of oppression

Origin: "Comes from the Latin *sedere*, to sit. It refers to a basic tactic of ancient warfare—that is, an army surrounds a fort or castle and remains there ('sits') until enemy resistance breaks down because the defenders are cut off from aid and supplies." (From *Fighting Words*, by Christine Ammer)

Some hummingbirds hold their nests together with spiderwebs.

BEDLAM

Meaning: Madness, uproar, or confusion

Origin: "*Bedlam* is a Middle English form of *Bethlehem* (the city where Jesus is said to have been born). Its current meaning comes from the Hospital of Saint Mary of Bethlehem in London, which was incorporated as a lunatic asylum in 1547." (From *Wilton's Etymology*, by Dave Wilton)

ADDICT

Meaning: A person with an uncontrollable (usually bad) habit

Origin: "Slaves given to Roman soldiers as a reward for performance in battle were known as *addicts*. Eventually, the term came to refer to a person who was a slave to anything." (From *Etymologically Speaking*, by Steven Morgan Friedman)

FIZZLE

Meaning: To make a hissing sound; to fail or end weakly

Origin: "Derives from the word *fisten*, 'to fart.' Its original definition, according to the *Oxford English Dictionary*, is 'the action of breaking wind quickly.'" (From *Take My Words*, by Howard Richler)

LEWD

Meaning: Vulgar or lascivious

Origin: "Comes from the Anglo-Saxon *loewede*, which meant 'unlearned,' and referred to the mass of the people as opposed to the clergy, just as we now talk of laymen in this sense. From 'unlearned' it came to mean 'base, coarse and vulgar.'" (From *To Coin a Phrase*, by Edwin Radford and Alan Smith)

HALIBUT

Meaning: A bottom-dwelling fish

Origin: "A Middle English term for any flatfish, including flounder and fluke, was *butte*. Fish was often eaten on holy days, so butte was compounded with *haly*, a form of 'holy,' thus giving Middle English *halybutte*, which became our modern halibut." (From *Webster's Word Histories*)

When an apple falls to the Earth, the Earth slightly moves toward it as well. (Very slightly.)

COURT TRANSQUIPS

Here's more real-life courtroom dialogue.

Q: "How did you get here today?"
A: "I had a friend bring me."
Q: "The friend's name?"
A: "We call him Fifi."
Q: "To his face?"

Q: "When you said that, there was some hesitation. Have you heard of others that you haven't heard about yet?"

Q: "What did you do to prevent the accident?"
A: "I just closed my eyes and screamed as loud as I could."

The Court: "What's the problem?"
Bailiff: "Oh, a cockroach was on the exhibit table, Your Honor."
Plaintiff's Counsel: "Motion to quash."
The Court: "Granted."

Mr. Jacobs: "Don't wave at me, or I will wave at you."
Mr. North: "You did wave."
Mr. Jacobs: "You can wave and I'll wave. Why don't we take five minutes to wave at each other."
Mr. Black: "Why don't we stipulate that all waves will be waived."

Defendant: "But Judge, I can't do 61,500 years!"
Judge: "Well, just do as much of it as you can. And have a nice day."

Q: "Do you remember the context in which your husband brought the issue up?"
A: "Not really. I try not to listen when he talks."

Q: "Do you speak Spanish, Officer?"
A: "Yes, I do."
Q: "Are you fluent in Spanish?"
A: "Yes, I do."

Q: "Doctor, before you performed the autopsy, did you check for a pulse?"
A: "No."
Q: "Did you check for blood pressure?"
A: "No."
Q: "Did you check for breathing?"
A: "No."
Q: "So, then it is possible that the patient was alive when you began the autopsy?"
A: "No."
Q: "How can you be so sure, Doctor?"
A: "Because his brain was sitting on my desk in a jar."
Q: "But could the patient have still been alive nevertheless?"
A: "It is possible that he could have been alive and practicing law somewhere."

Q: "How many times have you committed suicide?"

Animal instinct: Only about 3% of mammals practice monogamy.

THE WIZARDS OF FIZZ

Uncle John recently bought a book by Sydney Perkowitz called Universal Foam *because he wanted to read about science for a change. Wouldn't you know it, the first story he turned to was this brief history of carbonation.*

THE BIRTH OF SODA

Soft drinks have not always been carbonated. Pedestrians in 17th-century Paris, for instance, could buy lemonade from vendors who sold it from tanks strapped to their backs. Artificially carbonated drinks—now a worldwide industry with annual sales over $50 billion in the United States alone—were created for a more compelling reason than refreshment. They were made in imitation of naturally effervescent waters that poured from certain springs, waters believed to have therapeutic effects. In fact, although the mineral content of spring waters may have value, effervescence has no proven medicinal properties, other than the ability to settle nausea.

Nevertheless, people were willing to pay for natural bubbliness in waters such as Perrier, which emerges from a spring near the French city of Nîmes and was first bottled and sold in 1863. Once the bubbliness of spring water was recognized as coming from dissolved carbon dioxide, eminent scientists began looking for ways to artificially put the gas into water, creating a carbonated beverage.

FOUNDING FATHER

The first to succeed was Joseph Priestley, the 18th-century British scientist who identified oxygen as the active part of the atmosphere (and also discovered the nitrous oxide that pushes whipped cream out of an aerosol can). Priestley made carbonated water by using beer, or at least the carbon dioxide produced by its brewing. He visited a brewery in the city of Leeds, and holding two containers over the surface of the mash as it fermented, poured water back and forth until the liquid was charged with CO_2. In 1772, he developed equipment to carbonate water more conveniently. At about the same time in France, Antoine-Laurent Lavoisier, a founder of modern chemistry, developed a similar apparatus.

Q. How many times was the city of Winchester, Virginia,

Entrepreneurs eagerly adopted this new technology. One of the first was the Swiss jeweler Jacob Schweppe. He made and sold carbonated mineral water in Geneva, and later in London, providing two different formulations for medicinal purposes. To prevent the gas from escaping, his product came in corked bottles with rounded (convex) bottoms; such a "drunken" container could not stand upright, guaranteeing that its cork would remain damp and swollen so as to provide a tight seal.

GOOD FOR YOU

Apart from any perceived medical virtues, people drank sparkling water because they enjoyed its fizz and its slightly sour flavor, which comes because carbon dioxide in water yields highly diluted carbonic acid. There is also evidence that the fizzing action and perhaps the acidity affect the taste buds so they are more sensitive to food flavors. The popularity of bubbly water spread rapidly; by 1851, the Schweppes firm was selling well over two million bottles a year. A natural next step for other entrepreneurs was to add flavoring, such as ginger and lemon. And the first cola soft drink, based on caffeine-bearing nuts from the tropical kola nut tree, came along in 1886, when John Pemberton invented Coca-Cola in Atlanta, Georgia.

Today, the production of carbonated soda involves massive quantities of CO_2. At Coca-Cola, the world's biggest beverage company, carbonation is not carried out at one central location but rather at regional bottling plants. First the basic Coca-Cola syrup (whose recipe is a well-guarded secret) is blended with water. Then the mixture is chilled to a few degrees above freezing, which makes it easier for it to take up CO_2 and reduces the tendency to foam. After the liquid has been vaporized in diffusers (which makes it more permeable to the gas) the gas is added in stainless steel tanks. Different brands of soda, and different product lines by the same manufacturer, have different degrees of carbonation, which is controlled by varying the pressure in the tank. The typical value for Coca-Cola is sixty pounds per square inch, twice the pressure in an automobile tire and much higher than atmospheric pressure—a far cry from Joseph Priestley's groundbreaking but low-tech carbonation over fermenting beer mash.

MISTAKEN IDENTITY

*Next time someone says, "Y'know, you remind me a lot of
(someone's name)," don't simply laugh it off—GET PARANOID!
According to the BRI's extensive files, a case of
mistaken identity can lead to...*

HARASSMENT

Background: Slobodan "Dan" Milosovic (spelled with two 'o's), has lived in London, England, since 1980. Unfortunately for him, he has the same name—more or less—as Serbian ex-president Slobodan Milosevic (spelled with an 'e').

What Happened: During the Kosovo war, reporters assumed there was some connection between the two and camped out on Milosovic's doorstep. They not only harangued him with questions, they even began quizzing his neighbors. Eventually, Milosovic had to file a complaint with England's Press Complaints Commission to protest all of the attention. "Milosovic was fed up with being hounded by the media," said the media.

LAWSUITS

Background: Kevin Moore, a 45-year-old Florida resident, was contacted some years ago by a woman named Anne Victoria Moore, who assumed she had finally located her ex-husband, also named Kevin Moore. He assured her she had made a mistake.

What Happened: Ms. Moore refused to believe him. At last report, she had spent more than eight months filing legal actions against Kevin Moore. First, she placed a claim on his house...then on his bank account...and then charged him with failure to pay child support. She persists, although numerous government agencies have informed her that this Kevin Moore is "11 years older than, six inches shorter than, and facially dissimilar to, her ex-husband."

UNEMPLOYMENT

Background: In 1990 Bronti Wayne Kelly, of Temecula, California, had his wallet stolen. The guy who stole it was then caught for shoplifting, and "pretended to be Kelly when he was arrested."

What Happened: Kelly wound up with a criminal record. And according to news reports, after losing his wallet in the theft, he also "lost his apartment, car and most of his belongings between 1991 and 1995 because no one would hire him....Every time potential employers did a background check, they found the shoplifting arrest....The same man apparently also pretended to be Kelly when he was arrested for arson, burglary, theft, and disturbing the peace." Today Kelly carries a special document that distinguishes him from the impostor, but—amazingly—"he cannot have the criminal record carrying his name erased unless the fake Kelly is found."

IMPRISONMENT

Background: In 1993, a "woman with long blonde hair" broke into the house of a Mississippi man named Darron Terry. He caught her in the act...but she escaped. Following the burglary, Terry looked through some photographs and identified Melissa Gammill, "a carefree single woman working at a mall food court." as the culprit. Three months later, Gammill was arrested.

What Happened: Gammill could not provide an alibi, because she couldn't remember where she'd been on the night of the burglary. She was charged with the crime, convicted, and sentenced to ten years in prison. Luckily for Gammill, her lawyer, Debra Allen, believed that her client was innocent and developed a hunch that a lookalike had actually committed the crime. She pursued her theory until she stumbled across a mugshot of Pauline Meshea Bailey, who looks so much like Gammill that their photographs are practically interchangeable. In April 1995, Terry admitted he'd mistakenly identified the wrong person, and Gammill was set free after serving 10 months in prison.

ASSASSINATION

Background: During World War II, England's prime minister, Winston Churchill, was targeted by Nazi agents for assassination. They were constantly on the alert, waiting for an opportunity to strike. In 1943, their moment came. At an airport in Lisbon, Portugal (a neutral country), they saw Churchill, famous as "a portly, cigar-smoking Britisher," board a commercial flight to England.

What Happened: According to Churchill in his 1950 memoir, *The Hinge of Fate:*

> The daily commercial aircraft was about to start from the Lisbon air-field when a thickset man smoking a cigar walked up and was thought to be a passenger on it. The German agents therefore signalled that I was on board. Although these neutral passenger planes had plied unmolested for many months between Portugal and England and had carried only civilian traffic, a German war plane was instantly ordered out, and the defenseless aircraft was ruthlessly shot down. Fourteen civilian passengers perished, among them the well-known British film actor, Leslie Howard.

The "portly, cigar smoking Britisher" was in reality one Alfred Chenhalls. "The brutality of the Germans was only matched by the stupidity of their agents," Churchill wrote. "It is difficult to understand how anyone could imagine that with all the resources of Great Britain at my disposal, I should have booked passage on a neutral plane from Lisbon and flown home in broad daylight."

THE DESTRUCTION OF AN ENTIRE CIVILIZATION

Background: When Hernán Cortés landed in Mexico with his 600 soldiers in 1519, the Aztecs were in control of most of present-day Mexico. They had been since around the year 1200.

Religion was a major part of Aztec life...and according to legend, the god Quetzalcoatl, who had light skin, light eyes, and a beard (just like Cortés) was supposed to return to earth. So when Cortés and his men started to march toward the Aztec capital city of Tenochtitlán (now Mexico City), word passed that Quetzalcoatl had come back.

What Happened: In the capital city, the Aztec king, Montezuma, received the visitors "in fulfillment of the ancient prophecy." The Spaniards were greeted with food, gold, and women. Montezuma is quoted as saying to Cortés, "Our lord, you are weary. The journey has tired you, but now you have arrived on the earth. You have come to your city....You have come here to sit on your throne, to sit under its canopy." Cortés, in reply, assured Montezuma he had come in peace. Actually, he had come to conquer, and quickly took Montezuma hostage. The Spaniards then proceeded to wipe the Aztec civilization out.

DUMB JOCKS

They give an awful lot of interviews, but sports stars aren't always the most articulate people. Maybe they should keep their mouths shut. Nah.

"Some of the great Oedipuses in the world have been built by Donald Trump."
—Don King

"Sure I've got one. It's a perfect 20-20."
—Dallas Cowboy Duane Thomas, *on his IQ*

"Even Napoleon had his Watergate."
—Baseball manager Danny Ozark

"I'm a four-wheel-drive-pickup type of guy, and so is my wife."
—Outfielder Mike Greenwell, *describing his personality*

"That was the nail that broke the coffin's back."
—Basketball coach Jack Kraft, *after his star player fouled out*

"He'll take your head off at the blink of a hat."
—Joe Theismann, *on an NFL draft pick*

"I look up in the stands and I see them miss balls, too."
—Outfielder Devon White, *after fans booed him for dropping a fly ball*

"Next up is Fernando Gonzalez, who isn't playing tonight."
—Broadcaster Jerry Coleman

"My grandmother told me it was good for colds."
—Outfielder Kevin Mitchell, *on why he eats Vick's VapoRub*

"You mean the great home-run hitter?"
—N.J. Net Yinka Dare, *asked about Beirut*

"I'm in favor of it, as long as it's multiple choice."
—L.A. Laker Kurt Rambis, *on drug tests*

"Maybe I'm not getting enough saltwater to my brain."
—Frankie Hejduk, U.S. soccer team member and surfer, *on his hamstring injuries*

"If a guy is a good fastball hitter, does that mean I should throw him a bad fastball?"
—pitcher Larry Anderson

"David Cone is in a class by himself with three or four other players."
—George Steinbrenner, *on his ace pitcher*

BEHIND THE HITS

Here are a few "inside" stories about popular songs.

The Artist: The Champs
The Song: "Tequila"
The Story: An accidental hit. In 1958, a group of studio musicians recorded an instrumental called "Train to Nowhere" for Gene Autry's Challenge label. For the B-side, Danny Flores, the saxophone player, suggested a song he'd written in Tijuana. While arranging the song, someone jokingly told Flores to shout "Tequila!" in a low voice during the breaks. None of the musicians took it seriously...or even stuck around the studio long enough to hear a playback. On a whim, they named the group after Gene Autry's horse, Champion.

"Train to Nowhere" went nowhere...until DJs discovered the flip side. "Tequila" shot to number one, and the Champs won the first Grammy ever awarded for "Best R&B performance."

The Artist: R.E.M.
The Song: "Losing My Religion"
The Story: When R.E.M. recorded their album *Out of Time*, in 1991, this was the song that stood out as an obvious single. The only problem was Warner Bros. execs didn't want to release a record with religious symbolism. But according to lead singer Michael Stipe, the song actually has nothing to do with religion. "The phrase 'losing my religion' is Southern slang," he explained. "It means 'fed up' or 'at the end of your rope.'" R.E.M. insisted that it be released, and Warner Bros. finally gave in. Good decision: It was a Top 5 single that won a Grammy for Best Song in 1992.

The Artist: Todd Rundgren
The Song: "I Saw the Light"
The Story: Many of the biggest hits of all time were created spontaneously, in a few minutes—including this Top 20 hit. But just because a song's popular doesn't mean that the writer likes it.

"I wrote this song in fifteen minutes from start to finish." Rundgren says, "and it was one of the reasons that caused me to change my style of writing. For me, the greatest disappointment in the world

---

Jellyfish are 99% water.

is not being able to listen to my own music and enjoy it. 'I Saw the Light' is just a string of cliches. It's absolutely nothing that I ever thought, or thought about, before I sat down to write the song."

The Artist: Los Del Rio
The Song: "Macarena (Bayside Boys Mix)"
The Story: Spanish duo Los Del Rio wrote this song about a girl named Macarena, a common name in their native Seville. Their original version was already a big hit in Spanish-speaking countries when Miami radio stations started getting requests for it. A local DJ and two friends made this American version because it was the only way the program director would play the song on the air. They wrote English lyrics, restructured the melody (they used the Los Del Rio chorus and music tracks) and re-recorded it with a new singer—all in two days. It became a huge local hit, then a huge national hit, and was on the charts for an amazing sixty weeks.

Note: The deejay and his crew never even met Los Del Rio.

The Artist: Bob Dylan
The Song: "Lay Lady Lay"
The Story: There's nothing profound in this song—and that's the story. Dylan has always been known for his meaningful lyrics. But when he gave up smoking in the late 1960s, he was taken with the new sound of his voice, and suddenly seemed to care more about the music than the words. "Lay Lady Lay" typified the change. Dylan came up with the chord progression first. Then he added the melody, singing "la-la-la-la," which he conveniently turned into "lay lady lay." The song was originally commissioned as the theme for the film *Midnight Cowboy*. But Dylan didn't finish it in time...so the producers used Harry Nillson's *Everybody's Talkin'* instead.

The Artist: The Beatles
The Song: "Yesterday"
The Story: This song just popped into Paul McCartney's head when he woke up one morning. He ran to the piano immediately and plunked out the tune so he wouldn't forget it. His sleepy-eyed lyrics: "Scrambled eggs... / Ooooh baby how I love your legs." It was only after people close to the band convinced them that the song had real potential that Paul rewrote the lyrics.

THE BIRTH OF THE COMPACT DISC

*When CDs were introduced, we thought it was a conspiracy to
make us replace our record collection with CDs. Well, maybe
it was, but we have to admit that CD quality is pretty good.
Here's the story of how they were invented.*

AS SEEN ON TV

In 1974, the Philips Electronics company of the Netherlands started a revolution. They invented a laser video disc—the first product to make use of the "general induction laser" that had been developed at MIT in the early 1960s.

But LaserVision, as it was called, was a brand-new technology and it had a problem: poor error detection and correction—which resulted in inconsistent sound and picture quality. Philips built a prototype to show to several Japanese manufacturers, but the LaserVison player performed so poorly that only one of the Japanese companies—Sony—was willing to work with Philips to fix their new product.

At the time, Sony was a leader in both magnetic tape and digital recording technology. They had already built the world's first digital sound recorder—which used magnetic tape, weighed several hundred pounds, and was as large as a refrigerator...but it worked. And it gave Sony a head start in figuring out how to correct the problems that Philips was now experiencing with LaserVision.

DISC JOCKEYS

Sony put its digital magnetic tape system on the back burner and began developing a system that would record audio directly to a laser disc. It wouldn't be easy—on top of all the technical problems that had to be worked out, there was also strong opposition within the company to spending money on risky new technology.

Norio Ohga, the company's earliest and most enthusiastic proponent of digital sound recording, faced resistance from company founder Masaru Ibuka, and all but three of Sony's audio engineers. Creatures of the analog age, they had little faith in the basic con-

---

First Japanese flag displayed in the U.S. after WW II: In 1962, by Sony in NYC.

cept of digital technology—converting sound into numbers and then converting the numbers back into sound—and doubted it would ever improve on conventional analog recording. But Ohga, a former musician and aspiring symphony conductor, likened digital recording to "removing a winter coat from the sound," and insisted that the project be given the highest priority no matter what the cost.

STEP BY STEP

By the spring of 1976, most of the audio compact disc's bugs had been worked out, and the compact disc development team proudly presented Ohga with an astonishing technical marvel: a compact disc the same size as an LP record; but instead of having the same recording capacity as its vinyl counterpart, the CD could hold 13 hours and 20 minutes of sound.

So why aren't today's compact discs as big as an LP and capable of holding 13 hours of music? Because they'd cost too much to produce—something Ohga realized after taking one look at the prototype.

THE SIZE OF THINGS

Ohga sent his engineers back to the drawing board to come up with something that made more financial sense—a smaller CD that approximated the *capacity* of a vinyl record instead of its physical size. But exactly what size? The decision was still a few years off.

Back in the Netherlands, Philips Electronics was at work on its own version of a compact disc that was 11.5 centimeters across (about 4 1/2 inches) and capable of holding exactly 60 minutes of sound. Sixty minutes was a nice round number, and the discs were small enough to fit easily into players the size of automobile tape decks. But drawing from his background in classical music, Sony's Ohga pointed out a problem with the 11.5-centimeter standard that others had missed, as John Nathan writes in *Sony: The Private Life*:

> Ohga was adamantly opposed on grounds that a 60-minute limit was "unmusical": at that length, he pointed out, a single disc could not accommodate all of Beethoven's Ninth Symphony and would require interrupting many of the major operas before the end of

the First Act. On the other hand, 75 minutes would accommodate most important pieces of music, at least to a place where it made musical sense to cut them....The disc would have to be 12 centimeters to accommodate 75 minutes. In the end, Philips agreed to Sony's specifications.

FINAL TOUCHES

In March 1980, Sony and Philips tested their competing error-correction systems on discs that had been deliberately scratched, marked with chalk, and smeared with fingerprints. Sony's system worked better and was adopted by both companies.

Three months later, they submitted their prototype to the Digital Audio Disc Conference, which had been formed in 1977 to select a single worldwide standard for recording digital audio sound.

Two other companies submitted competing technologies: Telefunken, which recorded digital information mechanically, and JVC, which recorded digital sound electrostatically, the same way that a standard cassette recorder puts analog sound onto tape.

The Conference adopted both the Sony/Philips "Compact Disc Digital Audio System" and the JVC system, leaving Telefunken out in the cold. But the compact disc system quickly surpassed JVC's system because, unlike the JVC system, the compact disc's laser read the information on the CD without actually touching it—which meant that discs would last almost forever.

JUST SAY NO

While both companies continued work on perfecting their players, Sony's Norio Ohga and a Philips executive named Hans Timmer began preparing the recording industry for the introduction of CD technology. In May 1981, they brought Sony's prototype CD player to the International Music Industry Conference in Athens, Greece.

While they expected to dazzle the record company executives with CD technology, Ohga and Timmer also realized that they would encounter some opposition. But they were astonished by just how much opposition they did run into. The record companies had millions upon millions of dollars invested in LP record technology—all of which could become worthless if CDs ever took off. And because every compact disc manufactured was, in essence, a perfect "master" recording, counterfeiters could use them to make perfect bootleg recordings, something that had not been possible with LPs.

"Ohga must have been shaken, but he didn't show it," Timmer recalls. "He was calm and kept explaining that CDs would never scratch and that the sound was superior. But they shouted him down." Toward the end of Ohga's presentation, the executives stood up and began chanting, "The truth is in the groove! The truth is in the grove!"

"We barely escaped physical violence," Timmer says.

KEEP ON TRUCKIN'
Ohga was determined to continue developing CD technology, even if the entire industry was against him. Not that he had any choice: Sony's fortunes were now inextricably linked to the success of compact discs. Sony had taken a financial bath on its Betamax video recorders, which had been driven out of the marketplace by VHS-format, and the company sorely needed a hit product. Now they had invested tens of millions of dollars in CD technology. Compact discs *had* to succeed.

CD-DAY
On October 1, 1982, the world's first CD player—the Sony CDP 101—went on sale in Japan...and with it, the world's first CD albums, courtesy of CBS/Sony records.

The CDP 101 sold for $1,000 and compact discs sold for $16 to $18, twice the price of LPs. At those prices, the CDP 101 was a hit with audiophiles, but out of reach for most consumers. The *New York Times* wrote in March 1983:

> Some question whether the audio-disc will succeed. Even if prices come down—and industry experts expect they will—some analysts doubt whether consumers will be willing to sacrifice substantial investments in turntables and stacks of traditional recordings....The compact disc and player...is being likened in the music industry to the advent of stereophonic sound or the long-playing recording. Still, the CD's effect on record makers, manufacturers of audio equipment, and—most importantly—the music-loving consumer will probably be more gradual than the two previous revolutions, according to analysts.

The first CD to sell one million copies: Dire Straits' *Brothers in Arms.*

SUCCESS AT LAST

The analysts were wrong. In November 1984, Sony introduced a new CD player, the D-50, that was half the size of the CDP-101 and cost only $230. "The market came roaring back to life," John Nathan writes. By 1986, CD players were selling at a rate of more than a million per year and consumers had purchased more than 45 million compact discs. And that was just the beginning: Sales doubled to 100 million CDs by 1988, and quadrupled to 400 million CDs in 1992, compared to 2.3 million LPs sold that year, making them the fastest-growing consumer electronic product ever introduced.

* * *

REALLY BAD, AWFUL, TERRIBLE JOKES
Yes, we know these jokes are bad and you'll groan when you read them…and then you'll tell them to someone else.

A man walks into a psychiatrist's office with a banana up his nose and says, "What's the matter with me, Doc"
The psychiatrist says, "You're not eating properly."

Q: What do you call a cow with no legs?
A: Ground beef.

Q: Why couldn't the sesame seed leave the gambling casino?
A: Because he was on a roll.

Upon seeing a flock of geese flying south for the winter, the bird watcher exclaimed, "Migratious!"

Q: How many surrealists does it take to screw in a lightbulb?
A: To get to the other side.

Q: Did you hear about the dyslexic devil worshiper?
A: He sold his soul to Santa.

Q: What do you get if you don't pay your exorcist promptly?
A: Repossessed.

If you're swimming in the creek and an eel bites your cheek, that's *a moray.*

LUCKY FINDS

*Ever found something really valuable? It's one of the best
feelings in the world. Here's another installment of
a regular* Bathroom Reader *feature.*

U P IN SMOKE
The Find: A bunch of cigars
Where It Was Found: In the wine cellar of Temple House,
a 97-room manor built in Ireland in 1864
The Story: For more than thirty years, lord of the manor Sandy Perceval had been going into the cellar to scrounge up old cigars, which
had been there for as long as anyone in the family could remember.

Perceval never gave the smokes much thought until 1995, when a
friend, impressed by their quality, asked if he could take a few to be
appraised. It turned out that the cigars had been rolled in 1864,
making them the oldest smokable cigars in the world. They were
imported from the Orient by Perceval's great-great-grandfather. As
Sondra Bazrod writes in *The Hunt for Amazing Treasures*, "thanks to
the mist from a nearby lake, the Irish damp, and the temperature of
the wine cellar, the cigars survived in perfect condition in their own
natural humidor," until Perceval and his friends started smoking
them again 100 years later. Originally there were thousands of cigars, but by 1995 the collection had dwindled to a few strays plus
one unopened box of 500....Estimated value of that one box:
$1,000,000.

OFF THE WALL
The Find: "Large, poster-like cards" with movie stars on them
Where They Were Found: In the walls of a Victorian house in
Three Oaks, Michigan
The Story: About a week after Bill Moorehouse and Joseph Fox-
hood bought the vintage house, a huge storm hit and rain seeped in
through the leaky roof, ruining the plaster walls.

As workers tore down the plaster, they discovered old movie posters—thousands of them stuffed into walls in every room. It turned
out that the house had belonged to the manager of the town's movie
theater during the Great Depression. For years he'd brought several

---

Underwear in the news: Elvis's underpants are estimated to be worth $1,300.

"window cards" home each day...and used them as insulation, because they were just the right size to fit between the studs in the walls. Some of the window cards featured *The Girl from 10th Avenue*, starring Bette Davis, (the only one known to exist); *I'm No Angel*, starring Mae West; and *Song of Songs*, starring Marlene Dietrich. "These cards were entombed in the walls for sixty years," says Dwight Cleveland, a Chicago movie poster dealer, "and their condition was so good it was like they were in a time capsule."

Estimated value of the entire collection: hundreds of thousands of dollars. "It was like winning the lottery," Moorehouse said.

CANNED GOODS

The Find: A fire extinguisher canister

Where It Was Found: In a house in Ontario, Canada

The Story: Shortly after her husband died, Jean Weitzner sold her home of 30 years to Wilbert Herman, a local businessman. A few weeks later, the 89-year-old Mrs. Weitzner overheard some gossip at the hairdresser: cash had been found in her house.

Weitzner approached Herman to see if the rumor was true, and he admitted that $12,000 "plus a little bit more" was found in a fire extinguisher under the section of the house that had been her husband's office. Herman suggested that he, the contractor who found it, and Mrs. Weitzner split the loot three ways—$4,000 apiece. But when he showed up at her house with a document which said that the $4,000 represented "full payment" for any money found "in or around the house," Mrs. Weitzner refused to sign. Instead, she filed suit to recover the entire amount, which Herman later admitted was not $12,000, but actually $130,000, mostly in $50 and $100 bills. Apparently, Mr. Weitzner had been stashing away in small amounts for more than 40 years and never told his wife about it.

The judge ruled that the money belonged to Mrs. Weitzner, citing case law more than 300 years old that found that "finders keepers" only applies when the original owner's identity cannot be determined. Bonus: After interviewing the Weitzners' bookkeeper, the judge concluded that Harry Weitzner had already payed his full income taxes on the income—Mrs. Weitzner inherited the entire stash tax-free.

Got beef? Americans, on average, eat 100 lbs. of beef a year—about 50% of it as hamburger.

THE HATFIELDS VS. THE McCOYS

The facts about one of the most famous feuds in U.S. history.

The Contestants: Neighboring clans living on opposite sides of a stream that marked the border between West Virginia and Kentucky. The Hatfields, headed by Anderson "Devil Anse" Hatfield, lived on the West Virginia side. The McCoys, whose patriarch was Randolph "Ole Ran'l" McCoy, lived on the Kentucky side.

How the Feud Started: There was already animosity between the two clans by 1878. For one thing, during the Civil War, the Hatfields sided with the Confederacy, and the McCoys sided with the Union. But in 1878 Ole Ran'l sued Floyd Hatfield for stealing a hog—a serious offense in a farm-based economy—and McCoy lost. In 1880 relations worsened when McCoy's daughter Rose Anne became pregnant by Devil Anse's son Johnse and went across the river to live—unmarried—with the Hatfields.

Then on August 7, 1882, Randolph's son Tolbert stabbed Devil Anse's brother Ellison multiple times in a brawl that started during an election day picnic; when Ellison died a few days later, the Hatfields retaliated by tying three of the McCoy brothers to some bushes and executing them.

The feud continued for six more years. It ended after a nighttime raid on the McCoys on January 1, 1888. That night, a group of Hatfields surrounded Ole Ran'l McCoy's house (he was away) and ordered the occupants to come out and surrender. When no one did they set the house on fire. Ole Ran'l's daughter Allifair finally ran out and was gunned down; so was her brother Calvin. The house burned to the ground.

And the Winner Is: No one. This last attack was so brutal that officials in both Kentucky and West Virginia finally felt compelled to intervene. One Hatfield who participated in the raid was convicted and hanged for the crime. Several others were sentenced to long prison terms. With most violent offenders behind bars and the rest of the clan members weary of years of killing, the feud petered out.

Ouch! A typical porcupine has about 30,000 quills.

PRESIDENTIAL TRIVIA

Some interesting bits of American history from BRI member
Leland Gregory III's book Presidential Indiscretions.

Thomas Jefferson wrote the Declaration of Independence in 18 days.

James Garfield was the first president to use a phone in the White House. His first words to inventor Alexander Graham Bell, who was on the other end, were "Please speak a little more slowly."

Richard Nixon is the only president to have won an Emmy award. He received the Best Spoken Word award for an album made from the soundtrack of his television interview with David Frost.

George Washington was the first and only president elected by a unanimous electoral vote.

Richard Nixon was the only person ever elected twice to both the office of president and the office of vice president. He also holds the distinguished honor of being the only president ever to resign.

Andrew Jackson was the first president to be handed a baby to kiss during his campaign. He refused to kiss the infant and instead handed the baby over to his secretary of war.

Herbert Hoover was the only president who turned his entire salary over to charity.

Woodrow Wilson was the only president to have earned a Ph.D. He earned it from Johns Hopkins University in 1886.

During his youth, **Bill Clinton,** along with two other boys, performed in a jazz combo called the Three Blind Mice. They all wore sunglasses.

The only two politicians bound by law never to travel together are the president and the vice president.

At the time **President Abraham Lincoln** was assassinated, the only money he had on his person was a $5 Confederate note.

George Washington didn't have enough money to get to his own inauguration and was forced to borrow six hundred dollars from a neighbor.

While president of the United States, **Ulysses S. Grant** had his horse and carriage impounded and he himself was arrested for speeding on a Washington street.

While a high school student in the early 1930s, **Richard Nixon** worked for two summers as a barker for the wheel-of-chance at the Slippery Gulch Rodeo in Prescott, Arizona.

The Statue of Liberty's fingernails each weigh about 100 pounds.

WHERE'D THEY GET THAT NAME?

Ever wonder where the names of cities and towns come from? Think you know? Let's see how good you are—take this quiz and find out.

1. BOSTON, MASSACHUSETTS. This state capital was founded by Puritans in 1630. It's named after:

A. One of its original Puritan settlers.

B. A stone.

C. The tea company that owned much of the city until the 1800s.

2. LITTLE ROCK, ARKANSAS. Founded in 1722, this state capital is named after:

A. A little rock.

B. The French town of the same name (La Petite Roche).

C. The Frenchman Pierre de Rocqueville.

3. IDAHO. This state's name means:

A. "Good place to grow potatoes."

B. "Look, the sun is coming down the mountain."

C. "Place of refuge."

4. HONG KONG (CHINA). This city's name means:

A. Fragrant harbor.

B. Land of Dreams.

C. River of Water.

5. KALAMAZOO, MICHIGAN. This city, settled in 1829, is named after:

A. A Native American god.

B. A word meaning "he who smokes" or "boiling water."

C. A dried, salted fish.

If you've been struck by lightning, there's an 85% chance that you're a male.

6. BATON ROUGE, LOUISIANA. This state capital was founded in 1882. It's named after:
A. A local red-headed beauty.
B. A boundry marker.
C. A Creole word for lipstick.

7. CONEY ISLAND, NEW YORK. The name is derived from:
A. Bugs Bunny's ancestor.
B. The evergreen forest once located there.
C. The huge sno-cones sold at the famous amusement park.

8. ALCATRAZ. This island's name is derived from:
A. A kind of bird.
B. A Native American word for "rocky island."
C. The huge trash heaps—mainly empty alcohol bottles—deposited there by settlers. Native Americans thought they were "traz heaps."

9. TOPEKA, KANSAS. The name of this city means:
A. "Home of the singing bushes."
B. "Fermenting swamp."
C. "Good place to grow potatoes."

10. BOCA RATON, FLORIDA. This city's name comes from:
A. A game of chance.
B. A rock formation.
C. A nasty comment about the Native tribes living there.

11. WALLA WALLA, WASHINGTON. The name of this port city comes from:
A. A Native American fishing god.
B. A bird.
C. A swift, little river.

Answers on page 491.

"NO PANTS ALLOWED"

If you're too young to remember the 1960s, this may sound crazy to you, but back then, there were rules against women wearing pants in public places. This article appeared in the New York Times *in 1966.*

DILEMMA FOR RESTAURATEURS: WHERE DO SLACKS END AND PANTS START?

NEW YORK—Pants, tailored or formal, and the women in them, are being greeted with less than enthusiasm by the men who run many of New York's leading hotels and restaurants.

"It's easier to get into some places in lingerie," say some of the women who have tried both.

"I've taken to calling restaurants to see if I'm allowed in," says Mrs. Nora Jaffe, an abstract painter who believes she looks better in slacks than she does in most dresses. "I've been turned away from several places, but I'm not discouraged."

Mrs. Jaffe, a tall and slender brunette, has no such problems when she wears a $35 pink chiffon nightgown.

"I've worn it to several openings and it's been taken for a Grès design," she says of her double-layered nightgown that drapes to resemble a toga.

Giving Them the Slip

Eileen Ford, who together with her husband operates the Ford Model Agency, tells of going to the Golden Door at Kennedy International Airport with a model en route to Mexico.

"She was wearing a pinstriped pants suit in white flannel—really beautifully tailored," Mrs. Ford said. "They refused to allow her in so we went to the powder room and I gave her my black Paisley half-slip, trimmed with lace and bows. She put it on as a skirt. It was the funniest sight you've ever seen, but we got into the restaurant."

Anthony Nardin, general manager of the Golden Door, says his policy of "no pants" is prompted largely by women guests who object to them. "If a woman wearing slacks is on a delayed flight and comes in with the crew from the airline, we have no way to bar her. But

---

Father of his own country: President John Tyler (1841-45) had 15 children by 2 wives.

usually a group like that is put in a separate room anyway," he adds.

A Matter of Respect

Thomas Clinton, assistant manager of the Plaza Hotel, says, "Pants are pants, and if women wear them they'll be asked to leave."

"It doesn't matter what shape or form they take," he adds. "If we admitted one, we couldn't refuse others."

"We have a flat policy against them," says James Van Bortel, manager of the Top of the Sixes.

Mrs. Theodore Kwoh, the owner of the Mandarin East, believes it is a matter of respect for the restaurant. "You wouldn't wear slacks to a restaurant you respected," she says. "You have to draw the line somewhere—we might allow them in downstairs or late at night, but it's an exception."

Some restaurants disapprove in principle rather than in practice. "We usually don't permit them, but all rules are made to be broken," is the opinion of Dee Lawrence, manager of the 54th Street branch of P. J. Moriarty. "If the restaurant isn't too busy, we'll put them in a corner, but 99 per cent of the men who lunch here really don't like seeing women in pants."

"I'm Open-Minded"

"Evening pants are accepted anywhere," says Stuart Levin, director of the Four Seasons. "There's a difference between pants-pants and the feminine look."

Charles T. Carey, manger of the St. Regis-Sheraton, offers a similar viewpoint: "Formalized evening pants designed for parties are perfectly acceptable, but I'd have to look them over. We expect men to wear ties and jackets and women to be properly dressed."

One of the most receptive to the vogues and vagaries of fashion is Charles Masson, the owner of La Grenouille, a temple of fashionable dining. "I'm open-minded about the fashions of the times," he says, "but fashion is one thing and laissez-faire another.

"I will not permit slacks, but if a woman wears a well-made pants suit and they fit her personality, that is good taste. Exhibitionism is something else."

ACCORDING TO THE LATEST RESEARCH...

It seems as though practically every day there's a report on some scientific study with dramatic new info on what we should eat...or how we should act...or who we really are underneath all the BS. Some are pretty interesting. Did you know, for example, that science says...

YOU'D BETTER WATCH WHAT YOU SAY ABOUT PEOPLE

Researchers: Psychologists from Ohio State, Purdue University, and Indiana University

Who They Studied: College students

What They Learned: When a person attributes positive or negative traits to someone else, the listener will frequently attribute those same qualities to the speaker, a process known as "spontaneous trait transference."

"In other words," the researchers conclude, "politicians who allege corruption by their opponents may themselves be perceived as dishonest, critics who praise artists may themselves be perceived as talented, and gossips who describe others' infidelities may themselves be viewed as immoral....The gist of our research is that when you gossip, you become associated with the characteristics you describe, ultimately leading these characteristics to be transferred to you."

YOUR MEMORY GETS WORSE WITH LESS SLEEP

Researcher: Dr. Robert Stickgold, an assistant professor of psychiatry at Harvard Medical School

Who He Studied: Harvard undergraduates

What He Learned: Memory retention is linked to how much sleep you get. Stickgold tested this by conducting an experiment where Harvard undergraduates were trained to spot visual targets on a computer screen, and then press a button as soon as they were certain they had seen one. Conclusion: Students who were tested 3–12 hours later on the same day showed "absolutely no improvement" in speed or accuracy; neither did students who were tested the following day after getting six hours of sleep or less. "Only those who slept more than six hours," the study found, "seemed to improve in speed and accuracy."

YOUR MOOD INFLUENCES YOUR APPETITE
Researchers: Bernard Lyman and Janet Waters, two psychologists at Simon Fraser University in British Columbia
Who They Studied: Unknown
What They Learned: A person's mood influences the kinds of food they like to eat. "When people are lonely, they like liquid foods like soup or milk. When they 'want to be amused,' they like to eat spicy, salty, and crunchy foods. When they're worried, they prefer 'unheated sweets,' like candy bars and cookies. When they're angry, they like 'unheated solids' (whatever that means); and when they're happy, they like soft foods such as ice cream and yogurt."

SHOULD PEOPLE PRAY FOR YOU?
Researcher: William Harris of the Mid America Heart Institute in Kansas City, Missouri
Who He Studied: Heart patients
What He Learned: It seems as though having people pray for you when you're sick can help you get better. In the study, heart patients who had strangers praying for them had fewer complications than those who didn't. "It's potentially a natural explanation we don't understand yet," Harris says, "or, it's potentially a super- or other-than-natural mechanism."

THERE IS A KEY TO HAPPINESS
Researchers: David Blanchflower of Dartmouth College (USA) and Andrew Oswald of the University of Warwick (Great Britain)
Who They Studied: 100,000 people of different ages and backgrounds
What They Learned: Blanchflower and Oswald concluded that happiness tends to be the lowest around age forty, and goes up after that. Furthermore, "a lasting marriage brings about the same amount of happiness as an extra $100,000 in yearly income."

A VIEWER'S GUIDE TO RAINBOWS

Did you know there's a science of rainbow watching? We didn't, either. This article from the Christian Science Monitor *was based on a discussion with Raymond Lee, author of* The Rainbow Bridge.

THE RIGHT LIGHT

When it stops raining and the sun comes out, stand outside with your back to the sun. If conditions are just right, you'll see a rainbow. (But hurry—it will only last for 30 minutes or so.) As you gaze at the rainbow, here are some things you might observe:

• Notice that the sky *inside* the rainbow is brighter than the sky outside it. That's because water droplets inside the rainbow reflect and refract sunlight straight back to you. Raindrops above the rainbow send light *away* from you.

• See the base of the rainbow, where it appears to meet the ground? The rainbow is brighter there, because sunlight reflects off large and small raindrops at the base. Only small raindrops are at the top, and they reflect less light. This explains the legend of the "pot o' gold": When people saw the bright ends of a rainbow, they imagined that the glimmer had a magical explanation.

THE COLORS

The order of the colors of the rainbow are always the same. Have you ever heard of Roy G. Biv? That's the standard mnemonic device for remembering the proper order: red, orange, yellow, green, blue, indigo, violet. That's always the order—except when it's reversed, which is what happens in a secondary rainbow. For that, you need to remember Vib G. Yor. Some details:

• Look slightly above the rainbow. Do you see a second, faint rainbow above? It's a double rainbow—and if you do see it, notice:

1. The dark band of sky between the primary (main) and secondary rainbows. This is called "Alexander's band." It's named after Alexander of Aphrodislas.

2. Notice the order of the colors in the secondary rainbow. They're the reverse of the colors in the first rainbow. The second

---

The sun weighs about 4,000,000,000,000,000,000,000,000,000,000 pounds.

rainbow is created when light rays are reflected twice inside the raindrop. A triple rainbow is possible, too, but very difficult to see. Meteorologist Raymond Lee claims to have found three reliable accounts of triple-rainbow sightings, but had to scour 150 years of history to find them. The third rainbow is difficult to see because it's very near the bright sun.

THE WHOLE THING?

• Primary rainbows always appear 42 degrees above the top of the shadow cast by your head. (That's the simplest way to describe what scientists call the "antisolar point," the point directly opposite the sun.) The antisolar point is usually below the horizon. But if you get up high enough and conditions are right, you might see a rainbow as a circle, rather than as an arc. People in tall buildings, airplanes, and on mountains have seen circular rainbows.

• Often you see only part of a rainbow. This is because the conditions that create the rainbow don't extend all the way across the sky. Where water or sunlight are absent, so is the rainbow.

• Taking a picture of a complete rainbow can be frustrating, whether it's swooping across the sky or dancing across a spray of water from a hose. Here's why: Most 35mm cameras have a field of view of 40 degrees (out of 360). A rainbow takes up more than 40 degrees of sky. And because it's an image, not an object, you can't back up to fit more into your picture. Use a wide-angle lens.

THE RAINBOW YOU SEE IS YOUR OWN

There isn't one rainbow—there's one for each viewer. Everyone sees his own, personal rainbow.

Here's how it works: Picture a huge cone. It's on the ground, flat side down. Picture yourself standing at the point of the cone. The raindrops that are bending and reflecting the sunlight that reaches your eye as a rainbow are located on the surface of that cone. But someone standing right next to you is seeing a rainbow generated by a completely different set of raindrops along the surface of a different imaginary cone.

So next time you see a rainbow, remember—it's not in the sky, it's in your eyes...and you're the only one who can see it.

Takin' it easy: The top speed of a 3-toed sloth is .12 miles per hour.

"TRUST IN GOD, BUT TIE YOUR CAMEL"

You know that "a watched pot never boils," but there are count-less other proverbs that you may have never heard. Here are some of BRI's favorites from around the world.

"Remember to dig the well long before you get thirsty."
Chinese

"If you cannot catch a fish, do not blame the sea."
Greek

"It is not for the blind to give an opinion on colors."
Italian

"Trust in God, but tie your camel."
Persian

"Measure forty times, cut once."
Turkish

"He that blows into the fire must expect sparks in his eyes."
German

"Six feet of earth makes us all of one size."
Italian

"Fault denied is twice committed."
French

"Never send a chicken to bring home a fox."
Irish

"To lose a friend, make him a loan."
Greek

"Do not hit the fly that lands on the tiger's head.
Chinese

"A lovesick person looks in vain for a doctor."
West Africa

"Pearls are of no value in the desert."
Hindustan

"When one has no needle, thread is of little use."
Japanese

"When the elephant sinks in a pit, even the frog gives him a backward kick."
India

"The sky is the same color wherever you go."
Persian

"When the fox preaches, look to your geese."
German

"He that cannot dance claims the floor is uneven."
Hindustan

"When the ship has sunk, everyone knows how she could have been saved."
Italian

"Even the powerful ox has no defense against flies."
Chinese

"A good archer is known not by his arrows but by his aim."
English

"The road of by and by leads to the house of never."
Spanish

"The longer the expla-nation the bigger the lie."
Chinese

"I'm offended by political jokes. Too often they get elected." —Henny Youngman

THE BARBADOS TOMBS

The island of Barbados is known for its tropical climate, its sandy beaches—and its restless dead. Here are two legendary, unexplained mysteries surrounding people who have been buried on the island.

THE CHASE FAMILY CRYPT

Background Col. Thomas Chase and his family were wealthy English settlers living on Barbados in the early 1800s. They owned a large burial crypt in the graveyard of Christ Church. In 1807, Thomisina Goddard, a relative of the Chases, died and was interred in the crypt. A year later, Mary Chase, Thomas Chase's infant daughter, died mysteriously. (It was widely believed that Thomas Chase beat her to death; he was known as a violent man who beat his children—a number of whom showed signs of mental illness.) She, too, was placed in the crypt. But unlike Thomisina, who was placed in a wooden coffin, Mary's body was placed in a heavy lead coffin. After her casket was interred, the vault was sealed shut with a massive marble slab.

A Mysterious Happening

A few months afterward, Dorcas Chase (Thomas Chase's teenage daughter) starved herself to death. Like her infant sister, Dorcas was placed in a heavy lead casket and brought to the crypt. But when the family unsealed and opened the vault, they saw that something peculiar had happened: Mary Chase's tiny coffin had moved to the opposite side of the crypt—and it was standing on one end. Thomisina Goddard's casket had not been moved.

The family was shocked, but assumed the crypt had been broken into by grave robbers. They returned Mary's casket to its proper place, laid Dorcas's coffin next to it, and sealed the crypt even tighter than before—this time pouring a layer of molten lead over the marble capstone.

A Moving Experience

Thomas Chase committed suicide a month later. As with Mary and Dorcas, his body was placed in a heavy lead casket. This time when the crypt was opened, all the coffins were still in place. The crypt was again tightly sealed; it would not be reopened again by the family for another eight years.

In 1816 another child related to the Chase family died. This time when the vault was unsealed, the hinges on the doors were so rusty, they would not open; it took two strong men to finally pry them open wide enough to get the coffin inside. But when the family peered into the dark vault, they saw that the caskets had again been strewn about the crypt…except for Thomasina Goddard's, which was left untouched a second time.

The mourners were dumbfounded: the adult-sized lead coffins weighed more than 500 pounds each, and the child-sized ones weren't much lighter. It took four strong men to return each of the caskets to their proper places, and it seemed inconceivable that any natural forces could have tossed them around the tomb.

Keep on Moving

Less than a month after this latest interment, a woman visiting another grave heard groans and "loud cracking" noises coming from the Chase family crypt. Her horse became so agitated by the noises that it began foaming at the mouth and had to be treated by a veterinarian. And a week after that, something spooked several horses tied up outside Christ Church; they broke free, ran down the hill and jumped into the sea, where they drowned.

By now the goings-on in the vault were public knowledge and the source of wild speculation; when the next member of the Chase family died, more than 1,000 people came to the funeral—some from as far away as Cuba and Haiti. They weren't disappointed: when the crypt was unsealed, all of the coffins were out of place, each one standing on end against the walls of the crypt—except for Thomasina Goddard's.

You Move Me, Governor

After this funeral, the governor of the island decided to investigate. He attended the next funeral, and once again the coffins had been strewn about. This time, he tested the crypt's walls for secret passages (there were none), had the floor of the crypt covered with sand to detect footprints and other marks, had a new lock installed in the crypt's door, and had the crypt sealed with a layer of cement to be sure the door would not be opened. To top it off, he and other officials stamped the wet cement with their signet rings, making sure that it couldn't be tampered with without being detected.

On April 8, 1820, the vault was reopened to inter another member of the Chase family. The cement was still in place, but when the family removed it, something heavy leaning against the door of the crypt prevented it from being opened. Several strong men tried to force the door open…and when they finally succeeded, something crashed down inside the crypt. They opened the door all the way… and saw that it had been held shut because one of the coffins had been leaning against it. This time *all* the coffins had been disturbed—including Thomasina Goddard's.

The governor and several others examined the crypt closely to try and find an explanation. There was none; there were no footprints in the sand and none of the jewelry on any of the bodies had been stolen. Completely mystified, the governor ordered that the bodies be removed from the crypt and interred in another crypt on the island. They were never disturbed again; they rest in peace to this day.

THE McGREGOR CRYPT

Background The Chase crypt wasn't the only one on Barbados to have strange things happen to it: In August 1943, a group of Freemasons unsealed a crypt containing the body of Alexander Irvine, the founder of freemasonry on Barbados. (Irvine's remains were interred in the 1830s in the same crypt as Sir Even McGregor, the owner of the crypt, who was laid to rest in 1841.)

Strange Happenings

The McGregor crypt was even more tightly sealed than the Chase crypt: the inner door was locked tight and cemented with bricks and mortar, which itself was covered with a huge stone slab. When they unsealed the crypt, the inner door of the tomb would not open. Peeking in through a hole, they saw that a heavy lead coffin was standing on its head, leaning against the inner door. The masons carefully moved it and opened the door—only to discover that Irvine's coffin was missing; McGregor's was the one up against the door. The mystery was never solved; the island's burial records confirmed that both men had been interred in the crypt nearly 100 years before, but no evidence was ever found to explain the missing coffin.

TV'S MOST TASTELESS SITCOM?

Tasteless television is pretty common these days—from Baywatch
to Who Wants to Marry a Millionaire? *Many critics think* Hogan's
Heroes—*a 1960s sitcom based in a Nazi POW camp—belongs
in the same group. In fact, its outrageous premise might
qualify it as the most tasteless sitcom ever aired.*

CON JOB

In the early 1960s, two men named Bernard Fein and Albert
Ruddy teamed up to write a pilot for a TV sitcom. Neither
had any experience writing pilots—Fein was an actor who'd co-
starred in the *Sergeant Bilko* TV series, and Ruddy was an architect—
but that turned out to be an asset. If the pair had known how difficult it was to sell a TV pilot in Hollywood, they probably would not
have bothered. "If someone were to ask me today what their chances
of selling a television pilot are, I would say you might as well go to
Vegas," Ruddy says. "It's a million-to-one shot."

The pair came up with a sitcom about inmates in an American
prison who outwit the buffoonish warden and guards and are secretly
running the prison. Instead of stamping license plates and exercising
in the yard, the cons manufacture cigarette lighters and engage in
other moneymaking schemes to bankroll escape attempts.

Tough on Crime

The script was genuinely funny, but when Fein and Ruddy began
shopping it around, they realized the prison concept had an innate
problem: American audiences were not inclined to sympathize with
hardened criminals and probably wouldn't enjoy watching them escape each week. And potential advertisers knew it: "No one wanted
to sponsor 'a night in the slam,'" Ruddy says.

TURNABOUT

The pilot might have died right then and there—and with it, Fein
and Ruddy's writing careers—if the two men hadn't heard about a
show called *Campo 44* that was going into production at NBC. "We
read in the paper that NBC was doing a World War II sitcom set in

---

British explorer Robert Swan's claim to fame: 1st person to walk to the North *and* South poles.

an Italian prisoner-of-war camp, and we thought—perfect," Ruddy says. "We rewrote our script and set it in a German POW camp in about two days."

The revised script featured the exploits of Colonel Robert Hogan, recruited to lead an espionage/sabotage group behind enemy lines. Hogan and his men allow themselves to be captured by the Germans so they can set up a base of operations at the Stalag 13 POW camp—which is run by comically inept Nazis. From there, they sabotage the Germans while helping Allied prisoners escape.

HARD SELL

Fein and Ruddy pitched *Hogan's Heroes* to NBC, but the network turned it down—not because they thought the pilot was terrible, but because they thought it was so good that the series couldn't possibly live up to it. "If the pilot is this good," one NBC executive asked Ruddy after his sales pitch, "how could they sustain it week after week?"

CBS also rejected the series, but for an entirely different reason. After sitting through the sales pitch, CBS founder William Paley told Fein and Ruddy: "I find the idea of doing a comedy set in a Nazi prisoner-of-war camp reprehensible." But Ruddy kept pitching the show. "I literally acted out a half-hour of the show—the barking dogs, the machine-gun sound effects...It was hilarious!" At the end of it, Paley bought the show.

Hogan's Heroes premiered on September 17, 1965, and quickly became the most popular new show of the year. In fact, for several seasons it ranked in TV's top 20 programs...but it never escaped the controversy its premise engendered: Was it immoral to portray history's most evil killers as bumbling—even lovable—buffoons week after week, just to make a buck? One critic wrote: "Granted, this show is often funny and well-acted. But there's simply no excuse for turning the grim reality of Nazi atrocities into fodder for yet another brainless joke." Another wrote simply: "What's next? A family sitcom set in Auschwitz?"

CAST ASIDE

Ironically, the biggest apologists for the show were its Jewish cast members—including all four of the actors who played the regular Nazi characters—Colonel Klink, Sergeant Schultz, General Burkhal-

---

ter, and Major Hochstetter. Not only were they Jewish, but three were actually refugees from Nazi Germany:

- Werner Klemperer was the son of conductor Otto Klemperer, a Jew who left Germany in 1933 when Hitler came to power.
- John Banner (Sergeant Schultz), an Austrian Jew, was touring with actors in Zurich, Switzerland, in 1938, when Hitler invaded Austria. Unable to return home, he emigrated to the United States.
- Leon Askin (General Burkhalter) was an actor in Germany when Hitler became Chancellor. He was dismissed from the theater and was later arrested and beaten by the Gestapo. He fled to Paris, and emigrated to the United States in 1938.

A STRANGE CHOICE

If that's not weird enough, it turns out that Robert Clary, who played a character named LeBeau, had actually been imprisoned for three years in a Nazi concentration camp. His comment: "A lot of people have asked me how I could work on *Hogan's Heroes*. I tell them that '*Hogan's Heroes* was very different'...We were not really dealing with Nazism." Howard Caine, who played Major Hochstetter, was also Jewish. His defense: "I've had, over these years, many fellow Jews say to me 'How could you play a comic Gestapo like that?' Because I played him as a madman....My willingness to do it was to remain true to the concept that they wanted of the vicious killer, potential Nazi."

However, not everyone who worked on the show was comfortable with the concept. Actor Paul Lambert got out after only four episodes. "I always felt a little queasy about doing this show about 'funny Nazis,'" he says. "If it wasn't for the money, I wouldn't have done *Hogan's* at all." And Leonid Kinskey, who played a Russian POW in the pilot, turned down a regular part in the series. "The moment we had a dress rehearsal and I saw German SS uniforms, something very ugly rose in me," he said. "I visualized millions upon millions of innocent people murdered by Nazis. One can hardly in good taste joke about it. So in the practical life of the TV industry, I lost thousands of dollars, but I was, and am, at peace with myself concerning my stepping out of the series."

Ironic note: When *Campo 44* finally debuted on NBC (September 9, 1967), critics denounced it as a *Hogan's Heroes* rip-off, not realizing that it was really the other way around.

FOUNDING FATHERS

You already know the names. Here's who they belong to.

RICHARD REYNOLDS

Background: The nephew of cigarette mogul R.J. Reynolds. He spent ten years working for his uncle's tobacco company, then in 1912 struck out on his own. After several setbacks, he went back to his uncle and borrowed enough money to start the U.S. Foil Company—which made foil cigarette packaging for R.J. Reynolds Co.

Famous name: In the mid-1930s, Richard learned of a new type of foil made from aluminum. Sensing the product's potential, he built a plant to manufacture it. He began selling it as Reynold's Wrap.

TOM AND LOUIS BORDERS

Background: In 1971, they opened a college bookstore in Ann Arbor, Michigan. To manage the huge inventory, they developed one of the book industry's first computer systems. It helped them develop a reputation as the store where people could find almost any book imaginable...and made expansion possible.

Famous name: By 1996, the Borders Books chain had expanded to more than 115 stores around the country, with annual book (and music, added in the early 1990s) sales of more than $700 million.

WARREN AVIS

Background: In the 1930s he was a Ford salesman. Then during World War II he joined the Air Force and became a combat flying officer. He found that often, the hardest part of flying was figuring out how to get from the airport to his final destination.

Famous Name: In 1946, he started a car rental company at Detroit's Willow Run Airport. He talked Ford into selling him cars at a discount by convincing them that having renters "test-drive" new Fords would help the automaker sell its cars. By the time he sold Avis Rent-A-Car in 1954, the chain had expanded to 154 locations around the country.

GLEN W. BELL

Background: After he got out of the Marines in 1946, Bell sold his refrigerator for $500 and used the money to start Bell's Drive-In in San Bernardino, California. San Bernardino is also the birthplace of McDonalds, and when Bell realized how well the McDonald brothers were doing, he decided it would be easier to switch to Mexican' food than it would be to compete against them directly.

Famous Name: His first restaurants were called Taco Tia. But after a while he renamed them Taco Bell, after himself.

MAJOR GENERAL OLIVER OTIS HOWARD

Background: Howard commanded troops in important battles during the Civil War—including the First Battle of Bull Run and Antietam. After the war, he demonstrated such interest in the fate of the nearly four million recently freed slaves that President Andrew Johnson appointed him commissioner of the Bureau of Refugees, Freedmen, and Abandoned Lands.

Famous Name: As commissioner, Howard oversaw the establishment of numerous schools and training institutes for African Americans, including Howard University, named in his honor.

HEINRICH STEINWEG

Background: In 1815 Steinweg, who couldn't play a single musical instrument, got a job at an organ builder's shop in the German duchy of Braunschweig. In 1850 he and his wife and children emigrated to the United States, and in 1853 he opened his own piano manufacturing business that he named after himself . . . sort of.

Famous Name: Rather than stick with the original German spelling, Steinweg "Americanized" his name, calling his company Henry Steinway and Sons.

DR. KLAUS MAERTENS

Background: In the 1940s he made orthopedic support shoes for older women. He expanded his line to include shoes for people suffering from skiing injuries, and simple, functional work boots that could stand up to almost anything.

Famous Name: In 1959, Maertens licensed his designs to a small British shoe company, R. Griggs, which began selling English versions of the shoes under the anglicized trade name Dr. Marten's.

In the Congo, professional corpse painters charge admission to see their work.

ANIMAL SUPERSTITIONS

Superstitions are intriguing, even if you don't believe in them. Here are some pretty bizarre ones that people actually did believe.

"A swarm of bees settling on a roof is an omen that the house will burn down."

"It's bad luck for a miner to say the word 'cat' while down in the mine."

"More than seven spots on a ladybug is an omen of famine."

"Killing a bat shortens your life."

"It's bad luck to see three butterflies on one leaf at the same time."

"A swan feather sewn onto a husband's pillow will make him faithful to his wife."

"Carrying a badger's tooth brings good luck, especially at gambling."

"A white horse is a harbinger of bad luck—worse luck if a red-headed girl is riding it."

"A bull's heart stuck with thorns and put in the fireplace wards off witches."

"To make a sleeping woman talk, put a frog's tongue on her heart."

"Seeing an owl during the daytime is bad luck."

"If you make a wish when you see the first robin of spring, it will come true—but only if you complete the wish before the robin flies away."

"It's unlucky to burn a haddock."

"Pictures of an elephant bring good luck, but only if they face a door."

"Rats leaving one house and running into another mean good luck for the new house and bad luck for the old."

"Cows lifting their tails is a sure sign that rain is coming."

"If a frog hops into your house, it will bring good luck."

"Stuffing a cat's tail up your nose will cure a nosebleed."

"Don't let a pig cross your path—it's unlucky."

"It's good luck to say 'white rabbit' on the first day of the month, but bad luck to see a rabbit on the way to work."

A horse will win a sprint against a camel; a camel will win a marathon against a horse.

"E PLURIBUS UNUM"

This phrase appears on every U.S. coin...but what does it mean?
Don't think too hard—the answer's right here.

THE NATIONAL SEAL
Shortly after the signing of the Declaration of Independence in 1776, the Continental Congress created a committee of three—John Adams, Thomas Jefferson, and Benjamin Franklin—to design an official seal for the United States.

Adams wanted a picture of Hercules standing between two allegorical figures representing Virtue and Sloth; Jefferson wanted a depiction of "The Children of Israel in the Wilderness"; and Franklin suggested a representation of Moses parting the Red Sea. They couldn't agree, so they hired Swiss-born artist Pierre Eugene du Simitiere to come up with a compromise design. Du Simitiere combined the three themes, then added his own flourishes to the goulash. They hated it.

Seal of Approval. Frustrated, they hired a Philadelphia lawyer named William Barton to come up with something better. Barton proposed *his* mishmash of symbols, including an eagle and crest on one side of the seal and an unfinished pyramid on the other. But that wasn't right, either. Finally, Secretary of Congress Charles Thomson stripped away everything except the eagle and the pyramid, and added his own symbols, including a shield over the eagle's chest, an olive branch in one of the eagle's claws (symbolizing peace), and a bundle of arrows (symbolizing war) in the other. That's the seal that was finally adopted; you can see it on the $1 bill.

Salad Days. As it turns out, two elements of du Simitiere's original design *did* make it into the final seal: the all-seeing eye of Providence, which was placed atop the unfinished pyramid, and the motto *E Pluribus Unum*: "From Many, One," which is printed on a banner the eagle holds in its mouth. Where did du Simitiere get the motto? Believe it or not, historians speculate that he borrowed it from the masthead of *Gentleman's Magazine*, a popular publication in the late 1700s. The editors of the magazine, in turn, took it from *color est e pluribus unus*, a line in Virgil's poem "Moretum" that "refers to the making of a salad."

Teddy Roosevelt's opinion of Winston Churchill: A "shady self-promoter."

WEIRD GAME SHOWS

According to experts, the most important aspect of a game show is...the game. So what were the designers of these ridiculous shows thinking?

TV Champions (Japan). A different bizarre contest each week. One week contestants chug "rancid, evil-smelling soy bean gruel," another week they "allow themselves to be locked in cages and sworn at."

The Game of the Goose (Spain). Contestants move around a game board; each space represents a different challenge. One challenge: release a semi-nude model from an exploding bed. Another: try to escape from a box that's slowly filling with sand.

Dream House (U.S.). Young married couples move from room to room, competing to win furniture. Grand prize: An entire mobile home, "put anywhere in the USA."

Finders Keepers (U.S.). "Each day, the show is filmed on location at a different contestant's house. The film crew hides a prize in the contestant's living room, sets up cameras, and then lets viewers watch the contestant tear the room apart looking for it."

Italian Stripping Housewives (Italy). "A strange game show take-off on strip poker. Wives strip while their husbands gamble."

100 Grand (U.S.). Hollywood's response to the quiz show scandals of the 1950s: Contestants spend part of the show in an isolation booth writing their own questions. Amazingly, the first time the show aired, one contestant missed every single question. *"100 Grand* aired twice before sinking into oblivion."

Endurance (Japan). "Contestants are literally tortured....One of the stunts, for example, involves dragging contestants across gravel until they are injured." In another, they crawl through a cage of scorpions. When a contestant fails, the studio audience shouts, "Go Home!"

Gonzo Games (U.S.). A gentler version of *Endurance:* "Overanxious contestants vie to see, for instance, who can attach the most clothespins to their face." In another test of strength, "contestants stand on a barbecue grill until the pain forces them off."

A typical raindrop falls at about 7 miles per hour.

RAMBO, STARRING AL PACINO

Some roles are so closely associated with a specific actor that it's hard to imagine he or she wasn't the first choice. But it happens all the time. Can you imagine, for example...

G ENE HACKMAN AS HANNIBAL LECTER (*The Silence of the Lambs*—1991) Hackman wanted to direct the film and write the screenplay, so Orion Pictures bought the rights to the novel. Then Hackman dropped out. Director Jonathan Demme signed Anthony Hopkins for the part without telling Orion head Mike Medavoy, who was furious that "an Englishman" would play Lecter. Medavoy agreed on one condition: that Jodie Foster be cast as FBI agent Clarice Starling instead of Meg Ryan. Demme agreed; Foster won her second straight Oscar.

GOLDIE HAWN AND MERYL STREEP AS THELMA AND LOUISE (*Thelma and Louise*—1991) Streep wanted to test her comedic talents; Hawn's film *Private Benjamin* had made $100 million at the box office. They seemed perfect for the film, and wanted to work together. But their schedules were full. "We weren't available right then," Hawn says, "and the director, Ridley Scott, wouldn't wait." Michelle Pfeiffer and Jodie Foster turned down the film; so did Cher. So Scott gave the parts to Geena Davis and Susan Sarandon.

ELVIS PRESLEY AS THE MIDNIGHT COWBOY (*Midnight Cowboy*—1969) Desperate to be taken seriously as an actor, the King went shopping around for "a more serious movie role." The part of the male prostitute in *Midnight Cowboy* was one of the parts he considered, but he ultimately turned the film down and did one called *A Change of Habit* instead. Reason: "Since it was about a doctor (Elvis) and a nun (Mary Tyler Moore) in the ghetto, that qualified as being more 'serious.'" *A Change of Habit* was Elvis's biggest box office dud; *Midnight Cowboy* won the Oscar for Best Picture and turned Jon Voight into a star.

AL PACINO AS RAMBO (*First Blood*—1982) Pacino wasn't the first major star interested in the part of John Rambo. (Eastwood, De Niro, and Paul Newman turned it down.) He wanted Rambo to be "a little more of a madman," and had the script rewritten. But the new draft made the character too dark and nutty, so Pacino passed on the role. So did John Travolta, Michael Douglas, and Nick Nolte. Then Carolco Pictures bought the script and offered it to Sly Stallone, who rewrote the insane Vietnam vet into a misunderstood American hero, "kind of like a Rocky movie." *First Blood* was Stallone's first non-*Rocky* film that didn't bomb. It saved his career. The sequel, *Rambo*, established it for good.

DORIS DAY AS MRS. ROBINSON (*The Graduate*—1967) Day's Hollywood image was as "the perennial virgin." "There was something about taking that All-American housewife image and turning it all around," says producer Larry Turman. "I sent the script to her, but we never heard a thing." Day later explained that she read the script, but just couldn't see herself playing the role. So it was offered to Anne Bancroft, who could.

BURT REYNOLDS AS RANDALL P. McMURPHY (*One Flew Over the Cuckoo's Nest*—1975) When Marlon Brando turned down the part, director Milos Forman had breakfast with Burt Reynolds and told him he was one of two actors being considered for the part. Reynolds was thrilled. "If the other guy isn't Jack Nicholson," he replied, "I've got the part." When Forman stopped eating dead in his tracks, Reynolds knew he wasn't going to get the part. Nicholson got the role, and won the Oscar for best actor.

BURT REYNOLDS AS GARRETT BREEDLOVE (*Terms of Endearment*—1983) About ten years after Reynolds was turned down for *Cuckoo's Nest*, director James L. Brooks sent him the script for *Terms of Endearment*. The lead had been created especially for him, but Reynolds rejected it. "I'd promised…that I'd star in *Stroker Ace*," Burt explained later. So Brooks offered the part to Jack Nicholson, who jumped at it. "How many scripts make you cry?" he said. "I read hundreds of screenplays every year and this one made me think, 'Yeah, I know just how this guy feels.' It was terrific." *Stroker Ace* was one of the forgettable films of the year; *Terms of Endearment* won Nicholson his second Oscar.

HOW TO READ
TEA LEAVES

It used to be a common thing—go into a tea room or coffee shop and as you reached the end of your cup, a dark, mysterious stranger would offer to read your future for a few coins. After a ritual of stirring and dumping the cup's dregs, the reader would point out pictures in the leaves and tell you what they meant. It's a lost art. But now—thanks to the BRI— you can be the first on your block to practice it.

THE HISTORY OF TEA LEAF READING

T Tasseography—the art of telling the future by reading tea leaves and coffee grounds—has been around for so long there's no way to trace its history accurately. Legend, though, says it originated in China. The ancient Chinese foretold the future by reading the marks on the inside of bells. Apparently someone noticed that a teacup is shaped like an inverted bell—and that tea leaves left in a cup resemble the marks on a bell's interior. Since teacups were easier to handle than bells, reading tea leaves became more popular.

HOW DOES IT WORK?

Well, you have to use loose tea—not tea bags. And it's an art, not a science—like interpreting ink blots in a psychologist's office. This becomes obvious when you realize that it's awfully hard to differentiate between, for example, a tea leaf dog ("faithful friends") and a wolf ("jealous friends"), or between a toad ("unknown enemy") and a frog ("arrogance").

Throw in a reader who is also a good and intuitive judge of people, and you may have an effective "fortune-teller."

GETTING READY

• Use a cup with a wide opening, the kind that comes with a saucer—not a mug. The inside of the cup should be light colored and patternless so you can see the leaves clearly.
• Use loose tea, preferably with big leaves. If you can't find it in the store, cut open a tea bag or two and dump the contents into a cup. If

you're making coffee, dump the loose ground coffee (instant coffee won't work) right into the cup. Add hot water and wait for a few minutes before adding cream or sugar.

• The room should be peaceful, if possible. Clear your mind and relax, concentrating on your future and asking whatever power is involved for an accurate reading.

NOW SEE THIS

1. Don't drink to the last drop. Save the leaves or grounds with a little liquid in the bottom (one or two teaspoons is plenty).

2. Take the cup in your left hand and spin it three times clockwise.

3. Immediately after swirling it, turn the cup over on a saucer or plate. After all the liquid drains out, set it upright, with the handle pointing toward you. *Note:* The handle is like a *YOU ARE HERE* arrow on a map—it represents you and your home. So a symbol found near the handle indicates something that will literally strike close to home. Leaf configurations stuck near the rim represent your present; the walls, your immediate future; and the bottom, the distant future.

4. Look carefully into the cup, tipping it and noting the leaves or grounds stuck to the walls and the bottom from all angles. At first they may look like random clumps and glops, but see if their shapes remind you of anything. This will take some imagination (like looking for pictures in clouds). Also notice their size and relative positioning, because two images next to each other can influence each other.

INTERPRETING THE LEAVES

• The bigger and clearer an image is, the more significant it is. A small or blurry image has substantially less significance. If all the images are blurry, it indicates a delay before the events come to pass. If the cup itself is blurry, too, it signifies that you'll soon be receiving bad news from your optometrist.

• You may see just a few symbols, or dozens in one cup. The idea is to note all of them in a big picture and see how they interact with each other. As in life, each component influences and is influenced by the others.

The word "tragedy" comes from *tragos* and *ode,* Greek words for "goat" and "song."

• For example: Bad omens may be weakened or canceled out by nearby good omens and vice versa. A snake ("bad luck") that appears near the letter M may indicate that you should be on guard against an enemy whose name begins with M. A number 6 next to a travel symbol may mean you'll be gone for that many days, weeks...or even years.

• Start with the images near the rim ("the present"), then work your way into the bottom of the cup ("the future").

SYMBOL KEY

Below, we list some of the images you might see, along with their traditional meanings. In most guides there are literally hundreds to choose from. So when you see something in your cup, just ask yourself what it means to you and determine whether it's a good or bad omen. Have fun, and remember...they're only tea leaves!

Acorn: Good health, good luck

Airplane: Unexpected journey; shattered wings—danger

Alligator: Strength and power

Angel: Good news, lucky love

Apple: Long life, gain in business (maybe incompatibility with other PCs)

Arch: Trip abroad (or maybe just to McDonald's)

Arrow: A letter; if bent, bad news

Ax: Trouble

Basket: New family member

Bat: Fruitless endeavor (unless it's a fruit bat)

Bell: Good news, or a wedding

Birds: Good news

Boat: Friendly visitor

Bridge: Pleasant trip; if blurry, unfortunate ending

Bull: Enemies are out to get you

Bush: Success, fulfillment, presidential aspirations

Butterfly: Frivolous pleasure, squandered savings

Candle: Love, goodwill, education

Castle: Marrying into money

Cat: Treachery, insincere friends

Chain: Early marriage; if broken, an unhappy one

Coffin: Death of a person or one of your dreams

Comet: Unexpected visitor (or maybe clean sinks)

Cross: Trouble

Crown: Success

Dog: Faithful friend

Dot: Money

Egg: Some say good fortune; others, that you'll lose your savings

---

President John Adams was so short and fat that his nickname was "His Rotundity."

Elephant: Good luck, health, happiness

Envelope: Good news; if blurred, bad news.

Eye: Watch out, especially around money

Fan: Good luck with opposite sex

Feather: Frivolity, lack of responsibility

Fence (or other barrier): Obstacles

Fish: Good news from far away

Flag: Danger

Flowers: Loyal friends, happy marriage, success

Frog: Beware excessive pride, arrogance

Fruit: Success in new venture

Goat: You're surrounded by enemies

Grasshopper: A friend will leave, maybe not return (or you'll be cast in a remake of *Kung Fu*)

Gun: Trouble

Hand: Friendliness

Hat: Small success

Heart: A letter or lover is coming

Hen: New addition to family

Hourglass: Danger nearby

Key: Problems solved

Kite: Trip that will lead to valuable friendship

Knife: Danger

Ladder: Success, travel

Lizard: Treacherous friends

Monkey: Success

Moon: Fame and riches

Mouse: Thief nearby

Mushroom: Quarrel with lover

Owl: Failure, sickness, poverty, maybe death (but have a nice day anyway)

People: Generally good omen

Pig: Good luck, new member of family

Pitchfork: Deceitful opposite sex

Question mark: Beware all major decisions

Ring: Marriage

Screw: Just as implied, you'll be victim of injustice

Ship: Good news on its way

Snake: Enemy or threat

Spider: Unexpected inheritance

Square: Peace, or no marriage (actually, the two may go together)

Star: Achievement and success

Sun: Joy and power

Toad: Unknown enemy

Tree: Success, fulfillment

Tree branch: Better health

Umbrella: New opportunities

Volcano: Major upheaval

Wheel: Unexpected gift or inheritance

Windmill: Someone you helped will help you

Wolf: Jealous friends

Worms: Secret enemies

Wreath: Loss of loved one

Some beaver dams are more than 1,000 years old.

OFF YOUR ROCKER

We'll bet you didn't know your favorite rock singers could talk, too. Here are some of the profound things they have to say.

"I'm a mess and you're a mess, too. Everyone's a mess. Which means, actually, that no one's a mess."
—Fiona Apple

"It's really hard to maintain a one-on-one relationship if the other person is not going to allow me to be with other people."
—Axl Rose

"I only answer to two people—myself and God."
—Cher

"I'm not a snob. Ask anybody. Well, anybody who matters."
—Simon LeBon, Duran Duran

"There's a basic rule which runs through all kinds of music, kind of an unwritten rule. I don't know what it is."
—Ron Wood

"I want to go out at the top, but the secret is knowing when you're at the top. It's so difficult in this business—your career fluctuates all the time, up and down, like a pair of trousers."
—Rod Stewart

"I can't think of a better way to spread the message of world peace than by working with the NFL and being part of Super Bowl XXVII."
—Michael Jackson

"Damn, I look good with guns."
—Ted Nugent

"We use volume to drive evil spirits out the back of your head, and by evil spirits I mean the job, the boss, the spouse, the probation officer."
—David Lee Roth

"I should think that being my old lady would be all the satisfaction or career any woman needs."
—Mick Jagger

"God had to create disco music so that I could be born and be successful."
—Donna Summer

"I can do anything. One of these days I'll be so complete I won't be a human. I'll be a god."
—John Denver

"Just because I have my standards, they think I'm a bitch."
—Diana Ross

In 1970, an Englishman named A.P. Herbert cashed a check written on the side of a cow.

DUMB CROOKS

Here's proof that crime doesn't pay.

A BAD CALL

"When two service station attendants in Ionia, Michigan, refused to hand over the cash to an intoxicated robber, the man threatened to call the police. They still refused, so the robber, true to his word, called the cops and was arrested."

—**"The Edge,"** *Oregonian*

SHOULD'VE ELOPED

"Tennessee man Winston Swaggerty, 32, had an outstanding arrest warrant (on a theft charge), but that didn't stop him from having his wedding on the lawn of the Newport, Tennessee, courthouse. A deputy sheriff walking to work recognized the groom, handcuffed him, and led him upstairs to a cell. The bride's reaction? Said the deputy, 'She was really upset.'"

—**Associated Press**

DISAPPEARING THINK

"A pair of Indiana 19-year-olds thought they'd devised the perfect scam: signing checks with disappearing ink. They forgot to make something else disappear though: the name of Jeffrey J. Pyrcioch permanently printed at the top of the bogus checks. Pyrcioch and Heather M. Green were arrested on suspicion of fraud and theft."

—*Atlanta Journal*

ANGER MANAGEMENT

"Johnny Miller, 32, allegedly walked into a First Utah Bank, pulled a gun out of an envelope and robbed the teller. Miller got away with $34,000—but left behind the envelope. It contained a certificate for his completion of an anger-management course run by Utah's Department of Corrections. Miller was apprehended and currently awaits trial."

—*Stuff*

LEAST-COMPETENT CROOK AWARD

"Dennis Sullivan, 23, was arrested in January for the robbery of what he thought was an armored car, according to Manassas, Virginia, police. In reality, it was a laundry truck delivering towels and mops to a Bowl America. Said a police officer, '(Sullivan, holding a sawed-off shotgun), ran up to the (driver) and said, "Give it up." The (driver) said, "What?" Sullivan grabbed a bag and ran but soon realized he had a bag of mopheads.' Police spotted him running for his getaway car, and arrested him."

—News of the Weird

HE DIDN'T SEE THE ERROR OF HIS WAYS

"A blind man tried to rob a bank as a security guard who helped him to the teller's window stood nearby, police say.

"Bruce Edward Hall, 48, entered the bank Tuesday, accepted the guard's help, then gave a teller a note demanding money, police said. The teller mouthed 'It's a robbery' to a guard," and Hall was apprehended."

—Associated Press

ROAD RAGE

"A motorist was infuriated by the ticket that a Santa Monica traffic officer had just left on his windshield. So he reached into the officer's vehicle, pulled its keys from the ignition, and then sped off in his own car. Police nabbed him and the keys the next day. A police sergeant explained the easy arrest: 'We had his license plate number from the citation.'"

—Only in L.A., **Steve Harvey**

HE'S GOT A ROOM FOR 3 TO 5 YEARS

"A man registered for a motel room at the Meader Inn in Van Buren, Arkansas, then followed the clerk into the back room, robbed her, and fled. When police checked the registration card, they found that the thief had registered under his own name, Scott Brady, and even listed his address, which was local. The police went to Brady's home and arrested him."

—"The Edge," *Oregonian*

The word "million" was invented sometime around the year 1300 A.D.

"WITH THIS RING, I ME WED"

Marriage is a sacred institution…and some of these people probably belong in an institution.

AND WHAT A HONEYMOON! "Janet Downes thinks she has found the secret for a happy marriage: she's marrying herself on her 40th birthday. The Bellevue, Nebraska, woman says the wedding ceremony celebrates that she is 'happy with herself,' and plans to exchange vows with herself in the mirror. The ceremony will include a wedding gown, flowers, a traditional cake, and a choir."

—*News of the Weird*

CLOTHES ENCOUNTER. "Of the many marriages of inanimate objects that have taken place in Japan, few have equaled the splendor of the one which united two kimonos in Kyoto in 1934. In this wedding—solemnized with full Shinto rites and celebrated with an elaborate banquet—the bride was a renowned 232-year-old silk garment and the groom a distinguished 110-year-old cotton robe. The invitations were so highly prized that they have virtually become museum pieces."

—*The Mammoth Book of Oddities*

DRIVE ME CRAZY, BABY! "A man was turned down at the courthouse in Knoxville, Tennessee, when he tried to marry his car. After a depressing split with his girlfriend, the man applied for a marriage license to make his 1996 Mustang his bride, but his application was rejected."

—**Universal Press Syndicate**

TOO MUCH MONKEY BUSINESS. "An unusual wedding took place in 1936 in Surat, India. Wearing pearls and diamonds worth a fortune, the couple were joined in matrimony in a Hindu temple by a high-caste priest. Thousands witnessed the ceremony, and hundreds attended the wedding banquet for the happy bride and groom—a pair of monkeys."

—*Unbelievable…But True!*

TOOTH...OR CONSEQUENCES

When BRI stalwart Jack Mingo submitted this, Uncle John sent it to his dentist, Dr. Bamford, to review. Murphy's Law: The doctor returned it with his okay...along with a reminder that it was time for a check-up.

YOUR MOM WAS WRONG

What causes tooth decay? Decaying food, which acts as a bacteria sanctuary. So you can forget what your mom told you about avoiding sweets. Actually most candy and soft drinks are not that bad...*if* they're washed off quickly.

In fact, many "healthy" snacks can be the most deadly. Sticky dried fruit is particularly bad because it molders on and between teeth; so do carbohydrates like bagels, crackers, pretzels, and dry cereals. If you're looking for "tooth-healthy" snacks, go with fresh fruits and vegetables, dairy products, popcorn, nuts, chips, and unsweetened peanut butter.

TO TELL THE TOOTH

Companies make a lot of claims for toothpastes and mouthwashes. Research groups have debunked some obviously bogus ones, but it can still be hard to tell what's true or false. Some facts about "special ingredients," according to *Consumer Reports*:

• **Fluoride.** Really hardens teeth and prevents cavities. Buy toothpastes with it.

• **Whitening.** Researchers for *Consumer Reports* found no whitening agent in any toothpaste making that claim. The only method that works? Bleaching by dentists.

• **Tartar control.** Works, sort of. Doesn't take existing tartar off, but absorbs minerals in your saliva that could collect on your teeth.

• **Desensitizing.** Works if you have pain or sensitivity from receding gums, but not if you have pain from cavities or tooth-grinding, or other more common sources of most dental pain.

• **Baking soda.** Doesn't do a bit of good.

• **Hydrogen peroxide.** Doesn't do any good either. In fact, it may add more problems by drying out the mouth.

• **Triclosan.** Found in some toothpastes. A cautious yes on this—it seems to keep killing germs for hours after brushing.

"YOU HAVE BAD BREATH...*BAD BREATH!*"

People worried about bad breath spend $10 billion a year on gum, mints, and mouthwash—nearly all of it wasted.

No not even mouthwashes really stop bad breath for more than a minute or two—in fact, alcohol and hydrogen peroxide (a common ingredient) can actually worsen the conditions. While bad gums and teeth can have some affect on your breath, most bad breath comes from food and plaque forming a coating on the back of the tongue. What can you do about it? Suppressing the gag reflex, grasp your tongue with a washcloth and use a toothbrush or tongue scraper on it for two to three minutes, twice a day.

BITS AND BITES

• The patron saint of dentists: St. Apollonia. Why? She reportedly had her teeth pulled out in 249 A.D. by an anti-Christian mob.

• Despite the popular myth, George Washington didn't have wooden teeth—his four sets of dentures were made of hippopotamus bone, elephant ivory, and eight human teeth from dead people, held together with gold palates and springs.

• Thanks to fluoride and other preventives, Baby Boomers are probably the last generation that will have a lot of cavities in their permanent teeth.

• How about a tooth tattoo? Tiny gold images of hearts, butterflies, and the like have become popular among certain trendy groups. The downside is that from a distance of more than about three feet it just looks like you have food stuck in your teeth.

• Getting dentures was once considered a natural step in aging, but no longer. In 1959, dentists performed 34 extractions for every 100 people; now it's half that rate.

• Drugs can cause cavities. Antidepressants, antihypertensives, antihistamines, decongestants, and muscle relaxants all inhibit production of saliva, a natural bacteria destroyer.

• Hard to believe, but Colgate claims "Tooth Fairy" as a registered trademark.

VIDEO TREASURES

Ever found yourself at a video store staring at thousands of films you've never heard of, wondering which ones are worth watching? It happens to us all the time—so we decided to offer a few recommendations.

SWINGERS (1996) *Comedy*
Review: "This highly entertaining low-budget comedy features five young, Rat-Pack showbiz wannabees on the prowl for career breaks and beautiful 'babies.' Witty script and clever camera work make this one 'money, baby, money.'" (*VideoHound's Golden Movie Retriever*)

THE KILLING (1956) *Mystery/Suspense*
Review: "Strong noir thriller from Stanley Kubrick has Sterling Hayden leading a group of criminals in an intricately timed race-track heist. Excellent performances and atmospheric handling mark Kubrick, even at this early stage of his career, as a filmmaker to watch." (*Video Movie Guide*)

GET CARTER (1970) *Drama*
Review: "British gangster film set in the 1970s. The inspiration is Hollywood [in the] 1940s. Michael Caine is a cheap hood who returns home to investigate his brother's death. One of Caine's finest performances." (*Movies on TV*)

DEJA VU (1998) *Romance*
Review: "An unabashed love story, a glorious fantasy that's all the more meaningful because it involves grown-ups instead of the post-adolescents who usually star in movie romances. Unafraid to be sentimental, it has a certain wisdom about life, about the way we have to take chances and make hard decisions." (*Roger Ebert & The Movies—Capsule Summaries*)

EATING RAOUL (1982) *Comedy*
Review: "Delicious black comedy about the Blands, a super-square couple who lure wealthy swingers to their apartment and kill them, which both reduces the number of 'perverts' and helps finance their dream restaurant. A bright, original, and hilarious satire." (*Leonard Maltin's Movie & Video Guide*)

Ever seen it? *Nanook of the North* was the first documentary film ever made.

Q & A:
ASK THE EXPERTS

*Here are some more random questions, with answers
from books by some of the nation's top trivia experts.*

IN A LATHER

Q: *Do I really have to shampoo twice?*

A: "Of course not. Soaps are really efficient; one washing removes about 99% of the oil. But initially, that dirt and oil prevent the shampoo from forming the nice firm bubbles, which together make up lather. In fact, the only point of reapplying shampoo is that it's psychologically pleasing." (From *Why Things Are, Vol. II*, by Joel Achenbach)

POL POSITION

Q: *How did "left" and "right" come to represent the ends of the political spectrum?*

A: "According to the *Oxford English Dictionary*: 'This use originated in the French National Assembly of 1789, in which the nobles as a body took the position of honor on the President's right, and the Third Estate sat on his left. The significance of these positions, which was at first merely ceremonial, soon became political.'" (From *Return of the Straight Dope*, by Cecil Adams)

EAU DE CAR

Q: *What exactly is that "new car smell"?*

A: "There's nothing quite like it, and all attempts to reproduce it artificially for colognes and air fresheners have fallen short. It is a combination of scents from things one wouldn't normally smell voluntarily, condensed in intensity by the size of the relatively airtight passenger compartment. The odor components that go into it include fresh primer and paint, plastic, leather, vinyl, rubber, glues, sealers, and carpeting. The smell fades with time, as residual solvents leach away from exposure to light, heat, and air." (From *Just Curious, Jeeves*, by Jack Mingo and Erin Barrett)

The Man-o-War jellyfish can have tentacles up to 60 feet long.

CONCRETE JUNGLE

Q: *How do city street trees survive with only foot-square holes in the pavement?*

A: Actually, many of them don't. The average life of a street tree surrounded by concrete and asphalt is only 7 to 15 years—compared to the 30 to 40 years of similar trees in the wild. Why? "Tree roots are very superficial, occupying only the top three feet of soil—they spread out, not down. When the soil gets so compacted that the roots can't get in, the tree dies. But if the roots can get into the soil (or sewer), the tree has a decent chance of getting the water and nutrients needed to survive. People can help street trees by watering during dry periods and protecting them from dogs, bicycle chains (which can rub the thin bark that covers the tree's growth layers), bleach water from the scrub bucket, and motor oil." (From *The New York Times Book of Science Questions & Answers*, by C. Claiborne Ray)

APPLES AND ORANGES

Q: *What's the difference between horns and antlers?*

A: "The horns of antelopes and the antlers of deer, although comparable in function, differ considerably in structure. Horns, usually possessed by both sexes, are permanent features that continue to grow throughout the animal's life. They are bony projections from the skull, covered with keratin, which is tougher than bone. Antlers, by contrast, are pure bone and are formed and shed every year. They are normally grown only by male deer, with the exception of reindeer and caribou, whose females have them as well." (From *Can Elephants Swim?*, by Robert M. Jones)

HE GO BOOM!

Q: *How do they shoot off a "human cannonball" at the circus without blowing the poor guy to pieces?*

A: "Human cannonballs aren't blasted from the cannon with gunpowder. They're propelled by a catapult. The flash, loud noise, and smoke are supplied by firecrackers and such." (From *The Straight Dope Tells All*, by Cecil Adams)

In English, "four" is the only digit that has the same number of letters as its value.

FAMILY FEUDS

You can't always get along with everyone in your family...but these guys just out and out declared war on each other.

M ARS vs. MARS
The Contestants: Frank Mars, founder of Mars, Inc., chocolate company and his son Forrest Mars.

The Feud: The candy bars that Frank Mars invented—Snickers, Milky Way, and Three Musketeers—made him a very wealthy man. He lived in a mansion, drove expensive cars, and owned race horses and an airplane. He had plenty of money, but the country was in the middle of the Depression, so he wouldn't expand the company.

Forrest Mars was another story. He worked in his father's company, and wanted to expand it. "I wanted to conquer the world," he explained years later, and he soon began to chafe under his father's authority. "Things got bitter. I told my dad to stick his business up his ***. If he didn't want to give me one-third right then, I said, 'I'm leaving.' He said leave, so I left."

When Frank Mars died from kidney failure 15 months later (Forrest did not attend the funeral), his second wife, Ethel, inherited control of Mars, Inc. The will stipulated that Forrest would not inherit any Mars, Inc. stock until Ethel died, and even then he would only get half her shares. He was on his own.

Moving to France, Mars started a business selling shoe trees. When this failed, he went back to the candy business. He moved to Switzerland and took jobs in the world's great chocolate companies—Tobler and Nestle—to learn everything he could about chocolate from the best minds in the industry. (Frank Mars never knew anything about how to make chocolate—his candy bars were made with Hershey's chocolate.) "I was an hourly paid guy," Mars recounted years later. "They didn't know who I was. They never asked. They didn't care."

In 1933, Mars moved to London, reformulated his father's Milky Way recipe to suit English tastes, and began selling them under the name "Mars bars." By 1939, he had built his company into the third largest candy manufacturer in Britain. But when England passed a special tax on resident foreigners to raise money for World War II, Mars put his senior manager in charge of the company and returned to the United States to avoid paying the tax.

By now Forrest's stepmother and her family were firmly in control of Mars, Inc. So rather than go back to the family firm, Mars founded a new company, M&M, Inc., and began manufacturing candy-coated chocolates like the ones he'd seen during a visit to Spain (see page 170). Just as he'd done in England, Mars built M&M, Inc. into one of the largest candy companies in the country. But it wasn't enough—he still had one last score to settle.

And the Winner Is: Forrest Mars. When Ethel Mars died in 1945, he inherited half of her Mars, Inc. shares, making him a part-owner of the company he'd been shut out of. But he wanted it all. Mars spent the next 19 years battling executives for control. And he got it. In 1964—32 years after his father kicked him out of the company—it was his.

KRASILOVSKY VS. KRASILOUSKY VS. KRASILOSKY

The Contestants: Uncles, nephews, and cousins who worked at S. Krasilovsky & Brothers, a moving company in Brooklyn, N.Y.

The Feud: In 1939, nephew Mike Krasilovsky left the firm and started his own moving company, which he named Mike Krasilovsky Trucking & Millwright Company. The two companies began stealing each other's customers...and Mike began spelling his last name with a "u" instead of a "v" so his company would appear ahead of his uncle's in the telephone listings.

That was only the beginning: When cousin Milton started *his* moving company, he changed his name to Mick (because it looks like Mike), and spelled his last name Krasilosky so that it would appear ahead of both his uncle *and* his cousin. Mike retaliated by buying the Atlas-York Safe Corporation so that he would also appear in the "A" listings; then another cousin got into the business—the Acme Safe company—which prompted Mike to buy the Ace Trucking Company.

And the Winner Is: No one. But at the peak of the feud, Milton had 13 different listings in the phone book; Mike had 18. When another cousin, Marvin, came up with the idea for the AAA Acme Krasilovsky Safe Company, Mike finally gave up.

DON'T LEAVE HOME WITHOUT IT

You're at a restaurant and the waiter brings your check...You reach in your pocket and suddenly realize your wallet is at home. Or, you hand the waitress a credit card; she comes back and tells you, apologetically, that it's expired (or maxed out). Sound familiar? We figure there are two things to learn from the stories here: 1) Don't worry, it happens to everyone; and 2) Don't panic. If you're resourceful, you can deal with it.

EVEN THE PRESIDENT...

"President Bill Clinton was visiting Park City, Utah, on Monday. He picked out several books at Dolly's Books and handed over his American Express card for the $62.66 bill—only to be informed it had expired the day before." He paid cash.

—**Medford, Oregon, *Mail Tribune***

SORRY, NO CHECKS ACCEPTED

In April 1997, former British Prime Minister Margaret Thatcher tried to purchase $40 worth of groceries with a check. The clerk wouldn't accept it. "I can't override the system, so there was no way I could take her check," said cashier Shirley Taylor. "She was very good about it, tore the check up and paid cash. It was a bit embarrassing for her, I think."

—**Wire service reports**

THAT'S ME!

"After a young woman wrote a check at a clothes store in Marina del Rey, the clerk asked to see her driver's license. She explained apologetically that her wallet had been stolen. But, she added, she did have one form of ID. 'I was the May centerfold in *Playboy* magazine,' she said. 'I have the centerfold here in my purse if you want to see it.' She took it out. The smiles matched."

—***Only In L.A.*, by Steve Harvey**

Why did Grace Hopper coin the term "computer bug"? A moth shorted out her computer.

SAVED BY THE BUCK

"In 1979 Treasury Secretary Michael Blumenthal found himself in an embarrassing situation in Beethoven's, an expensive San Francisco restaurant. Blumenthal was confronted with a sizable dinner bill, an expired Visa card, and a waiter who wanted proof of signature to back up an out-of-town check. Blumenthal solved his predicament in a way only he could: He produced a dollar bill and pointed out his own signature, *W. M. Blumenthal*, in the bottom right-hand corner. The signatures matched, and Blumenthal's personal check was accepted."

—*The Emperor Who Ate the Bible,* Scott Morris

X-RATED

"NEW YORK—Sharon Mitchell, heroine of the X-rated *Captain Lust,* was having trouble cashing a check at a New York bank because she was not carrying a driver's license or any other identification.

"She was, however, carrying a magazine in which she appeared in the nude. She handed over the magazine, hitched her sweater up to her chin, and arranged herself in the same pose.

"They cashed her check."

—London *Sunday Telegraph Magazine*

*   *   *

BRI "FAVORITE ROLE MODELS"

Role Model: Abigail Boettcher, Pork Queen of Buena Vista County, Iowa
Setting an Example: In her farewell speech as reigning Pork Queen, the college freshman admitted to area pork producers that she "is, and always has been, a vegetarian."

Role Model: Diane Smith, of the Texas Dept. of Agriculture
Setting an Example: In 1996 Smith, the official in charge of promoting Texas's $8 billion beef industry, revealed that she'd been a vegetarian for the past 14 years.

New York City's Broadway was once known as Bloomingdale Road.

UNCLE JOHN'S FLATULENCE HALL OF FAME

It used to be that no one talked about farts...now, it's no big deal. You can't get away from it. Which is fine by us. Here we honor people who have made an art out of passing gas. (By the way— if this is your favorite part of the book, we recommend a tome called Who Cut the Cheese?, *by Jim Dawson.)*

Honorees: Simon Brassell, Karen Chin, and Robert Harman
Notable Achievement: Finding a way to discuss dinosaur farts without making people laugh
True Story: In 1991, the three scientists published a paper proposing that millions of years' worth of dinosaur farts may have helped make the Earth more hospitable for humans and other mammals. How? The methane gas passed by dinosaurs during the Cretaceous period, they suggested, "may have been a...contributor to global warming."

Honoree: King Louis XIV of France
Notable Achievement: Turning a fart into a compliment
True Story: "It is said," Frank O'Neil writes in *The Mammoth Book of Oddities*, "that Louis XIV expressed his admiration for the Duchess of Orleans, by doing her the honor of breaking wind in her presence."

Honoree: Randy Maresh, an employee at the Albertson's supermarket in Gresham, Oregon
Notable Achievement: Making someone so mad at his farting that they sued him
True Story: In the mid-1990s, Tom Morgan sued co-worker Randy Maresh for $100,000, claiming in court papers that Maresh "would continually and repeatedly seek out the plaintiff on the premises of Albertson's [supermarket] while plaintiff was engaged in his employee duties. That defendant, after locating plaintiff, would posi-

tion himself in the proximity of plaintiff so as to direct his 'gas' toward plaintiff, humiliating plaintiff and inflicting severe mental stress upon plaintiff." (In his written response to the suit, Maresh's lawyer argued that farts are "expressive behavior," and as such, are protected by the First Amendment.) No word on the outcome.

Honoree: Dr. Michael Levitt of Minneapolis, Minnesota
Notable Achievement: Inventing a Breathalyzer-type test that can detect a propensity for excessive farting
True Story: Dr. Levitt's test checks for elevated levels of hydrogen in a patient's breath. If it's there, the patient is likely to be gassy. (Not everyone is impressed with Dr. Levitt's scientific breakthrough: "If Levitt is checking his patients' breath for flatulence," Jeffrey Kluger writes in *Discover* magazine, "I wouldn't even ask how he'd propose to conduct dental work.")

Honoree: Canelos Indians of Ecuador
Notable Achievement: Turning a fart into a supernatural experience...and a free meal
True Story: "The Canelos Indians," Eric Rabkin writes in *It's a Gas*, "are particularly scared by their farts because they believe the soul escapes the body along with the smell. They have developed a ritual to counter this escape. When in a group someone breaks wind, one of the rest, the quickest, will clap him on the back three times and say, '*Uianza, uianza!*' The meaning of this word is unknown but it does signify a feast by that name which the person who farted is obliged to prepare....Alternatively, he can discharge his obligation by rewarding the clapper's kindness with three big clay vessels of manioc beer."

Honoree: Ned Lowenbach, assistant district attorney in Tuolumne County, California
Notable Achievement: Using farts as a legal strategy
True Story: In 1988, a defense attorney appealed his client's conviction, protesting that Lowenbach had disrupted trial proceedings by passing gas. 'He farted about one hundred times,' the attorney said. 'He even lifted his leg a few times.'"

In German, a partypooper is called a *partymuffel.*

DOG FOOD FOR THOUGHT

A page of canine quotes for dog lovers.

"Dogs need to sniff the ground; it's how they keep abreast of current events. The ground is a giant dog newspaper, containing all kinds of late-breaking dog news items."
—**Dave Barry**

"I wonder if other dogs think poodles are members of a weird religious cult."
—**Rita Rudner**

"Did you ever walk into a room and forget why you walked in? I think that's how dogs spend their lives."
—**Sue Murphy**

"When a man's dog turns against him it is time for his wife to pack her trunk and go home to mamma."
—**Mark Twain**

"My dog is half pit bull, half poodle. Not much of a guard dog, but a vicious gossip."
—**Craig Shoemaker**

"The nose of the bulldog has been slanted backward so that he can breathe without letting go."
—**Winston Churchill**

"Some days you're the dog; some days you're the hydrant."
—**Anonymous**

"People who keep dogs are cowards who haven't got the guts to bite people themselves."
—**August Strindberg**

A dog is the only thing on this earth that loves you more than he loves himself."
—**Anonymous**

"When a man's best friend is his dog, that dog has a problem."
—**Edward Abbey**

"If dogs could talk, perhaps we would find it as hard to get along with them as we do with people."
—**Karel Capek**

"The average dog is a nicer person than the average person."
—**Andy Rooney**

"My dog is worried about the economy because Alpo is up to 99 cents a can. That's almost $7.00 in dog money."
—**Joe Weinstein**

Do all dogs bark? Almost. The Basenji, an African breed, is the only kind that doesn't.

IT'S A DOG'S LIFE

Here's an article that should warm the heart of anyone who's ever dreamed of getting back at telemarketers and junk mail purveyors. It's by Lee Coppola, and it first appeared in Newsweek *magazine.*

A DOG WITH A NUMBER

Ever wonder what happens when a pet takes on a persona? Ashley could have told you, if he could have talked. Ashley was our family mutt, an SPCA special, part Beagle and part Spaniel.

For years—most of them after he died—he also served as the family's representative in the local telephone book. He was picked for the role quite haphazardly one day when I tried to keep my number out of the book to avoid getting business calls at home. When I balked at the $60-a-year fee, the cheery telephone company representative suggested I list the number in one of my children's names.

I was munching on a sandwich at the time and Ashley followed me around the kitchen waiting for a crumb to fall. "Can I put the phone in any name?" I asked the rep as I sidestepped Ashley. "Certainly," she answered, and therein gave birth to 10 years of telephone calls and mail to a dog.

THINK OF THE POOR PUPPIES!

"A remarkable new book about the Coppolas since the Civil War is about to make history—and you, Ashley Coppola, are in it," touted one letter asking Ashley to send $10 right away for "this one-time offer." Ashley received hundreds of pieces of mail, the bulk soliciting his money.

The most ironic pitches for cash were from the SPCA and the Buffalo Zoo—a kind of animal-helping-animal scenario. And we wondered how the chief executive of a local cemetery might react if he knew he was asking a canine to buy a plot to give his family "peace of mind." Or a local lawn service's thoughts about asking a dog who daily messed the grass, "Is your lawn as attractive as it could be?"

Then there was the letter offering Ashley "reliable electronic security to protect your home." One of the kids asked if that wasn't Ashley's job.

Cruel and Unusual Punishment? The musical *Cats* ran on Broadway for 18 years.

HE DIED CHASING A CAR...

The kids soon got into the swing of having their dog receive mail and telephone calls. "He's sleeping under the dining-room table," one would tell telemarketers. "He's out in the backyard taking a whiz," was the favorite reply of another. My wife would have nothing of that frivolity preferring to simply reply, "He's deceased."

But that tack backfired on her one day when our youngest child took an almost pleading call from a survey-company employee looking for Ashley. "I'm Ashley," the 17-year-old politely replied, taking pity on the caller. He dutifully gave his age and answered a few questions before he realized he was late for an appointment and hurriedly cut short the conversation. "Can I call you again?" the surveyor asked. "OK," our son said as he hung up.

Sure enough, the surveyor called again the next day and asked for Ashley. But this time Mom answered and gave her standard reply. "Oh my God," exclaimed the caller. "I'm so, so sorry." The surveyor's horrified grief puzzled my wife until our son explained how he had been a healthy teenage Ashley the day before.

MR. & MRS. PUPPY

It seemed direct mailers had a tough time figuring out Ashley's sex and marital status. He was named by our daughter at the time she was reading *Gone With the Wind* and was smitten with Ashley Wilkes. "Dear Mr. Coppola," his mail sometimes would begin. More often, though, Ashley's mail came to Mrs. Coppola or, on those politically correct occasions, Ms. Coppola.

Sometimes we worried about our dog's fate. You see, he broke several chain letters urging him to copy and send 20 others or risk some calamity. After all, Ashley was warned, didn't one person die nine days after throwing out the letter?

Did I mention credit cards? Ashley paid his bills on time, judging from the $5,000 lines of credit for which he "automatically" qualified. Made us wonder about the scrutiny of the nation's credit card industry.

AN ETHNIC FLAVOR

Of course, Ashley was no ordinary dog. He was an *Italian* dog. How else to explain the solicitation to Mr. Coppola that came all the way from Altamura, Italy, and sought donations to an orphanage? Then there was the offer to obtain his family's cherished crest, "fashioned hundreds of years ago in Italy," and purchase the Coppola family registry that listed him along with all the other Coppolas in America.

Is there some message in all this? Think of the saplings that were sacrificed to try to squeeze money from a canine. Or the time, energy, and money that were wasted each time a postage or bulk-mail stamp was affixed to an envelope being sent to a mutt. We did feel sheepish about the deception when the mail came from the self-employed trying to make a buck. We wondered if a local dentist really would have given Ashley a "complete initial consultation, exam, and bitewing X-rays for ONLY THREE DOLLARS." And what might have been the expression on the saleswoman's face if Ashley had shown up for his complimentary Mary Kay facial?

Ashley did appreciate, however, the coupon for dog food.

*   *   *

STRANGE-BUT-TRUE NAMES

Denis O'Pray, rector of the Church of Our Saviour in San Gabriel.

Jesse James, Harry Hollywood, and Sherman Oaks, LAPD officers.

Daniel Waters and Norman Powers, officials in the Department of Water and Power.

Jim Crooks, chief of L.A. County criminal justice computer system.

George Crook, L.A. lawyer. After he won a Golden Moniker Award from *California Lawyer* magazine, he wrote to the publication, "I am not a Nixon."

Susan Tellem, public relations executive.

Norm Reeder, in charge of Torrance library programs.

Steve Bear, an Angeles National Forest ranger.

Michael Park, a city Recreation and Parks supervisor.

Mark Ussery, loan department employee at Western Federal Savings and Loan.

John Argue, L.A. lawyer.

WHY WE EAT OATMEAL

It seems like people have been eating oatmeal forever, but that isn't the case. If it wasn't for the efforts of three men—one who figured out how it make it, another who figured out how to steal it, and a third who figured out to sell it—oatmeal might never have become a popular breakfast food at all.

STRONG MEDICINE

For thousands of years, humans have created meal and flour from by grinding grain between two *millstones*—flat stones that lay atop one another and rotate in opposite directions. In the process, the grain trapped between them is ground into flour.

But when raw oats are ground between millstones, the result is a floury meal that takes three or four hours to cook…and produces a lumpy, pasty gruel. Benjamin Franklin and others touted "oatmeal gruel" as a health food. But it tasted so terrible, and was so difficult to make, that it remained something sold by druggists and kept in the medicine closet, to be brought out only when necessary for "invalids and convalescents." With the exception of German, Scottish, and Irish immigrants who'd eaten it as a staple food in the old country, anyone healthy enough to eat something else usually did. Oats were something you fed to *horses*, not people.

MAN OF STEEL

Then in 1877 a miller in Akron, Ohio named Ferdinand Schumacher developed a process that used steel knives to convert hulled oat kernels into coarse meal. Because the knives cut the oats into flakes instead of grinding them into floury powder, the resulting porridge no longer had the consistency or taste of lumpy paste, and was much easier to prepare.

Schumacher's German American Oatmeal Factory had the improved method of milling oats all to itself…but not for long. Within a year, an employee named William Heston figured out how to improve the machine's cutting process. Then he went and secured a patent for the improvement—in effect using patent law to steal control of the machine. Heston quickly licensed the improvement back to Schumacher to prevent him from retaliating, but the damage was done—now someone else had the ability to mill oats into something that people actually *wanted* to eat.

Heston didn't waste any time setting himself up in business. He opened a mill 16 miles away in Ravenna, Ohio, and began producing steel-cut oats to compete directly with Schumacher. Heston was of Quaker descent, and understood that the Quaker reputation for simplicity, thrift, and hard work would reflect well upon his product. So he named his company the Quaker Mill Company and in 1877 registered as a trademark "the figure of a man in Quaker garb"—the first trademark for a breakfast cereal in the U.S.

In spite of all his advantages, Heston proved to be a terrible businessman; and in 1881 the mill went bankrupt.

That November an evangelical Christian named Henry Parsons Crowell bought Heston's mill, his oatmeal patents, and his Quaker trademark. The world of breakfast foods would never be the same.

DIVINE INTERVENTION

Crowell was on a mission from God. Seven years earlier when he was at death's door with tuberculosis (which had also killed his grandfather, father, and two brothers), he'd made a pact with God: If his health was restored, he'd devote the rest of his life to raising money for Christian causes. His health *was* restored, and Crowell became focused on raising as much money as possible…then donating 65% of it to Christian charities. (Ironically, there is little evidence to suggest that he ever gave any of his money to the Quakers.)

By now, thanks largely to Schumacher's efforts, demand for steel-cut oatmeal was enormous. In 1883 he built a huge new 5-story mill, appropriately named the Jumbo Mill, to meet it. His oatmeal production increased to 360,000 pounds a day; and because demand for oatmeal was growing so fast, other millers were trying to enter the business—usually by infringing on Schumacher's and Crowell's patents. As the supply of oatmeal increased, prices fell and profits disappeared.

Crowell realized he needed a better way to sell oatmeal. He tried to form a cartel of the largest oatmeal producers—which would have limited productions and raised prices—but Schumacher refused to join. Then in 1886, Schumacher's Jumbo Mill burned to the ground. It was not insured against fire.

THINKING OUTSIDE OF THE BOX

Crowell was determined to take advantage of Schumacher's misfortune, and he was in good position to do so.

In the mid-1880s, all oatmeal was sold in bulk—shopkeepers had a huge, 180-lb. wooden barrel of oatmeal in their stores, and when a customer wanted to buy some, it was scooped into a bag.

Crowell decided it made more sense to package oatmeal in individual 2-pound cardboard cartons—which had only been invented seven years earlier. The cartons were a revolution in packaging. Because they lay flat when unfolded, they could be fed into a printing press and become miniature billboards for the product inside.

Crowell made the most of this new advertising space. He used a colorful printing process that featured a picture of a Quaker on the box, plus cooking instructions and recipes for new dishes that helped increase demand. A free spoon was included in every box to encourage brand loyalty, and customers were invited to cut the Quaker off of the box and mail it in for more freebies.

YOU DIRTY RAT

Crowell also blanketed his sales territories with advertising, painting the Quaker Oats trademark on the sides of buildings and posting it on billboards, on the sides of streetcar cards, and in grocery store windows—even on the back of Sunday church bulletins. "In the space of only a few years," Thomas Hine writes in *The Total Package*, "Quaker Oats became the most promoted product ever."

At the same time, Crowell launched an assault on millers who still sold their oatmeal in bulk barrels. "This grocer dumps oats into a bin," the company's magazine *The Daily Quaker* reported, "Sets his rat traps on top of oats. Catches two rats the first night."

Quaker Oats was now set on the path that would make it America's bestselling cereal by the turn of the century…but there was still one thing left to do: In 1888 Crowell finally succeeded in convincing seven of the country's largest millers—including Schumacher, who'd been humbled by the Jumbo Mill fire—to join together as the American Cereal Company.

Schumacher and Crowell battled for control of the company for the next eleven years, until Crowell finally shoved Schumacher out in 1899 and made himself president. In 1901, American Cereal changed its name…to the Quaker Oats Company.

CLASSIC HOAXES

We've got a whole library full of books on hoaxes. It's amazing how many times people have pulled off clever scams...and how much fun it is to read about them. Here are a few of our favorites.

THE BOSTON BABY MEDIUM

Background: In the 1880s, a Boston "spiritualist" named Hannah Ross became famous for her ability to bring deceased infants back to Earth temporarily, so grieving parents could not only talk to them, but also see and touch them. Ross's séances were always held in dark rooms: She would go into a large cabinet and pull a curtain closed behind her, at which point she would summon the baby back from beyond the grave. Moments later, the baby's head—but never the rest of its body—would poke through the curtain. Ross would then call the parents forward to kiss, cuddle, and caress the ghostly baby's head, which was as warm to the touch as if it were still alive.

Exposed! In 1887, some news reporters teamed up with the Boston police to look into the séances...and exposed them as a hoax. Ross had accomplished the illusion by "painting the face of a baby on her breast and poking it through a slit in the cabinet curtain."

THE COUNTRY CLUB ELIMINATION ACT

Background: In 1971, the *Saturday Review* published in its April 3 issue a Letter to the Editor from a reader concerned about H.R. 6142, a little-known piece of legislation "introduced by Congressman A. F. Day and cosponsored by some 40 members of the House," that would abolish all private parks larger than 50 acres in size and all public recreation areas larger than 150 acres and used by fewer than 150 people a week.

The concerned reader, who identified himself as K. Jason Sitewell, explained that he'd grown up with Congressman Day and knew that Day suffered "a long history of golf-related family tragedies," including a grandfather who "perished in a sand trap," and his father, who died from a heart attack after hitting 19 balls in a row into a pond. The following week, the magazine printed a letter from Congressman Day himself, which cited statistics that in an average year, golf caused 75,000 coronary occlusions, 9,300 golf-cart fatalities, and 60,000 ruined marriages.

News of the bill sent the golfing world into an uproar. Concerned golfers all over the country contacted their congressmen, golf clubs held emergency meetings, and a popular weekly golfing magazine reprinted Sitewell's letter.

Exposed! Then in its May 8 edition the *Review's* editor Norman Cousins admitted the whole thing was a hoax—Congressman A. F. Day's name was short for "April Fool's Day," and K. Jason Sitewell was an "imperfect anagram for 'It's a joke, son.'"

THE CORNELL RHINO

Background. One winter morning in the 1920s, students at Cornell University discovered a set of large footprints in the snow around the campus. Zoology professors examined the prints and declared that, beyond a doubt, they were rhinoceros tracks. But where did the animal go? A horde of students followed the tracks across campus and out across the frozen surface of Beebee Lake, the source of the university's drinking water. There the tracks stopped . . . right next to an enormous hole in the ice. It seemed obvious that the rhino had walked onto the lake, fallen through the ice, and drowned. Many students and faculty swore off drinking tap water for the foreseeable future. Those who continued drinking it swore they could taste a subtle hint of rhino.

Exposed! A few days later, university officials received an anonymous letter from a Cornell student admitting he and a friend had made the tracks...using a rhinoceros-foot wastebasket.

THE GREAT SOVIET FUR SWINDLE

Background: Minks and sables are among the most valuable fur-bearing animals in the world. In the early 1950s, the Soviet Union had sables; Canada had minks. The Soviets proposed a swap: In exchange for two breeding pairs of Canadian minks, they would give the Canadians two pairs of sables. Sable furs were worth more than minks, so the Canadians accepted and sent the minks to Russia.

Exposed! They were ecstatic when the four Soviet sables arrived in return...until they realized that the two females had been sterilized prior to shipment.

After the U.S. Civil War, the U.S. charged England $15.5 million for *not* annexing Canada.

LIFE AFTER DEATH

Plenty has been written about people who nearly die, get a glimpse of the "other side," and then somehow make it back to the land of the living. Here are four examples of another kind of "rebirth": people who were thought to be dead, but were actually quite alive.

DECEASED: 32-year-old Ali Abdel-Rahim Mohammad, of Alexandria, Egypt

NEWS OF HIS DEATH: In 1999 Mohammad blacked out while swimming off the coast of Alexandria. His body was recovered and taken to the morgue.

RESURRECTION: After about three hours in the morgue refrigerator, Mohammad was awakened by a loud banging sound—an attendant was trying to close the refrigerator drawer in which Mohammad had been placed. So the "corpse" reached up and grabbed the attendant's hand. According to one news account, "his firm grip sent the attendant and a family who had apparently come to identify the body of a loved one stampeding out of the morgue yelling, 'Help us!'"

DECEASED: Henry Lodge, a 63-year-old California man

NEWS OF HIS DEATH: In 1986 Lodge was fixing some fuses when he had a heart attack. He was pronounced dead, and his remains were transported to the Los Angeles morgue.

RESURRECTION: Just as the morgue's Dr. Philip Campbell was preparing to make an incision in the remains, Lodge opened his eyes and screamed, "HELP!" Lodge made a speedy recovery and was soon released from the hospital; Dr. Campbell took a leave of absence from work for "nervous exhaustion."

DECEASED: Xue Wangshi, an 81-year-old Chinese woman

NEWS OF HER DEATH: On December 2, 1995, Ms. Wangshi collapsed and stopped breathing. She was pronounced dead and sent to a nearby crematorium.

RESURRECTION: Workers put Ms. Wangshi on a conveyor belt that fed the deceased into the furnace, but in classic cliffhanger fashion, moments later they saw her move her right hand. So they stopped the conveyor belt, "and Mrs. Wangshi sat up."

DECEASED: Musyoka Mutata, 60, who lived in the village of Kitui in Kenya

NEWS OF HIS DEATH: In 1985 Mututa contracted cholera and was thought to have died. Funeral arrangements were made, and at the appointed hour pallbearers arrived in his home to take the body away for burial.

RESURRECTION: When the pallbearers sprayed Mutata with insecticide to ward off flies, he suddenly sat up and asked for a drink of water. According to newspaper reports, this was Mutata's second near-death experience: in 1928 his parents mistook him for dead after an illness, and when "his body, wrapped in sheets and blankets, was being lowered into its grave, the three-year-old let out a scream and was saved."

Update: Four months after his 1985 near-death experience, Mutata died again, this time for real. Rather than bury him right away, however, his family waited two days to be sure that he was really, really dead.

DECEASED: The entire Naua tribe, which until the turn of the century had made its home in the Amazon rain forest in Brazil

NEWS OF THEIR DEATH: No word on precisely when the tribe is thought to have gone extinct; the last known report on the tribe was a 1906 newspaper article titled, "Last Naua Woman Marries."

RESURRECTION: The Naua weren't dead—as far as anyone can tell, they were just hiding. After avoiding contact with the rest of the world for nearly a century, in August 2000, more than 250 members of the tribe emerged from deep in the rain forest to protest the Brazilian government's plan to incorporate the Naua native lands into a national wildlife park. It's too early to tell what will happen, but as the law stands now, the Naua are considered trespassers on their own land. "We thought there were no more Naua," one Brazilian government told reporters. "Our job now is finding them land. No humans are allowed in the park, just the forest and the animals."

SMARTER THAN THE AVERAGE MONKEY

Maybe it's all the Tarzan research we had to do for this edition (see page 185), but for some reason we've been fascinated with monkeys lately. We're not swinging from trees yet, but we did dig up some interesting info on assorted primates. The following is from the Guinness Book of Animal Facts and Feats, *by Gerald Wood.*

THE BRAINS OF THE BUNCH

The most intelligent monkey is the baboon. Probably the most famous example was a male chacma baboon named "Jack," who used to work the railway signals at Uitenhage Station, about 200 miles north of Port Elizabeth, Cape Colony, South Africa.

According to the story, a railwayman named Wylde lost both his legs as the result of a train accident in 1877 and was later given a job as a signalman at Uitenhage Station. To make the journey between his wooden shack and the signal-box—a distance of about 150 yards—he built a trolley, and propelled himself along the track with the aid of a pole. One day he saw Jack for sale in the local market and purchased him as a pet. The baboon soon became extremely devoted to his master. During the next few months Wylde trained the baboon to fetch water, sweep out the shack, and even to hand a special key to passing engine-drivers who used it to adjust certain "points" further up the line.

ON THE JOB

When Jack heard an engine approaching, he would rush to the signal-box and take down the key from the wall. The signalman also taught the baboon to push him on his trolley to the signal-box, where the animal would sit and watch his master pulling the levers with great interest.

Jack learned to operate the signals for the Graaff Reinet and Port Elizabeth trains by himself while Wylde sat on the trolley ready to correct any mistakes that were made. Eventually, however, the baboon became so proficient at his job that he was able to carry out the whole operation by himself while his master remained in the shack. He was never known to make a mistake.

There are an estimated 20 billion billion molecules in a cubic centimeter of air.

The amazing partnership lasted for over nine years until Jack died from tuberculosis in 1890.

At the time of this writing, another chacma baboon called "Jock" is working as a signalman on a branch-line near Pretoria, South Africa. Unlike Jack, however, this baboon is paid 6 rand (82¢) a day and gets a bottle of beer every Saturday night!

RHESUS PIECES

In Australia there is a rhesus monkey (*Macaca mulatta*) called "Johnnie" who drives a tractor.

This remarkable animal is owned by Mr. Lindsay Schmidt, who runs a sheep-farm at Balmoral, some 200 miles west of Melbourne, Victoria.

Says Mr. Schmidt: "Johnnie is almost human. He was a pet to start with, then he started to follow me about the farm. Now he can open and shut paddock gates and, at shearing time, he picks burrs out of the wool. I couldn't keep him away from the tractor, which is now virtually his special job about the place. He'll never press the tractor starter button if it's in gear. He makes sure it's in neutral, then presses the button and springs smartly into the driving seat to take the wheel."

Johnnie then steers a straight or curved path according to the commands of his master, who stands at the rear of an attached truck and throws out fodder for the grazing animals.

When lunch-time comes the pair sit down in the shade of the tractor and enjoy separate lunch-bags consisting of sandwiches, fruit, and soft drinks. When the meal is over the monkey carefully puts his litter back into the bag (humans please note).

Johnnie has proved to be so valuable that Mr. Schmidt has been given a tax deduction of £140 a year by the Australian government for his services.

Last...and Least

• The least intelligent of the primates: lemurs. Some tests have found them less intelligent than dogs...and pigeons.

• The oldest known monkey was about 46 years old when he died. He was a mandrill named "George," living in the London Zoological Gardens. He was brought to Europe from Africa in 1869, and died in 1916.

Most crowded U.S. state: New Jersey, with an average of 1,000 people per square mile.

BRI BRAINTEASERS

We're back with another "regular" installment of brainteasers.
Many of these were sent in by BRI member A. J. Kori,
who collects hundreds of these puzzles.

1. During a high-stakes bridge tournament preceded by a sit-down dinner, Jay, Jennifer, Jeff, and John played together. At the end of the night, all four had more cash than when they had arrived. In other words, none of them lost, although they were playing for money.

How could this be?

2. What belongs to you alone, but is mostly used by others?

3. Two French diplomats who have never seen each other meet at the French consulate in New York and decide to have a drink together in a near-by bar. Incidentally, one is the father of the other one's son. How is this possible?

4. You're at a cocktail party with your date. Strangely enough, there's something in the room that everybody can touch—and so can you, but only with your left hand. What is it?

5. What word is always spelled incorrectly?

6. I dig out tiny caves, and store gold and silver in them. I also build bridges of silver and make crowns of gold. Sooner or later everybody needs my help, yet many people are afraid to let me help them. Who am I?

7. What is greater than God
More evil than the Devil
Poor people have it
Rich people need it
And if you eat it, you die?

8. You have to get to the hospital. At a fork in the road you meet Joe and Moe, a pair of identical twin boys. You can't tell them apart, but you know that Joe always tells the truth and Moe always lies. You can ask one of them only one question. What question will guarantee that you take the correct fork...and which twin do you ask?

9. The person who made it had no use for it; the person who bought it didn't want it; and the one who finally ended up with it, never even knew about it. What was it?

Answers are on page 492.

Inflation: A newborn baby's body contains 26 billion cells; an adult has 50 trillion.

BRAM STOKER'S DRACULA

It was a dark and stormy night…no, it really was. And that was the perfect setting for telling one of the scariest stories of all time. Here's how it happened.

CABIN FEVER

It all started in the summer of 1816. Percy Bysshe Shelley, the famed English poet, was vacationing along the shores of Lake Geneva in Switzerland with his 18-year-old future wife Mary Wollstonecraft. In adjoining villas were their friends, the poet Lord Byron, and Lord Byron's personal physician Dr. John Polidori. "It was a wet, ungenial summer," Mary Shelley later wrote, and the rain "confined us for days."

The group passed some of their time reading German horror stories. Then, inspired by the tales, Lord Byron announced to the group, "We will each write a ghost story." And with that challenge, *two* of the most enduring monsters in English literature came into being.

DYNAMIC DUO

Mary Wollstonecraft wrote a tale about a mad scientist who assembles a monster out of body parts stolen from cadavers and then brings the monster to life. Polidori, she recounted later, "had some terrible idea about a skull-headed lady, who was punished for peeping through a keyhole." Percy Shelley came up with a story "founded on the experiences of his early life"…and Lord Byron created a story about a vampire.

Wollstonecraft spent the rest of the summer turning her story into a novel—*Frankenstein*. Lord Byron never did complete his story, but Dr. Polidori was so intrigued by the vampire idea that he scrapped the skull-headed lady and, borrowing from Byron, later wrote *The Vampyre*, the first vampire novel of any substance to appear in English literature. *The Vampyre* was published in the April 1819 edition of *New Monthly Magazine*, and earned Polidori £30.

Vanilla comes from orchids.

REVENGE!

The Vampyre might have been just another simple retelling of the traditional vampire legends of Eastern Europe, were it not for the fact that Polidori and Lord Byron had once been lovers. Cooped up in the villa in Geneva that summer, they were driving each other crazy. Polidori was jealous of Byron's increasingly close friendship with Percy Shelley, and, perhaps because of this, he decided to make the vampire character a parody of Lord Byron.

The vampires of Eastern European lore were not that different from today's conception of werewolves: They were scary, uncivilized creatures, more animal than human. But Polidori's character was different. His vampire was a nobleman, and an immoral, sinister antihero named Lord Ruthven—not unlike Lord Byron, whose numerous sexual liaisons were the scandal of English society.

The name Ruthven was another dig at Byron. Polidori took the name from Ruthven Glenarvon, the main character of *Glenarvon*, a popular novel, written by Lady Caroline Lamb, another of Byron's former lovers. Lamb, too, had intended her character to be a satirical slap at Byron.

PULP FICTION

The Vampyre was modestly successful, but not a hit. Two years after it was published, Polidori, despondent over his failures both as a physician and a writer, committed suicide. Yet, for all its failings, *The Vampyre* was indirectly responsible for launching Europe's first vampire fad.

"In Paris," David Skal writes in *Hollywood Gothic*, "the theatrical possibilities of Polidori's tale were quickly grasped." The first offering—a play entitled *Le Vampire*—generated huge interest. "The production was reportedly thrilling, controversial—and an immense success," Skal writes. "The public appetite for vampire dramas prompted a veritable stampede of imitations." Within just a few years, one Parisian theater critic would complain:

> There is not a theatre in Paris without its Vampire! At the Potre-Saint-Martin we have *Le Vampire*; at the Vaudeville *Le Vampire* again; at the Varietés *Les trois Vampires ou le clair de la lune*.

The nobleman-vampire was a common theme in these French works. By the time an Irish writer and civil servant named Bram

Stoker arrived in London, England, in 1878, vampires had become a common theme in English drama and popular literature, as well.

NUMBER-ONE FAN

Stoker had been hired to manage the Lyceum Theatre, the most famous theater in London. He was also the personal assistant of Henry Irving, owner of the Lyceum and the man considered the greatest actor on the Victorian stage. And on top of that, Stoker also liked to write novels in his spare time. He had already written three: *The Snake's Pass*, *The Watter's Mou'*, and *The Shoulder of Shasta*. None of them had sold very well or won him much acclaim.

Some time around the year 1890, Stoker decided to try his hand at writing his own vampire story.

TRUE TO LIFE

Stoker decided to make the novel seem more authentic by setting the story in the present and inserting as many authentic details as possible. But where would the story take place? Who would the main character be?

Like Polidori, Stoker made his vampire a nobleman, and gave him the name Count Wampyr…but the name didn't sound right. Stoker renamed him Count Ordog, from the Romanian word for Satan…and then Count Pokol, from the Romanian word for Hell. That didn't work either.

At some point, as he was sketching the outlines of his vampire tale, Stoker stumbled upon the name of Prince Vlad "The Impaler" Dracula, a tyrannical 15th century warlord (see page 257). No one knows for certain when or where Stoker learned of the existence of Dracula, but according to one theory, he made the discovery in 1890 while vacationing in the seaside town of Whitby, North Yorkshire. Stoker, who made the village the center of action for much of his vampire story, reportedly found a book on Vlad the Impaler in the Whitby Library.

Some time later while researching his novel, Stoker met Arminus Vambrey, a professor from the University of Budapest. Vambrey had traveled extensively in Eastern Europe and Central Asia, and knew many Dracula tales, which he shared with Stoker over dinner. "After Vambery returned to Budapest," Raymond McNally writes in *In Search of Dracula*, "Bram wrote to him, requesting more

---

Ex-President Gerald Ford's favorite food: "Cottage cheese with A-1 Sauce."

details about the notorious 15th-century prince and the land he lived in. Transylvania, it seemed, would be an ideal setting for a vampire story."

Working in the circular Reading Room of the British Museum Library, Stoker read up on the superstitious beliefs of Romanian peasants, and scoured every book and map he could find that described the geography and features of Transylvania (which he'd never visited). He also placed much of the story in Whitby, and even named the ship in the story the *Demeter*, after a Russian ship that had run aground there in 1885. He may also have drawn some "inspiration" from the crimes of Jack the Ripper, who terrorized London from August to November 1888.

FINISHED!

After spending more than seven years researching and writing *Dracula*, Stoker finally finished the book in early 1897.

By the time he'd completed his novel, Stoker had worked for Henry Irving for nearly 20 years. He idolized Irving, and is said to have modeled Dracula's character after some of Irving's finest stage performances. Stoker hoped to turn his novel into a theatrical vehicle for Irving, and even arranged for a dramatic reading of *Dracula* at the Lyceum Theatre in May 1897.

The book, Stoker must have hoped, would demonstrate that he was as talented a writer as Irving was an actor. But it was not to be. "Legend has it," Stoker's grand-nephew and biographer Daniel Farson writes, "that Sir Henry Irving entered the theater during the reading and listened for a few moments with a glint of amusement. 'What do you think of it?' someone asked him as he left for his dressing room. 'Dreadful!' came the devastating reply, projected with such resonance that it filled the theater."

CURSE OF THE VAMPIRE

Stoker had hoped that even if Irving rejected *Dracula*, the novel might be a financial success. His wife Florence expected as much, predicting that *Dracula* would earn a lot of money for the family, perhaps even enough for Stoker to quit his job at the Lyceum Theatre and either retire or take up writing full time.

"The prediction turned out to be mistaken," Leonard Wolf

writes in *Dracula: The Connoisseur's Guide*. "Though it had a steady small sale, in Stoker's lifetime it did not earn enough to change the Stokers' standard of living."

Stoker continued writing an average of one novel a year—none of which were very successful—and working at the Lyceum Theatre until October 1905, when Henry Irving died suddenly and the theater closed. He spent the next few years moving from one theatrical project to another until May 1909, when he suffered a stroke that made it impossible for him to continue working. By 1911 he was virtually destitute, and had to apply to the Royal Literary Fund for assistance (he received £100). He died broke on April 20, 1912, at the age of 64. A year later, Florence Stoker was forced to sell her husband's working notes for *Dracula* at a public auction. They sold for under £3.

For more on Dracula, turn to page 257.

*　　*　　*

IT'S NOT A WORD, IT'S A SENTENCE

Some comments about marriage.

"Marriage is a great institution, but I'm not ready for an institution."

—Mae West

"Marriage is the best magician there is. In front of your eyes it can change an exciting, cute little dish into a boring dishwasher."

—Ryan O'Neal

"Love is blind—marriage is the eye-opener."

—Pauline Thomason

"Whatever you may look like, marry a man your own age—as your beauty fades, so will his eyesight."

—Phyllis Diller

"Only two things are necessary to keep one's wife happy. One is to let her think she is having her own way, and the other, to let her have it."

—Lyndon B. Johnson

People have been living in Damascus since 2000 B.C.—longer than any other city in the world.

BAD JOKES

Heard any good jokes lately? Not here, you haven't.
Our jokes are awful and we love them that way.
Heard any bad ones? Send them to us.

Q: What has four legs and one arm?
A: A rottweiler.

Q: Hear about the ship that ran aground carrying a cargo of red paint and black paint?
A: The whole crew was marooned.

A bus stops at a bus station. A train stops at a train station. Now you know why they call it a work-station.

Q: What is the difference between ignorance, apathy, and ambivalence?
A: I don't know and I don't care one way or the other.

Did you hear about the corduroy pillows? They're making headlines.

Q: Did you hear about the Buddhist who refused novacaine during his root canal?
A: He wanted to transcend dental medication.

Q: What do the letters DNA stand for?
A: National Dyslexics Association.

Q: Did you hear about the two antennas that got married?
A: The wedding was terrible, but the reception was great.

Did you know that name-dropping is the worst thing you can do? My friend Bobby DeNiro told me that.

Q: What's the difference between mashed potatoes and pea soup?
A: Anyone can mash potatoes.

Q: How much do pirates pay for their earrings?
A: A buccaneer.

Q: What is bright orange and sounds like a parrot?
A: A carrot.

So these two cannibals are eating a clown and one says, "Does this taste funny to you?"

Q: How many narcissists does it take to change a lightbulb?
A: One. He holds the bulb while the world revolves around him.

I like your approach…let's see your departure.

Q: If you're American when you go into the bathroom, and American when you come out, what are you when you're in the bathroom?
A: European.

Q: What do you call a midget fortune-teller who escaped from prison?
A: A small medium at large.

FRIENDS IN HIGH PLACES

We don't believe that the key to success is who you know. But connections sure can help. And, as you will see from the following accounts, it doesn't matter whether the help is behind the scenes, or in public...as long as it's from the right person.

SCRABBLE

Powerful Friend: Jack Strauss, chairman of Macy's department store, one of the nation's largest and most influential retailers in the 1940s and 1950s

Background: Alfred Botts and James Brunot launched Scrabble in 1949...and saw it go virtually nowhere. By 1952, they'd sold a little more than 15,000 copies of the game and were barely breaking even.

A Friendly Hand: In 1952 Strauss happened to play Scrabble with some friends during a summer holiday. He loved it—but when he returned to work and found that Macy's didn't even stock the game, he was shocked. He ordered the store to buy a quantity of the game, and run a big promotion for it—which sparked a Scrabble craze in New York City. Soon the craze spread to the rest of the country, and more than 4.5 million copies of the game were sold in less than five years. Sales have remained strong: Today Scrabble is the most popular word game and the #2 board game (after Monopoly) in the country.

M&M's

Powerful Friend: William Murrie, president of the Hershey Chocolate Company, the #1 chocolate manufacturer in the U.S. and exclusive chocolate supplier to the U.S. Armed Forces

Background: Forrest Mars was the son of the candymaker who invented the Snickers and Milky Way bars. They had a falling out (see page 144), and the elder Mars banished his son to Europe where, in the late 1930s, Forrest founded his own candy company. He had big plans to market a candy-coated chocolate he'd "invent-

---

How did Picasso keep warm in his early days?   By burning his paintings.

ed" after seeing similar candies in Spain. The thick sugary shell kept the chocolate from melting, even on hot summer days. Mars had everything he needed to start the company—money, experience, candy-making equipment—except for access to sugar and cocoa. Both were rationed during World War II, and without these ingredients, the new company would go nowhere.

A Friendly Hand: The Hershey Company had plenty of sugar and cocoa because it manufactured chocolate for the war effort, and Murrie was happy to sell some to Mars. Why? Because he wanted to help his son Bruce Murrie, who'd recently graduated from college.

Murrie had known Mars's father, so Forrest Mars used the connection to approach him with a proposal: In exchange for 20% of the startup capital and a steady supply of raw materials from Hershey, he'd make Bruce the executive vice president of the new company. Mars even offered to name the candy after him. "We'll call them M&M's, for Mars and Murrie," he explained. William Murrie took the deal, and even threw in technical assistance from Hershey engineers.

M&M's went on to become the most popular candy worldwide... but Bruce Murrie was gone by then. Once Mars had the company up and running, he forced Murrie out.

"Bruce expected to manage the company, much the way his father had managed Hershey for the past 50 years," writes Cynthia Brenner in *The Lords of Chocolate*. "But as time wore on it became painfully obvious that Forrest never wanted a real business partner; he just needed Murrie's connections."

PROFILES IN COURAGE

Powerful Friend: Arthur Krock, influential *New York Times* columnist and friend of the Kennedys

Background: Freshman Senator John F. Kennedy of Massachusetts had presidential ambitions in 1952, but his reputation was more that of a wealthy playboy than a future president. "By all outward appearances," Christopher Matthews writes in *Kennedy and Nixon*, "Kennedy seemed a genial dilettante destined for a long, no-heavy-lifting career in the Senate."

While recovering from back surgery in 1954, however, Kennedy, (with help from aide Ted Sorensen) wrote a book called *Profiles in*

Courage, an account of eight different American political leaders who took principled but unpopular stands on controversial issues… and paid heavy political prices for their integrity.

A Friendly Hand: Years earlier, Krock had served on the Pulitzer Prize committee. When he read an early, unfinished draft of *Profiles in Courage*, he suggested that it might win a Pulitzer—and Kennedy rushed to finish the book. Then Krock went to work, lobbying members of the Pulitzer board, most of whom he knew personally. "I thought *Profiles* had better be taken in hand by somebody and it might as well be me," Krock recalled years later.

Profiles in Courage did win the Pulitzer in 1957, establishing JFK as one of the Democratic Party's intellectual heavyweights and an up-and-comer for the presidency.

"In January 1957, the Gallup Poll showed that…41% of all Democrats preferred Senator Estes Kefauver as the party's next nominee and 33% favored Jack," Peter Collier writes in *The Kennedys*. "In March, after *Profiles in Courage* had been awarded the Pulitzer Prize, the order was reversed: 45% for Jack, and 33% for Kefauver."

THE HUNT FOR RED OCTOBER

Powerful Friend: President Ronald Reagan

Background: In 1984, a Maryland insurance broker named Tom Clancy wrote *The Hunt for Red October*, a naval thriller about a Soviet submarine captain who tries to defect to the United States. Clancy, a military buff, had never published a book before—his only "author" credits were for a three-page article on the MX missile, and a single Letter to the Editor. And the Naval Institute Press had never published a work of fiction. But they liked Clancy's manuscript, so they bought it and printed 14,000 copies.

A Friendly Hand: President Ronald Reagan read *The Hunt for Red October* after it was recommended to him by a friend…and that's when a reporter just happened to ask what he was reading. Reagan praised the book as "the perfect yarn" and "non-put-downable." That did the trick. *The Hunt for Red October*, which until then had received little attention and was selling slowly, shot up the bestseller lists. Ultimately, it sold more than 5.4 million copies, setting Tom Clancy on a course to become one of the best-selling authors of the 20th century.

WINE BY THE FOOT

We can't help you pick out a good bottle of wine…but here are a few vintage facts you can use to fool your friends into thinking you're an oenophile (pronounced "ee-nuh-file" —that's your first fact; it means "wine connoisseur").

STEP BY STEP

What's the first thing that comes to mind when you think of Italian wine? Grape stomping, right? You've seen it in old paintings…*Fantasia*…and that classic "I Love Lucy" episode where Lucy turns purple after a brawl in an Italian treading vat.

But do winemakers really crush grapes with their feet? Well, they don't anymore. And it's probably just as well, because stomping grapes is harder than you'd think.

For example, keeping your footing is difficult because the grape mass gets really slippery. Ancient Egyptians invented a grid of overhead bars for treaders to hold onto because they kept falling in and drowning. Wine treaders making port in Portugal kept from falling in by linking their arms around their neighbors' waists in a tightly linked chain that looked like a chorus line. And drowning isn't the only potential danger: Over long days and nights of treading, the grapes would start to ferment, releasing large quantities of carbon dioxide that sometimes asphyxiated treaders.

THAT WINE HAS LEGS

Still, despite the hazards, stomping the grape harvest sounds like fun. Songs were sung to keep a regular pace. Sometimes a little band played. But there was nothing romantic about it—it was hard work—tiring and monotonous. And when the grapes were finally completely crushed, treaders ended up stepping on pips and stalks at the bottom of the vat—described in 1877 as "something like the pilgrimages of old when the devout trudged wearily along, with hard peas packed between their feet and the soles of their shoes."

VIN DE SWEAT

A visiting American winegrower described this scene from Burgundy, in the late 1800s:

> Ten men, stripped of all their clothes, step into the vessel, and begin
> to tread down the floating mass, working it also with their hands.
> This operation is repeated several times if the wine does not ferment
> rapidly enough. The reason...is that the bodily heat of the men aids
> the wine in its fermentation.

The American later declined his host's offer of a glass of red wine,
choosing an untreaded white instead. Fortunately, foot treading is
now just a historical footnote, as it were. Today, almost all grapes are
pressed by machines.

Want another taste of wine? See page 377.

Want another taste of wine? See page 377.

*   *   *

WINE TRIVIA: A DROP OF
THIS, A DROP OF THAT

• King Louis XVI of France believed that a refusal to drink wine was
a sign of fanaticism. In his last letter before he lost his head in the
French Revolution, he blamed the political savagery of the revolu-
tionaries on the fact that their leader, Robespierre, drank only water,
not wine.

• Louis Pasteur first developed pasteurization in the 1850s as a way
to prevent the spoiling of wine. Afterward, he realized it could also
be used on other substances, such as milk.

• The first large-scale American winegrowing region was not on either coast, but in Cincinnati, Ohio. In fact, in the 1850s, it was
known as the "Rhine of America." In 1870, America's largest winery
was located on Middle Bass Island, just off the grape-growing town of
Sandusky, Ohio.

• Many people think that California wine is a relatively recent phenomenon. However, both the Napa and Sonoma wine industries
were started by Franciscan monks, who in 1824 started growing
grapes and making wine at the Solano Mission in Sonoma. The
winemaking they began continues to the present, interrupted only
by Prohibition early in the last century.

It takes Pluto 25 years to receive as much solar energy as the Earth receives in 1 minute.

WHY DIDN'T *WE* THINK OF THAT?

It's the ultimate American fantasy—invent a hot product and become a zillionaire overnight. That's why people work long, hard hours on their pet projects. Have you ever heard of any of these? They're available.

Entrepreneur: Bruce Lambert, Swedish inventor
Brilliant Idea: The See-through Refrigerator
Description: The door is a one-way mirror—so when a light is switched on inside the fridge, you can see what's inside without opening the door. You save energy...and pounds, Lambert figures: "The mirror encourages dieting, because people can see their reflections as they approach the door."

Entrepreneur: John D. Haley, of Boise, Idaho
Brilliant Idea: Rape-L
Description: Haley manufactures skunk scent vials that wearers can clip to their undergarments to fend off sexual assaults. When attacked, the wearer simply pinches the vial and douses themselves with the scent, which is harvested from real skunks at a skunk ranch in upstate New York. The kit also contains a second vial filled with ordinary tap water—"For practice," Haley explains. Suggested retail price: $19.95.

Entrepreneurs: John Lisanti and Cary Schuman, founders of Peace Missile, Inc.
Brilliant Idea: The Peace Missile II Putter And Driver
Description: The golf clubs are manufactured out of material recycled from American A-3 Polaris and Soviet SS-23 nuclear missiles. Lisanti says he got the idea while golfing with Schuman. "I mentioned how Cary hits the ball like a rocket," Lisanti says, "and then we thought, 'wouldn't it be great if we could melt down discarded Russian nuclear missiles and make some fabulous golf clubs out of them?'" Suggested Retail Price: $79 for the putter, $199 for the driver.

He wasn't blind, but Thomas Edison preferred reading in Braille.

Entrepreneur: Lino Missio, a 26-year-old Italian physics student

Brilliant Idea: Beethoven Condoms

Description: The condom will play a bit of Beethoven if it breaks during use. According to news reports, "the condom is coated with a substance that changes electrical conductivity upon rupture, setting off a microchip that produces sound." Missio has also proposed an alternative to music: a verbal warning to the participants to stop what they're doing immediately."

Entrepreneur: The Sigma Aldrich chemical company, which manufactures products for search-and-rescue-dog training

Brilliant Idea: Pseudo Scents

Description: Scents that mimic the odor given off by cadavers, to assist in the training of search-and-rescue-dogs. The product line includes Pseudo Corpse I (deceased less than 30 days); Pseudo Corpse II (more than 30 days); Drowned Victim Scent; and Distressed Body Scent Trauma and Fear (the victim is injured but not deceased). According to one report, trainers like the pseudo scents "because they're easier to tote around than the blood, bones, or bits of corpse typically used in training. That's less muss, less fuss, and no threat of hepatitis infection." No smell, either: Only canines can detect them.

Entrepreneurs: Scientists at five German zoological institutes

Brilliant Idea: Raise money for scientific research by "selling sponsors the right to name newly-discovered plant and animal life"

Description: The scientists got the idea when Manfred Parth, a researcher, tennis fan, and admirer of Boris Becker, named a new species of snail *bufonaria borisbeckeri* after the tennis great. (No word on whether Becker knows about his snails.) Suggested Retail Price: $5,000 "minimum."

And don't forget... Pedal and Play, "a slot machine mounted on an exercise bicycle," available in casinos in Atlantic City and Las Vegas, and on Carnival cruise ships.

UNDERWEAR
IN THE NEWS

Here's a question you've probably never considered: When is underwear newsworthy? We've got the answer because we've been studying the news to find out. The answer is, when it's...

ROYAL UNDERWEAR

In February 2000 Captain Nick Carrell, once a member of the queen of England's elite bodyguard unit, "admitted trying to steal Queen Elizabeth's underwear and being caught red-handed by the monarch."

The incident occurred in 1992 during a fire at Windsor Palace, when Carrell was helping remove belongings from the queen's private apartments (which were threatened by the fire). "I was planning to steal a pair of the queen's knickers," Carrell admitted to London's *Sunday People* newspaper. "I was helping to clear out her private apartment when I pulled open a chest of drawers. I was amazed to see it was filled with the queen's underwear and I put out my hand to take a pair. Suddenly, I realized she was standing right behind me, watching my every move. I don't know what she thought, but she didn't say a word. It was all very embarrassing."

LIFE-SAVING UNDERWEAR

"In 1994, fisherman Renato Arganza spent several days at sea clinging to a buoy after his boat capsized off the Philippines. Once rescued, he remarked that he had survived by eating his underpants."

DEADLY UNDERWEAR

In 1999, two women sheltering under a tree in London's Hyde Park during a thunderstorm were killed when lightning struck the tree. According to medical examiners, the two women died because the metal underwire in their bras acted as an electrical conductor. "This is only the second time in my experience of 50,000 deaths where lightning has struck the metal in a bra causing death," Westminster coroner Paul Knapman told the media. "I do not wish to overemphasize any significance." (*In These Times*)

CELEBRITY UNDERWEAR

• "At the 1998 auction of Kennedy memorabilia, Richard Wilson paid $3,450 for a pair of JFK's long johns. Mr. Wilson plans to exhibit the underwear next to a slip and a pair of panties formerly owned by Marilyn Monroe." (*Presidential Indiscretions*)

• In the early 1990s, an upset young man paid a visit to Father Fambrini, pastor at Hollywood's Blessed Sacrament Church. The man confessed that he'd raided Frederick's of Hollywood's lingerie museum and stolen some celebrity undies. Now, consumed with guilt, he wanted to return them, but didn't have the courage...so he asked Father Fambrini to do it. Father Fambrini agreed and returned the two stolen items: a bra belonging to actress Katey Sagal, and "the pantaloons of the late actress Ava Gardner." ("The Edge," *Oregonian*)

LIFESTYLE-ENHANCING UNDERWEAR

• In 1998, Monash University's (Australia) Institute of Reproduction and Development announced the invention of air conditioned mens' briefs, which the Institute says will prevent heat buildup in the nether regions that is believed to inhibit fertility. Why not just ask infertile males to switch from snug-fitting briefs to looser, cooler boxer shorts? "Because," says the Institute's David de Kretser, "some men don't like the freedom."

• In 1998, Florida entrepreneur Victoria Morton announced that she'd invented a bra that she claims can increase a woman's breast size by repositioning body fat, and she doesn't mean just body fat on the chest. "If a woman has extra tissue anywhere above her waist," Morton explained in a press release, "even on her back, she can use this bra to create bigger, firmer breasts." (Universal Press Syndicate)

ARTISTICALLY INSPIRED UNDERWEAR

American artist Laurie Long wasn't just offended when she learned that some vending machines in Japan dispense panties worn by schoolgirls, she was also inspired: She stocked a vending machine with her own used panties, "which have labels describing what she did while she wore them." (*Stuff* magazine)

Each cell in your body has more molecules than there are stars in the entire Milky Way galaxy.

WORD ORIGINS

Here are some more interesting word origins.

FEISTY

Meaning: Spunky, quarrelsome

Origin: "A 'fart' word. First appeared in the 13th century meaning 'a breaking of wind' or 'to break wind.'" (From *Take My Words*, by Howard Richler)

PUNDIT

Meaning: A critic/commentator on current events or politics

Origin: "Comes from the Hindi word *pandit*, meaning 'learned man.'" (From *Word Mysteries and Histories*, by the Editors of the *American Heritage Dictionary*)

SINCERE

Meaning: True to your word, not lying

Origin: "Came from two Latin words *sine*, 'without,' and *cera*, 'wax.' Legend has it that Roman artisans used wax for filling cracks or holes in furniture, so *sine cera* would mean 'without flaw': pure, clean." (From *Thereby Hangs a Tale*, by Charles Earle Funk)

NIGHTMARE

Meaning: A very bad dream

Origin: "*Mare* is an Old English term for a demon, known as incubus (male) or succubus (female), that descended on a sleeper, paralyzing and suffocating them...and sometimes having sexual relations with them. Over the centuries the meaning—'night demon'— has become generalized to any frightening dream." (From *Wilton's Etymology*, by Dave Wilton)

KHAKI

Meaning: A light shade of brown; cloth or pants of that color

Origin: "The name comes from the Urdu word for dust or dust-colored...which came from the Persian *khak*, for dust. First introduced into English in the mid-19th century by British troops serving in India." (From *Fighting Words*, by Christine Ammer)

The Hunza people of Kashmir (India & Pakistan) have a 0.00% cancer rate.

I, MADONNA

Madonna has somehow managed to keep herself in the media spotlight for the past 20 years. Here are some thoughts from America's most notorious "virgin."

"If I weren't as talented as I am ambitious, I would be a gross monstrosity."

"Manipulating people, that's what I'm good at."

"I always want more. That's me. I'm a bitch."

"I always said I wanted to be famous. I just love all the glamour and the attention."

"I've always known this was going to happen to me. My success was something that was meant to be."

"I wouldn't have turned out the way I was if I didn't have all those good old-fashioned values to rebel against."

"It's a great feeling to be powerful. I've been striving for it all my life. I think it's just a quest of every human being—power."

"I act out of instinct just like an animal."

"Shut up so I can talk!"

"Power is a great aphrodisiac, and I'm a very powerful person."

"When you're your own person and not so concerned with impressing, then the other person is very impressed."

"I'm tough, ambitious and I know exactly what I want."

"Losing my virginity was a career move."

"Rejection is the greatest aphrodisiac."

"Where other people are obsessed with the idea that I am always reinventing myself, I'd rather think that I'm shedding my layers, and slowly revealing myself. It feels to me like I'm just getting closer to the core of who I really am."

"I am my own painting. I am my own experiment. So, I am my own work of art."

"If you don't say what you want, then you're not going to get it."

MODERN MYTHOLOGY

These mythological characters may be as famous in our culture as Hercules or Pegasus were in ancient Greece. Here's where they came from.

NIPPER (THE RCA DOG). Nipper, a fox terrier, was originally owned by the brother of English painter Francis Barroud; when the brother died, Francis inherited the dog. According to legend, when a recording of the brother's voice was played at his funeral, the dog recognized his master's voice and looked into the horn of the phonograph. "Barroud depicted this incident in a painting that showed his brother's coffin, with the dog sitting on top listening to the Victrola. The image (minus the coffin, of course) became the symbol of RCA Victor."

PAUL BUNYAN. Paul Bunyan is commonly thought to be a character from traditional folklore, but he is actually what is known as "fakelore"—"an ersatz creation developed to meet the American need for instant homegrown folk heroes." Paul Bunyan was actually created in 1920 by an advertising agent named W.B. Laughead, to serve as a fictional spokesperson for the Red River Lumber company. "As such," Richard Shenkman writes in *Legends, Lies and Cherished Myths of American History*, "Paul is about as authentic a folk hero as Mr. Clean or the Jolly Green Giant—that is to say, not very authentic at all."

SPUDS MacKENZIE. "Some guy in our Chicago agency drew a rough sketch of a dog called the Party Animal, for a Bud Light poster," Anheuser-Busch's marketing director told *Sports Illustrated*. "So we had to find a real dog that looked like this drawing." They picked Honey Tree Evil Eye, a female English bull terrier. The poster was only supposed to be distributed to college students, but "orders for the poster of this strange-looking dog were monumental. We still can't explain it. It's like everything else in advertising. You just hope you get it right, but you never know for sure." After Spuds made his (her) TV debut during the 1987 Super Bowl, Bud Light sales shot up 20%. But Spuds was retired in controversy a few years later when Anheuser-Busch was accused of using him (her) to encourage underage drinking.

THE TACO BELL CHIHUAHUA

The most famous fast-food character of the 1990s was invented by chance, when two advertising executives named Chuck Bennett and Clay Williams were eating lunch at the Tortilla Grill in Venice, California. "We saw a little Chihuahua run by that appeared to be on a mission," Bennett says. "We both looked at each other and said, 'That would be funny.'"

THE CALIFORNIA RAISINS

In 1986 California raisin growers were facing a double whammy: declining raisin sales *and* a bumper raisin harvest coming—which would depress prices. So the California Raisin Board asked their ad agency, Foote, Cone, and Belding, to come up with a campaign to help increase sales. The agency turned the assignment over to two young copywriters, Seth Werner and Dexter Fedor...who couldn't think of anything. One evening they confessed their worries to some friends. "We'll probably do something stupid like have raisins sing 'Oh, I Heard it Through the Grapevine,'" Werner told the friends. That got a laugh...so the next morning Werner and Fedor began thinking about really doing the commercial that way—never realizing what a huge hit the characters would become. "No one can really explain the idea," Werner says. "In fact, the more people try to put their finger on it, the stupider it sounds."

Our Little Secret: In most press reports, Claymation pioneer Will Vinton, who filmed the ads, is credited with creating the raisin characters. But the truth is—and you'll never read this anywhere but here—by the time Vinton was hired, the raisins were already designed. The artist who designed them, Michael Brunsfeld, has also created every *Bathroom Reader* cover.

Fedor and Werner didn't have any idea what the raisins should look like, and Brunsfeld, a director at Colossal Pictures, submitted a design for an animated test commercial. "Raisins were difficult to make into appealing characters," Michael recalls. "It was like putting eyes on a wrinkled blob." The solution: Drawing them in the "rubber hose" style of the '30s and giving them oversized sneakers for balance. "That made them feel loose and funky." By the time the test ad was done, everything was in place. Vinton could just copy it. Everyone else got rich from the ads—but all Brunsfeld got were the original drawings—which are mounted on his wall today.

WHY ASK WHY?

Sometimes the answer is irrelevant—it's the question that counts.
These cosmic queries have been sent in by BRI readers.

Why isn't there mouse-flavored cat food?

Shouldn't there be a shorter word for *monosyllabic*?

Why is *dyslexic* so hard to spell?

Why are they called *stands* when they're made for sitting?

Why are there flotation devices under plane seats instead of parachutes?

If it's illegal to drink and drive, why do bars have parking lots?

Do you need a silencer if you are going to shoot a mime?

How does the guy who drives the snowplow get to work in the mornings?

If nothing sticks to Teflon, how do they make Teflon stick to the pan?

Why do they call it a *building*? Why isn't it a *built*?

Why is *verb* a noun?

Are there seeing-eye humans for blind dogs?

What does Geronimo say when he jumps out of a plane?

Do pediatricians play miniature golf on Wednesdays?

How can a house burn up while it burns down?

Why is the third hand on the watch called the *second hand*?

Is it good if a vacuum really sucks?

Why do we sing "Take me out to the ball game" when we're already there?

Why is it called *after dark* when it really is *after light*?

Why do we press harder on the buttons of a remote control when we know the batteries are dead?

Before drawing boards, what did they go back to?

How many stars in the Seven Sisters (also called the Pleiades)? About 250.

HONK IF YOU LOVE PEACE AND QUIET

Every year, BRI member Debbie Thornton sends in a list of real-life bumper stickers. Have you seen the one that says…

When everything's coming your way, you're in the wrong lane and driving against traffic.

A DAY WITHOUT SUNSHINE IS LIKE NIGHT.

You never really learn to swear until you learn to drive.

If you think nobody cares, try missing a couple of payments.

Originality is the art of concealing your sources.

You have the right to remain silent.

Shin—Device for finding furniture in the dark

WHICH IS THE NON-SMOKING LIFEBOAT?

COLE'S LAW:
Thinly sliced cabbage.

Experience is something you don't get until just after you need it.

I CAN RESIST ANYTHING BUT TEMPTATION

No sense being pessimistic. It wouldn't work anyway.

I intend to live forever. So far, so good.

You're just jealous because the voices only talk to me.

DYSLEXICS OF THE WORLD, UNTIE.

Beauty is in the eye of the beer holder.

Be nice to your kids. They'll choose your nursing home.

Clones are people two.

Does the name Pavlov ring a bell?

EVER STOP TO THINK, AND FORGET TO START AGAIN?

If you can read this, I can slam on my brakes and sue you.

THE BIRTH OF TARZAN, PART I

Tarzan was the first modern superhero—the first pop icon whose fame spread to every corner of the globe. That makes him the forefather of Superman, Batman, Star Wars, Madonna, and Michael Jordan. "Before Tarzan," writes one critic, "nobody understood just how big, how ubiquitous, how marketable a star could be." Here is the inside story of how—and why—Tarzan came to be.

OCCUPATIONAL HAZARD

In 1911, a paunchy, balding, 35-year-old named Edgar Rice Burroughs took a job selling pencil sharpeners. He wasn't very good at it; for that matter, he didn't seem to be very good at anything. As a young man he was denied admittance to West Point, and from there he'd gone on to fail at a number of professions, including cowpunching, goldmining, selling lightbulbs, running a newstand, advertising, and peddling quack medicine door-to-door.

"Two decades later," John Taliaferro writes in *Tarzan Forever*, "when Burroughs drew up an outline for his autobiography, he summarized the period between 1905 and 1911 with the simple, dreary statement: 'I am a flop.' "

KILLING TIME

A few years earlier, while selling a "remedy" for alcoholism door-to-door, Burroughs had been responsible for reading magazines to make sure the company's ads appeared as promised and were error-free. "After our advertisements were checked," he recalled later, "I sometimes took the magazines home to read"—a habit he kept up even after he switched jobs and began selling pencil sharpeners.

"There were several all-fiction publications among them," Burroughs remembered, "and although I had never written a story, I knew absolutely that I could write stories just as entertaining, and probably more so, than any I read in those magazines. If people were paid for writing such rot as I read, I could write stories just as rotten."

BEDTIME STORIES

Coming up with story ideas was no problem; the troubled Burroughs had become an insomniac. To distract himself as he lay in bed each night, he had developed the habit of telling himself adventure stories featuring heroes whose lives were nothing like his own. "While drifting through the unsatisfactory real world," Gabe Essoe writes, "Burroughs would console himself with a fantasy world in which he was handsome, virile, and capable of success, the idol of whole civilizations, beyond the limits of credulity."

"Most of the stories I wrote," he later admitted, "were stories I told myself just before I went to sleep."

OUT OF THIS WORLD

Burroughs started work on his first story in July 1911, and by mid-August he'd completed a 43,000-word manuscript he called *A Princess of Mars*, about a Civil War veteran who falls into a trance in Arizona, wakes up on Mars, fights a war against the Martians, and then marries a Martian princess.

Burroughs was actually latching onto a popular topic of the early 1900s. In 1879, Italian astronomer Giovanni Schiaparelli detected what he thought were *canali* ("canals") on the Martian surface; and in 1906 another astronomer, Percival Lowell, wrote a book that proposed that the canals were irrigation ditches built by an advanced race of Martians. People were excited by the prospect of life on the Red Planet...which is probably why Burroughs decided to write about it. He couldn't afford typing paper—he had a wife and two babies to support and had just lost his job selling pencil sharpeners—so he wrote on the backs of old letterhead that he picked up at his brother's stationery company.

PAYDAY

Burroughs finished the story and sent the manuscript to *Argosy* magazine, and with a few changes, *A Princess of Mars* was accepted for serial publication in *Argosy*'s sister publication, the *All-Story*. Price: $400. "I shall never make a million dollars," Burroughs wrote in his autobiography, "but if I do it cannot possibly give me the thrill that that four-hundred dollar check gave me."

Thomas Newell Metcalf, managing editor of the *All-Story*, invited Burroughs to submit another story, "a serial of the regular romantic type, something like, say, *Ivanhoe*." Three weeks later, Burroughs turned in a short story called "The Outlaw of Torn," a 13th-century tale about a fictitious son of England's King Henry III. But Metcalf didn't like it, so it was shelved.

GOING APE

In March 1912, Burroughs wrote back to Metcalf that he was already at work on his next tale:

> The story I am now on is of the scion of a noble English house—of the present time—who was born in tropical Africa where his parents died when he was about a year old. The infant was found and adopted by a huge she-ape, and was brought up among a band of fierce anthropods.
>
> The mental development of this ape-man in spite of every handicap, of how he learned to read English without knowledge of the spoken language, of the way in which his inherent reasoning faculties lifted him above his savage jungle friends and enemies, of his meeting with a white girl, how he came at last to civilization and to his own makes most fascinating writing and I think will prove interesting reading....The boy-child is called Tarzan, which is ape talk for "white skin."

Metcalf was impressed: "I think your idea for the new serial is cracker-jack and I shall be very anxious to have a look at it. You certainly have the most remarkable imagination of anybody whom I have run up against for some time."

SIGN OF THE TIMES

Again, Burroughs's story was built around popular topics of the day: Charles Darwin's theory of evolution and the mysterious continent of Africa, which had only recently begun giving up its secrets to Western explorers.

It also reflected his interest in another popular theory of the day: eugenics. In 1869, 10 years after Darwin published *On the Origin of Species*, his cousin, Francis Galton, wrote *Hereditary Genius*. In it, he argued that some human bloodlines were, by the law of natural selection, more advanced than others. According to Galton, the way a person could tell how advanced their bloodline was was to count the number of distinguished ancestors they had in their family tree: If you were descended from kings, Pilgrims, or the Founding Fathers, you were a member of a very advanced bloodline. If

Take one million cloud droplets and squish them together—what do you get? A single raindrop.

you were descended from criminals or peasants, you weren't very evolved at all.

This book made Galton the father of "eugenics," the theory that "selective breeding" could be used to improve the bloodlines of the human race. By 1912, the eugenics movement was so strong that universities all over the country offered courses in it; one organization called the American Breeders Society had even begun compiling a list of "America's Most Effective Blood Lines," literally a Who's Who of natural selection.

Perhaps in response to his own personal failings, Burroughs liked to brag that he came from exceedingly "good stock"—he shared a common Pilgrim ancestor with American Red Cross founder Clara Barton, Morse code inventor Samuel Morse, and (future) president Calvin Coolidge. The greatest gift his mother gave him, he later wrote, was "the red blood of the Puritan and the Pioneer, bequeathed…uncontaminated."

It was this fascination with bloodlines and natural selection that drove the new story. Could good breeding triumph over adversity?

GOING TO PRESS

In May, Burroughs finished work on *Tarzan of the Apes* and sent it to Metcalf. "I did not think it was a good story," Burroughs recalled, "and I doubted it would sell." As he'd done so many times before, Burroughs was also beginning to doubt whether he really wanted to be a writer. "I was sort of ashamed of it as an occupation for a big, strong, healthy man," he admitted later.

Metcalf disagreed with Burroughs's appraisal of the story: *Tarzan* was good—very good, he wrote to Burroughs later that summer:

> If you will stop and realize how many thousands and thousands of stories an editor has to read, day in, day out, you will be impressed when we tell you that we read this yarn at one sitting and had the time of our young lives. It is the most exciting story we have seen in a blue moon, and about as original as they make 'em.

Neither Burroughs nor Metcalf had any idea just *how* good *Tarzan of the Apes* was until October, when the *Tarzan* issue hit the newsstands. Within just a few days, *Tarzan* fan letters began pouring into the *All-Story* offices praising the story…and begging for more.

Aaaiieeeahhh! Grab a vine and swing to page 285 for Part II.

A newborn kangaroo could fit in the palm of your hand.

MILITARY SURPLUS: THE STORY OF CARROT CAKE

Our good friend Jeff Cheek has been writing about food ever since he left the CIA (the spy agency, not the food institute—no kidding!). He wrote this column for a local newspaper; we decided it was worth sharing with all our BRI members.

THE FRUIT MAN

George C. Page was a Nebraska farm boy who arrived in Los Angeles in the mid-1920s with a dream...and $2.30 in his pocket. He found a job as a busboy/dishwasher and worked double shifts until he'd saved $1,000. Then he rented a vacant store and founded Mission-Pak, shipping exotic Southern California fruits as holiday gifts. It was an overnight success. Ten years later, he was a millionaire, with eight packing plants and over a thousand workers.

In 1941, after the Japanese bombed Pearl Harbor, Page volunteered for active duty. He discovered, however, that the government had classified him as an "essential industrialist," and wouldn't let him serve in the military. Instead, they arranged for him to go to the University of California at Berkeley to learn how to dehydrate vegetables. With German submarines sinking our ships, every shipload had to count. Dehydration, and rehydration after delivery, seemed like the answer.

WAR SURPLUS

When the atomic bomb brought the Pacific war to an end, Page's government contracts were canceled. He was left with thousands of five-gallon cans of dehydrated carrots...and no place to sell them.

Page went back to his old boss at the restaurant where he'd started out. They tried everything. Baked carrots. Stewed carrots. Fried carrots. No luck; customers sent these tasteless dishes back. Finally, they dumped a few cups of shredded dried carrots into a cake mix. It was an instant hit. Other restaurants and bakeries wanted to add carrot cake to their menus. Page sold them five-gallon cans of dehydrated carrots, along with a printed recipe for carrot cake. Within a few months he'd gotten rid of his surplus carrots, and carrot cake was being served as dessert all over America.

According to the *Weekly World News*, Heaven's fax number is 011-972-2-612222.

MYTH-CONCEPTIONS

*"Common knowledge" is frequently wrong. Here are
some examples of things that many people believe…
but according to our sources, just aren't true.*

Myth: Crickets chirp by rubbing their legs together.
Fact: They rub their wings.

Myth: In the Old West, pioneers circled their wagons to protect
against Indian raids.
Fact: When they did circle the wagons, it was to keep livestock in.

Myth: Mosquitoes bite.
Fact: They can't bite—they have no teeth. They punch a needlelike
proboscis into the skin of their victim.

Myth: Lightning comes out of the sky and strikes the ground.
Fact: Scientists now believe that the lightning bolt we see is actually moving from the ground up to the sky.

Myth: Some people are double-jointed.
Fact: No one is truly double-jointed. Some people are just more
flexible than others.

Myth: You can only eat oysters in months that have an "r" in their
name.
Fact: Before refrigeration, oysters (and other foods) were more likely
to spoil in May, June, July, and August. It is no longer the case.

Myth: The lion is the king of the jungle.
Fact: The lion doesn't live in the jungle; it lives on the plains,
where it can run and chase its prey.

Myth: Stepping on a rusty nail will give you tetanus.
Fact: The bacteria that causes tetanus, or "lockjaw," can enter the
body through any cut, including a puncture from a nail. It has nothing to do with rust.

Eat one lump of sugar, and you've eaten the equivalent of 3 feet of sugar cane.

Myth: A strong cup of coffee will help a drunk person get sober.
Fact: It's the alcohol in a person's bloodstream that makes them drunk, and no amount of coffee, no matter how strong, will change that.

Myth: A sudden fright can turn a person's hair white overnight.
Fact: The age at which your hair turns white is determined by heredity. Seeing a ghost will have no effect on your hair color.

Myth: On a clear night, you can see millions of stars.
Fact: The most stars you could *possibly* see without a telescope is about 4,000.

Myth: Dogs sweat through their panting tongues.
Fact: Panting may help them cool off, but they sweat through their feet.

Myth: The sky is blue.
Fact: The sky is black. Dust particles and droplets of moisture in the air reflect the sun's light and make it appear blue.

Myth: A penny is made of copper.
Fact: Pennies minted after 1982 are 97.5% zinc and 2.5% copper.

Myth: Constant cracking of your knuckles will make them get bigger.
Fact: Go ahead and crack them—it's harmless.

Myth: In the French tale written by Charles Perrault in 1697, Cinderella's slippers were made of glass.
Fact: They were made of fur. The goof comes from a poor translation; someone interpreted *vair*, "fox fur" as *verre*, "glass."

Myth: St. Bernards wear kegs of brandy around their necks when they go out to rescue stranded travelers.
Fact: They never have. The popular idea comes from a series of paintings by Sir Edwin Landseer in the 1800s that depicted the dogs wearing brandy casks.

Uh-oh: About 1 in 4 Americans aren't sure if the Earth travels around the sun, or vice versa.

THE GOLDEN RULE

Every once in a while we throw in something serious—you can take it, can't you? Did you know that there's a version of the Golden Rule in most (maybe all) major religions? Here are eight translations of religious texts...and one secular commentary.

CHRISTIANITY

"Therefore all things whatsoever ye would that men should do to you, do ye even so to them, for this is the law and the prophets."
—Matthew 7:12

JUDAISM

"What is harmful to you, do not to your fellow men. That is the entire Law; all the rest is commentary."
—Talmud, Shabbat, 312

HINDUISM

"This is the turn of duty; do naught unto others which could cause you pain if done to you."
—Mahabharata, 5, 1517

CONFUCIANISM

"Surely it is the maxim of loving-kindness: Do not unto other that you would not have them do unto you."
—Analects, 15, 23

TAOISM

"Regard your neighbor's gain as your own gain and your neighbor's loss as your own loss."
—T'ai Shang Kan Ying P'ien

BUDDHISM

"Hurt not others in ways you yourself would find hurtful."
—Udana-Varga 5, 18

ZOROASTRIANISM

"That nature alone is good which refrains from doing unto another whatsoever is not good for itself."
—Dadistan-i-dinik, 94, 5

ISLAM

"No one of you is a believer until he desires for his brother that which he desires for himself."
—Sunnah

SECULAR VIEW

"Do not do unto others as you would that they should do unto you. Their tastes may not be the same."
—George Bernard Shaw

ACCORDING TO THE LATEST RESEARCH...

More "scientifically proven" info about you and your world.
(See page 113 for other important scientific studies.)

AMERICANS ARE REALLY GULLIBLE
Researchers: DiMassimo Brand Advertising
Who They Studied: Friends and neighbors of 200 volunteer liars
What They Learned: "Americans will believe anything, as long as it comes from a friend or a neighbor." The ad company recruited 200 people to tell fibs to their friends, then polled the friends a week later. Sample results: "27% repeated the lie that 'Just Do It!' was the slogan of Ex-Lax instead of Nike; 22% believed that milk was 'the other white meat,' rather than pork; 23% thought Amazon.com was a fashion Web site for large women; 29% agreed that Kenneth Starr was the president of Starbucks."

POETS REALLY ARE CRAZY
Researcher: Professor Arnold Ludwig, M.D., of the University of Kentucky
Who He Studied: 1,000 "original thinkers" of the 20th century
What He Learned: "Crazy people tend to choose creative jobs," and the most consistently off-kilter are poets. To be more precise: "Ludwig's study, 'Method and Madness in the Arts and Sciences,' reports that nearly 9 out of 10 poets surveyed have had diagnosable mental disorders." On the other end of the spectrum, only about 28% of physicists and biologists have mental disorders—the lowest percentage tested. The crazy runners-up: fiction writers are second, at 77%; theater people are at 74%; visual arts, 73%; musicians, 68%.

YOUR PETS KNOW WHEN YOU'RE COMING HOME
Researcher: Rupert Sheldrake, a British biologist
Who He Studied: Dogs in 1,500 different homes around the world

---

Most popular name for a goldfish in Great Britain: Jaws.

What He Learned: "Animals appear to sense when their owners are returning home and actually prepare for the event." He observed that almost half the dogs he studied actually "began preparing for their owner's return an hour before they got home....Besides becoming visibly agitated, the animals started going to the window to watch for their owner." He noticed cats and birds doing it, too.

ONIONS ARE GOOD FOR YOUR BONES

Researchers: Swiss scientists

Who They Studied: Female rats

What They Learned: "An onion a day keeps bone fractures away." *Newsweek* reported in its October 11, 1999 edition: "To study the effects of herbs and vegetables on osteoporosis, [the scientists] removed the ovaries from female rats. That made the rats' hormone fluctuations resemble those of post-menopausal women, who are at most risk for bone loss. After four weeks, the rats that were fed a gram of dried onion a day had significantly thicker and stronger bones. An onion, as well as other typical salad ingredients, reduced bone loss by 20%—slightly more than the popular anti-osteoporosis drug called calcitonin."

MARRIAGE CAN BE DEPRESSING

Researchers: Professor of psychology Daniel K. O'Leary and colleagues at the State University of New York at Stony Brook

Who They Studied: Women with significant marital problems who had no history of depression in their families

What They Learned: If you're depressed, you might need to do something about your marriage rather than simply take antidepressants. "For decades, people—particularly women—have been treated with antidepressants by well-meaning practitioners," explains O'Leary. "They get on medication, and nobody does a thing about the relationship." In the study, O'Leary and his crew interviewed women who were in the throes of marital difficulty. "We were able to pretty clearly conclude that if they were depressed, the depression was caused by the marital problems," he says. "They should seek help not only for the depression, but for the relationship problem."

THE HISTORY OF THE IQ TEST, PART II

As you read in Part I, (page 65), the IQ test had its origins in Victorian England and France. But it came into its own when the Americans got their hands on it. Here's another piece of the controversial story.

SO THAT'S WHAT IT MEANS

In 1916 a Stanford University psychologist named Lewis Terman modified the Binet-Simon test to create a new test. He called it the Stanford-Binet test...and if you've ever taken an IQ test, you may have experienced it firsthand. The original 1916 test and its descendants are still among the most widely-used intelligence tests in use today.

Drawing from a concept first suggested by German psychologist, William Stern, Terman developed a new formula for comparing a child's intelligence to that of other children the same age. He did it by dividing the test taker's "mental age," as determined by the test, by the test taker's chronological age. Then he multiplied the result by 100 to get a whole number:

$$(\text{Mental Age} \div \text{Chronological Age}) \times 100$$

Terman called this number the "intelligence quotient," or IQ for short. According to this formula, a 10-year-old child with a mental age of 12 would have an IQ of $(12/10) \times 100 = 120$. Likewise, a ten-year-old child with a mental age of eight would have an IQ of 80, and any child with the same mental and chronological age—indicating normal intelligence—would have an IQ of 100.

WISE GUY

Though Terman based his test on Alfred Binet's, he had an entirely different purpose in mind. Binet's test was designed to identify children who needed extra help in learning, so that they could be placed into special "mental orthopedics" courses that would bring them up to speed with kids whose scores were higher.

Terman had a different theory: He believed very strongly in the concept of "innate intelligence," the idea that a person's intelli-

---

By the time you finish reading this, the Earth will have traveled almost 100 miles through space.

gence was as unchangeable as the color of their eyes. Thus, he concluded, there was no point providing assistance to slow learners, because it wouldn't do any good. Since intelligence was immutable, educating the unintelligent was a waste of time.

A BREED APART

Like Francis Galton before him, Terman was an enthusiastic supporter of the eugenics movement. He believed that "selective breeding" of intelligent people with one another, combined with discouraging—or even forbidding—unintelligent people from reproducing at all, would increase the general intelligence of the human race.

Terman was also convinced that the Stanford-Binet test was an important breakthrough in psychological research. Unlike Binet, who saw his test as a rough measure of a child's level of knowledge relative to his peers, Terman believed that he had invented a diagnostic tool that could accurately and precisely measure the intellectual capacity of the human brain. He was determined to put the test to work for the benefit of mankind. As he wrote when the first Stanford-Binet test was published in 1916:

> There is no investigator who denies the fearful role played by mental deficiency in the production of vice, crime, and delinquency....
> In the near future, intelligence tests will bring tens of thousands of these high-grade defectives under the surveillance and protection of society. This will ultimately result in curtailing the reproduction of feeblemindedness and in the elimination of an enormous amount of crime, pauperism, and industrial inefficiency....
>
> There is no possibility at present of convincing society that they should not be allowed to reproduce, although from a eugenic point of view they constitute a grave problem, because of their unusually prolific breeding.

"Organized charities," he observed the following year in a paper titled "The Menace of Feeble-Mindedness," "often contribute to the survival of individuals who would otherwise not be able to live and reproduce."

Feeling smart enough to read more?
Turn to page 270 for Part III.

At its peak, a growing blue whale gains between 200 and 300 pounds a day.

MOVIE BOMB: *THE LAST ACTION HERO*

Some films don't set out to be disaster films, but they still end up that way. This one, for example, starred Hollywood's most bankable actor. He could do no wrong...until he picked this.

UNLIKELY SCENARIO

It was the kind of thing that's supposed to happen only in the movies: In 1991, two recent graduates of Wesleyan University, Zak Penn and Adam Leff, wrote a script called *Extremely Violent*, about a troubled boy who goes to adventure movies to escape his problems, and one day finds himself in the middle of a film starring his favorite action hero. "Their friends in the lower ranks of show business helped promote it," Thom Taylor writes in *The Big Deal*. "The script landed Penn and Leff with the agent of their choice...and suddenly it became a priority-event movie for Columbia Pictures."

Then came Ah-nold.

Fresh from the success of *Total Recall* and *Terminator 2: Judgment Day*, Arnold Schwarzenegger was the world's biggest movie star in 1992. At Columbia's urging, he read the script—and liked it. He agreed to do the film...as long as there were changes.

What Arnold wanted, Arnold got. He was considered "bulletproof" in the industry—everything he touched turned to money. So the studio eagerly had the script redone by new writers, who gutted it beyond recognition. Under Arnold's direction, they turned what had been a promising script into *Last Action Hero*, the Schwarzenegger vehicle that made it onto the screen. (The script was so thoroughly reworked that Penn and Leff lost their screenwriting credit, and are credited only with developing the story.)

Meanwhile, acting as producer, Arnold set to work giving the film his own personal touch. Using his newfound box-office clout, Arnold assumed a greater degree of creative control than he'd had on any other film. "Before, I always felt a little bit like I was butting in," he told a reporter, "I always felt I was stepping over the line." Not this time—Arnold was in the driver's seat. As Nancy Griffin and Kim Masters write in *Hit & Run*:

> Acting as a producer for the first time in his career, Schwarzenegger operated like a field marshal out of his 40-foot trailer on the Sony lot. Equipped with a special telephone that allowed him to punch directly into [the studio's offices], he would summon executives— who would immediately be seen streaking out of their offices and tearing across the lot to Camp Arnold.

Destroying the original script and letting Schwarzenegger call the shots seemed like a good idea at the time, even as *Hero*'s cost nearly doubled from $65 million to $120 million—making it the most expensive film ever made at the time.

The first hint of trouble came on May 1, 1993, when a rough cut of the film was shown to a test audience to gauge their reactions. The audience roared with approval when told they were there to watch Arnold Schwarzenegger's latest movie, but as the film progressed the excitement degenerated into boredom; by the end of the film the audience was "almost catatonic," according to one account. "The movie lay there like a big fried egg," one witness remembers, "and the executives (including Schwarzenegger, who was present) looked like a group of people who had just gotten on a ship and saw the name *Poseidon*."

Normally the studio would have tabulated audience survey cards to see how many people rated the film "good" or "excellent," but this time nobody bothered—the cards were quickly fed, unread, into a paper shredder before word of how bad the film was could get out.

Too late—within hours Hollywood was swirling with rumors that Schwarzenegger's magnum opus was doomed. Weeks of round-the-clock editing and the addition of newly filmed scenes didn't change a thing: When *Last Action Hero* opened on June 13, audiences stayed away from theaters and critics tore the film apart.

In its opening weekend, *Last Action Hero* came in second place behind *Jurassic Park*, which had already been in theaters a week. *Hero* dropped to fourth place the second week, behind *Jurassic Park*, *Sleepless in Seattle*, and even *Dennis the Menace*, and dropped out of sight soon after that. Estimated loss: $35 million.

"It's a bad feeling to stand around a giant premiere when they spend $200,000 on a blow-up doll of Arnold," says Chris Moore, the agent who sold Penn and Leff's original script to Columbia, "and feel, 'Wow, it's just not that good.'"

JOIN THE CLUB: THE SALVATION ARMY

The Salvation Army may be the most famous charitable organization in the world. Here's how it got started.

FOUNDED BY: William Booth, a London preacher in the 1860s. Booth's experience as a pawnbroker's apprentice gave him insight into the problems of England's underclass, and he made it his mission to minister to the poor.

HISTORY: Booth became a Methodist minister in the mid-1850s, but after several years he came to feel that God wanted more from him. He also felt that he should do more to reach ordinary people. So he began preaching in the streets of the East End of London, one of the city's poorest districts.

Booth never had any intention of starting his own church—his original goal was to convert "the poor and wretched" and send them to the established churches nearby. But he soon realized that many of his converts didn't feel welcome in other churches "because they could not afford a special Sunday suit...and many of the regular churchgoers were appalled when these shabbily dressed, evil-smelling people came to join them in worship."

So in 1865 Booth formed the East London Christian Mission (later shortened to the Christian Mission) and began focusing on meeting his converts' clothing and other material needs—as well as their spiritual needs.

How did the Christian Mission become known as the Salvation Army? In May 1878 Booth asked his son Bramwell to read the draft of the Christian Mission's Annual Report. Bramwell took one look and immediately objected to the first statement on the first page, which read:

"The Christian Mission is a Volunteer Army."

Bramwell argued that he wasn't a volunteer, because he felt compelled by God to work with the poor. So Booth crossed out the word; in its place, he wrote the word "Salvation"...and the Salvation Army had its name.

Elephants adopt orphans.

THE BIRTH OF THE SUBMARINE, PART II

68 years before Jules Verne wrote about an imaginary submarine called the Nautilus *in his book* 20,000 Leagues Under the Sea, *a failed-artist-turned-inventor named Robert Fulton invented a real submarine called the* Nautilus. *Does the name Fulton sound familiar? It was only after his sub failed to attract any interest from the leading naval powers of the day that Fulton went on to build the thing he is most famous for: the steamboat. Here's Part Two of our history of the submarine. (Part I is on page 79.)*

RUE BRITTANIA

Twenty years after David Bushnell built the *American Turtle*, another American inventor, Robert Fulton, took the concept a step further when he drew up plans for a submarine he called *Nautilus* (Greek for "sailor"). Fulton, a pacifist at heart, hated the way the British were able to use the Royal Navy to control international trade in the mid-1790s, so he approached France, then at war with England. Convinced that submarines could be used to break the Royal Navy's blockade of French ports, he thought that France would jump at the chance to buy them. But he was wrong—France wasn't interested in his submarines, at any price. After all, while Fulton had drawn plans for his submarine, he'd never actually built one, and the French were skeptical that such a strange boat—even if it could be built—would ever be as effective in battle as Fulton claimed.

Fulton sweetened his offer: he'd build and man the subs at his own expense and send them into battle against the British. All France had to do was pay him 4,000 francs for every large English warship he sunk, and 2,000 francs for every small one. Still no deal…but Fulton persisted, and finally, three years later, in 1799, France agreed to pay him 10,000 francs to build a single experimental submarine.

THE NAUTILUS

By June 1800, Robert Fulton had completed his submarine and was

---

ready for a public demonstration. To the crowds that gathered on the Seine River to witness the spectacle, the *Nautilus* might have looked like something from another planet, as Robert Burgess writes in *Ships Beneath the Sea*:

> She was twenty-one-feet-three inches long and six-foot-four inches wide....With her forward-mounted observation dome, the *Nautilus* bore a remarkable resemblance to a modern-day research submersible. She was operated by a three-man crew.
>
> Power was provided by a hand crank geared to a screw propeller at the rear. The boat would submerge upon flooding her hollow iron keel....Pumping the water ballast from the keel brought her to the surface, where she could be sailed.

After sailing a short distance up the Seine, the two men on deck folded up her fan-shaped sail, lowered the mast onto the deck, and disappeared inside the ship. As the *Nautilus* continued to make its way upstream without any visible means of propulsion, the vessel slowly sank beneath the waves. Five minutes later it resurfaced a little farther up the river, proceeded for a short distance, then sank again. Minutes later, the *Nautilus* surfaced even farther up river, after which the the two men came back up on deck, raised the mast and unfolded the sail, and sailed away.

No one had ever seen anything like it.

BOMBS AWAY

In his next demonstration, Fulton attacked a 40-foot "target" ship. Towing a bomb containing 20 pounds of gunpowder on a long rope, Fulton sailed to within 650 feet of the target ship and then dove below the surface and continued underwater, passing underneath the target ship and continuing onward until the towed bomb made contact with the hull and exploded.

The French were finally impressed; Napoleon himself asked for a demonstration. But Fulton replied with a bombshell of a different sort. He told Napoleon that he had dismantled and destroyed the sub. Furthermore, he refused to rebuild it or even show his drawings until he and Napoleon came to a financial agreement. Otherwise, he feared France would use his idea without paying him.

Destroying the submarine was a huge gamble and Fulton lost. "Napoleon did not even give Fulton the courtesy of a reply," Robert Burgess writes in *Ships Beneath the Sea*. "As time passed, Fulton heard

---

A greyhound (the *dog*, not the bus) can run as fast as 41 miles per hour.

that the French dictator was calling him a charlatan and a swindler bent on obtaining money under false pretenses."

SWITCHING SIDES

By now Fulton had shed his idealism and was determined to earn fame and fortune from his submarines, even if that meant building submarines for the hated Royal Navy. Having worn out his welcome in France, he accepted an offer from the British government to continue his work in England.

But on October 21, 1805, the Royal Navy destroyed the combined Spanish and French fleets in the Battle of Trafalgar, before Fulton had a chance to build even a single sub for Britain.

"Victory at Trafalgar," Cynthia Owen Philip writes in *Robert Fulton: A Biography*, "made Great Britain the undisputed ruler of the seas and secured the island kingdom from the threat of French invasion. It also abruptly changed the government's attitude toward Fulton. His unorthodox weapons, still unproven in battle, were now superfluous. So that there would be no chance of misunderstanding his position, the government stopped paying his monthly salary."

STEAMED UP

After more than a decade of futile effort, Fulton finally gave up on the submarine and returned to the United States to work on another interest of his—the steamboat. "With wealthy backer Robert Livingston he built the famous steamboat *Clermont*," Burgess writes, "and with the assistance of a steamboat monopoly, it brought him the fame and fortune he had long sought elsewhere." The submarine was dead...until it found a new champion.

See page 349 for part III.

*　　*　　*

A REEL QUOTE

"I told you 158 times I cannot stand little notes on my pillow. 'We are out of corn flakes, F.U.' It took me three hours to figure out F.U. was Felix Unger."

—Walter Matthau, *The Odd Couple*

Every second, your body loses and replaces 8 million blood cells.

Q & A:
ASK THE EXPERTS

*Here are some more random questions, with answers
from books by some of the nation's top trivia experts.*

VERY CAREFULLY

Q: *How do they get all that shaving cream into an aerosol can?*

A: "They don't. Shaving cream is basically soap and water,
put into the can along with compressed butane gas. Without the
gas, all you have is soapy liquid. When the valve is pressed, some
of the gas mixes with the soap and water and expands to make
foam." (From *The New York Times Book of Science Questions &
Answers*, by C. Claiborne Ray)

PARTLY SILLY

Q: *What is the difference between "partly cloudy" and "partly sunny"
in a weather report?*

A: "The expression 'partly sunny' was brought to you by the same
folks who brought you 'comfort station' and 'sanitary engineer.' As
a technical meteorological term, 'partly sunny' doesn't exist. So
while you might assume that a partly sunny sky should be clearer
than a partly cloudy one, the two terms signify the same condition.
You have merely encountered a weathercaster who prefers to see
the glass half full rather than half empty." (From *Imponderables*, by
David Feldman)

QUIT WINE-ING

Q: *What are the "sulfites" I see listed on some wine labels, and why do
all American wines seem to have them?*

A: "They are preservatives. In wine they're used to prevent discoloration, bacterial growth, and fermentation. They're also used to
prevent discoloration in shrimp, raisins, potatoes, lettuce, and other vegetables. But that's not all they do. Sulfites are the only addi-
tives now in use that are known to kill people. Fortunately, deaths
are rare and result from what amounts to an extreme allergic reac-

How do scientists study the moisture in clouds? By studying the dew on spider webs.

tion. If you've drunk your share of wine and you're still breathing, you're probably safe." (From *Return of the Straight Dope*, by Cecil Adams)

YOU'RE GROUNDED!

Q: *In a lightning storm, will rubber tires insulate a car from being hit by lightning?*

A: "No. Lightning is strong enough to travel through or around the rubber. According to the Boston Museum of Science, your tires would have to be solid rubber a mile thick to actually insulate you from a lightning bolt. Does that mean, then, that you should avoid your car in a thunderstorm? No, the good news is that your car is the safest place to be if you're outside during a storm—the lightning will most likely travel around the metal shell of your car and not do any damage to it or you. That is, if you have a metal car and don't park under a tree or touch the metal. The bad news is that if you have a convertible or plastic car, or if you touch the metal skin of your automobile when lightning strikes, you may be in for a profoundly shocking experience." (From *Just Curious, Jeeves*, by Jack Mingo and Erin Barrett)

BEE-HAVE

Q: *How can I tell whether I was stung by a wasp or a bee?*

A: "The easiest way to tell if a wasp or a bee caused the sting is to look at the perpetrator. Both yellow jackets (the most common) and honeybees have yellow-and-black markings, and they look very much alike, but honeybees have hairy bodies, whereas the bodies of yellow jackets are smooth.

"If the insect that stung you has flown away, you can sometimes identify the culprit by looking at the sting. Wasp stingers are smooth like needles. After piercing your skin and injecting its venom, the wasp slides its stinger out and flies away. Honeybees have barbed stingers that remain even after the bee has gone. When the bee leaves behind its stinger, it also leaves its venom sac. The muscles in the sac can continue pumping venom into the wound for up to 20 minutes." (From *101 Questions & Answers About Backyard Wildlife*, by Ann Squire)

Space dust increases Earth's weight by as much as 6 tons a day.

THE DUSTBIN OF HISTORY

Think today's big newsmakers will go down in history for what they've done? Don't count on it. These folks were well known in their time...but they're forgotten now. They've been swept into the Dustbin of History.

FORGOTTEN FIGURE: John Billington, "a foul-mouthed miscreant" who came to America in 1620 on the *Mayflower*

CLAIM TO FAME: Billington, his wife, and their two sons were among the 67 non-Pilgrim passengers on the ship. The Billingtons were, Governor William Bradford later wrote, "...one of the profanest families aboard the ship." They made enemies of just about everyone during the 66-day voyage and things did not improve on land.

In the summer of 1630, Billington shot a man, John Newcomen, in the woods near Plymouth Colony. Apparently he thought he'd finished him off...but he was wrong. When Billington returned to the colony, he learned that Newcomen was still alive and had identified him as the assailant. Newcomen died a few days later and Billington was charged with murder—the first ever in the colonies. Tried and convicted, Billington was hanged in September 1630.

INTO THE DUSTBIN: Amazingly, writes Peter Stevens in *The Mayflower Murderer and Other Forgotten Firsts in American History*, "Some Americans tracing their bloodlines back to the *Mayflower* proclaim proudly their kinship to the lout. And on the *Mayflower* Compact, the hallowed names of Brewster, Mullins, Alden, Bradford, and Standish abide for posterity with the scrawl of America's first convicted murderer: big, bad, John Billington."

FORGOTTEN FIGURE: Barney Oldfield, a race car driver

CLAIM TO FAME: In 1902, an obscure Detroit automaker named Henry Ford built a race car which he dubbed the "999." When his partner refused to drive it, Ford hired daredevil bicycle racer Barney Oldfield.

The bite of a King Cobra can kill a fully-grown elephant in less than 3 hours.

Oldfield had never been behind the wheel of an automobile in his life, but it didn't matter—Ford entered him in a race against Alexander Winton, then considered the fastest race car driver in the world.

"When race day came," Robert Lacy writes in *Ford: The Men and the Machine*,

> Oldfield charged 999 into battle with the happy ignorance of a neophyte. He slammed his foot down on the accelerator at the start and didn't raise it until he had crossed the finish line, not slackening in the slightest. Winton, who had christened his car "The Bullet," held the pace for a lap or so, then gave up.

The victory put Ford on the map and set Oldfield on a course to become America's first superstar race car driver. He became the first man in America to drive a gasoline-powered car at an average speed of 60 mph and by 1910 had pushed the land speed record all the way to an astonishing 131.25 mph, "the fastest ever traveled by a human being."

INTO THE DUSTBIN: Oldfield retired in 1918 at the age of 40 and spent the rest of his life watching one record after another fall to younger drivers in faster cars. "There is a story," Kernan writes, "that in old age he was stopped for speeding after a wild chase featuring three motorcycle cops. He watched calmly as the toughest of them strode up. 'Who do you think you are?' the cop snarled at him. 'Barney Oldfield?' "

FORGOTTEN FIGURE: Joshua Lawrence Chamberlain, Union general during the Civil War

CLAIM TO FAME: When the Civil War broke out, 33-year-old Chamberlain left his quiet life as a college professor to volunteer for the Union Army. Entering the army as a Lt. Colonel, he rose to the rank of Brigadier General. He fought with bravery in 24 major battles, including the battle of Gettysburg; he was wounded six times and had six horses shot out from under him.

On March 29, 1865, for example, a bullet went through his horse's neck, ricocheted off his arm, and struck him in the chest just below the heart. It probably would have killed him had it not been deflected by a pocket mirror. Instead, Chamberlain was knocked unconscious. When he came to, he was disgusted to see some of his men retreating. Bleeding profusely, Chamberlain grabbed his sword and charged the enemy. His men abandoned their retreat and joined him in the charge, turning the tables and winning the battle.

INTO THE DUSTBIN: General Grant rewarded Chamberlain's bravery by designating him to receive the formal surrender of the Confederacy at Appomattox. He later served four terms as governor of Maine, and in 1893 he was awarded the Congressional Medal of Honor. Nevertheless, historian Charles Calhoun writes, "Chamberlain largely faded from national view for most of the 20th century. No statue of him was ever erected at Gettysburg; few historians ever studied his campaigns."

*　　　*　　　*

FORGETTABLE FLOPS

• **Porcupine-flavored Potato Chips.** In 1984, Welsh bar owner Phil Lewis was discussing potato chip flavors with some Romanian customers. They told him of an old gypsy delicacy—porcupine baked in clay—and suggested the possibility of porcupine-flavored potato chips. Using a closely guarded recipe, Lewis set to work in his kitchen to produce the first packages. Customers compared the taste to smokey bacon but, as the venture attracted more and more publicity, animal-lovers protested. Lewis was forced to abandon it for more traditional flavors.

• **Attack Clock.** In 1919, John Humphrey of Connecticut invented an unusual alarm clock: The apparatus consisted of a timepiece attached to an adjustable rod with a rubber ball on the end. When the alarm on the clock went off, instead of a bell ringing, the rod would be activated, causing the ball to hit the sleeper. Humphrey deemed his device to be of great benefit to deaf people or invalids who might be upset by bells...but who presumably didn't mind being whacked over the head with a ball.

• **Floating Chairs.** Helium-filled furniture was the brainchild of William A. Calderwood of Peoria, Arizona. His 1989 patent envisioned furniture floating to the ceiling when not in use, thereby allowing extra floor space. When required, the furniture would be pulled back down to the floor by a rope.

—The Best Book of Lists Ever!

A stolen car is 200 times more likely to get into a crash than other cars.

HERE'S DAVE

Some jabs from late-night talk show host David Letterman.

"Based on what you know about him in history books, what do you think Abraham Lincoln would be doing if he were alive today? One, writing his memoirs; two, advising the president; three, desperately clawing at the inside of his coffin."

"People say New Yorkers can't get along. Not true. I saw two New Yorkers, complete strangers, sharing a cab. One guy took the tires and the radio; the other guy took the engine."

"Here's a bit of news. They spent $18 million on a little subway system between the Senate office building and the Senate chambers, just to move the senators back and forth. Well the train had a crash the other day and tragically, no one was injured."

"In the new sex survey they found out that 8% of people had sex four or more times a week. Now here's the interesting part. That number drops to 2% when you add the phrase 'with partner.'"

"New Yorkers have this funny habit. At Halloween, after they cut the pumpkin, they throw the knife in the East River."

"In Washington, D.C., the other day it was just a typical day with the squirrels gathering shell casings."

"Do you know what really kills me on this last election? The amount of money spent on their campaign. Ted Kennedy spent $17 million—of course he gets $2 million back when he returns his empties."

"Barbie is getting a bigger waist and a smaller chest. Not surprisingly, earlier today Ken announced he wants to start seeing other dolls."

"Donald Trump doesn't have much money invested in the stock market per se. Most of his money goes into junk blondes."

"Japanese prime minister Tomiichi Murayama apologized for Japan's part in World War II. However, he still hasn't mentioned anything about karaoke."

Life in the fast lane: The average bowling lane is 3' 6" wide and 60' long.

FAMILY FEUDS

Is blood thicker than water? Not when there's money involved.
Here are two feuds from the BRI files that prove the point.

KOCH vs. KOCH

The Contestants: Charles and Bill Koch, two sons of Fred Koch, the founder of Koch Industries, an oil refining company with annual revenues of $35 billion—making it the 2nd-largest privately-held company in the U.S.

How the Feud Started: When Fred Koch died in 1967, Charles Koch became company president. Two other sons, Bill and David, joined the company in the 1970s. Bill, who owned 21% of the company, became increasingly bitter about the way Charles ran things—he felt he was entitled to more power. He also was upset at being "limited" to a $10,000 expense account, and at having to report to non-family executives.

Then, in 1979, Bill learned that his brother Charles had commissioned a plan on how Bill's stake in the company would be distributed at his death. Enraged, he enlisted his brother Frederick—an "artist" who'd been written out of his father's will (but still owned 14% of the company)—to join him in a proxy fight against Charles. But they lost the fight.

Charles retaliated by firing Bill and then consolidated his control over the company by issuing shares to loyal executives. After that, it was tit-for-tat: Bill filed his first lawsuit against the company in 1982; Charles filed a $167 million countersuit for libel, also charging that Bill was "mentally unstable." In one of the lawsuits, the Koch's 80-year-old mother was dragged into court to testify only days after she is believed to have suffered a small stroke.

In 1983, Charles took out more than $1 billion in bank loans and bought Bill's and Frederick's shares, which should have been the end of it...but wasn't. In 1985, Bill sued again, accusing Charles of shortchanging him on the sale of his stock. Bill lost the suit, filed another one, then lost again in 1988. Then, armed with evidence that the company was shortchanging oil producers, Bill revived his 1985 lawsuit and also turned the information over to the U.S. Senate Select Committee on Indian Affairs.

Between 1873 and 1880, some U.S. doctors gave patients transfusions of milk instead of blood.

And the Winner Is: Split decision. Bill didn't get any more money for his shares…but he won the "shortchanging" lawsuit. A jury ruled that Koch Industries had defrauded the government in oil payments and had to pay over $200 million—25% of which Bill got. The company also had to pay his legal fees. Equally important, the verdict damaged the company's reputation. Bill announced that he was so pleased, he was celebrating with a backyard barbecue for his family and neighborhood kids.

JOHN KELLOGG vs. WILL KELLOGG

The Contestants: John Harvey Kellogg, a physician and bowel-obsessed health guru at the turn of the century, and his brother Will Keith Kellogg, an accountant.

The Feud: While searching for a new kind of breakfast food to help his patients get "regular," Dr. Kellogg invented the recipe for bran flakes; then he invented the recipe for corn flakes.

But he was an idealist: he saw corn flakes as purely medicinal and began selling them under the brand name "Sanitas," after his Seventh Day Adventist Sanitarium.

Will Kellogg was a businessman—he thought that Sanitas was a stupid name for a breakfast food (it reminded him of a disinfectant), and he thought the flakes would sell better if they contained a little sugar, which his brother opposed for health reasons.

While John Kellogg was on a trip to Europe, Will formed a cereal company and launched his own brand of corn flakes to compete against Sanitas. To add insult to injury, his packaging suggested that "Kellogg's Corn Flakes" were linked to his brother's famous sanitarium. John was furious when he found out. He filed suit to block the corn flakes and put his brother out of business.

And the Winner Is: Will Kellogg. John lost the suit. Not only that, when he retaliated by introducing "Kellogg's Sterilized Bran" to capitalize on his brother's thriving cereal business (just as his brother had earlier cashed in on the sanitarium's fame), Will filed suit to stop *him* from using the family name…and *won*. "The Battle of the Brans" had lasted more than a decade; by the time it was over, Dr. John Kellogg's sanitarium had fallen on hard times, while Will Kellogg's breakfast cereal business was booming, all thanks to an idea he'd stolen from his brother. The brothers rarely spoke to each other for the rest of their lives.

Plopp is the name of a candy bar sold in Sweden; Moron is the name of a wine sold in Italy.

WOULD YOU BELIEVE?

*Advice to our younger readers. It's a good idea to
pick your role models carefully. Here's why.*

CRUSADERS AGAINST CRIME

Role Model: Richard Pimental, a captain in the Taunton,
Massachusetts Police Department, known as "Captain
Good." He was the no-nonsense host of *Crime Watch,* a cable TV
show in which he profiled local crimes and denounced criminals as
"toilet-licking maggots."

Setting an Example: In March 1999, Captain Good was convicted
of stealing a gun from the department and sentenced to two years'
probation. The following year he was sentenced to six months' house
arrest after pleading guilty to obstruction of justice. He'd apparently
been tampering with witnesses while trying to fix the assault trial of
his nephew, who was charged with punching a bouncer in a bar.

Role Models: Art McKoy and Abdul Rahim, heads of a Cleveland,
Ohio, anti-crime organization

Setting an Example: In 1998, they were sentenced to prison for
spending $617,597 that the city of Cleveland, Ohio, accidentally de-
posited in the bank account of their organization. According to news
reports, the money landed in their account "when a city data operator punched in the wrong wire-transfer number while intending to
pay a utility bill."

CRUSADERS AGAINST ALCOHOL ABUSE

Role Model: Susan John, chairperson of Rochester, New York's
Committee on Alcohol and Drug Abuse

Setting an Example: In March 1997, she pleaded guilty for "driving
while impaired"—in other words, drunk driving. Her public statement: "This will give me additional insights into the problem of
drinking and driving, and I believe will allow me to do my job even
more effectively." Sure.

Role Model: Bethany Tosh, 21-year-old Miss Northeast Arkansas
for 2000

Setting an Example: She won the pageant on an anti-drunk driving platform. In March 2000, she surrendered her title after being convicted of driving under the influence of alcohol.

DEFENDERS OF PEOPLE'S RIGHTS

Role Models: Age Concern, a British organization "devoted to concerns of the elderly"

Setting An Example: In June 2000, a 69-year-old Englishman named Hector McDonald applied for a job at Age Concern. He was turned down for the job—because he was too old.

Role Models: The Texas Commission for the Blind, which was set up to provide workplace support to the visually impaired

Setting An Example: In 1999, it paid $55,000 to settle lawsuits filed by two blind employees. The commission had neglected to make "Braille and large-type employee manuals available to employees."

EXPERTS ON CONTROLLING ANGER

Role Model: A German youth worker who teaches anger control, identified only as "Herman K"

Setting An Example: In June 1999, Herman K was fined about $1,000 and given a 10-month suspended sentence. What for? He punched a policeman in the face, shouting "Here's something for your mouth!" after the officer ticketed his illegally parked car.

Role Model: Charles Mahuka, an anger management instructor

Setting an Example: In 1995, 32-year-old Miguel Gonzales was ordered to attend an anger management class after he assaulted his girlfriend. He showed up at the class drunk, which made Mahuka, his instructor, so angry that he beat Gonzales to death.

HITS AND MISSES

Role Model: The Reverend George Crossley, a televangelist

Setting An Example: In 1997, Crossley was convicted of trying to hire a hit-man to kill his arch-rival, whose estranged wife he was having an affair with. He'd inadvertently "hired" an undercover agent of the Bureau of Alcohol, Tobacco, and Firearms to do it.

TRISKAIDEKAPHOBIA

Triskaidekaphobia is literally "the fear of 3 plus 10" and millions of people suffer from it. According to experts, it costs America over a billion dollars a year in absenteeism, train and plane cancellations, and reduced commerce on the 13th of every month. Since this is our 13th Bathroom Reader, *we thought we'd take a look at the affliction.*

Fear of the number thirteen originated in Norse mythology. Aegir summoned twelve gods to a banquet in Valhalla. Guest number thirteenth showed up uninvited: Loki, god of evil. (To read the complete story, turn to page 441.)

Another possible connection comes from Christianity. Jesus and the 12 apostles dined together at the Last Supper, Judas, Christ's betrayer, being the 13th.

Predating the Christians, the Turks hated the number 13 so much that it was almost expunged from their vocabulary.

The Romans associated the number 13 with death and misfortune. There were 12 months in a year and 12 hours in a day (according to the Roman clock), so 13 was seen as a violation of the natural cycle.

Even before that, at religious feasts in ancient Babylon, 13 people were selected to represent the gods. At the end of the ceremony, the 13th "god" was put to death.

For ancient Egyptians, 13 represented the final rung of the ladder by which the soul reached eternity.

Thirteen is the number of members in a witch's coven.

The 13th card in the Tarot deck is the skeleton—Death.

According to *The Encyclopedia of Superstitions*, if 13 people gather in a room, one will die within a year. In 1798, *Gentleman's Magazine* explained the superstition by saying: "It seems to be founded on calculations adhered to by insurance offices."

On the other hand, consider the ill-fated Apollo 13 lunar mission, which left the launchpad at 13:13 hours on April 11…and then exploded, almost killing the entire crew.

AMAZING ANAGRAMS

In the Absolutely Absorbing BR, *we included a page of anagrams (words or phrases that are rearranged to form new words with—more or less—the same meaning). Now we've noticed that they're all over the Internet. We don't know who writes these things, but we love them.*

ASTRONOMERS
*becomes...*MOON STARERS

DESPERATION
*becomes...*A ROPE ENDS IT

CLOTHESPINS
*becomes...*SO LET'S PINCH

A DECIMAL POINT *becomes...*
I'M A DOT IN PLACE

THE CHECK IS IN THE MAIL
*becomes...*CLAIM "HECK, I
SENT IT (HEH!)"

PRENATAL
*becomes...*PARENTAL

TIRED NERVES
*becomes...*DRIVE TENSER

VALENTINE POEMS *becomes...*
PEN MATES IN LOVE

LATE-NIGHT CHINESE
FOOD PARTY *becomes...*
HEATING THE CRISPY
NOODLE FAT

A SHOPLIFTER
*becomes...*HAS TO PILFER

A DOMESTICATED ANIMAL
*becomes...*DOCILE, AS A
MAN TAMED IT

PAYMENT RECEIVED *becomes...*
EVERY CENT PAID ME

NEW YORK TIMES
*becomes...*MONKEYS WRITE

CIRCUMSTANTIAL EVIDENCE
*becomes...*CAN RUIN A
SELECTED VICTIM

MALES NEVER ASK FOR
DIRECTIONS *becomes...*
KEEN CRISIS OF MEN'S
ROAD TRAVEL

THE EYES
*becomes...*THEY SEE

And (as far as we're concerned) the all-time champion anagram:

TO BE OR NOT TO BE:
THAT IS THE QUESTION,
WHETHER 'TIS NOBLER IN
THE MIND TO SUFFER THE
SLINGS AND ARROWS OF
OUTRAGEOUS FORTUNE
*becomes...*IN ONE OF THE
BARD'S BEST-THOUGHT-
OF TRAGEDIES, OUR
INSISTENT HERO,
HAMLET, QUERIES ON
TWO FRONTS ABOUT
HOW LIFE TURNS
ROTTEN

Put 80 people in a room...and one bite from a black mamba snake could kill them all.

MORE EXECUTIVE DECISIONS

More dumb business decisions, made by U.S. executives.

SHOULD WE BUY THIS INVENTION?

Executive: William Orton, president of the Western Union Telegraph Company in 1876

Background: In 1876, Western Union had a monopoly on the telegraph, the world's most advanced communications technology. This made it one of America's richest and most powerful companies, "with $41 million in capital and the pocketbooks of the financial world behind it." So when Gardiner Greene Hubbard, a wealthy Bostonian, approached Orton with an offer to sell the patent for a new invention Hubbard had helped to fund, Orton treated it as a joke. Hubbard was asking for $100,000!

Decision: Orton bypassed Hubbard and drafted a response directly to the inventor. "Mr. Bell," he wrote, "after careful consideration of your invention, while it is a very interesting novelty, we have come to the conclusion that it has no commercial possibilities....What use could this company make of an electrical toy?"

Impact: The invention, the telephone, would have been perfect for Western Union. The company had a nationwide network of telegraph wires in place, and the inventor, 29-year-old Alexander Graham Bell, had shown that his telephones worked quite well on telegraph lines. All the company had to do was hook telephones up to its existing lines and it would have had the world's first nationwide telephone network in a matter of months.

Instead, Bell kept the patent and in a few decades his telephone company, "renamed American Telephone and Telegraph (AT&T), had become the largest corporation in America....The Bell patent—offered to Orton for a measly $100,000—became the single most valuable patent in history."

Ironically, less than two years after turning Bell down, Orton realized the magnitude of his mistake and spent millions of dollars challenging Bell's patents while attempting to build his own telephone network (which he was ultimately forced to hand over to

Chicken Little was right: Clouds don't float—they're actually falling very, very slowly.

Bell). Instead of going down in history as one of the architects of the telephone age, he is instead remembered for having made one of the worst decisions in American business history.

HOW DO WE COMPETE WITH BUDWEISER?

Executive: *Robert Uihlein, Jr., head of the Schlitz Brewing Company in Milwaukee, Wisconsin*

Background: In the 1970s, Schlitz was America's #2 beer, behind Budweiser. It had been #1 until 1957 and has pursued Bud ever since. In the 1970s, Uihlein came up with a strategy to compete against Anheuser-Busch. He figured that if he could cut the cost of ingredients used in his beer and speed up the brewing process at the same time, he could brew more beer in the same amount of time for less money…and earn higher profits.

Decision: Uihlein cut the amount of time it took to brew Schlitz from 40 days to 15, and replaced much of the barley malt in the beer with corn syrup—which was cheaper. He also switched from one type of foam stabilizer to another to get around new labeling laws that would have required the original stabilizer to be disclosed on the label.

Impact: Uihlein got what he wanted: a cheaper, more profitable beer that made a lot of money…at first. But it tasted terrible, and tended to break down quickly as the cheap ingredients bonded together and sank to the bottom of the can—forming a substance that "looked disconcertingly like mucus." Philip Van Munching writes in *Beer Blast*:

> Suddenly Schlitz found itself shipping out a great deal of apparently snot-ridden beer. The brewery knew about it pretty quickly and made a command decision—to do nothing.…Uihlein declined a costly recall for months, wagering that not much of the beer would be subjected to the kinds of temperatures at which most haze forms. He lost the bet, sales plummeted…and Schlitz began a long steady slide from the top three.

Schlitz finally caved in and recalled 10 million cans of the snot beer. But their reputation was ruined and sales never recovered. In 1981, they shut down their Milwaukee brewing plant; the following year the company was purchased by rival Stroh's. One former mayor of Milwaukee compared the brewery's fortunes to the sinking of the *Titanic*, asking, "How could that big of a business go under so fast?"

THE ORIGIN OF THE FORK

Of the three eating utensils we normally use, only forks have a modern origin. Knives and spoons are prehistoric—but as recently as 1800, forks weren't commonly used in America. Some food for thought...

KNIVES, BUT NO FORKS

Centuries ago, few people had ever heard of a "place setting." When a large piece of meat was set on the table (sometimes on a platter, sometimes directly on the table), diners grabbed the whole thing with their free hand...then pulled out a knife and sliced off a piece with the other hand. Most eating was done with fingers: Common people ate with all five, while nobles—who understood sophisticated table manners—ate with only three (thumb, forefinger, and middle).

At that time, there were no utensils. In fact, most men owned just one multipurpose blade, which, in addition to carving food, was used for fighting, hunting, and butchering animals. But wealthy nobles had always been able to afford a different knife for each purpose, and by the Middle Ages, they had developed a setting of *two* knives, for very formal dining. One knife was thrust into a large piece of meat to hold it in place on a plate, while the second was used to cut off a smaller piece, which the eater speared and placed in his mouth.

FORKS

One of the drawbacks of cutting a piece of meat while holding it in place with a knife is that the meat has tendency to "rotate in place like a wheel on an axle," Henry Petroski writes in *The Evolution of Useful Things*. "Frustration with knives, especially their shortcomings in holding meat steady for cutting, eventually led to the development of the fork." The name comes from *furca*, the Latin word for a farmer's pitchfork.

The first fork commonly used in Europe was a miniature version of the big carving fork used to spear turkeys and roasts in the kitchen. It had only two "tines" or prongs, spaced far enough apart to hold meat in place while cutting it; but apparently it wasn't something you stuck in your mouth and ate with—that was still the knife's job.

A FOOLISH UTENSIL

These first table forks probably originated at the royal courts of the Middle East, where they were in use as early as the seventh century. About 1100 A.D. they appeared in the Tuscany region of Italy, but they were considered "shocking novelties," and were ridiculed and condemned by the clergy—who insisted that "only human fingers, created by God, were worthy to touch God's bounty." Forks were "effeminate pieces of finery," as one historian puts it, used by sinners and sissies but not by decent, God-fearing folk.

"An Italian historian recorded a dinner at which a Venetian noblewoman used a fork of her own design," Charles Panati writes in *The Extraordinary Origins of Everyday Things*, "and incurred the rebuke of several clerics present for her 'excessive sign of refinement.' The woman died days after the meal, supposedly from the plague, but clergymen preached that her death was divine punishment, a warning to others contemplating the affectation of a fork."

FORK YOU

Thanks to these derogatory associations, more than 250 years passed before forks finally came into wide use in Italy. In the rest of Europe they were still virtually unheard of. Catherine de Medici finally brought them to France in the 1500s when she became queen. And in 1608 an Englishman named Thomas Coryate traveled to Italy and saw people eating with forks; the sight was so peculiar that he made note of it in his book *Crudities Hastily Gobbled Up in Five Months*:

> The Italians...do always at their meals use a little fork when they cut their meat....Should [anyone] unadvisedly touch the dish of meat with his fingers from which all at the table do cut, he will give occasion of offense unto the company, as having transgressed the laws of good manners, insomuch that for his error he shall be at least browbeaten if not reprehended in words....The Italian cannot by any means indure to have his dish touched with fingers, seeing all men's fingers are not alike clean.

Coryate brought some forks with him to England and presented one to Queen Elizabeth, who was so thrilled by the utensil that she had additional ones made from gold, coral, and crystal. But they remained little more than a pretentious fad of the royal court.

Forks became more common during the late 17th century, but it wasn't until the 18th century that they were widely used in continental Europe as a means for conveying food "from plate to mouth." The reason: French nobles saw forks as a way to distinguish themselves from commoners. "The fork became a symbol of luxury, refinement, and status," writes Charles Panati. "Suddenly, to touch food with even three bare fingers was gauche." A new custom developed—when an invitation to dinner was received, a servant frequently was sent ahead with a fine leather case containing a knife, fork, and spoon to be used at dinner later.

Making a New Point

But before this revolution took place, the fork had to be redesigned. The first forks were completely useless when it came to scooping peas and other loose food into the mouth—the gap between the two tines was too large. So cutlery makers began adding a third tine to their forks, and by the early eighteenth century, a fourth. "Four appears to have been the optimum [number]," Henry Petroski writes in *The Evolution of Useful Things*. "Four tines provide a relatively broad surface and yet do not feel too wide for the mouth. Nor does a four-tined fork have so many tines that it resembles a comb, or function like one when being pressed into a piece of meat."

Coming to America

One of the last places the fork caught on in the Western world was colonial America. In fact, forks weren't commonly used by the average citizen until the time of the Civil War; until then, people just ate with knives or their fingers. In 1828, for example, the English writer Frances Trollope wrote of some generals, colonels, and majors aboard a Mississippi steamboat who had "the frightful manner of feeding with their knives, till the whole blade seemed to enter the mouth." And as late as 1864, one etiquette manual complained that "many persons hold forks awkwardly, as if not accustomed to them."

What's the oldest letter in the alphabet? Experts say "O."

OOPS!

*More tales of outrageous blunders to let us know that
someone's screwing up even worse than we are. So
go ahead and feel superior for a few minutes.*

NAKED AMBITION

"Thirty-one-year-old stripper Roberto Pamplona suffered a broken nose and multiple injuries after performing his act in Milan, Italy. He was supposed to be stripping for a party in one room, but showed up next door...where the Catholic Mothers Against Pornography were meeting. The innocent mix-up angered the 'Mothers' and Pamplona's act erupted into a riot halfway through the show."

—**"The Edge,"** *Oregonian*

THE LIGHTS ARE ON, BUT...

"Police in Oakland, California, spent two hours attempting to subdue a gunman who'd barricaded himself inside his home. After firing 10 tear gas canisters, officers discovered that the man was actually standing right beside them, shouting pleas to come out and give himself up."

—*Bizarre News*

ROYAL CLOTHES

"On a visit to Kuala Lumpur, [former First Lady Nancy] Reagan was invited to tea with the Queen of Malaysia at the royal palace. The First Lady's entourage was cautioned not to wear yellow or blue, the royal colors, or white, because it is a funeral color. On the appointed hour, a misinformed Mrs. Reagan showed up in a white dress with blue flowers, blue shoes, and a blue straw hat."

—*Not a Good Word,* **by Jane Goodsell**

FIRE DOWN BELOW

"More than two hearts were enflamed as a couple became engaged on the night of November 13 near Medford, New Jersey. The groom-to-be—we'll call him Clifford—bought enough hay bales to spell 'Marry Me Ruth' and paid $200 more to hire a plane. As he and the lady flew over the bales, friends were supposed to illuminate them with car headlights. But the pals didn't arrive on time, so Clifford's brother Ric did the next best thing: He set the hay on fire. Fortunately for Clifford, Ruth saw the message and said 'yes.' Unfortunately for his brother, the flames also ignited surrounding vegetation. Firemen put out the blaze, but Ric was arrested and Clifford had to put up additional money—for that other type of bail."

—*Christian Science Monitor*

FRIENDS IN LOW PLACES

"As he pulled his car into the Yankee Stadium VIP parking lot, a driver claimed to be a friend of Yankee owner George Steinbrenner. He didn't realize the parking-lot attendant *was* Steinbrenner. 'He looked at me, and said, "Guess I've got the wrong lot,"' said Steinbrenner, who had decided to personally investigate traffic problems at the stadium."

—*Parade* magazine

RUSSIAN ROULETTE

"For high-ranking bureaucrats in the old USSR, nearly any special privilege was available. The mayor of Leningrad wanted nothing but the best for his daughter's wedding in January 1980. He used his clout to get the Hermitage Museum, which stores many of the nation's art treasures, to let him use Catherine the Great's china tea set, a prized antique, for the occasion.

"As the evening wore on, and the guests grew more exuberant, one reveler got to his feet and accidentally dropped one of the priceless teacups. Assuming that he had proposed a toast, the rest of the guests took this as a signal for the traditional Russian gesture of good luck, stood up and threw their teacups into the fireplace, smashing them."

—*Oops!*, by Smith and Decter

MAYBE IT WORKED

"Callers to a suicide hotline got a surprise when they heard a voice promising 'the naughtiest girls around.' The toll-free number had been given to an adult phone service after the suicide prevention folks stopped paying for it. 'This is not the kind of message a suicidal person needs to hear,' said a spokeswoman for the Alliance for the Mentally Ill in South Carolina."

—*Bizarre News*

Lonely parrots can go insane.

UNCLE JOHN'S BOTTOM 10

Most people have a list of Top 10 songs they listen to. But Uncle John has a Bottom 10. Here's the Official BRI Countdown— and we mean Down. They don't get much worse than this.

10. MERRY CHRISTMAS FROM THE BRADY BUNCH. "The six [Brady] kids were herded into a studio, where a producer barked out a list of songs that each would perform. He didn't bother to ask if they could sing, or even to learn their real names." Barry Williams, who played Greg Brady, tells the story of being forced to sing the difficult "O Holy Night," despite the fact that his pubescent voice kept cracking. His comment: "I think I made the recording guy's ears bleed." He adds: "Should you ever come across this particular album in a record store, I suggest you run screaming in the opposite direction."

9. RHAPSODY OF STEEL. From U.S. Steel. "A beautiful symphonic score over which people promote steel products."

8. ADRIAN MUNSEY AND THE LOST SHEEP. "A new category of popular music: Middle of the Field (MOF)." The album features Munsey and a bunch of baaa-ing sheep recorded live in a small English studio. "There are thirty million sheep and nineteen million lambs in the U.K.," he intones, "This record is about three of them." Munsey's follow-up: a disco tune called "C'est Sheep."

7. THE CANARIES: The Songs of Canaries with Music by the Artal Orchestra. "Mixes canary songs with waltzes such as 'Jeannie with the Light Brown Hair' and 'Wine, Women and Song.'"

6. PLANT TALK (Plant Talk Records). The jacket says it all: "Have you ever found yourself lying in bed at night and an idea hits you like a cold slap in the face?" Jim Bricker, owner of Reel Productions did and this album is the result...."Treat yourself by listening to Molly Roth (plant shop owner) talk to your Philodendron,

---

Food for thought: 99% of the pumpkins sold in the U.S. end up as jack-o-lanterns.

Schefflera, Palm Tree, and many others." Sample: "Do you speak English, Ivy? What's the matter, why are you so droopy? Oh I see, your person really poured water to you. You don't like wet feet, do you?" Not recommended for people with suicidal tendencies.

5. THE ELVIS TRIBUTES. A variety of awful discs. For example: "Welcome Home Elvis," by Daddy Bob ("All the angels have been waiting for their rock and roll star"); "Elvis," by Jenny Nicholas ("Where are you, Elvis? ...Where is the past that I embrace?"), "The Gate" by George Owens. (The gate at Graceland sings about how sad it is since Elvis died.)

4. SEBASTIAN SPEAKS! Your Watchdog on a Disc (Grr-r-records). Approximately 30 minutes of mean, growling dog sounds. The jacket says: "Sebastian was recorded live, at work in his own home. No stand-in dogs or sound effects were used."

3. LEARN CHARM THE WENDY WARD WAY! A two-hour, two-album, 20-day course in CHARM. OK, everybody sing along: "If she's perky and she's pretty and sparkles...if she's confident and knows what to say...she's a girl who knows about beauty...bet she learned it the Wendy Ward Way!"

2. WHY. Not included just because it is, as critics George Grimarc and Pat Reeder say, "one of those gooey, 'We Are the World'-type projects that naively seeks to alter ten thousand years of basic, vicious human nature with just a limp, sing-song melody, a children's chorus, and a lyric sheet that oozes sap like a Vermont maple tree." No, it's one of Uncle John's favorites because the lead voice is *Fantasy Island*'s inimitable Herve Villechaize ("De plane! De plane!"). And, yes, he sings the way he talks: "Why? Do pipple hef to fight?...Why don't dey know what cheeldren know?"

1. LET'S LOOK AT GREAT PAINTINGS. Feel inadequate when you visit art museums? No problem! "Understanding paintings is like learning how to swim or ice skate—it might be hard at first, but once we learn how, we can have fun for years!" Narrated by "the *rich, friendly* voice of Miss Ann Loring, who makes the paintings about which she talks *come to life*."

THE MYSTERY OF THE BEALE CIPHER

We weren't sure who sent this article to us, or how long we'd had it, but there it was in our files—the tale of a mysterious treasure that no one at the BRI had ever heard of before. Is it real...or a figment of someone's imagination? You decide. It was written by Hank Burchard, and first printed in the Washington Post *on October 5, 1984.*

TREASURE!
I know where $15 million in gold, silver, and jewels lies buried in the Blue Ridge Mountains of Virginia.

This vast treasure, amounting to four tons of gold and silver plus about a bushel of jewels, is known as the Beale Hoard. It's been there for more than 160 years, its location concealed by a code that the world's greatest cryptanalysts have tried and failed to crack.

WHERE DID IT COME FROM?

The treasure was mined—some say looted—in the Wild West by a party of 30 adventurers led by a Virginia gentleman named Thomas Jefferson Beale. The party set out in 1817 and explored as far west as Santa Fe and central Colorado, where they stumbled on an outcrop of rich gold ore. In 1819 and again in 1821, Beale brought back wagonloads of the precious metals and jewels and buried them near Buford's Tavern, now known as Montvale, a small community north of Roanoke and west of Lynchburg.

In 1822, before heading west for the third time, Beale left a locked iron box with tavernkeeper Robert Morriss, telling him to open it 10 years hence if nobody had called for it in the meantime. Neither Beale nor any of his companions was ever heard from again, all apparently having been killed by Indians.

A VALUABLE PUZZLE

Morriss was a busy man; it was 23 years—1845—before he got around to breaking open the box. In it he found three sets of ciphers and a letter describing Beale's adventures. There was also a note saying the key to the ciphers would be supplied later, which it wasn't, and that Beale would write Morriss from St. Louis, which he didn't.

Since the letter also said a portion of the treasure would go to Morriss for his trouble, he energetically undertook to crack the code. As the fruitless years went by, Morriss weakened. On his deathbed, in 1863, he gave the matter over to the hands of his friend James B. Ward, a prosperous and well-regarded citizen of Lynchburg. After years and years, Ward discovered that Code No. 2 was a "book cipher" based on the Declaration of Independence. The plain text read as follows (punctuation has been added for clarity):

> I have deposited in the county of Bedford, about four miles from Buford's, in an excavation or vault six feet below the surface of the ground, the following articles belonging jointly to the parties whose names are given in number 3 herewith: the first deposit consisted of one thousand and fourteen pounds of gold and three thousand eight hundred and twelve pounds of silver, deposited November 1819. The second was made December 1821 and consisted of nineteen hundred and seven pounds of gold and twelve hundred and eighty-eight pounds of silver; also jewels obtained in St. Louis in exchange for silver to save transportation, and valued at $13,000. The above is securely packed in iron pots with iron covers. The vault is roughly lined with stone and the vessels rest on solid stone, and are covered with others. Paper number 1 describes the exact locality of the vault, so that no difficulty will be had in finding it.

A FRUITLESS SEARCH

Ward labored the rest of his life to decipher Codes 1 and 3. In 1885, despairing of both the solutions and his life, he published the whole story in a pamphlet designed to sell for 50 cents, with this warning: "Before giving the papers to the public, I would say a word to those who may take an interest in them, and give them a little advice, acquired by bitter experience. It is, to devote only such time as can be spared from your legitimate business to the task, and if you can spare no time, let the matter alone. Should you disregard my advice, do not hold me responsible." That was your last warning. Ward died a pauper, and never even made anything on the pamphlet, because nearly the whole press run was destroyed in a fire at the printing plant in Lynchburg.

KEEP SEARCHING

But hot dog. The search goes on! Down in Bedford County the hills are crawling with folks who think they know where that vault is. The county also is bristling with angry landowners, some of them armed, who are damn tired of being badgered by treasure hunters. Searchers have been known to sneak in at night, sometimes with bulldozers and dynamite, hoping to grab the loot and scoot. Marilyn Parsons, 52, is back home in Reading, Pennsylvania, with her terrier Muffin, after spending two months in jail for felonious desecration of a cemetery near Montvale. She just knew Beale had hidden the stuff in plain sight, so to speak, using phony graves marked by coded gravestones. But the backhoe she hired turned up instead the thighbone of a citizen who hitherto had rested in peace. The graveyard theory is popular among Bealers, but it's wrong. I know because the real solution to Cipher No. 1 is as follows:

> From Bufords go north five miles on the Buchanan Road until the Peaks of Otter line up. Get down and follow the stream. Take the west fork to where it passes the double oak and the double pine. Two rods NNE [north-northeast] is a bolder [sic] graved with a B. From bolder [sic] nine rods south of west is a flat stone. Dig there.

IS THAT YOUR FINAL ANSWER?

That solution comes to you free of charge because that's the way it came to me, 13 years ago, from a correspondent who said he would get in touch with me later, after he shook the people who had been following him and tapping his phone. He said if I didn't hear from him in a year he'd be dead and the treasure would be mine.

Carl Hammer, Ph.D., who probably knows more about the Beale treasure than anybody else, was not surprised to hear that I had the solution. "I have seen dozens of solutions," he said. "Hundreds of solutions, I think. Some of them look very good, and all of them are very wrong. But there is a solution, I believe. The ciphers are real, not just random-number garbage." He grinned and waved his gin-and-tonic at the reams of documents spread out in his Georgetown living room.

THE BIG FOUR

There are four broad classifications of Beale researchers: the number-cruncher, the pencil-chewers, the historians, and the psychics.

• **Number-cruncher Hammer and his peers** use computers to seek subtle relationships among the Beale cipher digits.

• **The pencil-chewers combine a knowledge** of how ciphers are made with an intuitive sense of why people make them. Sometimes they take wonderful shots in the dark, but frustration and wishful thinking often lead them to force solutions.

• **The historians sift musty courthouse records** and files of crumbling newspapers. They've proved to just about everybody's satisfaction that Ward and Morriss existed, that Beale may well have, that such Western adventures were quite common at the time; and so on. There's a subset of historians who apply the tests of logic and likelihood to the documents. We enthusiasts don't like them much, because they keep asking uncomfortable questions, such as "Why did Beale tell us in Code 2 what Codes 1 and 3 contained, when presumably we'd have them all decoded at the same time?"

• **Most visible of all the searchers are the psychics**, such as a gentleman of Maine whose believes Cipher No. 1 "was in fact written by Thomas Jefferson..." He goes on to give a solution that says the secret's hidden behind a bed at Monticello, adding that "all of the foregoing speculation is as true and complete as my 'subconscious' biological computer and my imagination can make it..."

DEDICATED WACKOS

Beale correspondent Mrs. H.M.B.G. writes: "It took me 3 1/2 years to decode the Beale Ciphers. The Gold is not lost. It never has been lost. It is in the control of a group of rich people. It is not in Bedford County and never was. Thomas Beale is a code name for the man who brought the gold from the territory of Africa. It was a loan from the Bank of England..."

From a resident of Tampa comes the assertion that "Beale was an American agent in Europe; the ciphers tell of many intrigues of the American Revolution, and the jewels are the lost crown jewels of France." P.L.S., who said he had a solution come to him "by means other than decipherment," went to a place near Montvale with a metal detector and found a mattock bearing traces of gold, silver, and copper under a thick crust of rust. But it started to rain so he went home. Later he started to go back there, but his car broke down. And so it goes.

Hammer, who recently retired from Sperry-Univac, has never wavered in his conviction that there's a real message in the cipher. He's noodling out a Final Program designed to determine whether there are enough cracks in the surface of the code that it is even theoretically possible to power one's way in by computer. If he should find out that there's no way in, a lot of us hope he'll keep it to himself. (*Editor's note:* Is the Beale Treasure real? Absolutely, positively not....And if you find it, we get half.)

* * *

PRIMATE HALL OF FAME: CHEETAH THE CHIMP

Background. Cheetah appeared in more than two dozen Tarzan films between 1931 and 1968. The role was practically the same every time. When Tarzan was captured by poachers or unfriendly natives, Cheetah would sneak into their camp and free him. If there was an important message to be delivered ("Quick, Cheetah—take letter to Jane!"), Cheetah carried it. And Cheetah provided comic relief with somersaults or juvenile mischief at the family treehouse. Audiences loved these antics, but working with chimps created so many problems for directors that by the 1960s, Cheetah's part was cut back to almost nothing.

Tricks and Training. One of the reasons Cheetah always looked so convincing as a "thinking" animal was that many of the tricks the chimp already knew were written into *Tarzan* scripts. For example, the chimp that played Cheetah was adept at crawling on his stomach. So in *Tarzan and His Mate* (1934), a scene was included in which the chimp escaped from an attacking rhinoceros by crawling through the tall grass.

• Although Cheetah seemed angelic in the Tarzan movies, chimps can be dangerous to work with. During one scene in 1932, Jane's (Maureen O'Sullivan's) hair got in Cheetah's eyes, temporarily blinding the chimp. Cheetah went crazy on the set, and bit O'Sullivan. Another time, Cheetah was supposed to kiss Jane during a scene. As their faces met, the chimp sneezed all over her.

CRÈME *de la* CRUD

From the BRI files: A few samples of the worst of the worst.

HOLLYWOOD'S WORST CASTING DECISION
The Conqueror, starring John Wayne as Genghis Khan

John Wayne signed a two-picture deal with RKO Pictures in the mid-1950s, and owed the studio another film. He expected it to be a Western.

Unfortunately, RKO had a big-budget epic about Genghis Khan scheduled for theaters in 1956, and no star for it. They wanted Marlon Brando, and even wrote a screenplay for him—filled with the kind of "stylized, slightly archaic Elizabethan English" that Brando had mastered in the film *Julius Caesar*. But Brando wasn't available. "Faced with an expensive project with no leading man," writes Damien Bona in *Hollywood's All-time Worst Casting Blunders*, "the studio called in its chits." Wayne was Khan.

How did the Duke plan to play a twelfth-century Mongol warlord? The same way he played most of his characters—as a cowboy. "The way the screenplay reads," Wayne explained at the time, "it is a cowboy picture, and that is how I am going to play Genghis Khan. I see him as a gunfighter."

Who knows? It might've worked...except that Wayne was no match for the Brando screenplay. He sounded ridiculous saying things like "I am bereft of spirit," and "I feel this Tartar woman is for me. My blood says take her." He didn't look the part, either. As Bona writes, the Duke's Mongol warlord costume was an embarrassment:

> Wayne sports a Fu Manchu moustache and a toupee that calls to mind Moe Howard; his eyes are taped to give him a slight Asian flavor....The look does not become him. Clearly uncomfortable—and reportedly sauced much of the time—Wayne...is so unsteady in the role that ultimately he comes across like an amateur John Wayne impersonator wearing a funny costume.

Note: *This was one of the first movies we ever wrote about—it's not only terrible, but cursed. See BR#1, page 30.*

THE WORST NURSERY RHYME BOOK

The Struwwelpeter (Slovenly Peter), by Dr. Heinrich Hoffmann (1845)

We found this in William Maloney's book, *The Worst of Everything.* Maloney writes: "If you're a latent sadist and get your jollies from scaring small children, *The Struwwelpeter* is the book for you. Tuck the little ones in, turn down the light, and open to 'The Story of Little Suck-a-Thumb.' The kids will never suck their thumbs again, and they'll have lots of interesting stuff to tell their psychiatrists when they grow up....Editions of *Slovenly Peter* usually have some 35 stories in which children meet hideous ends for such naughtiness as romping, discontent, idleness, fidgeting, and crying. In 'The Cry-Baby,' a little girl who cries a lot goes blind, then her eyeballs fall out....The book was first published, as you might guess, in Germany." Want more? Probably not. But Maloney has kindly reprinted a page from an old edition anyway:

THE STORY OF LITTLE SUCK-A-THUMB

One day, Mamma said: Conrad dear,
I must go out and leave you here.
But mind now, Conrad, what I say.
Don't suck your thumb while I'm away.
The great tall tailor always comes
To little boys who suck their thumbs.
And ere they dream what he's about,
He takes his great sharp scissors out
And cuts their thumbs clean off—and then,
You know, they never grow again.

Mamma had scarcely turn'd her back,
The thumb was in, Alack! Alack!
The door flew open, in he ran,
The great, long, red-legg'd scissor man.
Oh! Children, see! The tailor's come
And caught out little Suck-A-thumb.
Snip! Snap! Snip! The scissors go;
And Conrad cries out, Oh! Oh! Oh!
Snip! Snap! Snip! They go so fast,
That both his thumbs are off at last.
Mamma comes home; there Conrad stands.
And looks quite sad, and shows his hands.
"Ah!" said Mamma, "I knew he'd come
To naughty little Suck-a-Thumb."

IT'S A WEIRD, WEIRD WORLD

Proof that truth really is stranger than fiction.

THAT VOODOO THAT YOU DO

"When her seventh-grade students refused to calm down, Monique Bazile, a substitute teacher in Irvington, New Jersey, threatened to burn down their houses and performed voodoo, causing some children to complain of itching."

—*Esquire,* January 1993

BEAN COUNTER

"A Nairobi physician, after removing a bean from a young girl's ear, jammed it back in when her parents came up short on cash for the $6 operation."

—"The Edge," *Oregonian*

DUCK, DUCK GOOSE

"A Tulsa, Oklahoma, physician, writing in a 1992 issue of the *Irish Journal of Psychological Medicine*, reported on a 32-year-old woman whose neighbors had a large satellite dish installed in their yard. The woman became convinced she was being wooed by Donald Duck and that the dish was put there to facilitate his communicating with her. After 'hovering' around the dish, she eventually undressed and climbed into it...where she later said she consummated marriage to Mr. Duck."

—*News of the Weird*

JUST CALL ME DAFFY

"A Wisconsin psychiatrist was accused of malpractice by one of his patients, Nadean Cool, who claimed he had convinced her that she had 120 separate personalities, including that of a duck, and then billed her health-care provider $300,000 for group therapy."

—*TV Guide*

California's Golden Gate Bridge isn't golden—it's "International Orange."

IRONIC, ISN'T IT?

There's nothing like a good dose of irony to put the problems of day-to-day life in proper perspective.

LIFE'S LITTLE IRONIES

• In 1999 the Mississippi state capitol in Jackson put up an artificial Christmas tree instead of a real one, out of concern for the fire hazard posed by real trees. "The artificial tree promptly caught fire, forcing the evacuation of the building."

• Tired of the other hunters who crowded into his favorite squirrel hunting grounds, in 1963 Pete Pickett strapped on some fake gorilla feet and tramped all over the place, hoping the prints would scare everyone else away. "Instead, the footprints drew mobs of Big Foot hunters."

• In 1999 Roger Russell began a 2,600-mile walk across South Africa to promote crime prevention. Two days into his walk, Russell was robbed at gunpoint.

IRONIC LIFE...

On a Friday the 13th, a man identified only as a 30-year-old Swede began choking on a piece of steak while at a restaurant in Norrkoping, Sweden. Paramedics could not dislodge the steak, and the man was dying in the back of the ambulance as it rushed to the hospital. Then, according to a Swedish newspaper account, "a few hundred yards from the hospital, the ambulance collided with a car. It was not a serious collision and no one was hurt. But the impact dislodged the chunk of beef, and the man resumed breathing."

...AND IRONIC DEATHS

• English novelist Arnold Bennett died in Paris in 1931. Cause of death? "Drinking a glass of typhoid-infected water to demonstrate that Parisian water was perfectly safe to drink."

• U.S. Army Surgeon John Blair Gibbs died while conversing with a reporter during the Spanish-American War. Gibbs was standing just inside his tent when he remarked to Thomas Steep, a correspondent with *Leslie's* magazine, "Well, I don't want to die in this

---

Moo. Country star Lyle Lovett is afraid of cows.

place…" Before he could finish his sentence, a bullet struck him in the head, killing him.

• "A Swedish man escaped from a blaze at a hunting cabin in central Sweden but froze to death as he fled, naked, on a snowmobile, a Swedish newspaper reported on Monday." (Reuters)

• "A 22-year-old man sliding down a ski run in California, crashed into a lift tower and died. He was sliding on a makeshift sled of yellow foam. The lift towers are meant to be cushioned by this foam, and the tower he hit was the one from which he had stolen the foam to make his sled." (*Fortean Times*)

CELEBRITY IRONY

• In 1995 singer Michael Jackson wrote to the British ambassador to the United States "to request a British knighthood." When asked what he should be knighted for, representatives of the "King of Pop" replied, "for his work with little children."

• "In the 1974 film *Chinatown*, Faye Dunaway's character famously tells Nicholson, 'She's my sister, she's my daughter….' Just as the film was about to open, Nicholson learned that the woman he thought was his older sister, 16 years his senior, was, in fact, his mother." (*Newsweek*)

• In the mid-1980s, sports fan and former President Richard Nixon was named to arbitrate a salary dispute between baseball owners and umpires. "Baseball needs clean, honest, well-paid umpires," Nixon told reporters.

• In the summer of 2000, English Prime Minister Tony Blair launched a public campaign against rowdy "yob culture" in England, in which he called for tougher laws against people who are drunk and rowdy in public. About three weeks into the campaign Blair's 16-year-old son Euan (who is too young to drink in public bars in England) was picked up by police after he was found "lying drunk and vomiting in a central London square."

• In 1988 Geraldo Rivera threatened to sue a couple who appeared on his show under false pretenses. "I'm very thick-skinned," Rivera told reporters, "but this is different. It affects the credibility of my program."

CAN CATS REALLY SEE IN THE DARK?

Calling all cat-lovers. This is your page. Here are some interesting cat facts from the book, Why Do Cats Sulk?, *by Arline Bleecker.*

Why does a cat roll over and show its stomach? This is a rare form of greeting—and the ultimate compliment. It indicates complete trust. Totally exposing its stomach reveals how secure a cat feels, because lying in this position exposes its most vulnerable part—and the cat knows it.

Why do cats "knead" when they're happy? When you relax and sit quietly, you're unwittingly giving your cat the same signal it got from its mother when it was a kitten—that Mom was ready to let her suckle.

A nursing kitten instinctively uses its paws to draw out the milk, gently pushing its mother's stomach to increase the flow. When older cats behave this way, it's a good sign that they're happy, content, and, very likely, recalling the best days of their lives.

Why does a cat bury its mess? While it's true that they are pretty picky characters, they don't bury their waste products because of fastidiousness alone. In the wild, only secondary cats bury their waste. The dominant feline, on the other hand, will actually display its feces prominently. This sends a strong message of its dominance.

However, in today's modern home, you are the dominant animal—and kitty chooses not to offend you. Another explanation is just as logical. Like most animals, cats bury their waste to protect their trail from predators.

Why do cats' eyes glow in the dark? A membrane, called *tapetum lucidum*, coats the eye and reflects light. When a cat is in the dark, its pupils open wide and light is reflected off them, but they're not actually glowing.

Can cats really see in the dark? They can't see in total darkness—

How do airports scare birds off their runways? One British airport plays Tina Turner albums.

and their daytime vision is only fair. But they can see better than humans in semi-darkness. They also can distinguish brightness seven times better than we can. As nocturnal hunters, their eyes are able to scoop up even the smallest scrap of available light. Their vision generally is blurred at the edges and they see best at 6 to 20 feet. But when it comes to movement, your cat doesn't ever miss a twitch.

Why doesn't your cat like refrigerated food? The reason they find cold food unappealing is because they're basically predators. In nature they would consume their kills fresh—at body temperature. Try serving food at room temperature, or give it a quick zap in the microwave.

Why do cats always land on their feet? The short answer is, they don't. Sure, they're the champs when it comes to landing safely—most of the time. But keep in mind that even if they land upright, they can sustain severe injuries from the impact.

Their amazing acrobatic skill is due to their natural "righting" reflex. This mechanism is very complicated and is governed by a complex organ in the inner ear that determines a specific sequence of events. Simplified, this organ sends information to the brain about the position of the cat's head in relation to the ground. In fractions of seconds, the brain commands the head to change position in order to protect it. When a cat's head is level, it first flips the top half of its body around to face the ground, then flips the rear.

In the process, it uses its tail to adjust for any overbalance. Finally, it's ready for landing and reaches the ground on all four feet with its back arched to cushion the impact.

The trick to its success, though, is time. A cat needs a minimum of 1.8 seconds to "right" itself. Though it is able to accomplish this in a fall as short as one foot, its chances of success are much better at greater heights (within limits).

How well can a cat hear? Actually, dogs have a greater range of pitch, but your cat's hearing far exceeds a dog's when it comes to picking out high-pitched sounds. Cats, after all, have brilliantly adapted to hunting by lurking in bushes—listening for the tiniest sound, the smallest rustle, the tiniest squeak. Their keen hearing also lets them know the precise direction and distance of their victims.

They can hear sounds up to an amazing 100,000 cycles per second which—no coincidence here—happens to be about the same sound pitch made by a mouse's squeal. A cat's hearing capability is five times greater than humans. (Dogs have only one-third the hearing ability of cats!)

Why do most cats hate water? Considering that cats evolved practically as desert animals in climates that were very dry, it's not so surprising that they aren't nuts about water. There just wasn't a whole lot of it around.

In reality, though, virtually any cat who has been exposed to water since kittenhood may enjoy it—and might even delight in taking a bath once in a while.

How long can a cat go without food or water? You won't have to drive yourself nuts worrying about a finicky cat that refuses to eat. It can survive without food much longer than we can. In fact, it can lose as much as 40% of its body weight and survive.

Your pet can actually go without food for two or three days without even getting very hungry—and up to two weeks with no ill effects. Water is another matter entirely. A 10% to 14% loss of the total water in your cat's body is fatal.

Why don't cats drink a lot of water? Originally, your cat's ancestors were desert animals. Because of this, their kidneys have adapted incredibly well to life without water. As a result, their kidneys can eliminate a lot of harmful toxins without needing a lot of fluid to do so. That's why their urine is so concentrated—and also why it smells so awful. Generally, the average healthy cat needs very little fluid to maintain its health. Research has shown that cats fed a steady diet of canned cat food—which is 70% water—may choose not to drink additional water. They may be getting all the fluid they need with the food. Nevertheless, fresh water should always be available to keep your pet healthy.

Q. What are bellysinkers, doorknobs, and burl cakes?   A. Nicknames for doughnuts.

YOU'RE MY INSPIRATION

More inspirations for famous fictional characters.

CROCODILE DUNDEE. In 1977, Rodney William Ansell was rescued from a remote part of the Australian outback. Against impossible odds, he'd survived on his own for two months after a giant crocodile attacked his boat and left him stranded. Watching him on TV, actor Paul Hogan and cowriters Ken Shadie and John Cornell were inspired to create Mick "Crocodile" Dundee for their 1986 film. Ansell was killed 22 years later in a shootout with police.

MURPHY BROWN. Inspired by Candace Bergen's friend, real-life newscaster Diane Sawyer.

CHARLIE'S ANGELS. The TV series was going to be called "Alley Cats"...until costar Kate Jackson suggested "Charlie's Angels." Producer Aaron Spelling asked where she got the idea, and Jackson pointed to a picture of three female angels—right behind him, on the wall of his office. It wasn't even Spelling's picture; he'd inherited the office (and the picture) from Frank Sinatra.

PEPE LE PEW. The Looney Tunes skunk was inspired by smooth-talking French actor Charles Boyer, who played a character named Pepe Le Moko in the 1938 film *Algiers.*

POE'S "THE RAVEN." Believe it or not, the immortal poem was inspired by a real raven. The bird was a gift to Charles Dickens in 1840, when he was researching ravens for *Barnaby Rudge.* "In 1841 Edgar Allen Poe, then a literary critic in Philadelphia, savaged Dickens's use of the raven in *Rudge,* saying a raven could be put to far better literary use." That's when he started working on his poem. Meanwhile, Dickens's pet raven died in 1842 and was stuffed. It was passed among collectors until 1971, when it was donated to the Philadelphia Library, "where the raven remains today, locked in a closet, next to a sign: *The Most Famous Bird in the World.*" (From *Wild Things,* by Mike Capuzzo)

LUCKY FINDS

Here's another look at some folks who found really valuable stuff...and got to keep it. We should all be so lucky!

PICTURE PERFECT

The Find: An ink-and-water color drawing of a dancer

Where It Was Found: In a thrift shop in Fort Myers, Florida

The Story: Jean Comey-Smith, 64, found the picture in 1998 and bought it for $1.99. She left it in her car for nearly a month.

"What caught my eye was the frame," Comey-Smith says. I flipped it over and saw the name A. Rodin....I thought, 'I know that name...' and remember thinking, 'I couldn't be that lucky. It's got to be a copy. It's got to be a print.'" Auguste Rodin is the French artist best known for his 1904 sculpture "The Thinker."

Comey-Smith *was* that lucky—Several appraisers turned down her offer to let them study her find, so she e-mailed the *Oprah Winfrey Show* after learning they were planning a program called Hidden Treasures. They invited her on the show to have the watercolor appraised by experts. "I was almost ready to cry when I found out how much it's worth," Comey-Smith said. The experts' finding: Her $1.99 painting, a genuine Rodin, was worth at least $14,000.

UNDERGROUND

The Find: Some coins

Where They Were Found: In a cornfield in Somerset, England

The Story: Since childhood, Martin Elliott had enjoyed playing with metal detectors. He never found more than junk—belt buckles, buttons, etc.—but he never lost enthusiasm for his hobby and was still going at it years later.

One afternoon in 1999, he paid a visit to his cousin Kevin Elliott, and taught him how to use the metal detector. Kevin started sweeping across his father's cornfield. He was just trying the detector out and didn't expect to find anything: the field, which was planted with corn, had been plowed over many times. But about four minutes later the metal detector sounded an alarm, so Elliott started digging. About a foot below the surface, he found an old Roman silver coin. Then he found another one…and then another, and another and another, eventually finding so many that he had to run and get some buckets to hold them all. In the end, he found 9,213 silver coins, worth an estimated $400,000—the largest hoard of Roman coins ever uncovered in Britain. Historians estimate that someone buried them in the field in about 230 A.D.

That was only the beginning—further excavations beneath the cornfield revealed "the presence of a major complex of Roman buildings," including an entire villa where the coins were buried, "a previously unknown and important Roman site."

STUCK IN THE MUD

The Find: A boat

Where It Was Found: Buried in the mud of the Sea of Galilee, in Israel

The Story: For years two fishermen, brothers named Yuval and Moshe Lufan, had dreamed of finding the remains of an ancient boat in the Sea of Galilee. But such boats, if there were any, would have been buried in the mud at the bottom of the sea and impossible to find. Then, in the 1980s, a severe drought struck Israel, and the water level in the Sea of Galilee dropped considerably. Much of the sea-floor that ordinarily would have been under water was temporarily exposed. So Yuval and Moshe spent the summer of 1986 combing the shore, looking for the oval outline of a boat….And amazingly, they actually found one. It appeared to be very old and, what's more, it was in very good condition.

The boat turned out to be even older than anyone imagined—carbon dating showed that it was built in the time Christ, about 2000 years ago. How'd it last that long without rotting away? Apparently the mud had acted as a preservative, keeping out corrosive elements in the air that would have caused the boat to disintegrate. It is the oldest example of its type ever found…and a true archaeological treasure.

*　　　*　　　*

REEL QUOTE

"He has every characteristic of a dog except loyalty."

—Henry Fonda, *The Best Man*

WHO SMELT THE IRON?

We all make dumb comments now and then, which we hope nobody notices...or that if they do, they're not writing them down. The people who made these bloopers weren't so lucky. Believe it or not, these are real.

KIDS' FAKE EXCUSES FOR SCHOOL ABSENCE

"Please excuse Mary for being absent. She was sick and I had her shot."

"Please excuse Ray Friday from school. He has very loose vowels."

"Please excuse Jimmy for being. It's his father's fault."

"Please excuse Harriet for missing school yesterday. We forgot to get the Sunday paper off the porch, and when we found it on Monday, we thought it was Sunday."

DOCTORS' MEDICAL REPORTS

"Patient was tearful and crying constantly. She also appears depressed."

"Patient has left his white blood cells at another hospital."

"When she fainted, her eyes rolled around the room."

"Discharge status: Alive but without permission."

COMMENTS FROM VISITORS TO U.S. NATIONAL PARKS

"We had no trouble finding the park entrances, but where are the exits?"

"The coyotes made too much noise last night and kept me awake. Please eradicate those annoying animals."

"Too many rocks in the mountains."

"Where does Bigfoot live?"

STUDENT SCHOOLWORK

"The inhabitants of Moscow are called Mosquitoes."

"A census taker is a man who goes from house to house increasing the population."

"Most of the houses in France are made of plaster of Paris."

"Iron was discovered because someone smelt it."

"The four seasons are salt, pepper, mustard, and vinegar."

QUESTIONS FOR CANADIAN FOREST RANGERS

"Where does Alberta end and Canada begin?"

"Can you help me? My husband's driving me crazy and he won't shut up."

"Do you have a glacier at this visitor centre?"

"Is this a map I'm looking at?"

"Don't all Canadians wear raccoon hats? Where can I buy one?"

The Great Wall of China is long enough to stretch from New York City to Houston.

"WE DON'T NEED NO DEVIL WAGONS"

This excerpt from Frank Donovan's book Wheels for a
Nation *reminds us how temporary even the most basic cultural
assumptions can be—and how quickly things can change.*

L OOKING BACK
Today, America is a "car culture." Most of us have built our
lives around the fact that we can always jump in a vehicle and
drive somewhere. Hard to believe that just 100 years ago, the automobile was such a novelty that most Americans expected (and
wanted) it to disappear quickly. If you'd been alive in 1900, the
chances are...

—You Might've Only Seen a Car Once
...as a Sideshow Attraction

Although few people had ever ridden in one by the year 1900, there
were occasional opportunities to see a car. Barnum and Bailey
brought a Duryea [*ed. note:* America's first car, built by the Duryea
brothers] with the circus as early as 1896, displaying it with other
"freaks and oddities." Montgomery Ward sent a car around the
country in a special railroad coach that same year as an advertising
stunt. And most state fairs in the last years of the old century displayed at least one of the horseless carriages that almost everyone
agreed would never replace the horse.

A few large cities had electric cabs, and there were reputedly between 2,000 and 3,000 cars of all kinds in the country, perhaps half
of them in and around New York. They ranged from expensive, imported Benzes and Peugeots to makeshift "blacksmith's cars" built
during long nights of trial and error in the backs of dingy shops and
stables.

—You Wouldn't Have Known What to Call It

A car was commonly referred to as a "horseless carriage," but that
really only explained what it *wasn't.* So in 1895 a Chicago newspaper offered a $500 prize for the best name for the new machine.
Hundreds of Midwesterners sent in names ranging from "autowain"

First American car race: Chicago, in 1895. Average speed: 7.5 mph.

to "petrocar," and the prize went to "motocycle." But that never caught on. Ironically, the French term "automobile"—a "bastard" mix of Latin and Greek that offended intellectuals—was not even considered. It was first mentioned in the *New York Times* in an editorial on January 3, 1899, which condemned not only the name but the vehicle itself:

> There is something uncanny about these newfangled vehicles. They are all unutterably ugly and never a one of them has been provided with a good or even an endurable name. The French... have evolved the word "automobile," which being half Greek and half Latin is so near to indecent that we print it with hesitation; while speakers of English have been fatally attracted by the irrelevant word "horseless." Other nations have been equally unfortunate and it really looks as if [we will never] find a respectable name for this noisy and odorous machine.

As the 19th century ended, the intellectuals admitted defeat. People seemed to like "automobile" (from the Greek *autos*, meaning "self," and the Latin *mobilis*, meaning "moving"). In 1900, the *Times* changed its index to classify these things as automobiles instead of horseless vehicles. Eventually, the term was used by everyone.

You Would Have Had "Good Reason" to Hate Cars

There were very specific reasons for the public's early dislike of the automobile:

• *Only the rich had them.* There was the traditional resentment of the "have-nots" toward the "haves" who owned cars. The clanking machines were becoming a disruptive influence that frightened horses. They were (and are) smelly and noisy. Even in 1900, editorials commented about pollution. One newspaper complained that common people were forced "to inhale the fumes which poison the atmosphere of our best avenues and to be either driven from their homes by the noise of the autos or choked by the dust which they raise."

• *They were too fast.* A school of medical thought held that the mind might not be able to sustain its equilibrium under the speeds of which some cars were capable. And certainly they were not good for women. One physician cautioned: "A speed of fifteen or twenty miles an hour in a motor car causes them acute mental suffering, nervous excitement, and circulatory disturbances...extending far into the night and causing insomnia."

• **They would inflate prices for essential goods.** At least one economist theorized that the increased use of leather and rubber in automobiles would raise the price of boots and shoes. "The more people ride," he warned, "the more the man who walks pays for going afoot."

• **They were all owned by "city slickers."** American farmers, who then comprised more than half the population and owned 18 million horses and mules, had a special hatred for the chicken-killing, horse-frightening, cattle-disturbing juggernauts that made occasional appearances on country roads. Eventually, Farmers' Anti-Automobile Leagues were formed to combat the evil machine. In Pennsylvania, the farmers' anti-car group reportedly even set up these "rules of the road":

> 1. "Automobiles traveling on country roads at night must send up a rocket every mile, then wait ten minutes for the road to clear."
>
> 2. "If a driver sees a team of horses, he is to pull to one side of the road and cover his machine with a blanket or dust cover that has been painted to blend into the scenery."
>
> 3. "In the event that a horse refuses to pass a car on the road, the owner must take his car apart and conceal the parts in the bushes."

• **They were evil.** Even the clergy was against automobiles. Many sermons were preached on the iniquity of the "devil wagons."

And the best reason of all to hate cars…

• **The French liked them.** A final reason for the distrust of the American public for the automobile was that gasoline-powered cars, the worst offenders in terms of smell and noise, were of French origin, and anything French was considered somewhat immoral by most Americans.

BUT ON THE OTHER HAND…

To "high society," what was French was right; and if the automobile was the rage of Paris…those who set the social pace in the New World could no longer be faithful to the horse. As *Vogue* reported from Paris at the close of the spring season:

> What a revolution the automobile is causing! The railway carriage is being ignored in certain circles of France, the members of which,

when they leave town for some château or watering place, make the trip in their own motor cars....The King of the Belgians makes the trip from Brussels to the French capital in his automobile, thus avoiding all the crowds at railroad stations and dependency upon time tables. Is it not truly a royal way of getting about?

What royalty and nobility could do in Europe, the scions of railroad fortunes, banking fortunes, fur fortunes, real-estate fortunes, and pork-packing fortunes could do in America. As soon as automobiles were considered indispensible by the rich, the automobile was assured of a permanent place in American society. It would, however, take a while for their tastes and habits to "trickle down" to the American public at large. Still, a decade later—by 1910—you probably would have been either driving a car...or saving your money for one.

*   *   *

REDUNDANT REDUNDANCIES

BRI member Derek DellArciprete sent this list of common 2-word phrases that repeat themselves. How many have you used lately?

Added bonus	Advance warning
Closed fist	Future plans
Future potential	Lag behind
True fact	Close proximity
Revert back	Foreign imports
Prior history	Convicted felon
Sum total	Past experience
End result	And etc.
Temper tantrum	Attach together
Free gift	Circulate around
Bare naked	Classic tradition
Unique individual	Descend down
Total abstinence	Duplicate copy
Join together	Exact replica

Close Encounters of the Third Kind **is a remake of Spielberg's 1964 amateur film** *Firelight.*

MOVIE BOMB: CUTTHROAT ISLAND

*Some films don't set out to be disaster films, but they still
end up that way. Take this one, for example—it's
the most expensive flop in Hollywood history.*

CUTTHROAT CASTING

Fresh from his success directing *Cliffhanger* and *Die Hard 2*,
Finnish director Renny Harlin was searching for a script that
would help his future wife, actress Geena Davis, make the leap from
light comedies into big-money action films. Harlin found his script
in *Cutthroat Island*, an *Indiana Jones*-type epic about a pirate's daughter who searches for her murdered father's treasure.

But Harlin worried that Davis didn't have enough star power to
attract the large audiences needed to justify the cost of a big-budget
action film. So he began looking for a male star to complement her.
He picked Michael Douglas, who agreed to do the film on two conditions: 1) It had to start filming immediately, because he was only
available for a short period of time; and 2) his part had to be rewritten to give his character the same amount of "screen time" as Davis.

THE FIRST SIGN OF DISASTER

Harlin agreed, hired "script doctor" Susan Shaliday, and began
building sets. He decided to film it in Thailand and on the Mediterranean island of Malta—two beautiful locations, but more than
5,000 miles apart...adding greatly to the expense and complexity
of completing the picture. The film's budget was set at $65 million,
making it one of Carolco Picture's most expensive films to date.

Several rewrites later, Geena Davis' role was actually expanding
at the expense of Douglas...so Douglas dropped out. "We spent
money like crazy, and the script was being rewritten like crazy,"
one executive recalls. "But it was becoming Renny's film for Geena.
Michael got upset when he realized what was happening. I don't
fault him; it was an impossible situation."

Now that Douglas was out, Geena Davis wanted out too. "Let's
be serious," one production executive says, "Everyone wanted off

---

The first canned foods appeared in 1811. But the can opener wasn't invented until 1855.

this picture when Michael Douglas left." But Davis was contractually obligated to finish the film whether Douglas was in it or not. So she stayed.

Harlin, left with expensive, half-built sets in two foreign countries, and no male lead, began working his way down the roster of Hollywood's "A-list" stars, trying to find someone—anyone—willing to take the part. Nobody would—Liam Neeson turned down the role; so did Ralph Fiennes, Keanu Reeves, and every other major star. So Harlin pulled out the "B-list" and began looking for second-tier actors to fill the part.

At this point in the film, Harlin should have been supervising the construction of the sets, the rewriting of the scripts, and other details. But he was so occupied by his mad scramble to find a male star that the work went forward without him. By the time he cast actor Matthew Modine for the part, much of the work was done.

ONE DISASTER AFTER ANOTHER

Unfortunately, it wasn't to Harlin's liking. He decided that the shooting script was "totally unshootable," and the enormously expensive sets all had to be redone. And that was only the beginning: one of the directors of photography broke his leg falling off a crane, some broken pipes caused raw sewage to pour into the water tank where the actors were supposed to swim, and when Harlin fired the chief camera operator following a dispute, more than two dozen crew members quit with him.

By the time *Cutthroat Island* limped into theaters its cost had mushroomed from $65 million to more than $115 million. Even worse: the critics hated it. "This film is too stupidly smutty for children," a *New York Times* film critic wrote, "and two cartoonish for sane adults." Ticket sales were disappointing even for a movie that everyone knew was bad and that no one wanted to make. Pulled from theaters after only a few weeks, *Cutthroat Island* made only $10 million at the box office, bringing the total loss to more than $105 million. Not only was it the most expensive film ever made, but also the most expensive flop in Hollywood history. But the studio responsible for this bomb, Carolco Pictures, wasn't around to see it: In the hole to the tune of $47 million, Carolco filed for bankruptcy six weeks before *Cutthroat Island* reached theaters.

LITTLE THINGS MEAN A LOT

"The devil's in the details," says an old proverb. And in the profits, too. The littlest thing can cost big bucks. Here are a few examples from our files.

A PAINT SCRAPER

The Story: In September 1978, a sailor accidentally dropped a 75¢ paint scraper into the torpedo launcher of the nuclear sub, U.S.S. *Swordfish*. The sub was forced to scrap its mission so repairs could be performed in drydock. Cost to U.S. taxpayers: $171,000.

A DECIMAL POINT

The Story: In 1999, Lockheed Martin signed a contract to sell military aircraft to "an international customer" (The company won't say who). Unfortunately, whoever drew up the contract misplaced a decimal point in the formula for determining the price. The mistake wasn't discovered until *after* the contract was signed, and the customer insisted on sticking to the wording of the contract exactly. Cost to Lockheed Martin: $70 million.

THE WORD 'PLEASE'

The Story: In 1995 Pacific Bell Telephone told its 4,500 directory assistance operators to answer calls with either: "Hi, this is _____, what city?"or "Hi, I'm _____, what city?" According to Pac Bell, these new greetings take 1.2 seconds to say, compared to 1.7 seconds when "please" is used. The phone company calculated that shaving half a second off of each call makes it possible for operators to handle 135,000 more calls per hour.

A FEW WASHERS

The Story: The $1.6 billion Hubble Space telescope was launched into orbit on April 24 1990, and immediately needed repairs. Cost of the rescue mission: $86 million. Cause of the problem: a few 25¢ washers that technicians used to fill in a gap in an optical testing device. No one noticed they were there...until they shook loose.

Tallest mountain on Earth: Not Everest—it's Hawaii's Mauna Kea, 31,800 feet from the ocean floor.

UNCLE JOHN'S CAFFEINE QUIZ

Since you're a bathroom reader, you probably know at least one thing about caffeine—that it's a laxative. Here's a quiz to see how much else you know about the world's most popular stimulant. (Answers on p. 493.)

1. You're an average American coffee drinker. That means you consume…
   a) 1 cup a day b) 2 cups a day c) 3 cups a day

2. True or false: If coffee says "decaffeinated" on the label, you can assume there's no caffeine in it.

3. How long does it take to get the peak caffeine rush from a cup of coffee?
   a) 5 minutes b) 15 minutes c) 30 minutes

4. True or false: You get more caffeine in a cup of espresso than in a mug of coffee.

5. True or false: The way you can tell how much caffeine is in coffee beans is how dark or light they are.

6. Do people get more sensitive or less sensitive to caffeine as they get older?

7. True or false: Coffee is the world's second most popular drink.

8. On average, how long will it take your body to get rid of the first half of the caffeine you've drunk?
   a) 2 to 3 hours b) 3 to 6 hours c) 6 to 8 hours

9. Roughly what percentage of the world's adults drink coffee every day?

10. Who rids their bodies of caffeine quicker—men or women?

11. True or false: Drinking moderate amounts of coffee can reduce your chance of getting colon cancer by as much as 30%.

12. Where does most of the caffeine used in soft drinks come from?
   a) The kola nuts used in flavoring
   b) Decaffeinated coffee
   c) A lab in Omaha, Nebraska

13. Why is caffeine put in soft drinks?

14. True or false: Drinks containing caffeine make you urinate more.

TOILET TECH

Better living through bathroom technology.

THE GEIGER TOILET

Inventor: Wolfgang Lehmann

Product: A toilet for the nuclear power industry. It tests nuclear plant workers' exposure to radiation by measuring the radioactivity of their urine.

How it Works: "If the urine discharged is normal, it is flushed," Julie Horan writes in *The Porcelain God*. "Urine showing dangerous levels of radiation is prevented from leaving the bowl and is transferred to a special holding tank," where it is saved for further study.

TRAILER TRASH

Inventor: Jungle Inc., a California company.

Product: The Bumper Dumper—a toilet seat that can be attached to a trailer hitch for use during camping trips, emergency situations, "and other situations where a sanitation situation may occur," says the company's website. "No more looking for the right spot, no more trying to balance while squatting, no more unstable, flimsy, rickety, under-sized porta potty, no more smelly, unsanitary outhouses, and no more surprises from creepy critters.

How It Works: "Just park your vehicle in a nice secluded spot, attach the Bumper Dumper to your trailer hitch, and VOILA!! A portable toilet sturdy enough to hold 500 lbs. and just as comfortable as using the bathroom at home. You can even set up a privacy screen for complete comfort. It's Super Sanitary!"

WHEN THE BIG ONE IS DROPPED...

Inventors: Robert O'Brien and Kenneth Milette

Product: Fallout shelter toilet. O'Brien and Milette patented it in 1961, at the height of the Cold War bomb-shelter craze. Because the occupants of a fallout shelter would have to seal themselves off from the outside world for two weeks or more after a nuclear attack, taking care of an entire family's bathroom needs presented a difficult technical challenge. Any toilet would have to work without

---

Old American weather superstition: If you see a dog eating grass, it will rain.

electricity, use very little water, produce very little sewage, and limit the amount of odor released into the bomb shelter.

How it Works: The toilet "used the waste water produced from the shelter's showers, and the collection of urine, to flush the toilet," Horan writes. "Fortunately, the urine was also deodorized. The toilet operated by a manual pump that created enough velocity to flush one quart of water, cleaning the bowl. The contents of the bowl were stored in a closed sewage tank." Today, they're collector's items.

OTHER ITEMS

• **LidAlert,** an alarm that warns people when they've left the toilet lid up. When the toilet is flushed and the lid is not returned to the down position, LidAlert plays Twinkle Twinkle Little Star "until the lid is put down or the tank is refilled, whichever comes first."

• **Illuminated Commode Training Kit.** Teaches kids to find their own way to the bathroom at night. "Footsteps in a mat that glows in the dark show the way to the bathroom; a glow-in-the-dark ring surrounds the toilet, marking its presence as well as that of the toilet paper holder....It works equally well for people who have had too much alcohol."

• **The Mayfair Majesty,** a "super-sized" toilet seat for people with king-sized bottoms. According to its Wisconsin manufacturer, they created it at the request of customers, "who claim that regular-sized toilet seats just aren't comfortable anymore."

• **The Zoë Toilet Seat.** Made by Toto USA, a division of Japanese plumbing fixture giant Toto. "This $699 wonder features a fan that sucks fumes through a deodorizing filter, a heated seat, and a remote-controlled bidet nozzle with three pressure settings. Push one button, and a whoosh of water masks your bathroom noises. Push another, and the seat cleans your bum with a spray of cool water and a jet of warm air. The Zoë has also been engineered with our SoftClose seat which eliminates annoying 'toilet seat slam.'"

• **The Lady P.** A urinal for woman, made by the Dutch company Sphinx Gustavberg. Price: $4,300. "The Lady P resembles a male urinal, but hangs lower on the wall and has a wider, more rounded bowl. To use it, women simply turn their backs to the wall, unzip, and bend at the knees."

A newborn baby's brain weighs only 3 ounces; the average adult's weighs 3 pounds.

PUTTING LIBERTY ON A PEDESTAL

*Anyone who says one person can't make a difference
has never heard the story of the Statue of Liberty.*

BIRTHDAY GIRL
In 1865 a young French sculptor named Frédéric-Auguste Bartholdi went to a banquet near the town of Versailles, where he struck up a conversation with Edouard de Laboulaye, a prominent historian.

De Laboulaye, a great admirer of the United States, observed that the country's centennial was approaching in 1876. He thought it would be a good idea for France to present America with a gift to commemorate the occasion. But what? Bartholdi proposed a giant statue of some kind…and thought about it for the next six years.

COMING TO AMERICA
By 1871 Bartholdi had most of the details worked out in his mind: The American monument would be a colossal statue of a woman called "Liberty Enlightening the World." It would be paid for by the French people, and the pedestal it stood on would be financed and built by the Americans.

The idea excited him so much that he booked passage on a ship and sailed to New York to drum up support for it. As he entered New York Harbor, Bartholdi noticed a small, 12-acre piece of land near Ellis Island, called Bedloe's Island. He decided it was the perfect spot for his statue.

Bartholdi spent the next five months traveling around the U.S. and getting support for the statue. Then he went back to France, where the government of Emperor Napoléon III (Napoléon Bonaparte's nephew) was openly hostile to the democratic and republican ideals celebrated by the Statue of Liberty. They would have jailed him if he'd spoken of the project openly—so Bartholdi kept a low profile until 1874, when the Third Republic was proclaimed after Napoléon III's defeat in the Franco-Prussian War.

Bartholdi went back to work. He founded a group called the

Franco-American Union, comprised of French and American sup-poters, to help raise money for the statue. He also recruited Alex-andre-Gustave Eiffel, soon to become famous for the Eiffel Tower, to design the steel and iron framework to hold the statue up.

A WOMAN IN A HURRY

By now the centennial was only two years away. It was obvious that the huge statue couldn't be designed, financed, built, shipped, and installed on Bedloe's island in time for the big celebration. But Bar-tholdi kept going anyway.

Raising the $400,000 he estimated was needed to build the stat-ue in France wasn't easy. Work stopped frequently when cash ran out, and Bartholdi and his craftspeople missed deadline after dead-line. Then in 1880 the Franco-American Union came up with the idea of holding a "Liberty" lottery to raise funds. That did the trick.

In the United States, things were harder. There was some enthu-siasm, but not as much as in France. It was, after all, a *French* statue …and not everyone was sure the country needed a French statue, even for free. The U.S. Congress did vote unanimously to accept the gift from France…but it didn't provide any funding for the ped-estal, and neither did the city of New York. Neither did the state.

By now the Statue of Liberty's right hand and torch were fin-ished, so Bartholdi shipped it to the Philadelphia Centennial Exhi-bition and had it put on display. For a fee of 50¢, visitors could climb a 30-foot steel ladder up the side of the hand and stand on the balcony surrounding the torch. Two years later the statue's head was displayed in a similar fashion in Paris, giving people a chance to climb up into the head and peek out from the windows in the crown. But while events like these generated a lot of enthu-siasm, they didn't raise as much money as Bartholdi hoped for.

LADY'S MAN

In 1883 the U.S. Congress voted down a fresh attempt to provide $100,000 toward the cost of the pedestal; the vote so outraged Jo-seph Pulitzer, publisher of the *New York World*, that he launched a campaign in the pages of his newspaper to raise the money.

"The Bartholdi statue will soon be on its way to enlighten the world," he told his readers, "more appropriate would be the gift of a statue of parsimony than a statue of liberty, if this is the apprecia-

tion we show of a friendly nation's sentiment and generosity."
After two months of non-stop haranguing, he managed to raise
exactly $135.75 of the $200,000 needed to build the pedestal.

NOTHING TO STAND ON

In June of 1884, work on the statue itself was finished. Bartholdi
had erected it in a courtyard next to his studio in Paris. The original plan had been to dismantle it as soon as it was completed, pack
it into shipping crates, and send it to the United States, where it
would be installed atop the pedestal on Bedloe's Island....

But the pedestal wasn't even close to being finished. So Bartholdi left the statue standing in the courtyard.

In September 1884 work on the pedestal ground to a halt when
the project ran out of money. An estimated $100,000 was still
needed. When it appeared that New York was coming up empty-
handed, Boston, Cleveland, Philadelphia, and San Francisco began
to compete to have the Statue of Liberty built in their cities.

IF AT FIRST YOU DON'T SUCCEED...

Furious, Joseph Pulitzer decided to try again. In the two years since
his first campaign, his newspaper's circulation had grown from a
few thousand readers to more than 100,000. He hoped that now
his paper was big enough to make a difference. For more than five
months, beginning on March 16, 1885, Pulitzer beseeched his readers day after day to send in what they could. No reader was too
humble, no donation too small; every person who contributed
would receive a mention in the newspaper. "The statue is not a gift
from the millionaires of France to the millionaires of America," he
told readers, "but a gift of the whole people of France to the whole
people of America. Take this appeal to yourself personally."

This time, the campaign began to get results: By March 27,
2,535 people had contributed $2,359.67. Then on April 1, Pulitzer
announced that the ship containing the crated parts of the statue
would leave France aboard the French warship *Isere* on May 8th.
The excitement began to build, prompting a new wave of giving.
By April 15 he'd raised $25,000, and a month later another
$25,000—enough money to restart work on the pedestal.

At this point, the makers of Castoria laxative stepped forward to
help. They offered to chip in $25,000, "provided that for the period

of one year, you permit us to place across the top of the pedestal the word 'Castoria.,'" they wrote. "Thus art and science, the symbol of liberty to man, and of health to his children, would be more closely enshrined in the hearts of our people." The offer of a laxative for Miss Liberty was politely declined; Castoria kept its money.

ON A ROLL

By now the race to fund the pedestal had captivated the entire country, and money really began to pour in. People sent in pennies, nickels and dimes...and they also began buying copies of the *World* each day to keep track of the race; by the time the dust settled, the *World's* circulation had exploded to the point that it was the most widely-read newspaper in the entire Western Hemisphere.

On June 19, the fundraising passed the $75,000 mark; on July 22, the *Isere* arrived in New York Harbor and began unloading its cargo; bringing the excitement—and the giving—to its peak.

Finally on August 11, Pulitzer's goal was met. "ONE HUNDRED THOUSAND DOLLARS! TRIUMPHANT COMPLETION OF THE *WORLD'S* FUND FOR THE LIBERTY PEDESTAL. More than 120,000 people had contributed to the effort, for an average donation of about 83¢ per person.

Work on the pedestal now moved at a steady clip; by April 1886 it was finished, and the pieces of the statue itself were put into place. The internal steel and iron framework structure went up first; then the pieces of the statue's outer skin were attached one by one. Finally on October 28, 1886, at a ceremony headed by President Grover Cleveland, the statue was opened to the public....more than ten years after the original July 4, 1876 deadline.

The statue was late—*very* late. But better late than never.

A WOMAN OF FEW WORDS

The verse most closely associated with the statue, "Give me your tired, your poor, / Your huddled masses yearning to breathe free..." weren't added to the pedestal until 1903... and only after officials realized what an inspiration the statue had become to the waves of immigrants arriving at nearby Ellis Island. The verses are part of "The New Colossus," a sonnet composed by New York poet Emma Lazarus in 1883; she donated it to an auction at the New York's Academy of Design to raise money for the statue's pedestal.

What do a brick and a plate-glass window have in common? They're both made from sand.

MORE STRANGE LAWSUITS

Here are more real-life examples of unusual legal battles.

THE PLAINTIFF: Lorenzo Grier

THE DEFENDANT: The United States of America

THE LAWSUIT: In 1995, Grier sued the government for fraud, breach of contract, and discrimination. The basis for his suit? "Appellant alleged that former President Ronald Reagan did not respond when Appellant invented the multiplication tables and sent them to the White House, but instead stole Appellant's invention and implemented it in the public schools." Grier asked for $900 billion in damages.

THE VERDICT: Case dismissed

THE PLAINTIFF: Edna Hobbs

THE DEFENDANT: The Joseph Company, makers of The Clapper (a device that activates appliances when someone claps)

THE LAWSUIT: Hobbs filed suit because she had to clap so hard, she injured her hands trying to get the appliances to go on. In fact, she was in so much pain, she said, "I couldn't peel potatoes," adding: "I never ate so many baked potatoes in my life."

THE VERDICT: Case dismissed. The judge ruled that Hobbs "had merely failed to adjust the sensitivity controls."

THE PLAINTIFF: The parents of Daniel Dukes, "a 27-year-old drifter with a criminal record"

THE DEFENDANT: Sea World, in Orlando, Florida

THE LAWSUIT: When Dukes' body was found in the park in 1999, he was wearing only underwear and was draped on the back of a killer whale. Cause of death: drowning. His parents sued for millions, claiming Dukes had been *pulled* into the water (though that wouldn't explain how his clothes were removed). Plus, they insisted the park should have posted a sign warning that a killer whale can kill. The *San Antonio Express-News* commented: "If his

---

In 1977, you could have bought a seat on the New York Stock Exchange for $35,000.

parents couldn't teach Dukes the dangers of playing with a five-ton whale, Sea World cannot be expected to do much better."
THE VERDICT: Unknown

THE PLAINTIFF: Larry W. Bryant
THE DEFENDANT: Gov. James Gilmore of Virginia
THE LAWSUIT: In June 2000, Bryant filed suit to get Gilmore to call a grand jury to look into alien abductions, and to make sure the National Guard knew how to deal with alien attacks. Bryant was quoted as saying he was especially concerned about some "dark, silently floating triangles," which Gilmore had done nothing about.
THE VERDICT: Case dismissed

THE PLAINTIFF: The mother of a newborn girl in an unnamed Tennessee hospital
THE DEFENDANT: The hospital
THE LAWSUIT: About 12 hours before the woman went into labor, she was injected with blue dye as part of a test for a urinary tract infection. Result: when the baby was born, it was dyed blue (only temporarily). Amused hospital workers referred to the baby as "Smurfette." The not-so-amused mother sued the hospital for $4 million, saying their "callous remarks" about the "Smurfette" caused "permanent emotional damage, humiliation, and ridicule."
THE VERDICT: Unknown

THE PLAINTIFF: S, a California lawyer
THE DEFENDANT: R, his next-door neighbor—also a lawyer
THE LAWSUIT: In 1991, R asked S, whose family was playing basketball, to quiet down. S refused…so R sprayed the family and their basketball court with a hose. S sued, claiming emotional distress. Then R countersued, saying S had reduced the value of his home. And to prove it, he introduced "scientific testimony from acoustical engineers, architects, and real-estate appraisers."
THE VERDICT: At first the court restricted S to six hours of basketball a day…But an appeals court ruled that R should just close his window.

The first motion picture, copyrighted in the U.S., shows a man sneezing (1894).

VLAD THE IMPALER: THE *REAL* DRACULA

On page 164, we told you about Bram Stoker's book,
Dracula. *Here's a short history of the man*
who inspired it, Vlad the Impaler.

SEEING IS BELIEVING

In 1431, Holy Roman Emperor Sigismund invited Prince Vlad II of Wallachia (part of modern-day Romania) to join the Order of the Dragon, a religious order of knights sworn to defend Christendom from the Muslim Turks. The Prince traveled to Nuremburg to accept the honor, and returned carrying a large flag with the image of a dragon on it.

"It seems probable," Raymond McNally and Radu Florescu write in *In Search of Dracula*, "that when the simple, superstitious peasants saw Vlad bearing the standard with the dragon symbol, they interpreted it as a sign that he was now in league with the devil." Prince Vlad soon became known as Vlad Dracul—Vlad the "dragon" or, since dragons and devils were synonymous in 15th-century Romania, Vlad the Devil. Prince Vlad's son, who was also named Vlad, was nicknamed Dracula, "son of the devil."

The nicknames weren't too far from the truth: Both Vlads were bloodthirsty tyrants.

YOUNG TURKS

Born some time between 1428 and 1431, Dracula had a fairly uneventful childhood. Then in 1442—when Dracula was a teenager—Sultan Murad II of the Turks, suspecting the loyalty of Vlad Dracul, imprisoned his family. Dracul managed to talk his way out of prison, but his sons, Dracula and Radu, were forced to remain hostages as a further "guarantee." There they were educated by some of the finest tutors of the Ottoman Empire, and learned to speak Turkish with near-perfect fluency. At the same time, McNally and Florescu write, Dracula "developed a reputation for trickery, cunning, insubordination, and brutality, and inspired fright in his own guards."

Critter rule of thumb: If it's a mammal, it has a tongue (or at least *had* one at one point).

In and Out of Power

In 1447, Vlad Dracul was assassinated on the orders of the Prince of nearby Transylvania. Dracula, still a hostage of the Sultan, managed to escape the following year and was installed as the new Prince of Wallachia. He was overthrown two months later, and didn't reclaim the throne until 1456, eight years later.

It was during this second reign that Dracula earned his legendary reputation for cruelty. In fact, for centuries Vlad Dracula was better known as Vlad Tepes—"The Impaler"—for his method of torturing and executing thousands of his enemies—and even his own countrymen—by impaling them upon wooden poles.

Dracula was a certifiable psycho. He enjoyed watching people suffer, and made sure an impalement took several hours—sometimes even days. There were even various forms of impalement depending upon age, rank, or sex.

Yet amazingly, in spite of his legendary cruelty, Dracula is thought of as a hero in Romanian history, because he used the terror of his reign to maintain public order and defend the country against foreign invasion. "On one atrocious occasion," David Skal writes in V is for Vampire, "20,000 Turkish captives were exterminated in this manner (impaling) and displayed in a mile long semicircle outside Dracula's capital city, Tirgoviste, to ward off oncoming enemy troops. It worked."

THE END...AND A NEW BEGINNING

After years of successfully waging war against the Turks, in 1462, the tide turned and Dracula was on the verge of defeat. Desperate, he turned to Matthias Corvinus, the King of Hungary. But rather than help Dracula as he had earlier promised, Corvinus had Dracula arrested and thrown into prison. He languished there for another nine years.

No longer able to torture people, Dracula turned his attention to insects and animals. "Dracula," McNally and Florescu write, "could not cure himself of the evil habit of catching mice and having birds bought at the marketplace so that he could 'punish them' by impalement.

Dracula was finally freed in 1475 when a powerful cousin inter-

---

Yes? No? Depends on where you go: In Greece and Bulgaria, nodding up and down means "no."

ceded on his behalf. By November of 1476 Dracula was back on the throne in Wallachia. But this reign was even shorter the second time around. In late December or early January, Dracula died in battle fighting a rival for the Wallachian throne, and his head was sent to the sultan. According to legend, monks from a nearby monastery found Dracula's body and buried it—without the head—somewhere in their church. The church still stands today, but Dracula's grave has never been found.

TALES OF VLAD THE IMPALER

Dracula's barbarism was extreme even by medieval standards, and tales of his crimes made him a legendary figure across much of Europe within his own lifetime. "His cruelties," McNally and Florescu write, "were committed on such a massive scale that his evil reputation reached beyond the grave to the firesides where generations of grandmothers warned little children, 'Be good, or Dracula will get you!'"

*   *   *

LIFE AFTER DEATH

Deceased: Max Hoffman, a 5-year-old boy living in the U.S. in the 1860s

News of His Death: In 1865 a cholera epidemic swept the town where Hoffman lived; he became infected and as far as anyone could tell, died. Soon afterwards, he was given a proper funeral and was buried.

Resurrection: For two nights after his funeral, his mother had such incredibly vivid nightmares of him still being alive that she insisted that her husband dig up the coffin. Perhaps just to ease his wife's fears, Mr. Hoffman did just that, and when he pried open the coffen saw signs of life and was able to revive his son. Five-year-old Max made a full recovery, lived to the age of ninety, and kept the handles from the coffin as a keepsake for the rest of his life.

SOAP OPERA BLOOPERS

Soaps are relentlessly dire and serious, so soap lovers really treasure those moments when their soap stars blow it and show they're human. Here are a few classic moments.

When soap operas first appeared on TV, there was no videotape and no teleprompters. All soap operas were broadcast live. Anything could—and did—happen.

• Radio actor Ralph Locke, trying to make the transition to early TV soaps as part of *One Man's Family*, froze on his lines, simply announced he had no more to say and walked off the set. The scene was taking place on an airplane, so the viewer was left to imagine him falling to his death.

• Apparently, the thought of being seen by an audience thousands of times larger than the biggest theater was just too much for many early TV dramatists. Actor John Raby tells the story of an actress in *A Woman to Remember* who panicked on live TV and tried to run off the set. He grabbed her, pushed her into a chair and spoke his lines, as well as hers.

• On *Last Year's Nest*, Leonard Valenta was in a love scene with a woman when a set fell on her. She did the rest of the scene holding it up.

• Haila Stoddard, playing Pauline on *The Secret Storm* was supposed to say to her mother, "I always thought she was a bit of a witch." Instead, there on live TV, in front of millions, she said, "whit of a bitch." Her astounded mom, instead of going on with her regular lines, responded, "Oh dear, Pauline, you didn't mean to say that!" It took the actors ten minutes to get back to the script.

• On *Search for Tomorrow*, Jerry Lanning, playing hit man Nick D'Antoni, choked Liza Walton (Sherry Mathis) so hard, she literally turned blue. They were married in real life a week later.

• On *One Life to Live*, Max Holden (Nicholas Walker) and Gabrielle Medina (Fiona Hutchinson) were supposed to do a candle-lit love scene, then, symbolic of their passion, the place was to go up in flames. The candles set Walker's hair on fire.

• On *The Edge of Night*, John Larkin (Mike Carr) leapt through the door, did a few pirouettes and barked, "Hello, all you folks out there in TV land." Fellow cast members were not laughing, they knew it was live TV. He thought it was a dress rehearsal.

• "I'd like you to make (instead of meet) Anne," said Eileen Fulton as she introduced Anne to a man on *As the World Turns*.

• On *Concerning Miss Marlowe* the prop telephone wasn't a prop. It rang. It wasn't in the script, so thinking fast, actress Val Dufour answered it, said, "It's for you," handed it to a French maid in the scene and walked off. Frantic, the maid faked a scene talking on the phone.

• On *First Love*, it was supposed to be a "Friday cliffhanger." The actress was supposed to say "Chris cracked up his plane." The pilot's wife and another woman were supposed to react with shock and horror, and the audience was supposed to tune in on Monday. But she flubbed it, saying "Chris crapped (pause—horrified tiny voice) up his plane." The show closed on the women screaming with laughter.

• An actor on *The Edge of Night* repeatedly rehearsed a phone conversation by speaking into his hand. He got so used to it that, when the phone rang on live TV, he did his lines into his hand. Part way through, he saw himself on a monitor, talking into his hand like an idiot, but decided there was nothing he could do.

• The toupee of Dean Santoro (Paul Stewart) on *The Edge of Night* fell off during a live scene. What else could he do? He put it back on.

• Nearsighted Ed Zimmerman, playing a surgeon on *The Guiding Light*, had to remember oodles of medical terms for an operation. They became a jumble in his mind, but he knew, if he had to, he could save himself by reading the teleprompter. Suddenly, his contact lens fell out into the patient's "wound." Rattled, he started barking random orders to the nurse. By then, they had departed from the script and Ed found the teleprompter man running the script backwards, trying to find their place. Doctor Ed forgot to sew up the incision. He sewed up his glove instead.

U.S. Government stats: Most common job for women in 1890: Servant. In 1990: Secretary.

DO GEESE SEE GOD?

In the last few Readers, we've included clever but simple palindromes. They're fun and impressive—after all, it takes a special skill to see when something can be spelled the same forward and backward. But they seem to be getting weirder and more complex. Who comes up with these things? Don't they have jobs…or families…or any other way to spend their time? Well, weird or not, we're hooked. Here are some new ones.

May a moody baby doom a yam?

Do geese see God?

Step on no pets.

Satan, oscillate my metallic sonatas!

Al lets Della call Ed Stella.

Straw? No, too stupid a fad; I put soot on warts.

Anne, I vote more cars race Rome to Vienna.

Some men interpret nine memos.

Dennis sinned.

No, it never propagates if I set a gap or prevention.

God saw I was dog.

Too bad—I hid a boot.

Campus motto: Bottoms up, Mac.

'Tis in a DeSoto sedan I sit.

No trace; not one carton.

Oozy rat in a sanitary zoo.

Was it Eliot's toilet I saw?

Lisa Bonet ate no basil.

A relic, Odin! I'm a mini, docile Ra!

"Do nine men interpret?" "Nine men," I nod.

He did, eh?

Is Don Adams mad? (A nod.) Si!

Eva, can I stab bats in a cave?

Live not on evil, madam, live not on evil.

No sir! Away! A papaya war is on.

Dogma: I am God.

Oh, no—Don Ho!

So many dynamos.

Are we not drawn onward, we few, drawn onward to new era?

To: Dr., et al. / Re: Grub / Ma had a hamburger / Later, Dot.

We panic in a pew.

Norma is as selfless as I am, Ron.

Sun at noon, tan us.

Lapses? Order red roses, pal.

NUDES & PRUDES

It's hard to shock anyone with nudity today. But stupidity is always a shock. These characters demonstrate that whether you're dressed or naked, you can still be dumber than sin.

NUDE…"Bernard Defrance, a high school teacher near Paris, told his students that each time they stumped him with a riddle, he'd shed a piece of clothing—starting with his trademark bow tie. As it turns out, the kids were too smart for him. During one round of the game in November, the 51-year-old Defrance was left standing naked before his class. He was later suspended."

PRUDES…"In 1934, eight men were fined $1 apiece for bathing 'topless' at Coney Island. 'All of you fellows may be Adonises,' said the presiding magistrate, 'but there are many people who object to seeing so much of the human body exposed.' A year later, a mass arrest of 42 topless males in Atlantic City, New Jersey, fattened the municipal coffers by $84. The city fathers declared: 'We'll have no gorillas on our beaches.' "

NUDE…"A 41-year-old Allentown man known to police as 'The Naked Bandit' pleaded guilty to robbing a string of convenience stores while in the nude, authorities said on Thursday. 'His logic was that the last time he did some robberies, he had clothes on and was identified by his clothes,' said Lehigh County District Attorney James Anthony." (Reuters)

PRUDES…"Matt Zelen dived into the pool to start the 100-yard butterfly, then remembered something: He'd forgotten to tie his racing suit. When the St. John's University junior felt his suit sliding off, he decided to kick it off and finish the race. Zelen, a contender for the 2000 Olympics, would have won the race by more than two seconds but he was stripped of more than just his suit—he was disqualified for violating a uniform code." (*Parade* magazine)

NUDE…"Police in Vinton, Louisiana, were bemused when a Pontiac Grand Am hit a tree and disgorged 20 nude occupants. It

In an average year, 46 million people from foreign countries visit the U.S.

turned out that they were the Rodriguez family, Pentecostalists from Floydada, Texas. Police Chief Douillard commented, 'They were completely nude. All 20 of them. Didn't have a stitch of clothes on. I mean, no socks, no underwear, no nothin'. Five of them were in the trunk. The Lord told them to get rid of all their belongings and go to Louisiana."

PRUDE…"The Mayor of North Platte, Nebraska, kept his promise to walk naked down the street. Mayor Jim Whitaker said he'd walk 'naked' if the Paws-itive Partners Humane Society raised $5,000. When his plan drew national attention—and angry calls— Whitaker revealed that he actually planned to walk a dog named 'Naked' instead of walking in the buff himself."

NUDE…"A bare-breasted mermaid perched on a rock is causing a stir along Lyse Fjord in Norway. 'One man jumped off a boat and swam over to me,' Line Oexnevad, 37, said of her job as a siren. 'Most people just look and cheer.' Ms. Oexnevad, naked except for a blonde wig and a fish-tail, was hired as a tourist attraction."

PRUDES…"At the turn of the century (1900, that is), Boston, Massachusetts, refused to accept shipments of navel oranges from Los Angeles, terming the fruit's name 'indelicate and immodest.'" ("Only in L.A.," the *Los Angeles Times*)

NUDE…"Police arriving at the scene of a two-car collision in Los Angeles found a totally nude woman behind the wheel of one car. The 35-year-old L.A. resident reportedly told police that when she began her drive, she thought she was a camel in Morocco, and when she saw the palm trees lining the downtown streets, she was sure of it…." (*Bizarre* magazine)

PRUDE…"Animal control workers in California recently received a call from a woman who insisted she needed to get a marriage license for a male and a female cat 'before they breed.'" ("Only in L.A.," the *Los Angeles Times*)

First person to appear on the cover of *Rolling Stone* magazine: John Lennon.

WORD GEOGRAPHY

Did you know that many words are taken from place names? Here are some examples, from a book called Toposaurus, *by John D. Jacobson.*

GHETTO
From: Il Geto, an island of Venice, Italy
Explanation: In 1516, the city fathers of Venice decreed that all of the city's Jews had to live on the island of Geto. The practice spread throughout Europe, and the Jewish quarters of all cities came to be known as *ghettos*. Today, however, a ghetto segregates people by income and ethnicity rather than by religion.

PARCHMENT
From: Pergamum, an ancient Greek city-state
Explanation: In 190 B.C., the residents of Pergamum, deprived of papyrus by an Egyptian cartel, developed a substitute. *Parchment*, a durable and highly portable writing surface, was produced from the skins of sheep, goats, and other animals. (Parchment is still used for some diplomas, and as a result we often refer to such documents as "sheepskins.")

BABBLE
From: Babylon (near Baghdad in modern Iraq)
Explanation: According to the Bible, the ancient people of Babylon once tried to build a mighty tower (the Tower of Babel) to reach the heavens. But the Lord was not happy with this and "confounded the tongues of the people that they might not understand one another's speech." The result provides us with the English word *babble*, a meaningless confusion of words and sounds.

COACH
From: Kocs, a small town in northwest Hungary
Explanation: The first horse-drawn *coach* was invented there in the 15th century. The use of these large passenger vehicles quickly spread throughout Europe, because they provided cheap transportation for commoners who couldn't afford their own conveyances. A century later, the word *coach* became synonymous with English university tutors, apparently because they, too, carried their students along, albeit educationally.

Marvel comics put a hyphen in Spider-Man's name so he wouldn't be confused with Superman.

BLARNEY

From: Blarney, Ireland

Explanation: In 1602, an Irishman by the name of Cormack McCarthy sweet-talked the British, who had encircled his castle (located in Blarney), into delaying its takeover indefinitely. McCarthy's verbal success subsequently resulted in the term *blarney*, meaning "smooth, flattering talk."

TARIFF

From: Tarifa, a Spanish seaport

Explanation: This southern port, a one-time Roman settlement, was controlled by African pirates during the Moorish occupation of Spain. The Mediterranean freebooters forced ships passing through the Straits of Gibraltar to pay duties, a form of blackmail that came to be known as a *tariff*.

COLOGNE

From: Köln, Germany

Explanation: In 50 A.D., this city was founded by the Romans and named Colonia Agrippina (Agrippina's Colony) because it was the birthplace of Agrippina, wife of the popular Roman general, Germanicus Caeser, and mother of the Emperor Caligula. The name of the city was later shortened to Colonnia. And while the German word for the city is now Köln, during its French occupation it was called *Cologne* and gave its name to the perfumed water produced there since 1709.

BALONEY

From: Bologna, Italy

Explanation: At one time this district was best known for its sausage which was of dubious quality. The original Bologna sausage was supposedly stuffed with odds and ends, such as chopped guts and seasoned ground meat. The perception that baloney sausage was inferior was transferred to anything worthless, nonsense, or pure *baloney*.

BAYONET

From: Bayonne, France

Explanation: According to tradition, a dagger called a *bayonet* was manufactured in that city in 1490. The name was later used for a knife that is attached to the muzzle of a rifle.

Double relief: Experts say that a belly laugh can help relieve constipation.

NIETZSCHE KNOWS

We don't only quote Madonna, you know. Here are some thoughts from the great 19th-century philosopher Friedrich Nietzsche (1844–1900).

"Insanity in individuals is something rare, but in groups, parties, nations, and epochs it is the rule."

"Love is a state in which a man sees things most decidedly as they are not."

"What does not destroy me, makes me strong."

"He who denies his own vanity usually possesses it in so brutal a form that he instinctively shuts his eyes to avoid the necessity of despising himself."

"Wishing is a symptom of recovery."

"After a quarrel between a man and a woman, the man suffers chiefly from the thought that he has wounded the woman; the woman suffers from the thought that she has not wounded the man enough."

"Perhaps I know why it is man alone who laughs; he alone suffers so deeply that he had to invent laughter."

"The surest way to corrupt a youth is to instruct him to hold in higher esteem those who think alike than those who think differently."

"No one lies so boldly as the man who is indignant."

"The author must keep his mouth shut when his work starts to speak."

"He who fights with monsters might take care lest he thereby become a monster. And if you gaze for long into an abyss, the abyss gazes also into you."

"How did reason come into the world? As is fitting, in an irrational manner, by accident. One will have to guess at it as at a riddle."

"There are no eternal facts, as there are no absolute truths."

"Morality is the best of all devices for leading mankind by the nose."

"My time has not yet come; some are born posthumously."

Goldfish were originally green; the Chinese bred them to be many different colors. Gold stuck.

THE POLITICALLY CORRECT QUIZ

As we've always contended, "political correctness" isn't as bad as it's made out to be—after all, there's nothing wrong with becoming more sensitive to people's feelings. On the other hand, people can get pretty outrageous with their ideas of what's "appropriate." Here are 8 real-life examples of politically correct—or "incorrect" behavior. How sensitive are you? Can you spot the "correct" one? (Answers on page 494.)

1. In 1994 cellist Anne Conrad-Antoville resigned from the Eureka Symphony Orchestra rather than perform *Peter and the Wolf*. Why?

a) "The story encourages cruelty to wolves."

b) "The suggestive overtones of the name 'Peter' should be obvious to everyone."

c) She wanted the part of Peter to be played by a girl, to show that females are "just as self-sufficient and strong as males."

2. New York Parks department officials became alarmed when they saw a picture of "Man & His Dog," a life-size bronze statue scheduled to be unveiled in a public park the following month. Why?

a) The dog was not on a leash.

b) His hind leg was lifted.

c) The man "did not appear to be wearing anything beneath his trench coat."

3. In 2000 a British state employment center removed words from its job ads. Which words…and why?

a) "Sober" and "nice smile" It didn't want to be seen as discriminating against substance abusers and people with bad teeth.

b) "Hard-working" and "energetic." It didn't want to be seen as discriminating against folks who aren't hard-working and energetic.

c) "Clean" and "pleasant." It didn't want to discriminate against people with poor hygiene.

4. In 1995 the board of Walworth County, Wisconsin changed the language of an antibigotry resolution. In the new language, the Ku Klux Klan was referred to as what?

a) "White-race enthusiasts" instead of "racists."

b) An "unhappy group" instead of a "hate group."

c) "Diversity challenged" instead of "bigoted."

5. In 1995 the Oxford University Press published *The New Testament and Psalms: An Inclusive Version.* How was it different from other versions?

a) All of the characters in the Bible and Psalms are described as "people of color" because they probably were.

b) All pets and livestock are referred to as "companion animals," so as not to offend animal rights activists.

c) All references to the right hand of God are omitted "so as not to offend the left-handed."

6. In the 1960s, the *Pittsburgh Press* refused to include what phrase in its obituaries?

a) "Died in his / her sleep."

b) "Please omit flowers."

c) "Next of kin."

7. Joseph Paul Franklin, who murdered more than a dozen people, objected on principle to the way he was characterized in the media. Which specific phrase did he object to?

a) "Serial Killer"

b) "Cold-blooded"

c) "Sociopath"

8. To avoid offending people, the city council of Longmont, Colorado voted to change the wording of a street sign. Which one?

a) "Dead End" ("too macabre") was changed to "No Outlet."

b) "Stop" ("too rude") changed to "Please Stop…Thank You!"

c) "No Right Turn" and "No Left Turn" ("too political") were changed to "No Turn."

Not only is Lake Titicaca the highest navigable lake in the world, it's also the most fun to say.

THE HISTORY OF THE IQ TEST, PART III

If you're really intelligent, you've already read Part II on page 195. Here's the darkest, ugliest part of the story. It may seem unbelievable…but it's all true, folks.

SPOILS OF WAR

Not long after the United States entered World War I in 1917, Robert Yerkes, the president of the American Psychological Association (and like many others in the history of the IQ test, a believer in eugenics) proposed that psychologists could contribute to the war effort by administering IQ tests to military draftees. The military approved the plan. Lewis Terman and other eminent psychologists set to work creating a standardized test they called "Alpha," which was then administered to the troops.

"The tests appear to have had little practical effect on the outcome of the war," Leon J. Kamin writes in *The Politics of IQ*. "They were not, in fact, much used for the placement of men. The testing program, however, generated enormous amounts of data, since some two million men were given standardized IQ tests."

There was enough raw data to keep statisticians busy crunching numbers in every conceivable combination for years to come.

BRIGHAM DUMB

One of the number crunchers was a Princeton University professor named Carl Brigham. For some reason he was completely focused on immigrants. In 1923, he published a book entitled *A Study of American Intelligence*, in which he analyzed the IQs of immigrants who'd been drafted during World War I. Brigham concluded, among other things, that immigrants who'd lived in the United States for 20 years or more tested just as intelligent as native-born Americans; but that immigrants who'd lived in the United States for five years or less scored poorly on IQ tests and were "essentially feeble-minded."

As Brigham saw it, intelligence was directly related to how long the immigrants had lived in the country. Immigrants who'd been in the country for 10 years tested more intelligent than immigrants who'd been in the country for 5 years, but less intelligent than immigrants who'd been in the country for 15 years.

Brigham used this information to conclude that newer arrivals to the United States were simply dumber. "We are forced to…accept the hypothesis," he wrote, "that the curve indicates a gradual deterioration in the class of immigrants examined in the army, who came to this country in each succeeding five-year period since 1902."

ANOTHER LOOK

That was one interpretation of the Alpha Test results. But the fact that the test was peppered with multiple-choice questions such as

> The Brooklyn Nationals are called the (1) Giants,
> (2) Orioles, (3) Superbas, (4) Indians

and

> Revolvers are made by (1) Swift & Co., (2) Smith &
> Wesson, (3) W.L. Douglas, (4) B.T. Babbit

…wouldn't it also be possible to conclude that the test was heavily biased in favor of people who (1) could read English, and (2) had lived in the country long enough to know the names of American baseball teams and handgun manufacturers? Was it possible that, instead of measuring innate human intelligence, the test was actually measuring literacy and familiarity with American mainstream culture?

Brigham rejected this possibility out of hand—he insisted that failure to answer the questions correctly was direct proof of an inferior IQ. He urged his colleagues to reject "feeble hypotheses that would make these differences [in intelligence] an artifact of the method of examining."

So why were newly arrived immigrants less intelligent than the ones who had been here a while? Brigham had an explanation for this—something he called the "race hypothesis:" Whereas, before 1890 the bulk of immigrants to the United States had come from England, Germany, and other "Nordic" countries, in recent years immigration patterns had shifted. The huge waves of immigrants from southern and eastern European countries, such as Italy and Russia, had come to be known in academic circles as the "New Immigration."

A 7.0 magnitude earthquake is 900 times more powerful than a 5.0 earthquake.

The Italians, Slavs, and Eastern European Jews that made up the New Immigration, Brigham concluded, must be innately less intelligent than the Dutch, English, and German immigrants who had preceded them. "Our test results," he wrote, "indicate a genuine intellectual superiority of the Nordic group."

AS IF THAT WEREN'T ENOUGH

Brigham also pointed out that, like southern and eastern Europeans, American blacks scored lower on IQ tests than American whites did. Once again, he dismissed the possibility that racism, segregation, lack of equal access to education, or the fact that slavery had ended barely 60 years earlier might have played a role in the low test scores. No—he was convinced that the IQ test proved that blacks were intellectually inferior to whites, and warned of what this meant for the future of the United States:

> We must face a possibility of racial admixture here that is infinitely worse than that faced by any European country today, for we are incorporating the Negro into our racial stock, while all of Europe is comparatively free from this taint….The decline of American intelligence will be more rapid than the decline of the intelligence of European national groups, owing to the presence here of the Negro.

THE IMMIGRANTS ARE COMING!

Brigham urged the government to take defensive action. But the idea of controlling who was allowed to immigrate to the United States was a relatively new concept. For most of the country's history, there were no federal laws regulating immigration. The first was in 1875, when three "classes" of people—"coolies," convicts, and prostitutes—were denied entry for the first time. Everyone else was admitted.

Then, in 1921, Congress passed a special law establishing "national origin quotas" for each foreign country. The law restricted each nationality to 3% of the number of nationals already living in the United States, with census figures from 1910 used to set the quota for each individual country. If 1,000,000 immigrants from France were counted in the 1910 census, for example, French immigration would be capped at 30,000 people per year. But that law was supposed to be a temporary measure.

THE GOOD OLD DAYS

That was before Brigham and a number of like-minded psychologists brought their "scientific" findings to the U.S. Congress. In 1924, a new, more severe bill called the Johnson-Lodge Immigration Act was passed into law.

The act made two major changes in U.S. immigration policy: it cut the quota for each country from 3% to 2%; and rather than use U.S. population figures from the just-completed 1920 census or even stick with the numbers from the 1910 census, the new law required that national quotas be calculated using numbers taken from the 1890 census. Why? According to Leon J. Kamin in *The Politics of IQ*:

> The use of the 1890 census had only one purpose, acknowledged by the bill's supporters. The "New Immigration" had begun after 1890, and the law was designed to exclude the biologically inferior peoples of southeastern Europe. The new law made the country safe for Professor Brigham's Nordics....[But] the law, for which the science of mental testing may claim substantial credit, also resulted in the deaths of literally hundreds of thousands of victims of the Nazi biological theorists. The victims were denied admission to the United States because the "German quota" was filled.

BACK TO SCHOOL

In the mid-1920s, colleges and universities began to hire Brigham and other IQ experts to administer intelligence tests to college applicants. But because college applicants were, on average, better educated than World War I draftees, their scores were so high that they tested off the Alpha Test's charts. So Brigham rewrote the questions to make them harder...and while he was at it, he renamed the test. From now on, it would be known as the Scholastic Aptitude Test, or SAT for short.

NOW HOLD ON A MINUTE

The very first SAT was administered for Princeton University, on June 23, 1926, to 8,040 high school students around the country. Soon afterward the Army decided to use the SAT to test applicants for West Point, and in 1930 it was used at the U.S. Naval Academy for the first time. From there it spread to Harvard, Yale, and then to other colleges in the Ivy League. By the mid-1930s, the SAT was well on its way to becoming a major factor in American college life.

Strange coincidence: Yoko Ono and Linda McCartney both attended Sarah Lawrence College.

There was one problem—Brigham had begun to question every-thing he believed about the "science" of intelligence testing.

"At the same time he was promoting the SAT to universities," Nicholas Lehman writes in *The Big Test*, "Brigham was undergoing a momentous intellectual change. He had come to the view that the central tenet held by IQ testers—that the test measured a bio-logically grounded, genetically inherited quality that was tied to ethnicity—was false."

Well, looks like we're not making IQ tests part of the BRI entrance requirements anymore.
So it's okay to turn to page 413 for Part IV.

*　　*　　*

ACCORDING TO THE LATEST RESEARCH... SUNLIGHT MAKES YOU A BETTER STUDENT

Researchers: An energy consulting firm in Orange County, California

Who They Studied: 21,000 students in California, Colorado, and Washington states.

What They Learned: Kids do better in school when they work in natural light than when they work in artificial light. Specifically: "Elementary students in classrooms with more natural illumination scored up to 26% higher on standardized tests in reading and up to 20% higher in math."

"No one knows for sure why sunlight has such a strong tie to stu-dent achievement, but the study's authors have some theories," the *Los Angeles Times* reported. "They believe that the light is a mood lifter for students and teachers alike. Sunlight might also boost overall health, and may make it easier for students to see their books and blackboards."

BOOP-OOP-A-DOOP!

If you're a cartoon fan but have never seen the original Betty Boop cartoons of the late 1920s and early 1930s, do yourself a favor next time you rent a movie: rent some Betty Boop cartoons, too. Here's a look at the origins of one of the earliest and most controversial cartoon "superstars." Boop-oop-a-doop!

BOUNCING ALONG

It was 1928. Grim Natwick had just landed a job at Fleischer Studios, an animation company famous for its "follow-the-bouncing-ball" sing-along cartoons. Founders Max and Dave Fleischer were hard at work trying to find a cartoon character to compete with Mickey Mouse, who had made his screen debut that year in "Steamboat Willie." The brothers' first attempt, "Bimbo the Dog," wasn't nearly as popular as Disney's mouse. They knew something was missing.

What if they gave him a girlfriend?

FIRST BOOP

As Natwick would recall years later, Dave Fleischer had an idea:

> One morning [he] came over to my desk and handed me the music to the [popular] song "Boop-Oop-A-Doop," by Helen Kane, and asked me to design a girl character to go with it. At that point, the only character the Fleischers had in their sound cartoons was Bimbo. So without bothering to ask if they wanted a human, I started drawing a little girl dog. I had a song sheet of Helen Kane and the spit curls came from her. I put cute legs on her and long ears. I suppose I used a French poodle for the basic idea of the character.

And drawing from his years of experience, Natwick also gave her something that few female cartoons had ever had before: genuine feminine curves. "Years of art school and night classes, drawing thousands of naked models," Natwick said. "I knew all the sexy angles and shapes, from the turn of the ankle to the shape of the heel of her shoe."

One more influence on the character's look: from their Times Square office, Natwick and the other animators "made careful observation of the exaggerated strutting of that neighborhood's ladies of the night," and incorporated their strut into the character.

What did actress Dolores Hart do after starring in two movies with Elvis? She became a nun.

RISING STAR

The as-yet unnamed female dog debuted in a cartoon called "Dizzy Dishes," in a supporting role as a dancer in a nightclub where Bimbo, the main character, was a waiter.

As usual, Bimbo did not light any fires with the audience. But his female costar was another story—audiences loved her…and Paramount Pictures, Fleischer Studio's distributor, quickly asked for more cartoons "with that girl in them."

When he realized how popular she was, Max Fleischer had the animators turn her into a human. "Somebody changed those ears into earrings," Natwick recalled nearly 60 years later. "Maybe I did. Everyone thought that as long as she looked like a girl anyway, let's just make her all girl." (Bimbo wasn't so lucky—he stayed a dog.)

And starting with the 1931 cartoon "Betty Coed," Betty Boop finally had a name.

RISQUE BUSINESS

Betty Boop may have been the Fleischers' answer to Mickey Mouse, but she was a world apart. Disney sought to entertain without offending anyone, creating characters and stories with not a *hint* of adult themes or controversy. In contrast, Natwick explained, "Betty was a suggestion you could spell in three letters: S-E-X. She was all girl."

Freak gusts of wind blew up her skirt, and stray branches tugged at her top. In the 1934 cartoon "Betty Boop's Rise to Fame," one of Betty's naked breasts is seen on film for a fraction of a second.

WOMAN OF THE WORLD

Betty Boop was one of the most successful cartoon characters of the early 1930s, not just in the U.S. but also all over the world. She had tremendous appeal for increasingly independent young women growing up in the 1930s. Luminaries such as Jean-Paul Sartre and Gertrude Stein were fans, and her likeness—stamped onto products as diverse as dolls, playing cards, nail polish, and cigarette cases—was one of the most mass-marketed images of the Depression era. Her cartoons also gave important exposure to jazz greats like Cab Calloway and Louis Armstrong, introducing their music to audiences who might never have heard it otherwise.

Armstrong's performance of "I'll Be Glad When You're Dead, You Rascal You" was one of his first screen appearances ever. However, it was just the musicians' voices that the Fleischers used—they actually made cartoon characters out of the singers, using a device called rotoscope. So next time you see the walrus ghost dancing in "Minnie the Moocher," (one of Betty's best cartoons), look a little closer—you're actually watching a performance by Cab Calloway.

HEAVENS TO BETTY!

Betty's innocent sexuality was her strongest drawing card, a fact that was unfortunately proven in the mid-1930s, when Paramount Pictures—under pressure from the Hayes office, Hollywood's official censor—told Fleischer Studios to clean up Betty Boop's act.

"Naturally," Fleischer historian Leslie Cabarga writes, "Betty was never the same." Betty's short, sleeveless, backless dress was replaced with a much longer dress with sleeves and a collar; her garter belt was never seen again. No longer a nightclub singer pursued by lecherous men, Betty was now portrayed as a schoolteacher, secretary, housewife, or babysitter; about the only man in her life was an elderly, protective professor named Grampy.

Whether or not censorship was to blame, by the end of the '30s the Betty Boop craze had run its course. Fleischer Studios ended the original series with "Yip Yip Yippy," released in August 1939.

*   *   *   *

BOOP-OOP-A-LAWSUIT

Raising Kane. One person definitely not a Betty Boop fan was the original "Boop-Oop-a-Doop" girl herself, singer Helen Kane. She was furious that Betty's success seemed to come at the expense of her own singing career. In April 1934, Kane filed a $250,000 lawsuit against Max Fleischer, alleging that Betty was "a deliberate caricature of me," and had robbed her of both her popularity and her livelihood by imitating her method of singing. Fleischer's strategy was to deny the obvious link between Kane and Betty.

But what decided the case in the Fleischers' favor was a film clip of a Black singer named Baby Esther singing a song containing the phrase "boop-oop-a-doop." Fleischer introduced testimony that Kane had heard Baby Esther sing back in 1928. That was covincing enough so the judge threw the case out of court.

The voice of Betty Boop, Mae Questel, was also Olive Oyl's voice...and occasionally Popeye's, too.

MYTH-UNDERSTANDINGS

Sometimes cultural "truths" are really only half-truths.

HIPPOCRATES

Myth: Hippocrates was the father of modern medicine.

The Truth: Thanks to the Hippocratic oath, which is still administered during the graduation ceremonies of many medical schools, the name of the ancient Greek physician has become virtually synonymous with the practice of medicine. He may have tried to heal people, but like all doctors of his era, Hippocrates knew virtually nothing about the workings of the human body. And almost all of what he did believe—for example "that veins carried air, not blood, and illness was caused by vapor secreted by undigested food from unsuitable diets"—was dead wrong.

"WAY DOWN UPON THE SWANEE RIVER..."

Myth: The song "The Old Folks at Home" was inspired by the Suwannee River in Florida.

The Truth: Although the Swanee River in the song *is* the one in Florida, Stephen Foster, who wrote the song, had never seen it. He was writing tunes for a minstrel show and asked his brother Morrison for the name of a Southern river with two syllables. Morrison suggested Yazoo, in Mississippi. Stephen didn't like that, so Morrison ran his finger down a map and came up with the Suwannee. Now it's the Florida state song.

TEDDY ROOSEVELT AND THE TEDDY BEAR

Myth: Teddy Roosevelt liked Teddy Bears. The tale of how the Teddy Bear got its name is legendary (and true): On a hunting trip, President Roosevelt refused to shoot a little bear that had been tied to a tree for him. A political cartoonist named Clifford Berryman depicted the incident in a cartoon, and a toymaker who saw the cartoon began selling stuffed bears as "Teddy's Bears." The cuddly bears became a fad.

The Truth: As the bears grew in popularity, Roosevelt came not

---

Whew! When Jerry Lewis wanted to make *Catcher in the Rye* into a film, J. D. Salinger said no.

only to hate Teddy Bears, but also to fear them. He was convinced that they were bad for children, and issued numerous statements attacking them as poor substitutes for human dolls.

"Take away the little girl's dolly," he warned in one diatribe, "and you have interfered with the nascent expression of motherhood. You have planted the race suicide where it will work the most harm—in the very arms of the babies themselves."

THE CIA

Myth: The CIA was meant to be America's top spy agency, policing the world and protecting American interests with elaborate clandestine activity.

The Truth: It may be a spy agency today, but, according to Jonathan Vankin in his book *Conspiracies, Coverups and Crimes*, that wasn't the original idea:

> The CIA was never meant to do its own spying. And it certainly wasn't meant to conduct clandestine operations. The original purpose of the CIA was to summarize and analyze information turned up by the other intelligence operations. It was a report-writing department.
>
> The CIA's one loophole is a fuzzy phrase in the 1947 law [that created the agency]. According to the bill signed by Truman, the Central Intelligence Agency would perform "other functions" at the discretion of the National Security Council. The language of the act is fairly specific. Those "other functions" relate only to intelligence. Nowhere does it mention clandestine operations. Even so, the "functions" clause has been the rationale for what has become a...government-sanctioned, secret society.

MORSE CODE

Myth: The dot-dash code for telegraphs is named after the code's creator, Samuel Morse.

The Truth: The code *is* named after Morse—actually, he named it after himself. But many historians think his collaborator, Alfred Vail, actually created it. Morse's original notes from 1832 suggest that he was planning a code that assigned each word in the dictionary a number. But six years later, someone came up with an alphabet code, using dots and dashes to signify letters. An apprentice, William Baxter, said it was Vail's innovation. But Morse insisted he'd done it, and history books simply take his word for it.

There really is a unit of time called a "jiffy." It's exactly 1/100th of a second.

VIDEO TREASURES

Some more BRI video recommendations.

LOCAL HERO (1983) *Comedy*
Review: "Burt Lancaster plays a Houston oil baron who sends Peter Riegert to the west coast of Scotland to negotiate with the natives for North Sea oil rights. This film is blessed with sparkling little moments of humor, unforgettable characters and a warmly human story." (*Video Movie Guide*) *Director:* Bill Forsyth.

INTO THE NIGHT (1985) *Drama*
Review: "Campy, offbeat thriller about a middle-aged, jilted deadbeat who meets a beautiful woman when she suddenly drops onto the hood of his car (with a relentless gang of Iranians pursuing her) and their search for the one person who can help her out of this mess." (*VideoHound's Golden Movie Retriever*) *Director:* John Landis.

BROADWAY DANNY ROSE (1984) *Comedy*
Review: "A New York talent agent, loyal to a stable of acts that would break your heart, promotes a bloated Sinatra-wannabe and gets mixed up with the Mob and the crooner's screeching mistress. A sweet screwball comedy that revisits the earlier world of Woody's little people." (*Seen That, Now What?*) *Director:* Woody Allen.

RUN, LOLA RUN (1999) *German/Drama*
Review: "A quick stop for cigarettes derails the normally prompt Lola, and now she has 20 minutes to save her boyfriend Manni. The movie mixes film, video, and animation to show how Lola's journey affects those she encounters during her mad dash. A flawless, 81-minute love story perfect for a generation raised on Sega and MTV." (*Roughcut Reviews*) *Director:* Tom Tykwer

THE SNAPPER (1993) *Irish/Comedy*
Review: "Wonderful adaptation of Roddy Doyle's novel about a working-class Irish family, and the teenage daughter who finds herself pregnant—with the circumstances too embarrassing to discuss. Vivid, funny, and believable, sparked by good performances." (*Leonard Maltin's Movie & Video Guide*) *Director:* Stephen Frears.

Paul Newman played Billy the Kid in *The Left Handed Gun*. One problem: Billy was right-handed.

POLITICALLY INCORRECT TOOTHPASTE

Next time you go to buy a tube of toothpaste, look at the packaging. See anything besides a pearly-white smile? If you'd been looking for some in the 1920s, you might have seen something dramatically different... and offensive. Here's the story of a formerly racist toothpaste.

TOOTHPASTE BLACKENS COLGATE'S REPUTATION

Darlie toothpaste, owned by Colgate-Palmolive, is one of the more popular toothpastes in Asia. But it has a little secret: Until recently, it was called "Darkie" toothpaste, and the package was adorned with an offensive logo of a minstrel man in blackface. Apparently the man who created it in the 1920s had come to the United States and seen Al Jolson in his "blackface" show. He was impressed with how white Jolson's teeth looked, and thought that image could sell toothpaste.

Stereotypes of this sort were not unusual in packaging before World War II. What was unusual was that Darkie's racist name and logo were still intact in 1985 when Colgate bought the brand from Hong Kong's Hawley & Hazel Chemical Co.

Just Business?

Here's where the story gets a little twisted. According to Alecia Swasy in her book *Soap Opera*, Colgate's arch-rival, Procter & Gamble, learned about the sale and immediately used it to their advantage. Both companies were releasing a tartar-control formula that year, and P&G decided to give itself an edge by hiring a public relations firm to surreptitiously leak information to activists and newspapers about Colgate's "racist" Asian brand.

The strategy worked. There was a storm of protest: stories and editorials in major newspapers, threats of boycotts, and even Eddie Murphy expressing his outrage on David Letterman's show. Colgate was perhaps unfairly attacked for a brand it had just purchased, but the attacks became more justified as the toothpaste giant dragged its feet on changing the name, apparently fearing a loss of business. Finally, nearly four years later, it announced that it was changing the name of Darkie to Darlie and making the man on the package an abstraction of indeterminate race.

The name change placated Western critics, who pointed out that the toothpaste actually sold better after the name change. What they didn't know, and apparently still don't, is that only the English was changed. The Cantonese name (*Haak Yahn Nga Gou*) stayed the same, and Chinese-language ads reassured users that, despite the cosmetic change to placate Westerners, "Black Man Toothpaste is still Black Man Toothpaste."

* * *

STRANGERS IN DENTIFRICE

Planning a trip to Asia? If you forget your toothpaste, you can buy a standard American brand like Crest, Colgate, or Pepsodent (they're everywhere). But if you're feeling a little adventurous, try one of the local brands. Many even have ads in English, so you'll know what you're getting...sort of.

• **Evafresh Spearmint Toothpaste (China)** "Is made of choice materials with scientific prescription. It does no harm to the animal and prevents the teeth from gum-boil..."

• **White Jade (China)** The Shanghai Toothpaste Company claims "Your teeth will be healthy and no usual oral disease can occur....It does no harm to animal, it for smokers quite well." They also make Bulb Poll brand for children, saying; "With fresh melon flavour... brushing teeth would be of interest for children."

• **Supirivicky Brand (Ceylon)** This herbal toothpaste promises to relieve "obnoxious odours, spongy gums, cough, vomiting, gripe, colic, and paralysis of tongue."

• **Heibao Toothpaste (Hong Kong)** For a mere $96 per tube, Heibao promises an even more profound rejuvenation: "You will find your hair loss to be reduced by up to 90%. You will look younger, move younger and feel younger TEN to FIFTEEN years back because your hair becomes darker (as your good old days) and thicker and most important of all, your organic systems will function at their best!...Suitable for all ages, sex and race without any bad side effect."

WORD GEOGRAPHY

Did you know that many words are taken from place names? Here are some examples, from Toposaurus, *by John D. Jacobson.*

BIKINI
From: Bikini Atoll, Pacific Marshall Islands

Explanation: On July 1, 1946, the United States detonated an atomic bomb as a test on the tiny atoll. Four days later, a French fashion designer, Louis Reard, introduced a very daring two-piece bathing suit.

Reard gave the name *bikini* to his creation because he suspected that it might have the same psychological effect on men that the A-bomb explosion had on the atoll.

HOOKER
From: Corlear's Hook on Manhattan Island

Explanation: The painted ladies of this district of old New York City were known as *hookers* in the early 19th century. Corlear's Hook was in the general vicinity of today's South Street Seaport. This hook-shaped piece of marshy land was later filled in by the shipbuilding industry that flourished there. (Note: Civil War General Hooker had nothing to do with the term.)

SELTZER
From: Niederselters (Lower Selters), Germany

Explanation: A source of naturally sparkling mineral water was found there in the mid-18th century. The name for this bubbly water first appeared as *Selterser Wasser* (Selters water), which was ultimately Anglicized and lowercased to *seltzer*.

NAUGAHYDE
From: Naugatuck, Connecticut

Explanation: *Naugahyde* was first produced in this manufacturing town in 1937. The word combines *Nauga*, the first element in Naugatuck, and *hyde* from hide, or animal skin. According to the *Oxford English Dictionary*, Naugahyde is a "fabric base coated with a layer of rubber or vinyl resin and finished with a grain like that of leather."

Good news: 13 boxes of jello are sold every second.

"IN GOD WE TRUST"

"And," as we say at the BRI, "in Uncle John, too."
Here's why this phrase is on every U.S. coin.

PENNIES FROM HEAVEN. In 1861, a Pennsylvania preacher named M. R. Watkinson wrote to Secretary of the Treasury Salmon P. Chase expressing his fear that future generations looking back on the Civil War era might see it as an unholy period in American history. "Would not," Watkinson asked, "the antiquaries of succeeding centuries rightly reason from our past that we were a heathen nation?" Watkinson came up a strange solution: For some reason, he felt the problem could be solved by invoking the name of the Almighty on U.S. coins.

In Coins We Trust. Secretary Chase, a pious man who reportedly liked to sit in his bath and read the Bible, thought it was a great idea…and took it upon himself to make it happen. "The trust of our people in God shall be declared in our national coins," he wrote to James Pollock, director of the U.S. Mint. "You will cause a device to be prepared without unnecessary delay with a motto expressing in the fewest and tersest words possible this national recognition."

Banking on God. Pollock suggested "One Country, Our God," but Chase preferred "Our God and Our Country," and "In God We Trust" (a popular Civil War battle cry inspired by the phrase "in God is our trust," from the fourth verse of the "Star Spangled Banner"). Chase ordered that one proposed new coin use the first slogan and another use the second. The first coin was never minted, but the second one (the 1864 two-cent piece) was…and by the turn of the century, "In God We Trust" was a standard feature on American coins. But the slogan wasn't mandated by law.

God and Money. In 1907, President Roosevelt felt concerns about linking God and money. So he had the phrase removed from the new $10 and $20 gold pieces being designed, which ignited a huge public controversy. Congress promptly passed a law *requiring* that "In God We Trust" be restored to all coins. Today, U.S. law requires that three inscriptions—"Liberty," "E Pluribus Unum," and "In God We Trust"—appear on every coin.

THE BIRTH OF TARZAN, PART II

Tarzan wasn't only an international superhero—he was also the corner-stone of an incredibly profitable business empire. (Part I is on page 185.)

CHECKS AND BALANCES

Burroughs was just getting started as an author, but his years of business experience, though financially disastrous, had given him a surprising amount of business savvy.

When the $400 check for his first story, *A Princess of Mars*, arrived from *All-Story* magazine in 1911, he noticed that the words "For All Rights" were typed on it. As far as Burroughs was concerned, he'd only sold the magazine the right to publish his story in *their magazine*—and for that matter, only once. "What other rights are there?" he wrote back before cashing the check (which would have implied that he accepted *All-Story*'s terms and was indeed signing over "all rights" to the story.) Few authors—let alone first-time authors with an unbroken, 15-year string of business and career failures—had the sense to ask that question.

OVER A BARREL

All-Story could not publish *A Princess of Mars* without Burroughs's consent, and after a flurry of correspondence, the magazine finally gave in. It sent Burroughs a letter agreeing that he would retain all rights to his characters and story after they published it once.

Refusing to cash that check until he'd won back the rights to his story—and then doing it again when he sold his first *Tarzan* story a few months later—were probably the most important business decisions of his entire career. They would earn him millions of dollars in the years to come. "Had Burroughs's innate genius not guided him at this crucial stage," Gabe Essoe writes in *Tarzan of the Movies*, "he would have had nothing to sell to film makers in later years."

In 1913, Burroughs made another smart move: he registered the name Tarzan as a trademark.

SHELF LIFE

Burroughs understood that the real money for Tarzan was in books, not magazines. Magazines disappeared from newsstands after only a month or two; but books might stay on the shelves for years. Now, armed with piles of fan letters and strong sales of the *Tarzan* issue of *All-Story* magazine, he pitched *Tarzan of the Apes* to book publishers.

They weren't interested. Every publisher Burroughs contacted turned him down, so he put the idea aside and signed up with a newspaper syndicator to publish his stories in newspaper serial form instead. It was a huge success—and convinced A.C. McClurg & Co., one of the publishers that had originally turned Burroughs down, to publish *Tarzan of the Apes* after all.

In the years to come, that first *Tarzan* novel would sell more than three million copies, earning a fortune for both Edgar Rice Burroughs and his publisher. But it was only the beginning: In his liftime, Burroughs would write 66 more novels, 26 of them *Tarzan* novels; and by the time he died in 1950, he'd sold more than 36 million books in 31 different languages all over the world. This made him the most successful author of the first half of the 20th century.

JACK OF ALL TRADES

Burroughs was more than just the most successful writer of his age: He was a pioneer in the art of marketing a character in every possible medium. After succeeding in magazines, newspapers, hardcover books (paperbacks had not been invented yet), and movies (see page 431), in 1932 Burroughs formed a radio division of his corporation. He created a 364-episode "Tarzan" radio serial that was sold to radio stations all over the country. (Burroughs's son-in-law, Jack Pierce—who played Tarzan in the 1926 film *Tarzan and the Golden Lion*—and his daughter, Joan Burroughs Pierce, provided the voices of Tarzan and Jane.)

In creating the "Tarzan" radio show, Burroughs actually "introduced the prerecorded radio show," Gabe Essoe writes. "Up to this time, all radio programs had been aired live. Tarzan's pioneering success in this field prompted a major trend toward 'canned' broadcasts."

The following year, Burroughs signed a deal with United Features Syndicate to create and distribute a "Tarzan" comic strip to newspapers. At its peak in 1942, the strip appeared in 141 daily papers and 156 Sunday papers around the world. Then in 1936, Burroughs took those same newspaper strips and relaunched them as comic books.

PUT A TARZAN IN YOUR TANK

Meanwhile, as Tarzan conquered one mass medium after another, Burroughs was busy licensing his hero's name and image to several hundred different manufacturers. They flooded the nation with hundreds of Tarzan products, including sweatshirts, wristwatches, masks and "chest wigs," candy, peanuts, bubble gum, trading cards, rubber toys, leg garters, bathing suits; and even Tarzan-brand coffee, bread, and gasoline. In Japan, *Tarzan* fitness magazine told people how to stay in shape just like Tarzan.

In 1939, Burroughs even founded the Tarzan Clan of America, which he hoped would one day rival the Boy Scouts. (It didn't.)

Perhaps the most interesting use of the Tarzan name was in 1928, when Burroughs subdivided the Southern California ranch estate he'd bought nine years earlier and began selling off parcels. On July 9, 1928, the U.S. Postal Service granted the former ranch its own post office and official recognition as a town, giving it the same name that Burroughs had bestowed upon it when he bought the property in 1919: Tarzana.

KING OF THE JUNGLE

Before Edgar Rice Burroughs came along, no one had ever tried to market a fictional character this way. For that matter, in creating so many different competing forms of the same character, Burroughs had done precisely the opposite of what the brightest business and marketing minds of his day would have recommended. Not just the inventor of one of the most enduring fictional characters of the twentieth century, he was also the inventor of an entirely new way of doing business, John Taliaferro writes in *Tarzan Forever*:

> Though marketing experts and syndication agents warned that Tarzan on the radio would compete with Tarzan in the comics or that serial motion pictures would steal audiences from feature motion

pictures, Burroughs was convinced that the total would exceed the sum of the parts. As he saw it, there was no such thing as overkill, and well before Walt Disney ever hawked his first mouse ears or Ninja Turtle "action figures" became film stars, Burroughs was already a grand master of a concept that would one day be known as multimedia....

In short order, Tarzan became a superhero, the first pop icon to attain global saturation. As such he was the forefather of Superman and more recent real-life marvels such as Michael Jordan. Before Tarzan, nobody understood just how big, how ubiquitous, how marketable a star could be.

Of course, without the successful series of films, Tarzan might never have become the mighty pop force he still is today.

The story of his film career begins on page 431.

*   *   *

GRAFFITI

Creative writing, from the hallowed walls of public restrooms across the country.

To kick the bucket is beyond the pail.

If voting could really change things, it would be illegal.

An elephant is a mouse drawn to government specifications.

WHO GIVES A DAMN ABOUT APATHY.

Add up the spinal column and get a disc count.

Reality is an illusion caused by lack of alcohol.

Democracy is letting the other fellow have your way.

When all else fails, read the instructions.

I used up all my sick days, so I'm calling in dead.

Democracy...three wolves and a sheep voting on what to have for lunch.

My boss has boots so shiny I can see my face in them.

A specialist is someone brought in at the last minute to share the blame.

I wish I were what I was when I was trying to become what I am now.

ATTACK OF THE MONKEY PEOPLE!

*Lock your door! Latch your window! Furry little primates
are headed for your town...and who knows what they'll
do next?!!! Here are a few reports from the field.*

JAPAN!

"Macaque monkeys are invading Japanese cities to ransack homes and stores for food. They're blamed for numerous incidents in which they've entered stores and taken candy bars, fruit, and vegetables right off the shelves. The cities of Hakone and Odawara built a $2 million preserve for the monkeys outside of the two cities to deter the urban attacks, but the monkeys apparently aren't interested."

—*Oregonian*

NEW YORK!

"A 66-year-old woman was waiting for a ride to church one Sunday morning when her doorbell rang. She looked out the window to see two rhesus monkeys standing on the porch, ringing her doorbell, knocking on the door, and trying to turn the doorknob." Police—who said the pair had escaped from their owner's house—were called to take them away.

—*Strange Tails*

PUNJAB, INDIA!

"The nothern Indian state of Punjab is opening a jail for *monkeys*. Wild monkeys—the alleged descendents of escaped laboratory monkeys—have been mugging women for their handbags and are terrorizing government officials. Once busted, the monkeys will be jailed until they are declared fit for release."

—*The Edge*

PENNSYLVANIA!

Becky Kelly found a monkey in a friend's backyard in Hollidaysburg, Pennsylvania took it home and put it in a cage. The monkey was ap-

---

There are two countries named Congo and they're right next to each other.

parently calm until the next day when, let out to play, it looked through a window and saw two men approach the house. "It went nuts," said another woman who lived in the house. The monkey grabbed a paring knife from the kitchen and a cigarette lighter and went on a rampage through the home for two hours, running and screaming and trying to flick the lighter on. It bit two women and used the knife to slice open bags of food in the kitchen cupboards, stopping to eat marshmallows, sugar, and bread. Police had to call in animal control officers to snare the animal."

—*Strange Tails*

TOKYO!

In Tokyo, monkeys have been swarming into orchards and swiping bushels of apples. The monkeys come well equipped…with plastic shopping bags."

—*The Edge*

AFRICA!

"A troupe of about 60 gorillas invaded the village of Olamze on the border with equatorial Guinea recently, after an infant gorilla was seized earlier in the day by a local hunter. Shortly before midnight the gorillas entered the village in single file, ignoring gunshots fired by villagers to scare them away. The next night they beat on doors and windows until the village chief ordered the hunter to release the baby gorilla. According to the Cameroon newspaper *L'Action*, the gorillas 'returned to the forest with shouts of joy, savouring their victory.'"

—*The Fortean Times*

*   *   *   *

WHERE ARE THEY HEADED NEXT?

Wild apes make sophisticated travel plans, says Dr. F. Sue Savage-Rumbaugh of Georgia State University. She studied pygmy chimpanzees, or bonobos, in the Congo and found that the monkeys head to different destinations…then meet at the end of the day at a specific spot chosen before they leave.

—*This Is True*

DUMB CROOKS

Here's proof that crime doesn't pay.

CONSUMER PROTECTION AGENCY

"Suspecting that a drug dealer had sold her counterfeit crack cocaine, Rosie Lee Hill complained to Pensacola, Florida, police. Good news: An investigating officer determined the two cocaine rocks were real. Bad news: Hill was arrested. She'd paid $50 for the drugs, she explained, but when she tasted them she thought they were baking soda."

—*Dumb Crooks*

NO BRAINS ALOUD

"A convict broke out of jail in Washington, D.C., then a few days later accompanied his girlfriend to her trial for robbery. At lunch, he went out for a sandwich. She needed to see him, so she had him paged. Police officers recognized his name and arrested him as he returned to the courthouse (in a car he'd stolen during lunch hour)."

—*Bizarre News*

OPEN-DOOR POLICY

"When clerk Lee Johnson of the Li'L Cricket store in Spartanburg, South Carolina, was robbed, he hit the silent alarm. A deputy sheriff responding to the alarm drove up, but apparently the robber didn't notice who it was. So Johnson asked if he could go out and tell the arriving 'customer' the store was closed. 'Sure,' the robber said. Johnson went to the door and let the deputy in to arrest Kim Meredith, 34, who was charged with armed robbery. 'This man needs to be on dumb crook news,' Johnson told reporters."

—*This Is True*

DOES THAT COME WITH A BENEFITS PACKAGE?

"Norman Hardy, Jr., 22, pleaded innocent in a Brattleboro, Vermont court, to charges of cocaine possession. Then he filled out a form requesting a public defender to represent him. Occupation? 'Selling drugs,' he wrote on the form. The judge granted the request for a public defender."

—*Associated Press*

Women blink nearly twice as much as men.

WHO WANTS TO BE AN IDIOT?

"Ms. Fareena Jabbar, 37, was arrested in Colombo, Sri Lanka, in October and charged with trying to pass a U.S. $1 million bill (a denomination that does not exist). Jabbar supplied a 'certificate of authenticity' signed by officials of the 'International Association of Millionaires.'"

—*News of the Weird*

BLIND JUSTICE

"David Worrell, 25, got a 12-year suspended sentence for his attempted bank robbery in London. Was the judge being soft on crime? No—he just didn't feel Worrell posed a significant threat to society. Worrell, a blind man, had tried to hold up a bank using his cane as a weapon. When he heard the police sirens outside, he panicked and ran smack into a door."

—*Oops!*, by Smith and Decter

SHOULD'VE PLED THE FIFTH

"Michael Carter was arrested for kidnapping and robbery in New Haven, Connecticut, though he insisted that he was innocent. When police officers asked him to return to the scene of the crime so witnesses could see him, Carter responded, 'How can they identify me? I had a mask on.'"

—*Oregonian*

PAPER TRAIL

"Three men in ski masks robbing a Rolling Hills Estates bank were in need of an empty bag for the money. So one of them emptied his bulging gym bag and filled it with cash. Among the gym bag's contents left behind on the bank floor: two traffic tickets bearing the robber's name and address. It only got worse. When the hold-up men couldn't start their getaway car, they jumped into another and sped away. Left behind in the disabled car were wallets with identification for two of them. Police gathered up the telltale papers and quickly tracked down the trio."

—*Only in L.A.*, by Steve Harvey

NOT-SO-DUMB JOCKS

Okay, okay. They're not all dumb. Here are some genuinely clever remarks from America's sports stars.

"I knew it was going to be a long season when, on opening day during the national anthem, one of my players turns to me and says, 'Every time I hear that song, I have a bad game.'"
—Baseball manager Jim Leyland

"I'm the most loyal player money can buy."
—Don Sutton

"Once you put it down, you can't pick it up."
—Pat Williams, NBA executive, *on Charles Barkley's autobiography*

"I thought I'd be shot or hung by the time I was 40 anyway, so it's no big deal."
—Bill Parcels, *on his 53rd birthday*

"It's called an eraser."
—Arnold Palmer, *on how to take strokes off your golf game*

"You win some, lose some and wreck some."
—NASCAR driver Dale Earnhardt

"It was a cross between a screwball and a change-up—a screw-up."
—Cubs reliever Bob Patterson, *on one that was hit out of the park*

"In 1962, I was voted Minor League Player of the Year. Unfortunately, that was my second year in the majors."
—Bob Uecker

"At first, I said, 'Let's play for taxes.'"
—Michael Jordan, *on playing golf with President Clinton*

"If he was on fire, he couldn't act as if he were burning."
—Shaquille O'Neal, *on Dennis Rodman's acting ability*

"[Tommy] Morrison proved that he is an ambidextrous fighter. He can get knocked out with either hand."
—Boxing expert Bert Sugar

"It's been a very good year. Excuse me, it's been a very fine year."
—Indy car driver Scott Pruett, *whose sponsor was Firestone*

Geography quiz: How many Great Lakes lie entirely within the U.S.? Just one—Lake Michigan.

ENGLISH AS SHE IS SPOKE

This is a great moment for Bathroom Readers—years ago we heard about a legendary guide to English that was so bad, it was hilarious. Well, we finally found a copy—and we're proud to present this excerpt to you.

In 1855 Senhor Pedro Carolino wrote and published *The New Guide of the Conversation in Portuguese and English*. Amazingly, Carolino knew *no English*—he did it all using a Portuguese-French phrase-book and a French-English dictionary. That may *sound* logical, but instead of creating a usable guide, Carolino ended up butchering the English language—inventing phrases like "I am pinking me with a pin." Even more amazing: it was used as a serious textbook in some foreign countries.

The English-speaking world first became aware of the book when a group of Tibetan tourists came to London in 1880 and tried to use *The New Guide* to carry on conversations. It quickly became known as a masterpiece of unintentional humor. Here are some excerpts from Carolino's "great experiment":

Familiar Phrases of English

"No budge you there."

"He laughs at my nose, he jest at me."

"Apply you at the study during that you are young."

"Dress your hairs."

"How do you can it to deny?"

"That are the dishes whose you must be and to abstain."

"Put you confidence at my."

"It pinchs me enough."

"This girl have a beauty edge."

"I am catched cold in the brain."

"I am pinking me with a pin."

"I dead myself in envy to see her."

"I take a broth all morning."

"I shall not tell you than two woods."

"Do no might one's understand to speak."

"Dress my horse."

"Where are their stockings, their shoes, her shirt and her petlicot?"

"The rose trees begins to button."

"One's find-modest the young men rarely."

"If can't please at every one's."

"Take that boy and whip him to much."

"We are in the canicule."

"Take care to dirt you self."

Norwegian Christmas tradition: Hide the brooms. Why? So witches can't find them, of course.

English Vocabulary

Of the Man

The brain
The brains
The fat of the leg
The ham
The inferior lip
The superior lip
The entrails
The reins

Defects of the Body

A blind
A lame
A bald
A left handed
An ugly
A squint-eyed
A scurf
A deaf

Properties of the body

Yawn
Good air
Sneesing
Ugliness
Mien
Action

Games

Foot-ball
Bar Gleek
Carousal
Pile
Mall
Even or non even
Keel

Objects of man

The boots
The buckles
The button-holes
The buskins
The lining
The wig
The morning-gown

Woman objects

The sash
The cornet
The pumps
The paint or disguise
The spindle
The patches
The skate

Kitchen Utensils

The skimming-dish
The potlid
The pothanger
The spunge
The spark
The clout
The jack
The draughts

Trades

Starch-maker
Coffeeman
Porkshop-keeper
Tinker, a brasier
Nailer
Chinaman
Founder
Lochsmith

Eatings

Some wigs
A chitterling sausages
A dainty-dishes
A mutton shoulder
A little mine
Hog fat
Some marchpanes
An amelet
A slice, steak
Vegetables boiled to a pap

Diseases

The scrofulas
The whitlow
The vomitory
The megrime

Quadruped's beasts

Lamb
Ass
Shi ass
Hind
Dragon
Young rabbit
Leveret
Ram, aries

Military objects

A frame of a cannon
The bait
An arquebuse
A baggage
The firepan
A cuirass
E kettle drum

Most visited mountain on earth: Mount Fuji, in Japan.

Familiar Dialogues *clean of gallicisms and despoiled phrases*

With a hair dresser

"Your razors, are them well?"

"Yes, Sir."

"Comb-me quickly; don't put me so much pomatum. What news tell me? all hairs dresser are news-monger."

"Sir, I have no heared any thing."

For to breakfast

"John bring us some thing for to breakfast.

"Yes, Sir; there is some sausages. Will you than I bring the ham?

"Yes, bring-him, we will cup a steak put a nappe clothe upon this table."

"I you do not eat?"

"How you like the tea."

"It is excellent."

"Still a not her cup."

To inform one'self of a person

"How is that gentilman who you did speak by and by."

"Is a German."

"Tongh he is German, he speak so much well italyan, french, spanish, and english, that among the Italyans, they believe him Italyan, he speak the frenche as the Frenches himself. The Spanishesmen believe him Spanishing, and the Englishes, Englisman."

"It is difficult to enjoy well so much several langages."

For to ride a horse

"Here is a horse who have a bad looks. Give me another; I will not that. He not sall know to march, he is pursy, he is foundered. Don't you are ashamed to give me a jade as like? he is undshoed, he is with nails up; it want to lead to the farrier."

"Your pistols are its loads?"

"No; I forgot to but gun-powder and balls. Go us more fast never I was seen a so much bad beast; she will not nor to bring forward neither put back."

"Strek him the bridle, hold him I the reins sharters. Pique strongly, make to marsh him."

"I have pricked him enough. But I can't to make march him."

"Go down, I shall make march."

"Take care that he not give you a foot kicks."

"Then he kicks for that I look? Look here if I knew to tame hix."

The French Language

"Do you study?"

"Yes, sir, I attempts to translate of french by portuguese."

"Do you know already the principal grammars rules?"

"I am appleed my self at to learn its by heart."

"Do speak french alwais?"

"Some times; though I flay it yet."

"You jest, you does express you self very well."

With a furniture tradesman

"It seems no me new."

"Pardon me, it comes workman's hands."

"Which hightness want you its?"

"I want almost four feet six thumbs wide's, over seen of long."

With a banker

"I have the honor to present you a ex-change letter, draw on you and endorsed to my order."

"I can't to accept it seeing that I have not nor the advice neither funds of the drawer."

"It is not yet happened. It is at usance."

"I know again the signature and the flourish of my correspondent; I will accept him to the day of the falling comprehend there the days of grace, if at there to that occasion I shall received there orders."

"In this case, I not want of to do to protest it."

"It can to spare him the expenses of the protest."

"Will you discharge this other trade what there is it? It is payable to the sight."

"Yes I will pay it immediately, I go to count you the sum."

"Would you have so good as to give me some England money by they louis?"

"With too much pleasure."

With a gardener

"What make you hither, Francis?"

"I water this flowers parterre."

"Shall I eat some plums soon?"

"It is not the season yet; but here is some peaches what does ripen at the eye sight."

"It delay me to eat some walnut-kernels; take care not leave to pass this season."

"Be tranquil, I shall throw you any nuts during the shell is green yet."

Idiotisms and Proverbs

"The necessity don't know the low."

"Few, few the bird make her nest."

"He is not valuable to breat that he eat."

"Its are some blu stories."

"There is not any ruler without a exception."

"A horse bared don't look him the tooth."

"Take the occasion for the hairs."

"To do a wink to some body."

"There is not better sauce who the appetite."

"Which like Bertram, love hir dog."

"It want to beat the iron during it is hot."

"He has a good break."

"It is better be single as a bad company."

"The stone as roll not heap up not foam."

"They shurt him the doar in face."

"He turns as a weath turcocl."

"Take out the live coals with the hand of the cat."

THE GAME OF UNO

Have you ever played the game of Uno? It's consistently been one of America's best-selling toys. Here's where it came from.

INVENTED BY: Merle Roberts, a barber from Cincinnati, Ohio

ORIGIN: In the 1960s Roberts created a simplified version of crazy eights, and sold it both out of the trunk of his car and at Kiwanis conventions. That might well have been all there is to write about it…if a neighbor hadn't played the game with an acquaintance named Bill Apple. Apple, in turn, showed the game to his brothers-in-law Bob Tezak and Ed Ackeman, on Thanksgiving Day in 1971.

"It was miserable weather that weekend so we just played game after game," Tezak recalls. He and Ackeman enjoyed it so much that they talked Apple into buying it. "We paid Roberts in the neighborhood of $100,000 for all rights to the game, which in 1972 was a considerable amount of money," Tezak says. "I got a lot of strange looks, but I did it. At the time I didn't know any better."

SELLING IT: Tezak was a florist and funeral home director. The trio set up shop in back room of his family's funeral parlor while Ackeman took a two years' leave of absence from his job as a bank teller to develop and sell UNO. In their first year of business, they sold 5,000 games and made $54 in profits—which they split three ways.

Their big break came in 1977, when Tezak made a sales presentation at the Wal-Mart headquarters in Bentonville, Arkansas. "I can see this guy isn't about to place an order," Tezak remembers, "but I'm still making my pitch when Wal-Mart's founder Sam Walton walks in and says, 'How ya' doin', son?' So I told him about UNO. When I got done, he was quiet for awhile. Then he said, 'Buy a couple gross from the boy.' That made us. What Wal-Mart buys, everybody buys."

Since then, UNO has sold more than 100 million decks, making it the #1 card game in the world (after playing cards).

He did kiss the sky: Jimi Hendrix made 26 jumps with 101st Airborn Paratroopers in 1961.

POLI-TALKS

Politicians aren't getting much respect these days—but then, it sounds like they don't deserve much, either.

"I think that the free-enterprise system is absolutely too important to be left to the voluntary action of the marketplace."
—Rep. Richard Kelly (R-Fla.)

"If a frog had wings, he wouldn't hit his tail on the ground."
—George Bush, on unemployment benefits

"I make my decisions horizontally, not vertically."
—Sen. Bob Kerry (D-Neb.)

"I hope that history will present me with maybe two words. One is peace. The other is human rights."
—Jimmy Carter

"The streets are safe in Philadelphia, it's only the people who make them unsafe."
—Frank Rizzo, mayor of Philadelphia

"If we don't watch our respective tails, the people are going to be running the government."
—State Sen. Bill Craven (R-Ca.), on state initiatives

"Democracy used to be a good thing, but now it has gotten into the wrong hands."
—Sen. Jesse Helms

"I don't see why the legislature should be in the business of artificial intelligence, real intelligence or any intelligence at all."
—Rep. Hunt Downer (D-La.)

"A zebra cannot change its spots."
—Al Gore

"Rarely is the question asked: Is our children learning?"
—George W. Bush

"We, as Republicans, need to start rowing with one oar."
—Rep. John Kasich (R-Ohio)

"I haven't committed a crime. What I did was fail to comply with the law."
—David Dinkins, former New York City mayor

"I don't have the brains for business. I want to go into politics."
—Mao Xinyou, grandson of Mao Zedong

FROM THE HUNNY JAR

Words of wisdom from Winnie the Pooh.

"Rivers know this: There is no hurry. We shall get there."

"To the uneducated, an A is just three sticks."

"When going 'round a spinney of larch trees Tracking Something, be sure it isn't your own footprints you are following."

"You can't stay in your corner of the forest waiting for people to come to you. You have to go to them sometimes."

"When you are a Bear of very little brain and you think of things, you find sometimes that a thing which seems very thing-ish inside you is quite different when it gets out into the open and has other people looking at it."

"Sometimes, if you stand on the bottom rail of a bridge and lean over to watch the river slipping slowly away beneath you, you suddenly know everything there is to be known."

"One advantage of being disorderly is that one is constantly making exciting discoveries."

"Those who are clever, who have a brain, never understand anything."

"If you secretly get into a kangaroo's pocket, and she begins to jump away, be prepared for a bumpy ride."

"Before beginning a Hunt, it is wise to ask what you are looking for before you begin looking for it."

"When you fall on somebody, it's not enough to say you didn't mean to, after all, he probably didn't mean to be underneath you."

"When having a smackerel of something with a friend, don't eat so much that you get stuck in the doorway trying to get out."

"It gets you nowhere if the other person's tail is only just in sight for the second half of the conversation."

"Don't underestimate the value of Doing Nothing, of just going along and not bothering."

TOO CLOSE FOR COMFORT

What happens when the real world intrudes into the fantasy world of movies and TV? It happens every now and then—some tragedy in the real world is a little too close to something on the screen....People get very uncomfortable, and a change is made. For example:

TAKE HER, SHE'S MINE (1963)

Background: The film, a romantic comedy starring Sandra Dee, contained one scene in which a character spoke to Jackie Kennedy on the phone...and two scenes in which one of the characters spoke in a voice that sounded like President John F. Kennedy.

Too Close for Comfort: The film opened on November 16, 1963 ...and President Kennedy was assassinated six days later. The studio immediately recalled all of the 350 prints in distribution, cut out the scene with Jackie Kennedy, and dubbed a new voice to replace the one that sounded like President Kennedy.

PROMISED LAND (1999)

Background: In 1999 the TV series, a drama set in Colorado and starring Gerald McRaney and Wendy Phillips, was in its third season. One of the episodes CBS was planning to run featured a shooting at a school.

Too Close for Comfort: Eerily, two days before the episode was scheduled to air, two students shot up Columbine High School in Colorado, killing 15 people. CBS pulled the episode.

SMALL SOLDIERS (1998)

Background: The film, about toy soldiers who come to life and start a war in an Ohio town, starred comedian Phil Hartman as the father of the boy who owns one of the soldiers.

Too Close for Comfort: The film was scheduled to open on July 10, 1998...and on May 28, 1998, Phil Hartman was shot and killed by his wife in a murder-suicide. Dreamworks quickly re-edited the

---

95% of the population of Egypt live within 12 miles of the Nile River.

film so that none of the soldiers are shown pointing their guns at Hartman, and removed a scene in which he says, "I think I'm having an aneurysm."

THE GREATEST AMERICAN HERO (1981)

Background: The lead character in the ABC series was named Ralph Hinkley. He finds a superhero suit with magical powers, but can't get it to work properly because he lost the instruction manual.

Too Close for Comfort: On March 30, 1981, 25-year-old John Hinkley, Jr., shot President Ronald Reagan. *Greatest American Hero* was already halfway through the broadcast season, but ABC officials decided to change Ralph Hinkley's name to Ralph Hanley. They didn't explain the change to the audience. They simply dubbed "Hanley" over "Hinkley." Eventually, the character's name was changed back to Hinkley—again with no explanation.

FOR GOODNESS SAKE (1994)

Background: *For Goodness Sake* was a 24-minute-long "corporate and educational training film promoting morality and ethical values" that was produced by a company called Mentor Media in 1994. The film featured a series of cameo appearances by Hollywood stars.

Too Close for Comfort: One of the stars featured was O.J. Simpson. When he was arrested for murder on June 17, 1994, Mentor Media quickly cut his two-minute scene from the film. But that move was protested by a group called "the Micah Center for Ethical Monotheism," which questioned the morality of removing Simpson, "because that would be like passing judgment on him." So Mentor made both versions of the film available to customers... and the one with Simpson sold better than the one without him.

*   *   *

A GROANER

The flood was over, and Noah told the animals to go forth and multiply. Two snakes remained on the ark, however. "Why aren't you going forth and multiplying?" asked Noah.

One replied, "Because, silly man, we're adders."

Q & A:
ASK THE EXPERTS

*Here are some more random questions, with answers
from books by some of the nation's top trivia experts.*

HE'S LATE, HE'S LATE...

Q: *How does a magician pull a rabbit out of a hat?*

A: "The magician's table is draped with a cloth to prevent
the audience from seeing a small shelf at the back of the table,
upon which the bunny sits, wrapped in a large handkerchief. At
the outset of the trick, the magician removes his hat and displays
the inside—empty. Then he sets it, brim down, near the back of
the table. While waving his wand with his right hand, he grasps
both the brim of the hat and the corners of the handkerchief with
his left. With a swift, graceful—and unseen—move, he turns over
the hat. The bundle drops into the hat and with another wave of
his wand—presto, he raises the rabbit into the air." (From *More
How Do They Do That?*, by Caroline Sutton and Kevin Markey)

VISUAL MATHEMATICS

Q: *When you close one eye, is your sight reduced by half?*

A: "No. There's considerable overlap in the range of vision of
each eye. When an eye is lost, sight is reduced by about 20%."
(From *1,000 Facts Someone Screwed Up*, by Deane Jordan)

ORANGE YA GLAD?

Q: *What's the difference between Florida and California oranges?*

A: "They're the same species of orange—*Citrus sinensis*. The differences are a result of climate, not botany.

"California oranges *look* more like oranges because the California nights get much cooler than Florida nights. Oranges are a
winter–early spring crop, and need a little nip in the night air to
develop full coloration. They do not ripen once they are picked.

"Because Americans prefer orange oranges, Florida growers
either color their oranges or sell them for juice. Florida oranges

---

Not much of a harvester: the harvest rat spends 22 hours a day looking for food.

are plumper, juicier, and thinner-skinned than California oranges due to the moist subtropical climate. The drier, thicker-skinned California fruits are generally sold as eating oranges. Since there is a greater demand for juice oranges, Florida's production far exceeds California's. Oranges are also grown commercially in Texas and Arizona." (From *Why Does Popcorn Pop?*, by Don Voorhees)

SOLID GOLD

Q: *What is "24-carat" gold?*

A: "A carat is a unit of measurement. In gold, a carat equals one-twenty-fourth part.

"Because pure gold is a very soft metal, it is frequently mixed with other metals, known as alloys, to give it greater strength and durability. Copper and silver are most often used as gold alloys. The amount of alloy added to the gold affects its color as well as its strength, with copper lending a deeper yellow or red hue, and silver giving a lighter appearance.

"If a piece of jewelry is 18 parts gold and 6 parts alloy, we say it is 18-carat gold; if it has 14 parts of gold to 10 parts of another metal, we say it is 14-carat gold. 24-carat is *pure* gold." (From *A Book of Curiosities*, by Roberta Kramer)

SAY CHEESY

Q: *What's the orange stuff on Cheetos?*

A: "It's a combination of various dyes and seasonings, and it's the only part of Cheetos that has any cheese whatsoever in it. The main part of these snacks is cornmeal, with whey and oil added, mixed into a dough, then squeezed out into a long worm shape by an extruder. When the dough meets the cooler air, it sort of explodes or puffs like popcorn. Blades cut it into bite-sized pieces, which are then fried.

"From there, the pale white morsels are shaken in colored and flavored powder. Real cheese, Yellow No. 6, annatto, and turmeric give the pieces that cheesy effect. A little more salt and vegetable oil are added for sticking power and flavor. Despite rumors, the powder coating is not toxic, but because it's brightly colored and relatively loose, it can be lethal to furniture and clothes." (From *Just Curious, Jeeves*, by Jack Mingo and Erin Barrett)

First president to have a "First Cat" at the White House: Abraham Lincoln.

"LAST KISS"

*There's a whole genre of rock known as "Disaster music." It usually
involves somebody dying...and somebody feeling really bad about it.
For some reason, the most consistently popular of these songs is a
grisly tale of a teenage car wreck; it's been a hit in three different
decades. A few years ago, Uncle John started wondering who
wrote this song...and why. He stuck with it until he found
R&B singer Wayne Cochran (he was a preacher by then)
in Florida. Here's the story Cochran told him.*

LIVING ON THE ROAD

In the 1950s, Wayne Cochran lived in a $20-a-month
shack on Route 1941 in Georgia. It was a main highway, and
he saw more than his share of auto accidents in the time he lived
there. One day he decided to write a song about them; in a half an
hour he composed the first half, but he wasn't sure how to finish it.
The inspiration came from a real-life tragedy.

Fifteen miles away, in Barnesville, Georgia, a young girl named
Belinda Clark went out on her very first date. She and her boyfriend and two other couples took off in a 1954 Chevy Impala, with
Belinda sitting in the middle of the front seat. It was sort of foggy
that night, and as the group approached a fork in the road, they
couldn't see that a flatbed truck was stalled in front of them. They
ran right under the truck. The accident was so gory that when a
man from a nearby gas station came to help take the bodies away,
he didn't recognize that one of the victims was his own daughter.

The emotional response in the community was intense, and
Wayne suddenly found that he could describe an entire accident
scene. So he finished his song and dedicated it to Belinda Clark.
He called it "Last Kiss" because that was the dramatic high point of
the song, and besides, there was a hit record called "Last Date" on
the charts at the time.

A LOCAL HIT

Wayne sang it around town, and people liked it. So he recorded it
for a tiny record label called Gala Records. Their method of distributing the record wasn't very sophisticated: they drove around and

sold it out of the trunks of their cars. Miraculously, it hit #1 in Georgia. But with that level of distribution, Gala couldn't do much more with it.

Later, Cochran signed with the much larger King Records (the label James Brown recorded on) and in 1964 they did a new version of the song. But Syd Nathan, King's owner, wouldn't promote it. Instead, a Texas promoter heard the song and did a version with a local band called J. Frank Wilson and the Cavaliers. On Josie Records, it reached #2 in the nation. When Cochran saw in Billboard that his song was a hit, he marched into Nathan's office. "Why didn't you promote 'Last Kiss'?" he asked. "Because it was a junk record. It shouldn't have been put out," Nathan replied. "Well then, why is it selling so many copies?" Cochran asked, showing Nathan the magazine. Nathan couldn't believe it.

J. Frank Wilson and the Cavaliers had a multimillion-selling, Top 5 record with "Last Kiss." Then it was revived in Canada by a group called Wednesday in 1975, and reached #1 there. And in 1999, Pearl Jam had their biggest single, a Top 5 version of the same tune.

Note: when Uncle John talked with Cochran, Wayne commented that he'd lost the Gold Record that had been presented to him for writing a million-seller back in 1964. "If you talk to anyone from the RIAA (Record Industry Association of America), ask them if I can get a replacement," he said. Well, we don't know if he's gotten a new one (maybe for Pearl Jam's version?), but if anyone reading this works in the record industry, maybe you can check for us. Thanks.

*　　*　　*　　*

Another Disaster Song:

After Teen Angel has been run over by a train (in the famous 1959 hit record by Mark Dinning), her boyfriend cries:

"What was it you were looking for that took your life that night?
They say they found my high school ring clutched in your fingers tight."

FOOD SUPERSTITIONS

What can you do with food, besides eat it? Use it to drive evil spirits away, of course. People once believed in these bizarre rituals.

"Sprinkle pepper on a chair to ensure that guests do not over-stay their welcome."

"If cooking bacon curls up in the pan, a new lover is about to arrive."

"Eating five almonds will cure drunkenness."

"If the bubbles on the surface of a cup of coffee float toward the drinker, prosperous times lie ahead; if they retreat, hard times are promised."

"Cut a slice from the stalk end of a banana while making a wish. If a Y-shaped mark is re-vealed, the wish will come true."

"Feed red pistachio nuts to a zombie—it will break his trance and allow him to die."

"When a slice of buttered bread falls butter-side-up, it means a visitor is coming."

"Put a red tomato on the windowsill—it scares away evil spirits."

"If bread dough cracks during baking, a funeral is imminent."

"It's lucky to see two pies, but unlucky to see only one."

"A wish will come true if you make it while burning onions."

"Feeding ground eggshells to children cures bedwetting."

"Stirring a pot of tea stirs up trouble."

"It's bad luck to let milk boil over."

"Bank up used tea leaves at the back of the fire to ward off pover-ty."

"If you find a pod with nine peas in it, throw it over your shoulder and make a wish. It will come true."

"Finding a chicken egg with no yolk is unlucky."

"If meat shrinks in the pot, your downfall is assured. If it swells, you'll experience prosperity."

"Beans scattered in the corners of a home will drive out evil spirits."

"It is unlucky to say the word salt at sea."

A PROVERB BY ANY OTHER NAME...

Here are a dozen familiar proverbs—things like "A rolling stone gathers no moss"—except they're virtually unrecognizable, because they've been translated into the most obtuse language possible. Can you figure out what they're supposed to be saying? From Take My Words, *by Howard Richler. Answers are on page 495.*

1. "If you retire with canines, you're prone to commence the next day alongside wingless blood-sucking insects of the order *Siphonaptera*."

2. "Exist and let your fellow Homo sapiens continue to be."

3. "Consolidation affects erection of our personhood, whereas bifurcation affects our declension."

4. "One-sixteenth of a pound of prophylactic is equivalent to sixteen ounces of alleviation."

5. "While sugary condiments provide supereminence, it must be admitted that fermented grain provides greater celerity."

6. "Never under any circumstance scrutinize the mastication orifice of a gratuitous herbivorous quadruped."

7. "Pulchritude does not extend beyond the profundity of the epidermis."

8. "Show extreme caution to those of Hellenic persuasion who are transporting goods for disposal on a noncharge basis."

9. "Habitual or customary performance of what you advise in your homilies is advisable."

10. "Penniless solicitors should not be expressing existential imperatives."

11. "Just because one can engage in accelerated locomotion does not imply that one will be successful in concealing one's precise location."

12. "He who administers to the somatic ailments of mankind should be applying balm to his own personhood."

Easy to remember: Alaska's state flower is the forget-me-not.

JOIN THE CLUB

*You've heard of these organizations—you might even be
a member of a few. Here's where they came from.*

T HE LEAGUE OF WOMEN VOTERS
Founded by: Carrie Chapman Catt, a leader of the womens'
suffragist movement, in 1919.

History: The League of Women Voters is an outgrowth of the National Woman Suffrage Association (NWSA), a 2 million-member women's organization formed in 1890 to push individual states to ratify suffrage amendments. Catt and her cronies believed that if enough states passed their own amendments giving women the right to vote, Congress would be forced to approve a federal amendment.

It worked. After more than 72 years of struggle, the 19th Amendment was added to the U.S. Constitution on August 26, 1920. Catt addressed the final NWSA convention. She suggested that rather than disband, they should alter their mission to educating women about the electoral process, and encouraging them to vote. The members agreed, and the League was born.

Today the League is a non-partisan organization with a focus on voter registration and voter education.

THE YOUNG MEN'S
CHRISTIAN ASSOCIATION (YMCA)

Founded by: George Williams, a self-described "careless, thoughtless, swearing young fellow" who converted to Christianity while working in the London clothing trade in the 1840s.

History: At a time when there were few recreational opportunities in the cities "other than saloons and brothels," Williams gathered together a group of like-minded religious young men who began meeting regularly for prayer and reflection; in 1844 this group became the first local YMCA.

For the first 45 years of its existence the YMCA was primarily a missionary group with a focus on "saving souls, with saloon and street corner preaching, lists of Christian boarding houses, lectures, libraries and meeting halls, most of them in rented quarters." (It wasn't until 1889 that the organization began to promote physical fitness.) The YMCA stood out in its time because it ignored the rigid lines that separated class from class, and church from church, in 19th century England. It grew fast. By the 1850s the group was in seven countries, with 397 branches.

Sidelight: If you read *Uncle John's Absolutely Absorbing Bathroom Reader*, you know the story of how the YMCA invented basketball in 1891. Here's another tidbit: By 1895, it was clear that basketball was too strenuous for some businessmen. So William G. Morgan, physical director of the Holyoke, Massachusetts YMCA invented a game called "mintonette." Like basketball, it could be played indoors during the cold winter months—but it wasn't as physically demanding. The name of the game was eventually changed when "a professor from Springfield college, noting the volleying nature of play, suggested calling it 'volleyball.'"

THE AMERICAN SOCIETY FOR THE PREVENTION OF CRUELTY TO ANIMALS (ASPCA)

Founded By: Henry Bergh, a philanthropist and diplomat from a wealthy shipbuilding family

Origin: Bergh, aka "The Great Meddler," was known "for using his walking stick to upbraid peddlers who beat their horses on city streets." He wasn't a conventional animal rights proponent—it was cruelty he detested more than anything else. (He later started the Society for the Prevention for Cruelty to Children.) When he founded the ASPCA in 1866, it was the first humane society in America.

Within a year, the ASPCA succeeded in prodding the New York Legislature to pass the country's first anti-cruelty law. The following year Bergh established an ambulance service for New York City's injured work horses, a full two years before Bellevue Hospital set up the world's first hospital ambulance service for humans. Bergh is also credited with developing and popularizing the clay pigeon in the 1870s, to discourage the sport shooting of real pigeons which was popular at the time.

During his lifetime, thirty-four states passed animal rights legislation.

More people are killed by donkeys every year than are killed in plane crashes.

SIGNS O' THE TIMES

Sometimes communication can be difficult...even in your native language. Here are actual signs posted across America.

At a Florida maternity ward:
No Children Allowed

At a Santa Fe gas station:
We will sell gasoline to anyone in a glass container.

At a radiator-repair garage:
Best place to take a leak.

At a Maine shop:
Our motto is to give our customers the lowest possible prices and workmanship.

In a Pennsylvania cemetery:
Persons are prohibited from picking flowers from any but their own graves.

At many military bases:
Restricted to unauthorized personnel.

At a long-established New Mexico dry cleaner:
38 years on the same spot.

In the offices of a loan company:
Ask about our plans for owning your home.

On a New York convalescent home:
For the sick and tired of the Episcopal Church.

In the window of a Kentucky appliance store:
Don't kill your wife. Let our washing machine do the dirty work.

In a funeral parlor:
Ask about our layaway plan.

In a Maine restaurant:
Open 7 days a week and weekends.

In the vestry of a New England church:
Will the last person to leave please see that the perpetual light is extinguished.

At a Los Angeles dance hall:
Good clean dancing every night but Sunday.

On a shopping mall marquee:
Archery tournament—ears pierced.

In a clothing store:
Wonderful bargains for men with 16 and 17 necks.

On a roller-coaster:
Watch your head.

On a Tennessee highway:
When this sign is under water, this road is impassable.

Population explosion: 127 runners ran the N.Y. Marathon in 1970. In 1998, 32,000 did.

OLDER & WISER

Some observations about aging from people who should know. They're from the book Older & Wiser, *by Gretchen B. Dianda and Betty J. Hofmayer.*

"Growing old is like being increasingly penalized for a crime you haven't committed."
—**Anthony Powell,
English author, at age 68**

"If you rest, you rust."
—**Helen Hayes, at age 88**

"I still have two abiding passions. One is my model railway, the other—women. But, at the age of 89, I find I am getting just a little too old for model railways."
—**Pierre Monteux,
French conductor, at age 89**

"The French are true romantics. They feel the only difference between a man of 40 and one of 70 is 30 years' experience."
—**Maurice Chevalier,
at age 70**

"I used to dread getting older because I thought I would not be able to do all the things I wanted to do, but now that I am older, I find that I don't want to do them."
—**Lady Nancy Astor,
at age 80**

"I'm celebrating my 75th birthday, which is sort of embarrassing because I'm 85."
—**Victor Borge, at age 85**

"I cut my own hair, now. I got sick of barbers because they talk too much. And too much of their talk was about my hair falling out."
—**Robert Frost, at age 88**

"I'm having a glorious old age. One of my greatest delights is that I have outlived most of my opposition."
—**Maggie Kuhn,
organizer of the
Gray Panthers, at age 86**

"Nobody grows old by merely living a number of years. People grow old only by deserting their ideals."
—**Douglas MacArthur,
at age 65**

"The lessons of life amount not to wisdom but to scar tissue and callus."
—**Wallace Stegner, at age 67**

"Hold every moment sacred."
—**Thomas Mann, at age 64**

THE STORIES BEHIND THE STORIES

Here are the origins of three classic children's books.

PIPPI LONGSTOCKING

Inspiration: A sick child's imagination…and a broken ankle.

How it Became a Book: In the early 1940s a young girl named Karin Lindgren fell ill with pneumonia and had to spend several days in bed. Her mother, a 38-year-old office worker, took some time off to care for her.

As Astrid Lindgren recounted many years later, her ailing daughter made an unusual request:

> Karen asked me to tell her about Pippi Langstrump [Swedish for Long-stocking]. She had invented that name at that very moment, but I didn't ask who this Pippi was. I just started to tell her about a girl with such a funny name. From then on, my daughter kept asking me to tell her everything about Pippi Longstocking.
>
> Shortly afterwards I broke my ankle and had to stay in bed for a few days, so I decided to write down the stories. I showed them to a publisher, and that was how it started.

Since then, more than 15 million Pippi Longstocking books have been sold, and they have been translated into 55 languages—making Astrid Lindgren the most successful writer in the history of Swedish literature.

PETER RABBIT

Inspiration: Another sick child; this time it was 5-year-old Noël Moore, the son of one of Beatrix Potter's friends.

In 1893 Noël contracted an illness that kept him in bed for months. Beatrix Potter lived too far away to visit very often, so she wrote him elaborate letters instead. When Potter had something interesting to write about, she included it in the letter; when she didn't, she just made up stories. One of the stories, told in a letter dated September 4, 1893, involved Peter, her pet rabbit:

> My Dear Noël, I don't know what to write to you, so I shall tell you a

story about four little rabbits whose names were Flopsy, Mopsy, Cottontail, and Peter.

They lived with their Mother in a sand bank under the root of a big fir tree.

'Now my dears,' said old Mrs. Bunny, 'you may go into the field or down the lane, but don't go into Mr. McGregor's garden...'

How it Became a Book: Potter wrote similar letters to other children she knew; they were so well received that it eventually occurred to her that they might make good children's books. In 1900 she wrote to Nöel Moore asking if he still had the "Peter Rabbit" letter she'd written eight years earlier. He did, and he lent it back to her so she could copy it.

Potter submitted *The Tale of Peter Rabbit* to at least six different publishers; each one turned her down...so she printed 250 copies using her own savings and sold them to family and friends. She also sent a copy to Frederick Warne & Co. Ltd., one of publishers that had originally turned her down, and they agreed to publish it. (This was no big vote of confidence, though—the company made Potter cover all expenses and take all the financial risks.) That was nearly 100 years ago; today Peter Rabbit still ranks as one of the top 10 best-selling childrens' books of all time.

BABAR THE ELEPHANT

Inspiration: A bedtime story

How it Became a Book: In the summer of 1930, a French woman named Cecile de Brunhoff told her sons a bedtime story about a little elephant named Babar. The story went on night after night; the boys enjoyed it so much that their father, a painter named Jean de Brunhoff, painted some pictures to go along with the story and assembled them into a homemade book. The book was passed from one relative to another among the extended de Brunhoff family that summer; it generated so much enthusiasm among family members that de Brunhoff decided to get it published.

In 1931, his brother-in-law, a fashion magazine editor, arranged to print *L'histoire de Babar, le petit elephant.* Though it was the middle of the Depression, the huge, expensive volume sold well... giving birth not only to the Babar series, but to the modern picture book as well.

DRACULA,
"I VANT TO BE A STAR"

Long before Dracula became a pop icon, he was just a character in a not-very-popular novel by novelist Bram Stoker (see page 164)…but everyone's got to start somewhere. Here's the story of how Dracula made his way into pop culture through the stage and screen.

IN THE MAIL

Nosferatu—who cannot die!

A million fancies strike you when you hear the name: Nosferatu!

NOSFERATU
does not die!

What do you expect of the first showing of this great work? Aren't you afraid? Men must die. But legend has it that a vampire, Nosferatu, "the undead," lives on men's blood! You want to see a symphony of horror? You may expect more. Be careful. Nosferatu is not just fun, not something to be taken lightly. Once more: beware.

That was the text of a movie advertisement sent to Bram Stoker's 64-year-old widow from Berlin in April 1922. In the ten years since her husband's death, Florence Stoker's financial situation had deteriorated. All of Stoker's books had gone out of print, except for *Dracula*, and sales of that were modest even in the best years. Mrs. Stoker, slowly going blind from cataracts, would have been destitute were it not for help from her son, Noel.

Now, to add insult to injury, came this advertisement in the mail. It was for "Nosferatu, A Symphony of Horrors," a German film which by its own admission was "freely adapted" from Bram Stoker's *Dracula*. All of Stoker's characters were in the film, only under different names: Dracula was renamed Graf Orlok; Jonathan Harker had become Hutter, his fiancée Mina was renamed Emma, and so on.

Mrs. Stoker was furious. She'd never given the filmmakers, Prana-Film, permission to adapt her husband's work. *Nosferatu* was stolen property, and she wanted it destroyed. So she sued.

Mmm-mm good: Peruvians eat about 65 million guinea pigs each year.

HONEST MISTAKE?

The makers of *Nosferatu* may not have meant any harm. Film-making was still in its infancy in the early 1920s, and Prana-Film, less than a year old, was owned by two businessmen who'd never made films before. But it turned out they were as impractical about making money as they were in obtaining permissions—and two months after Mrs. Stoker filed her lawsuit, the studio went bankrupt.

All existing prints of the film, including the original negative, scattered to the four winds with Prana-Film's dissolution. With no hope left of collecting any financial damages, most people would probably have left it at that. But Mrs. Stoker spent the next ten years hunting down every print of *Nosferatu* she could find...and had them all destroyed—including the original negative, which is believed to have been burned in 1925.

"Most 'lost' films have vanished through neglect," David Skal writes in *Hollywood Gothic*. "But in the case of *Nosferatu* we have one of the few instances in film history, and perhaps the only one, in which an obliterating capital punishment is sought for a work of cinematic art, strictly on legalistic grounds, by a person with no knowledge of the work's specific contents or artistic merit." Mrs. Stoker had never even seen the film she worked so hard to destroy.

Despite her dedication, though, she was unsuccessful in destroying every print—a handful survived.

First with the Most

It's fortunate that Mrs. Stoker failed in her attempt to kill *Nosferatu* because the film is not only the first Dracula film ever made, it's also considered by many film historians to be the best. "*Nosferatu*," Skal writes, "would go on to be recognized as a landmark of world cinema, elevating the estimation of *Dracula* in a way no other dramatic adaptation ever would, or ever could....It had achieved what Florence Stoker herself would never achieve for the book: artistic legitimacy."

DRACULA ON STAGE

In the mid-1920s a British actor named Hamilton Deane licensed the stage rights to Dracula from Mrs. Stoker and adapted the novel for the stage, creating a play that could be produced on a shoestring budget. He also recast the novel's only American character, a Texan named Quincey Morris, as a woman, so that the actresses in his troupe would have more parts.

But the biggest change he made was to clean up Count Dracula. He replaced the vampire's bad breath, hairy palms, and overall bad hygiene with cleanliness, formality, and proper manners. "Gentility and breeding added a new dimension to the character," Skal writes, "and served a theatrical function—he was now able to interact with the characters, rather than merely hang outside their bedroom windows."

Count Me Out

When he set to work adapting *Dracula* for the stage, Deane had himself in mind to play the part of Dracula. But he trimmed the role so much that he decided to play Dr. Van Helsing instead. Perhaps to soothe rocky relations with Mrs. Stoker and her agent, C.A. Bang, Deane cast Bang's brother-in-law, 22-year-old Raymond Huntley, as Dracula. Huntley was paid £8 a week for the part, and was required to provide his own costumes—including lounge suits, full evening tails, a dinner jacket, and a silk hat—all out of his own pocket.

About the only item he didn't have to provide was Dracula's cape, which was considered a stage prop. The cape's huge standup collar completely concealed Huntley's head when he turned his back to the audience, allowing him to "disappear" from the stage by slipping out of the cape and ducking out through a trapdoor in the floor. The trapdoor exit was later removed from the play, but the cape with the standup collar remains a standard part of the Dracula costume to this day.

ON THE ROAD

Hamilton Deane didn't intend his adaptation of *Dracula* to be high art: The play was what was known as a "boob catcher," a play that used gimmickry, sex appeal—and in *Dracula's* case, death—to draw common people into the theatre. For that reason Deane bypassed the London stage (and London theater critics, who would have savaged the production) and took his show on the road, hitting smaller cities and towns all over Britain.

What's Hugh of Provence famous for? He's the first person to wear glasses in a portrait (1352).

He stayed on the road for more than two years before finally opening at London's Little Theatre on February 14, 1927. As predicted, it was panned by the London critics. The show was at the end of its run...or so Deane thought. But as days turned into weeks, and weeks into months, the crowds didn't get smaller—they got bigger. Despite the bad reviews, by the end of summer *Dracula* was playing to capacity crowds and had to move to a larger theatre called the Duke of York's. "While glittering productions costing thousands of pounds have wilted and died after a week or so in the West End," the *London Evening News* wrote, "Dracula has gone on drinking blood nightly."

COMING TO AMERICA

In early 1927 an American theater promoter named Horace Liveright traveled to London to see *Dracula*. He enjoyed it so much that he saw it again three more times. "Although it was badly produced," he recalled later, "I got a kick out of it each time."

Liveright wanted to bring *Dracula* to Broadway....But he didn't think Hamilton Deane's adaptation was written well enough for New York audiences. So he got permission from Mrs. Stoker to write another adaptation, one that retained Deane's theatricality but improved his amateurish dialogue.

Liveright offered to take Raymond Huntley to the U.S., too, and Huntley agreed to go...providing Liveright agreed to raise his pay to $125 a week. No deal—Huntley stayed in London. The part of Dracula went to a Hungarian expatriate actor named Bela Lugosi.

Lugosi, 46, had established himself in Hungary and Germany by playing romantic parts and an occasional villain. But his American career was burdened by the fact that he could speak barely a word of English, and rather than work on his English, he preferred to memorize his lines phonetically.

The result of Lugosi's inability to speak English, Skal writes, "was the oddly inflected and deliberate style of speech now forever associated with the role of Dracula—and a professional albatross that would forever limit the roles offered to him."

VAMPIRE FEVER

Dracula opened at New York's Fulton Theatre on October 5, 1927.

It received better reviews than the London version, thanks in large part to the new script and to Lugosi's acting. Lugosi's experience as a romantic lead made his interpretation of *Dracula* markedly different from Huntley's in London, Skal writes:

> The London Dracula was middle-aged and malignant; Lugosi presented quite a different picture: sexy, continental, with slicked-back patent-leather hair and a weird green cast to his makeup—a Latin lover from beyond the grave, Valentino gone slightly rancid. It was a combination that worked, and audiences—especially female audiences—relished, even wallowed in, the romantic paradoxes.

Dracula was a hit. It played for 31 weeks and 241 performances before closing in 1928. Then, Liveright formed a national touring company, and in the process launched America's first vampire craze. By May of 1929, Liveright had made more than $1 million on *Dracula*, and would make a million more in less than a year.

A SIGN OF THINGS TO COME

Bela Lugosi was not so lucky: He'd joined the touring company for its west coast swing, but when it moved to the east coast he made the mistake of asking for a substantial raise, one that he felt was commensurate with his ability to draw his fans into the theater.

Liveright didn't see it that way, and replaced Lugosi with the man Lugosi had replaced in 1927—Raymond Huntley.

Lugosi, not for the last time in his career, was out in the cold.

For Dracula, "I Vant to Be in Pictures" turn to page 360.

*   *   *

A BRI "FAVORITE ROLE MODEL"

Role Models: The hundreds of thousands of people who gathered in New York City's Central Park on Earth Day 1990 to "express their support for environmental programs, and to display their concern for Mother Earth."

Setting an Example: They left behind more than 154.3 tons of litter, which took 50 park employees until 3 a.m. to clean up.

to gild the ceiling of a church in Rome. It's still there.

YES, VIRGINIA, THERE *IS* A SANTA… OR MAYBE THERE ISN'T

You've probably heard the phrase, "Yes, Virginia, there is a Santa Claus." But do you know where it comes from? Here's the original letter, the reply, and finally, a little scientific analysis to help you decide for yourself.

Y ES, VIRGINIA

One of the most famous Letters to the Editor ever to appear in a newspaper was this query from an 8-year-old girl. It was first printed in the *New York Sun* in 1897, along with a response by editor Francis P. Church. It proved so popular that it was reprinted every year until the *Sun* went out of business in 1949. It's now a part of American lore. But few people have read the original letters. Here they are.

The Question
Dear Editor:

I am 8 years old. Some of my little friends say there is no Santa Claus. Papa says, "If you see it in the *Sun*, it's so." Please tell me the truth, is there a Santa Claus?
Virginia O'Hanlon

The Answer
"Virginia, your little friends are wrong. They have been affected by the skepticism of a skeptical age. They do not believe except what they see. They think that nothing can be which is not comprehensible by their little minds. All minds, Virginia, whether they be men's or children's, are little. In this great universe of ours, man is a mere insect, an ant, in his intellect as compared with the boundless world about him, as measured by the intelligence capable of grasping the whole of truth and knowledge.

"Yes, Virginia, there is a Santa Claus. He exists as certainly as love and generosity and devotion exist, and you know that they abound and give to your life its highest beauty and joy.

The seven Gummi Bears are named Gruffi, Cubbi, Tummi, Zummi, Sunni, Gusto, and Grammi.

"Alas! How dreary would be the world if there were no Santa Claus! It would be as dreary as if there were no Virginias. There would be no childlike faith then, no poetry, no romance to make tolerable this existence. We should have no enjoyment, except in sense and sight. The external light with which childhood fills the world would be extinguished.

"Not believe in Santa Claus! You might as well not believe in fairies. You might get your pops to hire men to watch in all the chimneys on Christmas eve to catch Santa Claus, but even if you did not see Santa Claus coming down, what would that prove? Nobody sees Santa Claus, but that is no sign that there is no Santa Claus. The most real things in the world are those that neither children nor men can see. Did you ever see fairies dancing on the lawn? Of course not, but that's no proof that they are not there. Nobody can conceive or imagine all the wonders there are unseen and unseeable in the world.

"You tear apart the baby's rattle and see what makes the noise inside, but there is a veil covering the unseen world which not the strongest man, nor even the united strength of all the strongest men that ever lived could tear apart. Only faith, poetry, love, romance, can push aside that curtain and view and picture the supernal beauty and glory beyond. Is it all real? Ah, Virginia, in all this world there is nothing else real and abiding.

"No Santa Claus! Thank God! He lives and lives forever. A thousand years from now, Virginia, nay 10 times 10,000 years from now, he will continue to make glad the heart of childhood."

*   *   *

UH, WELL, VIRGINIA, ON SECOND THOUGHT...

"Can reindeer really fly? Is there really a Santa Claus?

To answer this question, we turned to the book *Cyber Jokes*, edited by Doug Mayer, and his careful analysis of four key factors:

1. Santa's Workload

"There are two billion children in the world, but since Santa doesn't appear to handle the Muslim, Hindu, Jewish, and Buddhist children, that reduces his workload to 15% of the total, or 300 million. At an average rate of 3.5 children per household, that's 85.7 million homes. Santa has 31 hours of Christmas to work with, thanks to the different time zones and the rotation of the Earth, assuming he travels east to west. This works out to 767.9 visits per second. So for each household with good children, Santa has about 1/1,000th of a second to park, hop out of the sleigh, jump down the chimney, fill the stockings, distribute the presents, eat whatever snacks have been left, get back up the chimney, into the sleigh and move on to the next house."

2. The Time/Distance Factor

"Assuming that these 91.8 million stops are evenly distributed around the Earth, we're talking about .78 miles per household, a total trip of 75.5 million miles."

3. Calculation of Estimated Speed

"This means that Santa's sleigh is moving at 650 miles per second, or 3,000 times the speed of sound."

4. Santa's Payload

"Assuming that each child gets nothing more than a medium-size Lego set (about two pounds), the sleigh is carrying 321,300 tons, not counting Santa, who is invariably described as 'heavy.' On land, normal reindeer can pull no more than 300 pounds, and even granting that flying reindeer could pull 10 times the normal amount, Santa's going to need 214,200 reindeer to pull his sleigh. This increases the payload to 353,430 tons, or four times the weight of the *Queen Elizabeth*."

CONCLUSION

"[A craft of] 353,000 tons, traveling at 650 miles per second, creates enormous air resistance. This will heat up Mr. Claus and his sleigh like a spacecraft reentering Earth's atmosphere."

Translation: If there is a Santa, he's toast.

*   *   *

Cayo's Law: The only things that start on time are the ones you're late for.

Best-selling passenger car ever: Toyota Corolla. At least 24 million have been sold since 1966.

THE ORIGIN OF THE SUPERMARKET

We take it for granted today, but less than 100 years ago, the supermarket seemed like some sort of bizarre fantasy. Wait a minute—that's what it seems like today, too. Well, anyway, here are some historical highlights.

TO MARKET, TO MARKET

At the end of the 19th century, a typical food-shopping trip wasn't as easy as it is today. Buying groceries would have included, for example:

• Stop at the butcher for meat. (You could also choose from a small selection of canned goods and bread.)

• A stop at the fruit store for fresh produce.

• Stopping on the street to buy from milk wagons, and from horse-and-wagon peddlers hawking their specialties—anything from baked goods to fish or ice.

• A final stop at the local grocer, who sold canned goods, potatoes, and sugar in 100-pound sacks, molasses, and sauerkraut in barrels, bacon in slabs, and butter in tubs. But strolling through the aisles was out of the question. At the counter, customers told the grocer what they wanted and a clerk would fill their order.

THE SELF-SERVE STORE

Then, in 1916 Clarence Saunders opened the Piggly Wiggly Store in Memphis, Tennessee. "Astonished customers," write the Sterns in their *Encyclopedia of Pop Culture*, "were given baskets (shopping carts weren't invented) and sent through the store to pick what they needed—a job formerly reserved for clerks." Although customers were a little bewildered by the dozens of stocked aisles at first, Piggly Wiggly was an immediate success. It grossed $114,000 in the first six months—with expenses of only $3,400. Before long, there were over 1,000 of them in 40 states. The self-serve grocery store began to spread.

ROAD WARRIORS

Amazingly, one of the biggest factors in the growth of the supermar-

---

What American author has had the most feature films made of his work? Edgar Allen Poe.

ket was the invention of the automobile ignition switch. Previously, housewives had to limit their shopping to stores within walking distance; it was too difficult and dangerous to turn the starter crank to get a car started. But once there was an easy way to start the car, housewives were set to travel miles to get a bargain.

This led to another significant innovation: the free parking lot. For the first time, parking was available right in front of a store, customers didn't have to look for a space on crowded streets. The attractiveness of this concept was demonstrated when the Kroger Grocery and Bakery Company opened in Indianapolis, surrounded on four sides by free parking lots. The store performed 40% above initial predictions, and a whopping 80% of customers arrived by car.

PRICE MAULING

When the Depression hit in 1929, families found themselves struggling to buy food. Michael Cullen, manager of a Kroger grocery store, suggested opening a huge self-serve store far from high-rent districts, selling everything a shopper needed under one roof. Kroger executives thought the idea was crazy. So Cullen did it on his own, using his life savings. King Kullen, the Price Wrecker, opened in March 1930 in an abandoned warehouse in Jamaica, Long Island.

Cullen knew the grocery business inside and out, which allowed him to buy drastically reduced merchandise from the surplus stocks of food manufacturers. Plus, his store's size gave him great buying power; he bought massive quantities at lower prices than his competitors could. Success came quickly. Two years later, Cullen was operating seven more stores, and the super-store concept was widely imitated. A few years later, in 1933, Cincinnati's Albers Supermarket became the first store to actually use the term "supermarket."

When Sylvan Goldman invented the shopping cart in 1937, supermarkets had everything they needed for long-term success. (See page 260 in *Uncle John's Absolutely Absorbing Bathroom Reader* for details.)

SUPERMARKETS' WEAK SPOT

As chain stores became more powerful, both the media and independent grocers began campaigns against them. Even *Time* magazine referred to them as "cheapies," assuring the American public that these giant disgraces were only due to bad times and would disappear soon. Independent grocers launched campaigns to boycott supermarkets because they used "unfair" methods to overcome their competition—such as staying open at night and selling items at or near cost. But customers were thrilled to be paying significantly less for food and continued to patronize them. In New Jersey a law making it illegal to sell food at or below cost was passed…and then quickly withdrawn when consumers raged that it was making them pay more for no good reason.

A SYMBOL OF DEMOCRACY

But the real explosion in new supermarkets came in the baby boom years. In 1951, *Collier's* magazine reported that more than three supermarkets were opening a day in the United States, a pace that only increased in the 1960s. In 1950, supermarkets accounted for 35% of all food sales in America; by 1960, that figure was 70%. Small groceries began to thin out.

Now the media reversed itself. Supermarkets were no longer a national disgrace—they were a unique symbol of American ingenuity. Beginning in 1956, the U.S. government even began using supermarkets as a propaganda tool to promote "the American Way." Soviet premier Nikita Kruschev and Queen Elizabeth both paid rapt attention as guides at supermarkets demonstrated how a steak was wrapped in cellophane. The U.S. Information Agency even arranged for the Pope to come and bless an American supermarket.

The government set up demo stores in several European cities, where people were amazed at the variety of food under one roof. Italians in particular were astonished by certain aspects of American supermarkets, such as pet food, which didn't exist in Italy. It drew such a large crowd that the pet food section had to be removed. Another was the concept of self-service. Italians were amazed that they could actually touch food before they bought it. Some even suspected that the United States had devious motives in introducing the supermarket. Left-wing newspapers were full of conspiracy theories.

Supermarkets are widespread in many countries today, but they remain an international symbol of American culture and know-how.

ship a corpse out of Daytona Beach International Airport.

NEVER SAY NEVER

A *few pearls of wisdom from 599* Things You
Should Never Do, *edited by Ed Morrow.*

"Never get in a battle of wits
without any ammunition."
—Anonymous

"Never ask old people how they
are if you have anything else to
do that day."
—Joe Restivo

"Never underestimate the
effectiveness of a straight cash
bribe."
—Claude Cockburn

"Never kick a mule and turn
your back."
—American adage

"Never drop your gun to hug a
bear."
—H. E. Palmer

"Never give black coffee to an
intoxicated person. You may
wind up with a wide-awake
drunk on your hands."
—Ann Landers

"Never hate a man enough to
give him his diamonds back."
—Zsa Zsa Gabor

"Never date a man whose belt
buckle is bigger than his head."
—Brett Butler

"Never let your schooling in-
terfere with your education."
—Mark Twain

"Never buy a fur from a veterinarian."
—Joan Rivers

"Never tell anybody to go to
hell unless you can make them
go."
—Sam Rayburn

"Never raise your hand to your
children—it leaves your mid-
section unprotected."
—Robert Orben

"Never get deeply in debt to
someone who cried at the end
of *Scarface.*"
—Robert S. Wieder

"Never trust a doctor who sells
cemetery plots on the side."
—Anonymous

"Never learn how to iron a
man's shirt or you'll wind up
having to do it."
—Michele Slung

"Never choose between two
good things; take both."
—American adage

Don't be greedy; There's enough gold in the ocean to give every human 9 pounds.

THE QUOTABLE VAMPIRE

A collection of favorite vampire quotes from books, TV, and film.

"All I know is I haven't had a suntan in one hundred and thirty-six years....I'd give anything just to go to the beach for at least fifteen minutes."

—Suzy the vampire,
Vampire Hookers (1986)

"There's no getting around it, kid, vampires drink blood. We suggest pigs' blood—B negative. I think you'll find it surprisingly, um, full-bodied, with a smooth flavor."

—Modoc, *My Best Friend Is a Vampire* (1988)

"Look. The night. It's so bright it'll blind you."

—The vampire Mae,
Near Dark (1987)

"This part of the seduction is quite simple, really. Just take away everything that she has, then give her everything she needs."

—The vampire Maxmillian,
Vampire in Brooklyn (1995)

"Fun? How would you like to go around dressed like a headwaiter for seven hundred years? Just once I'd like to go to dinner dressed in a turtleneck and a sports jacket."

—Dracula to Renfield, *Love at First Bite* (1979)

"I buried myself for 100 years to get away from you. Can't you take a hint?"

—The vampire Angelique,
Nightlife (1989)

"Humans are prey, they are sustenance, cattle. Do you converse with a hamburger before you eat it? Do you converse with a milkshake?"

—Jacob, *To Sleep with a Vampire* (1992)

"You shall pay, black prince. I shall place a curse of suffering on you that will doom you to a living hell. A hunger, a wild gnawing animal hunger will grow in you, a hunger for human blood."

—Dracula,
Blacula (1972)

"I'll take a lite...Blood Lite."

—Vampire in a vampire bar,
Nightlife (1989)

The real meaning of relief: The longest case of constipation ever recorded lasted 102 days.

"There's only one way you can be with me, but you have to do something you've never done before…commit yourself… forever."
—The vampire Louise, *The Girl with the Hungry Eyes* (1993)

"For centuries I have known the magical powers of blood—powers greater even than those of holy water. That fountain of youth that withstands the ravages of time."
—Countess Dracula, *Mama Dracula* (1980)

"I think I should warn you I have certain unusual habits. I'm a late riser, very late…. When I'm sleeping I must never be disturbed….And I'm on a liquid diet."
—The vampire Angelique, *Nightlife* (1989)

"Vampires get such a crummy deal," she complained. "Not only do we have to sleep in worm-eaten old coffins and wear these smelly old clothes, but we can't even look in the mirror when we want to fix ourselves up a little bit."
—The vampire Anna to her human friend Tony, *The Vampire Moves In* (1985)

"I may never see the sunrise, but I can take you to worlds beyond your dreams. I can teach you about the stars. We'll dance in their light—for eternity."
—The vampire Carmilla, *Carmilla* (1990)

"We have lived in this country for four generations. We're Americans—Carpathian-Americans. We work here, we live here, we pay taxes, we're entitled to the protection of the law. I think it's time we came out of the damn coffin."
—Harry, to his vampire family, *Blood Ties* (1991)

* * *

MONKEY MISCELLANY

"The most intelligent ape is the chimpanzee. At one time western anthropologists thought that the gorilla was smarter, but Africans familiar with both animals say, 'If you throw a spear at the *njina* [gorilla], he will spring out of its way; but if you throw one at the *nchigo* [chimpanzee], he will catch it in his hand and throw it back at you.'"
—*The Guinness Book of Animal Facts and Feats*

Experts say time *is* getting shorter: 280 million years ago, a year lasted 390 days.

ANOTHER LOOK AT MOTHER GOOSE

Many historians say nursery rhymes aren't as innocent as they seem—hidden behind the simple verses are political allegories and social commentary. That sounds enticing (heck, we bought it—see "Inside Mother Goose," page 210 in The Best of Uncle John's BR*), but it's not necessarily true. Here's another interpretation.*

ROCK-A-BYE BABY, on the tree-top..."
Some people believe... It's a lesson in humility. In fact, it first appeared in print about 1765, in a volume called *Mother Goose's Melody*, accompanied by the note: "This may serve as a Warning to the Proud and Ambitious, who climb so high that they generally fall at last."

Actually... The cradle is probably just a cradle. According to tradition, it was written by a Pilgrim who came to America on the Mayflower. He was "struck by the American Indian practice of hanging birchbark cradles on the branches of trees, where they rocked in the wind." Actually, since people in the Old World also used wind-rocked cradles, "Rock-a-Bye Baby" may even predate the Mayflower.

"HUMPTY DUMPTY sat on a wall..."

Some people believe... Mr. Dumpty was Richard III, who was killed after he fell from his horse in battle (that's what *we* wrote in *Bathroom Reader #2*)...or that he represents a high-born noble in Richard's time who fell from the King's favor.

Actually... It's probably just a riddle. Today everyone knows Humpty is an egg, but thousands of years ago—when the rhyme is believed to have first appeared—it would have been a challenge to figure out. Nearly identical riddle-rhymes appeared in Germany ("Humpelken-Pumpelken"), France ("Boule, Boule"), Sweden ("Thille, Lille"), Finland ("Hillerin-Lillerin") and other European countries. Experts guess that it was during the 18th century, when illustrations of Humpty began to appear, that he became known as a character rather than just a riddle. By the end of the 1700s, the term was so well known that it meant "a short clumsy person of either sex."

"LITTLE MISS MUFFET sat on a tuffet…"

Some people believe… "Miss Muffet represents Mary Queen of Scots (1542–87), and the unpleasant spider is Presbyterian reformer John Knox, who perpetually berated the Roman Catholic monarch about her religion."

Actually… Miss Muffet is more likely to have been Patience Muffet, daughter of a 16th-century English entomologist, Thomas Muffet. He was a big fan of spiders, and wrote a natural history called *The Silkwormes and their flies*. What's a "tuffet"? Probably "a grassy hillock," not the stool she's often pictured on.

"SING A SONG OF SIXPENCE, a pocket full of rye…"

Some people believe… The king is Henry VIII; the queen is his first wife, Catherine of Aragon; and the maid is Anne Boleyn, Henry's second wife—whose beheading is predicted in the line, "along came a blackbird and snapped off her nose." The blackbirds are black-robed monks of the monasteries Henry dissolved.

Actually… The rhyme probably commemorates a recipe found in a 1549 Italian cookbook, translated into English in 1598 as *Epulario, or, the Italian Banquet*. The recipe gives instructions on how to make pies containing live birds. When the pies were cut, the birds would fly out—"a party favor guaranteed to enliven any feast."

"RING AROUND THE ROSIE, a pocket full of posies…"

Some people believe… It refers to the Great Plague of London in 1665 or the Black Death of the 14th century. (We repeated that in *Bathroom Reader 2*.) "Ring around the rosie" is the red rash that afflicted plague victims, posies are the herbs carried to ward off infection. "All fall down," of course, is what happens when the plague strikes.

Actually… As intriguing as this sounds, most experts now discount it. The oldest known printed version of the rhyme is from 1790, more than 100 years after its supposed origin—and it's American, not English. More likely: The rhyme originated as a dancing game. One American expert, Philip Hiscock, suggests that it may have been invented as a way to avoid the ban on dancing enforced by some Protestant sects in England and America.

First country to give women the vote: New Zealand, in 1893.

TRUTH IN ADVERTISING

Did you laugh when you read this title? Well, okay, we agree—it is an oxymoron. And here's some proof.

THE AD SAID: The Coors Brewing Company was launching its "Pure Water 2000 Campaign" in the late 1980s, "Because it was the right thing to do." The company's 1990 annual report stated: "Pete Coors [great-grandson of company founder Adolph Coors] personally kicked off the Coors Pure Water 2000 program, a national commitment to help clean up America's rivers, streams, and lakes." TV and print ads showed him "standing streamside, extolling the virtues of clean water."

IN THE REAL WORLD: The *Denver Post* reported that Coors "officially became a toxic criminal on October 12, 1990, when they pleaded guilty to violating state environmental law by illegally pumping industrial solvents into Clear Creek from 1976 to 1989."

• And when a massive Coors beer spill wiped out all of the fish in a 5.2-mile stretch of the creek in 1991, company head Bill Coors told shareholders it was no big deal—the fish were only "junk fish," and Clear Creek "was not a prime fishing stream."

THE ADS SAID: 140 different retailers—including cruise lines, expensive stores, chic gift boutiques, and resort destinations "don't take American Express." So bring your Visa card.

IN THE REAL WORLD: "Some of the featured partners, Carnival Cruise Lines among them, took American Express until just before they appeared in Visa's commercials," The *Wall St. Journal* reported in 1999. "And, after reaping the national publicity at Visa's expense, quietly resumed taking American Express. Others didn't even go that far: 'We never really stopped taking Amex fully,' says Les Otten, chairman of American Skiing Company."

THE AD SAID: In 1999 American Express ran a "reality" TV commercial featuring a man named Robert H. Tompkins, identified as a card member since 1958. "Do you know me?" he asks viewers, then answers, "Probably not." The ad goes on to give viewers a glimpse of his life story: Tompkins moved to Paris 40 years ago to learn about wine, where he fell in love and became a vintner. In a voiceover, he thanks American Express for being there "even in the worst of times," as an air raid siren sounds and black-and-white footage of a tank rolling through the streets fills the screen. "Not to worry," an American Express representative tells him over the phone, "We've found a way to get you out."

IN THE REAL WORLD: "While there really is a Mr. Tompkins, he really is an American Express card holder, and he gave his consent to use his name in the ad, American Express later admitted that…none of the events depicted in the commercial had actually happened to him, not even one."

…Well, then, what was Mr. Tompkins' life really like? Hard to say—according to news reports, American Express "declined to give any further information about Mr. Tompkins."

AND MORE CLASSIC MOMENTS OF TRUTH...

• "Green Giant was ordered to tell consumers its 'American Mixture' variety of frozen vegetables is a product of Mexico."

• "Fabergé Company was fined because its ad campaign promising 'Now: More Brut!' was for a product containing less Brut than previous versions."

• "Allstate Insurance apologized for sending letters praising an agent as a winner of Allstate's 'Quality Agent Award' when the man had just been banned from the business in the largest agent misconduct case in California history."

• The John Hancock insurance company launched an advertising campaign featuring "real people in real situations." When a journalist asked to speak to these real people, a company spokesperson conceded that they were actors and 'in that sense they are not real people.' "

• "A New Jersey company was charged with fraud because its 'secret' hair replacement technique turned out to be sewing toupees to men's scalps."

—*The San Francisco Examiner*

Most destructive car chase ever filmed: *The Junkman* (1982); 150 cars were destroyed.

FAMILY FEUD

*Here's another example of what happens when families
are more interested in money than in each other.*

SHOEN vs. SHOEN

The Contestants: Leonard S. Shoen, founder of U-Haul
trailer rental chain and three of his sons, Joseph, James, and
Mark Shoen.

How the Feud Started: Shoen started U-Haul in 1945 using
$5,000 in savings. He built the first trailers with his own hands; by
the early 1970s, he'd turned the company into the nation's largest
do-it-yourself moving company.

Shoen figured that someday he would pass on the business to his
children, so he began transferring shares in Amerco, U-Haul's par-
ent company, in 1950. Too early, it turned out, and to too many
children: He had twelve kids—six children with his first wife, five
with his second wife, and one with his third wife. By the time he
was finished distributing shares to them, they owned 95% of the
company, leaving him with only a 5% stake, even though he was
the one running the company. Big mistake.

The 1973 oil crisis hit gas stations hard—including the ones that
were U-Haul dealers. Shoen decided to diversify into other rental
markets—Jet Skis, party supplies, porn videos, you name it. If it was
rentable, Shoen wanted to rent it.

Shoen's oldest sons saw things differently: they wanted to focus
on the company's core business—moving—and they were upset
that their father's neglect of the company's aging fleet was feeding
longtime customers over to its main competitor, Ryder.

The Shoen sons were also angry for personal reasons. They were
fabulously wealthy on paper, but their father plowed all of Amerco's profits back into the company and rarely paid dividends on
their stock. So they were always broke. "We were millionaires in
name only," Mark Shoen says. "We were told we were wealthy, but
we didn't have enough money to buy a car." By 1986 the brothers
had had enough. Joe, James and Mark Shoen forced their father
into retirement and seized control of Amerco for themselves.

England was the 1st country with regular TV service (1936). The U.S. was 2nd (1939).

The move split the family into two warring factions, and Leonard and six of his children—Sam, Michael, Cecilia, Katrina, Theresa, and Mary Anna—filed suit against Joe and Mark Shoen and the rest of Amerco's board of directors to win back control of the company.

And the Winner Is: Leonard, sort of. In 1994 he won a $1.48 billion judgement against Amerco's board of directors, including Joe, James and Mark Shoen. The verdict was reduced to $461.8 million on appeal, but the directors filed for bankruptcy, claiming they couldn't pay the judgement. The case was finally settled in 1996, when Amerco paid off the verdict in exchange for Leonard and the other "outsiders" surrendering all of their stock and ownership interests in Amerco.

Completely cut out of the company he founded 50 years earlier, Leonard Shoen moved to Las Vegas and bought a hotel. He hoped to turn it into a casino, but was refused a gaming license because of "doubts raised about his moral character." On October 29, 1999, 83-year-old Leonard rammed his car into telephone pole on a Las Vegas street and died from his injuries. Police called the death an apparent suicide. (Shoen's passing sparked a family feud over who would inherit the hotel.)

"Had Leonard Shoen spent $500 for a lawyer in 1950," said one associate, "none of the rest would have followed."

*　　　*　　　*

ACCORDING TO THE LATEST RESEARCH... GRANDMAS SMELL GOOD

Researchers: Scientists at Rutgers University's Monsell Chemical Senses Center

Who They Studied: 300 students, commenting on the underarm smells of 30 volunteers, "ranging from toddlers to 70-somethings"

What They Learned: People like the smell of older women. In the study, "the researchers collected underarm odors on gauze pads... and asked the students to assess their moods before and after sniffing the samples. 'Old women had an uplifting effect,' said Denise Chen of the Monsell Center." Smells from young men had "the opposite effect."

Golf was banned in England in 1457, because it was a distraction from archery.

SALT OF THE EARTH

A few facts you can use to spice up your conversation at dinner tonight.

SALT BECOMES YOU

- **Salt is life itself:** We each have about eight ounces of salt inside us. It's vital for regulating muscle contraction, heartbeat, nerve impulse transmission, protein digestion and the exchange of water between cells, so as to bring food in and waste out. Deprived of salt, the body goes into convulsion, paralysis and death.

- **Hypertension and salt:** Baby food makers have learned they can sell more if they salt it. Why? Because mothers are the ones who buy it and they like the taste better. Critics say babies don't need the salt and that hooking them on it early in life predisposes them to high blood pressure.

- **Salt can be poison:** It's healthy to eat about a third of an ounce of salt a day. If you eat more than four ounces at once, you'll die.

SALT SCIENCE

- Strangely enough, salt is made of two elements—sodium and chlorine—which, if put in your mouth by themselves, will either blow up (sodium) or poison you (chlorine). But merged into a compound—sodium chloride—they change into an essential of life. The salt taste comes from the chlorine—which is also vital for making the hydrochloric acid which digests food in our stomach.

- Scientists once thought the oceans were salty because rivers constantly washed salt out of soil and carried it to sea. But then they found pools of seawater trapped in underground sediments millions of years ago that show the ocean has always been about as salty as it is now.

- We can never run out of salt. There's enough in the oceans to cover the world 14 inches deep.

- Salt is the only mineral that can be mined by turning it into a liquid (by pumping water in). Then they pump out the brine and turn it back into a solid by evaporation.

- Salt is hygroscopic, which means it absorbs water. That's why you can't drink seawater; it will dehydrate you.

Where can you find a "short ton"? In the U.S.—it's 2,000 lbs. An English ton is 2,240 lbs.

- Salt is one of the four things the tongue can taste (the others are sweet, sour, and bitter). Only sweet and bitter are inborn; salt is an acquired taste.

- The hypothalamus at the base of the brain measures sodium and potassium in body fluids. When they get too high (from either not drinking enough water or eating too much salt), it triggers the sensation of thirst.

SALT MISCELLANY

- Only 5 percent of the salt we mine goes into food. The rest goes into making chemicals.

- When salt is made by vigorous boiling, it forms cubic crystals, but when it's naturally dried, it makes pyramid-shaped crystals. The pyramid-shaped crystals are particularly sought after for kosher use and in fine cooking.

- It takes four gallons of seawater to make a pound of salt.

- Salt is often found with oil and is often used by oil companies as an indicator of where to drill.

- For centuries, salt was served in a bowl, not a shaker. It couldn't be shaken, since it absorbs water and sticks together. The Morton Salt Co. changed that in 1910 by covering every grain with chemicals that keep water out—thus its famous slogan, "When it rains, it pours."

- The water in our bodies (we're 70% water) has the same saltiness as the seas from which we evolved. The amniotic fluid surronding fetuses in the womb is essentially saltwater.

SALT SUPERSTITIONS

- In Scandinavia, knocking over salt is considered bad luck...*if* the salt gets wet.

- In some cultures people believe that since salt corrodes, it destroys evil. As protection, they wear a sachet of salt around their neck and sprinkle it on brooms before sweeping their homes.

- Hebrews, Greeks, and Romans all salted their sacrifices.

- Bedouins won't attack a man if they've eaten his salt.

A 'TOON IS BORN

Here are the stories of how three popular cartoons were created.

THE JETSONS

Background: In 1960, Hanna-Barbera studios broke new ground with America's first prime-time cartoon series, *The Flintstones*. Airing at 7:30 on Friday nights, it became one of the Top 20 programs of the 1960–61 season. It did so well, in fact, that ABC wanted a second prime-time cartoon the following year.

Inspiration: So Hanna-Barbera just reversed the formula. "After *The Flintstones*, it was a pretty natural move," says Joseph Barbera. "The space race was on everybody's mind in the early 1960s...so we went from the cave days to the future, the exact opposite direction....If *The Flintstones* featured the likes of Stony Curtis, Cary Granite, and Ann Margrock, the Jetson family could go see Dean Martian perform in a Las Venus hotel such as the Sonic Saharia, the Riviera Satellite, or the Flamoongo.

On the Air: *The Jetsons* originally aired at 7:30 PM on Sunday night—traditionally a kids' time slot in the days before cable TV. But against *Walt Disney's Wonderful World of Color* (NBC) and *Dennis the Menace* (CBS), it flopped. *The Jetsons* was canceled after one season; only 24 episodes were made.

The following year (1963), however, ABC scheduled *Jetsons* reruns as a regular Saturday morning cartoon show (pre-cable). That's where it belonged. The show was so popular with kids that for the next 20 years, the same 24 episodes ran over and over again on Saturdays.

REN & STIMPY

Background: Fresh from his success animating *The New Adventures of Mighty Mouse* for television, in 1989 an animator named John Kricfalusi pitched the Nickelodeon channel an idea he had for a cartoon called "Your Gang."

Nickelodeon was interested in the show, but it insisted on buying all the rights to the characters, as part of its plan to create a stable of "evergreen" cartoons, like those at Walt Disney and Warner Brothers, that could be broadcast for decades to come.

Inspiration: Kricfalusi didn't want to sell the rights to his favorite "Your Gang" characters. Instead, "he sold Nickelodeon a show about two ancillary 'Your Gang' characters with whom he was willing to part: a paranoid Chihuahua named Ren (inspired by a postcard of a chihuahua in a sweater), and an excretion-obsessed cat named Stimpy (which originated as a doodle and was named after a college friend)."

On the Air: When *Ren & Stimpy* debuted in August 1991, Nickelodeon had only six completed episodes to broadcast. But the show was such a surprise hit—Nickelodeon's Sunday morning ratings doubled on the strength of "Ren & Stimpy" alone—that Nickelodeon aired the six episodes over and over again for about a year until new episodes were ready. The *Los Angeles Times* reported: "*Ren & Stimpy* [has] started a national craze that helped turn Nicktoons into a major force in children's animation."

Meanwhile, however, Kricfalusi and Nickelodeon had a falling-out. The cable station said the cartoonist was too slow with new episodes; Kricfalusi said that Nick was meddling creatively. In 1992, Nick fired *Ren & Stimpy*'s creator and replaced him with a former partner. The show lost its edge and faded away. However, it's still considered *the* breakthrough series for modern TV animation. "All new shows that have any kind of style have to tip their hat to *Ren & Stimpy*," says animation historian Jerry Beck. *Beavis and Butt-head* actually owes its *existence* to the show. *Ren & Stimpy*'s success was the reason the channel was willing to pay for its own animated show.

BEAVIS AND BUTT-HEAD

Background: In the early 1990s, a defense industry engineer named Mike Judge grew tired of his job working for a company that made components for the F-18 fighter jet. So he quit and became a musician. After a few months of playing guitar in a bar band, he bought a $200 animation kit and began making cartoons to amuse himself.

Inspiration: "One day in the summer of 1990," *Newsweek* reported, "Judge was trying to draw this kid he remembered from junior high. It didn't much look like the kid, but when he came back to it a week later, it made him laugh, and that was enough. This was the birth of Butt-Head, with his short upper lip and massive gums. 'The guy I tried to draw, he had that laugh: "Huh-huh, huh-huh-huh,"' says Judge....'Actually, my hair is really unmanageable, so I may have gotten Butt-head's hair from myself.'"

Judge adds, "There were probably four or five guys who inspired Beavis, just a little Bic-flipping pyro kid. I've noticed that 13-year-old metal heads haven't changed much over the years."

A few years later, Judge decided to make an antisocial cartoon called "Frog Baseball" featuring Beavis and Butt-Head playing baseball using a live frog for the ball. "I was thinking of when I was a kid and bored," Judge said. "There's nothing to do. That's when kids start blowing up lizards. You're this 14-year-old guy with no car, you just have a bike and testosterone. It's a dangerous situation."

"My mom didn't like 'Frog Baseball' at all. I showed it once at this guy's house. He was having this cartoon viewing party, and everything else was very cartoony, standard stuff. When 'Frog Baseball' came on, this girl kept looking at the screen and then at me. She says, 'He isn't actually going to hit the frog, is he?' And then Butt-head hits the frog, and she says, 'God, you look so normal.'"

On the Air: Judge entered "Frog Baseball" in a "Sick and Twisted" cartoon festival, and a week later a company called Colossal Pictures bought it for the MTV series "Liquid Television." But before they put it on the air, the channel tested it on a focus group to gauge their reaction. "The focus group was both riveted and hysterical from the moment they saw it," says Gwen Lipsky, MTV's vice president of research and planning. "After the tape was over, they kept asking to see it again. Then, after they had seen it again, several people offered to buy it from me."

MTV put Beavis and Butt-head on "Liquid Televison" for two weeks in March 1993. The reaction was so positive that in May it was back full-time. It quickly became MTV's most popular show, with ratings twice as high as any other show on the network.

*   *   *

AMAZING LUCK

"On February 2, 1931, a horse named Brampton was driving for the wire in a race in Dargaville, New Zealand, comfortably in the lead. But 40 feet from the finish line, the horse stumbled and fell, rolled over several times with his jockey clinging frantically to his back, and crossed the line the winner."

EMPEROR NORTON

Once he was Emperor of the United States. Now he's forgotten—swept into the Dustbin of History.

FORGOTTEN FIGURE: Joshua Norton, a wealthy 19th century businessman and speculator who settled in San Francisco.

CLAIM TO FAME: In 1853 Norton bet his fortune on the rice market and lost it all; by 1856 he was completely bankrupt. The experience left him mentally deranged, his head filled with delusions that he was Emperor of California. In 1859 Norton promoted himself to Emperor of the United States, and when the Civil War seemed inevitable, he issued proclamations abolishing the U.S. Congress and dissolving the republic, and assumed the powers of the American presidency.

No one listened, of course, but as the years passed, Californians—San Franciscans especially—began to treat Norton as if he really were an emperor: Riverboat companies and even the Central Pacific Railroad gave him lifetime free passes, and the California State Senate set aside a special seat for him in the Senate chamber. Theaters admitted him without a ticket, and audiences showed their deference by standing as the Emperor entered the hall. He printed 25¢ and 50¢ banknotes...which were accepted by local businesses.

When the San Francisco Police arrested him for lunacy, the judge dressed down the officers for detaining a man who "had shed no blood, robbed no one, and despoiled no country, which is more than can be said for most fellows in the king line."

Even City Hall played along, picking up the tab for Norton's 50¢-a-night "Imperial Palace" (a room in a boarding house), and buying him a new set of clothes from the prestigious Bullock and Jones tailors when Norton's "Imperial Wardrobe," which consisted of old military uniforms combined with a collection of crazy hats, became tattered and worn.

INTO THE DUSTBIN: Although largely forgotten today, when Emperor Norton I died penniless in 1880 at the age of 61, a millionaire's club picked up the tab for his lavish imperial funeral. More than 3,000 people attended the lying in state, making it one of the largest funerals ever held in San Francisco.

90% of Americans thought income taxes were fair in 1944; only 45% agreed in 1999.

JOIN THE CLUB

*Here are more stories about some of
America's most famous organizations.*

THE AMERICAN ASSOCIATION OF RETIRED PERSONS (AARP)

Founded by: Two people with entirely different motives:

• *Ethel Percy Andrus*, a retired California school principal, who'd started the National Retired Teachers Association (NRTA) in 1947 to help supply health insurance to retired teachers.

• *Leonard Davis*, an insurance salesman.

History: In the mid-1950s Andrus was looking for private health insurance for her retired teachers, who as a rule lost all their fringe benefits—including health insurance—when they retired. She wasn't having much luck: In those days insurance companies almost *never* sold insurance to people over 65, and more than 40 insurance companies had already turned her down, figuring she was a "crank," as Andrus later put it.

Then in 1955 Andrus met Davis, who'd already set up a similar insurance plan for some retired teachers in New York. Together they developed a policy that could be sold through the mail. "The policies sold by the tens of thousands," Charles Morris writes in *The AARP*, "and since the teachers turned out to be good risks, who paid their premiums on time, they were very profitable. Andrus and Davis were quickly besieged by other retired people, who were not teachers but who wanted to buy health coverage."

Sensing a business opportunity, Davis came up with $50,000 to found the AARP, a sort of NRTA for people who weren't teachers. The AARP went on to become perhaps the most powerful lobbying organization in the United States, with more than 32 million members. Davis became a very wealthy man, first by selling insurance to the AARP, then shrewdly started up his own company, the Colonial Penn Insurance Company—which became the exclusive insurance provider to AARP's members. The AARP provided a number of services to older Americans, including important lobbying efforts with the federal government. But beneath the surface, it was driven by a lucrative insurance business.

More than 1/2 of all the geysers in the world are in Yellowstone National Park.

"The AARP was not much more than a front for Davis' insurance company," columnist Andy Rooney wrote in 1996. "The AARP did not even have a list of its own members. That membership was kept under lock and key and in the offices of the Colonial Penn Insurance Company....For several years, Colonial Penn was the single most profitable company in the United States, even though the policies it sold AARP and NRTA members were rated poor." The AARP finally became independent from Colonial Penn in 1978, following a *60 Minutes* expose that revealed the ties between the insurance company and the AARP.

THE DAUGHTERS OF THE AMERICAN REVOLUTION (DAR)

Founded by: Mary Lockwood, a writer; and six other women living in Washington D.C., in 1890.

History: The celebration of the 100th anniversary of the Declaration of Independence 1876 led to an increase in patriotic fervor and interest in the American Revolution. A number of patriotic organizations were formed in the years that followed. One was the Sons of the American Revolution (SAR), which limited its membership to the descendants of men "who wintered at Valley Forge, signed the Declaration of Independence, fought in the battles of the American Revolution, served in the Continental Congress, or otherwise supported the cause of American Independence."

One of the first acts of the SAR was to deny membership to female descendants of revolutionary patriots, which offended Mary Lockwood enough to inspire an angry letter to the *Washington Post*, asking why women patriots couldn't be honored as well. That prompted other letters to the *Post*, including those from six women who began to organize the Daughters of the American Revolution. This female-descendants-only group was founded on October 11, 1890, with First Lady Caroline Scott Harrison, the wife of President Benjamin Harrison, serving as its first president.

Historical Footnote: The DAR is best known for its conflict with First Lady (and member) Eleanor Roosevelt. In 1939 the DAR refused to let Marian Anderson sing at its Constitution Hall solely because she was black. Roosevelt then quit the DAR and arranged for Anderson to give an Easter Sunday recital on the steps of the Lincoln Memorial. More than 75,000 people attended; the DAR has never lived the incident down.

WRONG ABOUT WRIGHT

Judging from what we've been told in history books, when the Wright brothers invented powered flight, they were rewarded with parades, medals and headlines. But that's a lie. The truth is, the U.S. government insisted that one of the greatest technological achievements of all time simply hadn't happened. Here's the true story.

CHANCE—THE UNINVITED GUEST

On December 8, 1903, Samuel Langley, head of the Smithsonian Institution and America's foremost expert on flight, was ready to make his most important attempt at manned flight. Since 1891 he'd been flying unmanned models powered by internal combustion engines; the U.S. government considered his experiments so promising that they'd given him $50,000 to continue. Now he planned to fly his gasoline-powered, manned plane off of a houseboat in the Potomac River. The press was on hand, waiting expectantly.

But it didn't happen. Unfortunately, the launching device, which was supposed to hurl the plane into the air, snagged the plane at the last second instead...and it went into the water "like a handful of mortar."

The *New York Times*, scornful of attempts at powered flight anyway, heaped abuse on Langley. They editorialized: "The ridiculous fiasco...was not unexpected. The flying machine might be evolved by the combined and continuous efforts of mathematicians and mechanicians in from one to ten million years."

THE REAL THING

It didn't take that long. Only nine days later, on December 17, two bicycle makers from Dayton, Ohio—Wilbur and Orville Wright—achieved the goal of all the world's would-be aviators: powered flight. It was a revolutionary development in the history of humankind...but few people even noticed. Only a few papers carried the Associated Press story of the flight. Most editors considered the whole thing a scam. When the Wrights set up the world's first airstrip outside Dayton in 1904 and flew daily all summer, only a few reporters came to see.

Oldest cat ever: Ma, an English tabby, who was 37 when she died in 1957.

In fact, the first published eyewitness account of flight appears, amazingly enough, in a bee-keeping journal called *Gleanings in Bee Culture*. And this almost a year after they started flying. The editor, A. I. Root saw the Wrights make aviation's first turn on Sept. 20, 1904 and wrote:

> I have a wonderful story to tell you, a story that in some respects outrivals the Arabian Nights fables…It was my privilege to see the first successful trip of an airship without a balloon to sustain it, that the world has ever made…These two brothers have probably not even a faint glimpse of what their discovery is going to bring to the children of men.

The scientific press was also slow to acknowledge the Wrights' accomplishment. As Sherwood Harris writes in *The First to Fly*:

> As late as January 1906, *Scientific American* had been skeptical of reports about the Wrights long flights, its editorial board feeling that if the reports were true, then certainly the enterprising American press would have given them great attention. When the reports persisted, the magazine finally obtained confirmation by letter from many reputable people who had witnessed actual flights. In its December 15 [1906] issue, the magazine stated its complete acceptance of the Wright flights.

MILITARY INTELLIGENCE

You'd think the U.S. government would leap to purchase one of the most revolutionary weapons ever. Not so. In 1904, after making flights of five minutes, the Wrights wrote their Congressman, Robert Nevin, offering to license their device to the government for military purposes. Their letter said they'd made 105 flights up to 3 miles long at 35 mph. The flying machine, they said, "lands without being wrecked" and "can be made of great practical use in scouting and carrying messages in times of war." (Interestingly enough, for many years the *only* use the Wrights could imagine for their creation was war.)

The War Department, under future president William Howard Taft, responded that they weren't interested. They'd gotten many requests for "financial assistance in the development of designs for flying machines" and would only consider a device that had been "brought to the stage of practical operation without expense to the U.S. government." But, they added, do get in touch "as soon as it shall have been perfected."

In Oct. 1905, the Wrights wrote that they'd built a better plane and made flights of up to 39 minutes and over 20 miles. The War Department again declined in a letter with almost the same wording—a form letter! Obviously, either no one was reading their letters, or no one understood what they were saying.

Showing incredible patience, the frustrated Wrights politely wrote back again. This time they said they'd build a flying machine to *any* specifications the government would name. The War Department, still clinging to the obvious impossibility of powered flight, wrote back saying it "does not care to formulate any requirements for the performance of a flying machine…until a machine is produced with by actual operation is shown to be able to produce horizontal flight and to carry an operator"—even though they had already produced it. They were so dejected that they didn't fly again for two and a half years."

ACCEPTED AT LAST

In 1907 a young balloon racer named Frank Lahm got a job with the Army Signal Corps office in Washington, D.C. He knew all the early flight pioneers and had heard from them about the miracle achieved by the Wrights. That, finally, was the Wrights' big break. Fred Howard writes in *Wilbur and Orville*:

> Lahm wrote a letter to the Board of Ordnance and Fortification (of the Army Signal Corps), urging that the brothers' latest proposal for the sale of a Flyer receive favorable action. It would be unfortunate, he said, if the U.S. should not be the first to take advantage of [the] unquestioned military value of the Wright Flyer. Lahm's letter had the desired effect.…
>
> Wilbur decided a fair price for the Flyer would be $25,000. The Board had only $10,000.…When Wilbur went to Washington to attend a formal meeting of the Board, his frankness of manner and self-confidence worked their usual magic and the Board assured him the entire $25,000 would be forthcoming by drawing on an emergency fund left over from the Spanish-American War.

MORE BUREAUCRATIC INSANITY

Apparently nothing much has changed: Even though the Wrights were the only ones in the world making practical airplanes, the U.S. government still had to put the matter out for bids. So in Dec. 23, 1907, it issued an "Advertisement and specification for a

Heavier-Than-Air Flying Machine," capable of carrying two men at 40 mph and staying up for at least an hour, then landing without serious damage. Critics howled. *The American Magazine of Aeronautics* wrote, "There is not a known flying machine in the world which could fulfill these specifications." Amazingly, the Signal Corps got 41 bids, with price tags ranging from $850 to $1 million. One was from a federal prisoner who would build a plane for his freedom. Another had plans written on wrapping paper and a third bidder offered to build planes by the pound.

The Wrights, of course, got the contract.

I SEE LONDON, I SEE FRANCE

Still, it was the French and British who first acknowledged the Wright Brothers' feats publicly. Shortly after winning the government contract (but before they'd proved themselves by building the U.S. a plane), Wilbur went to France to demonstrate their machine. The French were avid aviators, and welcomed him enthusiastically...at first. Then, as he rebuilt his plane (it had been damaged in shipping), working long hours and living simply in a nearby room, they became suspicious. Why wasn't he more flamboyant? Why didn't he attend the rounds of parties, like other celebrated French air pioneers?

Eventually, the French and British press decided he was a charlatan. But on August 8, 1907, they changed their minds. "To make a long story short," recalled an American named Ross Browne, who was there to see Wilbur's first European flight, "he got into the machine that afternoon, got into the air and made a beautiful circular flight. You should have seen the crowd there. They threw hats and everything."

STILL DUMB

Finally, four years after the first flight, the Wright Brothers were heroes. But there was one final insult: The Smithsonian Institution insisted that the first manned flight had been Langley's slam-dunk into the Potomac. They didn't want the Wright Flyer, so it sat in a shed in Dayton until 1928...when Orville finally gave it to the London Museum of Science. Only in 1942 did the Smithsonian bow to common knowledge, reverse its position, and humbly ask for the plane. The Smithsonian restored it and dedicated it in 1948, on the 45th anniversary of flight.

ANIMALS FAMOUS FOR 15 MINUTES

When Andy Warhol said, "Everyone will be famous for 15 minutes," he didn't have animals in mind. Yet even they haven't been able to escape relentless publicity.

THE STAR: Number 61, a chimpanzee

THE HEADLINE: *Monkey Has The Right Stuff*

WHAT HAPPENED: On January 31, 1963, NASA launched a Redstone 2 rocket into suborbital flight. The mission's "pilot" was Number 61, a chimpanzee and primate guinea pig for a scientific study on the impact of space flight on humans. He was renamed Ham (an acronym for Holloman Aerospace Medical Center).

His mission was scheduled to last 14 1/2 minutes, but a lot went wrong: A faulty component added 2 minutes to the flight, the oxygen nearly ran out, and as the rocket returned to Earth, Ham pulled 17 G's (17 times the weight of gravity) instead of the 12 G's the scientists had predicted. "Nevertheless," Ruthven Tremain writes in *The Animal's Who's Who*, "having been trained to respond to flashing lights by working various switches to avoid electric shocks, he performed so well he received only three shocks the entire flight."

THE AFTERMATH: Ham lived out the rest of his life at the National Zoological Park in Washington, D.C., where he was a star.

THE STAR: Hachiko, an Akita dog

THE HEADLINE: *Dog Remains Faithful to the End*

WHAT HAPPENED: For years Hachiko followed his master, Professor Eisaburo Ueno, to the Shibuya railroad station in Tokyo, where the professor caught the train to work; then he waited at the station until the professor returned from work at night. In May 1925, Dr. Ueno dropped dead at the university and never returned home. Hachiko waited at the train station until midnight, and then returned the next day and waited again. He returned to the train station to wait for his master every day until he died in 1934.

THE AFTERMATH: Hachiko's loyalty to his master made him

Diamonds are up to 90 times harder than corundum, the next-hardest mineral.

famous throughout Japan, and when he died a statue honoring him was erected in Shibuya station. The station has held an annual memorial service ever since.

THE STAR: Allan F-1, a black stallion born in 1886

THE HEADLINE: *Slow Horse Is Late Bloomer*

WHAT HAPPENED: One of the worst racing horses of his day, every owner who bought Allan F-1 invariably lost money on him and quickly resold him. One owner traded him for a mule, another had to settle for a donkey.

But the horse had one redeeming feature: when he did pace, he looked very pretty doing it. So in 1901 a breeder named James R. Brantley bred the 15-year-old horse to a Tennessee walking horse.

THE AFTERMATH: Allan F-1 wasn't the first walking horse, but he was so beautiful and so successful at transmitting his unique loose gait to his offspring that in 1938, the Tennessee Walking Horse Breeder's Association designated Allan its "foundation sire"—the father of the breed.

THE STAR: Blanco, a white Collie

THE HEADLINE: *First Dog Is Second Rate*

WHAT HAPPENED: When President Lyndon Johnson moved into the White House in 1963, he brought along his Beagles—Him and Her. The dogs made headlines on April 27, 1964, when LBJ picked them up by their ears. A photographer got a shot of Him and Her yelping in pain. The White House was deluged with calls and letters from angry dog lovers.

Her died in November 1964, after swallowing a stone, and Him died in June 1966, run over by a car while chasing a squirrel across the White House lawn. It made national news, and dozens of people wrote the White House offering the president a new dog. LBJ said no, but eventually accepted one. He chose Blanco, a white collie. Bad choice: When Blanco arrived at the White House, she began biting every dog and most of the people she came in contact with.

THE AFTERMATH: Blanco was kept on tranquilizers for the rest of LBJ's presidency, and according to one account, "when Johnson left office, he was finally persuaded to give Blanco away."

What do the cities of Denver and Orlando have in

THE BIRTH OF THE SUBMARINE, PART III

You've probably heard of the Monitor *and the* Merrimack…*but have you heard of the* CSS Hunley? *Here's part 3 of the our story on the origin of the submarine. (Part II is on page 200.)*

DAMN YANKEES

The situation was desperate. By 1863, the second year of the American Civil War, the U.S. Navy had succeeded in blockading Charleston, South Carolina, ports, halting virtually all Southern shipping. The Confederacy was willing to try just about anything to reopen its ports—including using submarines.

They came up with a class of small, cigar-shaped ironclad subs called *Davids* (from David and Goliath). Fatal design flaw: the *Davids* were steam powered, which meant that they had to run with a hatch open at all times to provide combustion air for the engine. Since the boats floated only a few inches above the water line, they were prone to swamping and sinking in even the calmest waters, which made them deathtraps.

ONE-HIT WONDER

But before the Confederacy abandoned the *Davids*, one managed an attack on the U.S.S. *New Ironsides* as she sat at anchor in Charleston harbor. The *David* closed in and detonated its bomb, but the *New Ironsides* didn't sink. The *David*, on the other hand, took on so much water that the crew had to abandon ship.

"Neither ship suffered serious damage, but the encounter did establish a historical first," Burgess writes. Charles Howard, the ensign who saw the *David* coming and sounded the alarm, was shot by a member of the *David's* crew and "earned the dubious distinction of being the first fatality of submarine warfare."

Another Confederate submarine was the *H. L. Hunley*, named by the inventor, Horace L. Hunley. Realizing the danger of steam power on a submarine, Hunley opted for manpower. Starting with two old boilers welded together to make a 25-foot-long hull, Hunley added stabilizing fins, diving planes, and a propeller shaft that ran the length of the ship and was powered by eight members of the crew turning hand cranks. Top speed: 4 mph.

DOWN SHE GOES

Confederate General P. G. T. Beauregard was so impressed with the design that he pressed the sub into immediate service. On her first trial, however, the *Hunley* swamped and sank like a stone. Seven crew members drowned. The ship was salvaged and put back in service but again sank, this time killing six of its crew. "It is more dangerous to those who use it than to the enemy," General Beauregard observed.

But Hunley was convinced that human error and bad training were the problem, so he set out to fix them by commanding the ship himself. Big mistake—on its next trip, the *Hunley* sank once more, this time killing everyone on board, including Hunley. "The spectacle was indescribably ghastly," wrote one Confederate general who was present when the *Hunley* was brought to the surface. "The unfortunate men were contorted into all sorts of horrible attitudes, and the blackened faces of all presented the expression of their despair and agony."

IF AT FIRST YOU DON'T SUCCEED...

"Since every trip made by this submarine seemed doomed to disaster," Richard Garrett writes in *Submarines*, "it was decided that the time for trials was over. If she was to kill more men, she might as well take a fragment of Yankee shipping with her."

At 8:00 p.m. on February 17, 1864, the *Hunley* attacked the USS *Housatonic*, a 1,400-ton steam-powered Union warship. The *Housatonic's* crew knew that the Confederacy was using submersibiles to attack Union ships, so as soon as they saw the *Hunley* coming they weighed anchor and began steaming away. But it was too late—the *Hunley* closed in on the *Housatanic*, placed a 90-pound explosive charge on her hull, backed away, and detonated the charge. The bomb blew a hole in the *Housatonic's* hull below the waterline, sinking her. It was a huge event in naval history: For the first time ever, a submarine had sunk an enemy warship in battle, something that would not be repeated until World War I more than 50 years later.

Bank on it: Before the American Revolution, there wasn't a single bank in America.

YOU WIN SOME, YOU LOSE SOME

True to form, though, at the moment of her victory the *Hunley*'s luck deserted her. The *Housatonic* settled in shallow water. The crew was able to climb up into the rigging and wait for help; in the end only one officer and four members of the *Housatonic*'s 160-man crew died in the attack.

But, as Dan Van Der Vat writes in *Stealth at Sea: The History of the Submarine*:

> The *Hunley*, having become the first submersible to sink an enemy vessel, promptly became the first such craft to be lost in action. Swamped in the turbulence caused by the unexpectedly violent explosion, the vessel sank with a loss of all nine aboard.

The *Hunley* had sunk one ship and killed five enemy seamen at the cost of the lives of 32 men. But by sinking the *Housatonic*, the *Hunley* proved that submarines could be lethal weapons in wartime, guaranteeing that more subs would be built.

LOST...AND FOUND

What happened to the *Hunley*? Workers clearing sunken ships from Charleston Harbor after the war discovered it, then lost it again. P. T. Barnum offered a $100,000 reward to anyone who could find the wreck, but it wasn't found until May 1995, buried beneath 3 feet of silt in 30 feet of water, four miles short of its intended destination. The sub was brought to the surface in August in 2000 and is now being restored.

* * *

BUGS IN THE MOVIES

Tarantulas have a reputation for being dangerous, and all of them look scary on-screen. But, according to Ray Mendez, an "insect wrangler" for film, TV, and commercials, many varieties are harmless.

"The Mexican Red-Knee tarantula and the American Desert tarantula are both passive," he says. "Almost all of the tarantulas on the screen are one of those types." So if James Bond finds a hairy tarantula in his bed, it's really just an innocuous spider? "That's right," Mendez laughs.

UNCLE JOHN'S STALL OF FAME

More memorable bathroom achievements.

Honoree: Richard List, a 47-year-old landscaper in Berkeley, California

Notable Achievement: Best artistic use of discarded toilets

True Story: List is the inventor of "plop art." In 1993, he moved 19 old toilets into a vacant lot, painted them Day-Glo orange, pink, and green and declared them the New-Sense (say it fast) Museum. Then, between the commodes, he gradually added decorated television sets…disembodied mannequins…weird sculptures…and a host of other odds and ends. "What can I say?" said a nearby retailer. "Art is whatever you can get away with, I guess. I'd much rather have a nice monumental Picasso or an ice skating rink, but we have the Toilet Museum."

Honoree: The government of Suwon, South Korea

Notable Achievement: Using clean bathrooms as a foreign relations tool

True Story: "In this era of globalization," declared one government official, "it is important to become the leader in the world in the cleanest bathrooms." According to news reports, the city has 580 "plush public restrooms….Toilet seats are heated, violin music plays, and tasteful paintings and flower arrangements adorn the rooms….There are weekly guided tours and according to officials, some people arrange to meet inside to have tea."

Honoree: Annabel Elliott Outhouse of Nova Scotia

Notable Achievement: Writing the only book about outhouses by someone named Outhouse

True Story: Her book is entitled *Outhouses of the Island*, and although it sounds as though it might be a family genealogy, it really is about outdoor toilets in Long Island, Nova Scotia.

Harley-Davidson tried to trademark its engine sound and the word "hog." Both attempts failed.

Honoree: The Dutch town of Bergen op Zoom
Notable Achievement: Most unusual way of handling dog poop
True Story: On city sidewalks, the town installed flushing toilets for dogs.

Honoree: *Weekly World News*
Notable Achievement: Best supernatural reporting about toilets
True Story: In 1999, a headline in the tabloid read: "PRIEST CALLED IN TO EXORCISE TOILET—*AFTER LADY VANISHES!*" The story explained that the woman was the fourth victim of "the cursed crapper," which had already claimed three plumbers. "There was something demonic dwelling in that toilet, according to the famed French exorcist who conducted the ceremony. 'It seems clear that those who vanished were sucked straight into Hell,' he said. 'And that, I'm sure, was not a pleasant experience.'"

Honoree: Bob Kelley, radio announcer for the Los Angeles Angels, a minor league baseball team in the 1940s and 1950s
Notable Achievement: Turning a potential bathroom disaster into entertainment
True Story: According to Steve Harvey in *Only in L.A.*: "Kelley re-created road games of the minor league Angels in the studio at KMPC. He obtained the play-by-play from Western Union and called the game as if he were there, using various sound effects. One Sunday...Kelley returned from a local bar to call the second game of a double-header...And he felt the call of nature—really bad....But he couldn't leave because there was no one to take his place. Finally he picked up a metal wastebasket and in a few moments he said, "Uh-oh, folks. It's starting to rain. I think you can hear it coming down on this old tin roof."'

Honoree: Koko, the gorilla that knows American sign language
Notable Achievement: Being the first member of the ape family to master "potty talk"
True Story: In the late 1990s, Koko participated in a live Internet chat on America Online. According to one account, "When asked about her boyfriend, Koko replied, 'toilet.'"

WIDE WORLD OF
WEIRD SPORTS

*Calling all jocks: Tired of baseball, football, etc.? Don't
fret—you've got plenty of options! Here are some
little-known sports that may tickle your fancy.*

BOG SNORKELING
Where They Do It: Llanwrtyd Wells, Wales

How It's Played: The idea is to completely immerse yourself in a bog, breathing through a snorkel. One description: "Snorkelers plunge into a smelly ditch near the village of Llanwrtyd Wells and embark on a furious downstream dog paddle. Their aquatic odyssey presents many daunting challenges: the bog's sludgy consistency, the disgusting brown backwash that the swimmers generate, and the determined water scorpions that like to burrow into one's bathing suit."(*Outside* magazine)

If that's not weird enough, there's also Bike Bog Snorkeling held in Powys, Wales. As *Bizarre* magazine describes it: "The idiots who took part in the inaugural mountain-bike bog snorkeling championship soon realized the error of their ways as they cycled into the slimy abyss. Visibility was down to a few feet, and despite the fact that the bikes had been specially prepared by having every orifice stuffed with lead shot, they did their best to float away....Riders competed against the clock to cycle round a post—with a special prize for anyone who could cycle back out of the bog—this proved to be impossible."

CANINE FREESTYLE DANCING
Where They Do It: Everywhere. There are more than 8,000 enthusiasts around the world.

How It's Played: Dancing with your dog for prizes? Not a sport, exactly, but who can resist? The idea is to move in time with a dog partner, but you're not allowed to hold the dog's paws, the way you would in "at-home dog dancing." In fact, you're not suppposed to touch the dog at all. According to the *New York Times*: "Costumed owners and their matching-collared pooches exhibit choreography to such tunes as 'The Yellow Rose of Texas' and 'Get Happy' and compete for prizes. "You will discover," says the national Canine Freestyle Federation, "that your dog likes music!...You'll see a new sparkle in his eye, feet stepping higher and a tail wagging harder."

WADLOPING

Where They Do It: In the Waddenzee, a shallow inlet separating the northern Netherlands mainland from the East Frisian Islands

How It's Played: Entrants leap off a dike on Holland's north coast into the knee-deep, sulfurous mud and trudge across the Waddenzee to Simonzand Island, four hours away by foot (when your feet are knee-deep in mud). "Some wadlopers suffer attacks of agoraphobia when they can see no land, just a 360-degree horizon of worm-pocked mud," the *Wall Street Journal* reports. "Veteran wadlopers hike to more distant islands. For the truly obsessed, there's the 'monster walk' to the German island of Borkum, 14 miles away. Borkum, the wadloper's Everest, has been reached by just three men, who waited three years for the lowest possible tide and even then had to walk four miles through neck-high water."

Rules of the Game: "A wrong turn or a change in the wind can put the wadloper in deep water, with no way back to land but to swim. About 15 years ago, a group of wadlopers went astray and had to be rescued by helicopter....The Dutch government has since banned freelance *wadlopen*, requiring wadlopers to travel with trained guides, who carry compasses, maps, two-way radios and rescue equipment."

AND DON'T FORGET...

• **Finnish Wife-Carrying.** According to *Parade* magazine: "The goal: carry a woman, preferably someone else's wife, over a 780-foot course through water, on sand, grass, and asphalt, and over two fences. Dropping the woman results in a 15-second penalty. The fastest man earns the big prize: The woman's weight in lemonade."

• **Welsh Shin-Kicking.** Also known as "purring." "Two men face each other, each holding the shoulders of his opponent. They kick each other's shins until one man loses his grip on his opponent. To add to the pain, their shoes are reinforced." (Update: "The sport has failed to catch on in other nations.")

Blister rule of thumb: Big blisters are called *bullae*, small ones are called *vesicles*.

LIMERICKS

*Limericks have been around since the 1700s. Here are a few
of the more "respectable" ones that our BRI readers have sent us.*

There was a young lady of Ryde,
Who ate some green apples and
    died;
The apples fermented
Inside the lamented,
And made cider inside her inside.

There was a brave girl of
    Connecticut,
Who signaled the train with her
    petticut;
Which the papers defined
As presence of mind,
But deplorable absence of ecticut.

There was a young curate of Kew,
Who kept a tom cat in a pew;
He taught it to speak
Alphabetical Greek,
But it never got further than $\mu\hat{\nu}$.

There was a young athlete named
    Tribbling,
Whose hobby was basketball
    dribbling;
But he dribbled one day
On a busy freeway—
Now his sister is missing a
    sibling.

A maiden at college named
    Breeze,
Weighted down by B.A.'s and
    M.D.'s,
Collapsed from the strain;
Said her doctor, "It's plain
You are killing yourself by
    degrees!"

There was a hillbilly named Shaw
Who envied his maw and his paw.
To share in their life
He adopted his wife
And became his own father-in-
    law.

There was a young belle of old
    Natchez
Whose garments were always in
    patchez.
When comment arose
On the state of her clothes,
She drawled, "When Ah itchez,
    Ah scratchez!"

There was a young lady from Lynn
Who was sunk in original sin.
When they said, "Do be good,"
She replied, "If I could....
But I'd do wrong right over
    again."

There was a young fellow of
    Leeds,
Who swallowed six packets of
    seeds.
In a month, silly ass,
He was covered with grass.
And he couldn't sit down for the
    weeds.

A cat in despondency sighed,
And resolved to commit suicide;
She passed under the wheels
Of eight automobiles,
And after the ninth one she
    died.

Acne treatment, circa 350 A.D.: "wipe pimples with a cloth while watching a falling star."

FAMOUS FOR 15 MINUTES

Here's more proof that Andy Warhol was right when he said that "in the future, everyone will be famous for 15 minutes."

THE STAR: Floyd Collins, a Kentucky farmer

THE HEADLINE: *Man Seeks Adventure Underground; Finds Fame—and Death—Instead*

WHAT HAPPENED: In 1925, while exploring a cavern near his farm, Collins's lantern failed. As he crawled around in complete darkness, somehow he dislodged a seven-ton boulder. It fell on his leg, trapping him in a "coffinlike straightjacket of a space" 8 inches high and 12 feet long. Friends and relatives tried, but could not pry him free.

Word of the dire events found its way to a 19-year-old reporter named Skeets Miller, who crawled into the cave and interviewed Collins. The story was picked up by newspapers all over the U.S.

Suddenly, the eyes of the entire country were focused on Collins. Scores of newspaper and radio reporters descended on the farm, as did film crews from six movie studios and more than 50,000 onlookers, not to mention the hot dog, soft drink, and souvenir vendors who set up shop at the mouth of the cave.

THE AFTERMATH: Two weeks later, the entrance passage collapsed and Collins was cut off from the outside world. Rescuers tunneled down from above, but by the time they reached him on February 16, he'd been dead for two or three days. (Skeets Miller, the reporter who broke the story, fared better: He won the Pulitzer Prize.)

THE STAR: Maria Barberi, a "homely 24-year-old seamstress" living in New York's Little Italy in the 1890s

THE HEADLINE: *Spurned At the Altar, Would-be Bride Gets the Chair Instead*

WHAT HAPPENED: In the 1890s, a bootblack named Domenico Cataldo seduced Barberi with the promise that if they set up house-

---

keeping together, they would marry "soon." Weeks later Cataldo admitted that Barberi was his 6th live-in girlfriend and he did not plan to marry her. Humiliated and enraged, she slashed Cataldo's throat with a folding razor.

Barberi confessed to the murder and was sentenced to death. But it was no ordinary death sentence: she was slated to become the first woman executed in New York's brand-new electric chair, the first of its kind in the world.

The prospect of executing a woman with 1,000 volts of electricity outraged people all over the country. More than 60,000 people signed a petition calling for a pardon, but Governor Levi Morton refused to get involved.

Eventually the court granted Barberi a new trial. And it became one of the most watched legal cases of its day. Barberi's lawyers argued that she was not guilty because she descended from a family of "degenerates" and committed the murder while suffering an attack of "psychical epilepsy."

THE AFTERMATH: After three weeks of trial, the jury deliberated for only 40 minutes before finding Barberi not guilty. Once again a free woman, Barberi returned to her life as a seamstress and disappeared into obscurity.

THE STAR: Dion Rayford, a 25-year-old defensive end for the University of Kansas in 1999

THE HEADLINE: *Football Player Becomes "Taco the Town."*

WHAT HAPPENED: On November 17, 1999, after an evening of drinking, Rayford picked up some fast food at the drive-through window of the Taco Bell in Lawrence, Kansas. Moments later, when he realized the restaurant had botched his taco order and had left out a chalupa, he got out of his car, walked back to the drive-through window, and started screaming. According to newspaper accounts, Rayford "inserted his head and shoulders into the window, and demanded a chalupa with such force that employees locked themselves into an office and called 911." When police arived minutes later, Rayford, still screaming for his food, was arrested and taken into custody.

The story probably might never have made it beyond the local media were it not for one tantalizing piece of misinformation:

The police initially reported—incorrectly—that Rayford had become wedged in the drive-through window.

THE AFTERMATH: Every major paper in the country carried the story. Rayford's "Chalupa Crisis" also made ABC's "World News Now," "The Tonight Show," and "Fox Sports News." The incident may have ruined Rayford's chances for a professional career. "It's a red flag," said Kansas Head Coach Terry Allen. "Professional football is such a competitive arena that some coach could say, 'Let's take this other guy because Dion is the Chalupa man.' "

THE STAR: Mahir Cagri, a 37-year-old Turkish journalist and music teacher

THE HEADLINE: *Nice Turkish Boy Caught in Web of Lies*

WHAT HAPPENED: In 1999, Cagri, a devout Muslim, set up his own webpage on the Internet. It wasn't all that unusual—it showed pictures of Cagri playing the accordion; it talked about his hometown of Izmir, Turkey, and his passion for Ping-Pong. That was it...until a teenage hacker broke into the site and added a few extras.

"Welcome to my homepage!!!!!! I kiss you!!!!!" the new site proclaimed. "I like sex....I like to take foto-camera (animals, towns, nice nude models and peoples)....Who is want to come TURKEY I can invitate—She can stay in my home."

Word of the "improved" website spread as people stumbled onto the site, had a laugh, and then e-mailed it to their friends. Cagri's website received more than 2.5 million hits. He was deluged with thousands of e-mails (including proposals for marriage) and phone calls.

He was profiled in *Time*, *USA Today*, *Entertainment Weekly*, and in scores of newspapers all over the world. When a company called eTour.com flew him in to the United States, he was mobbed by his American fans.

THE AFTERMATH: The furor died down after a few months. "I still invite everybody to come see Turkey and me," he says, "but I cannot accommodate everyone. I had a regular, normal life before this happened, and I have not changed. I am the same Mahir."

DRACULA, "I VANT TO BE IN PICTURES"

If Dracula had only made it onto the stage as a play (see Dracula,
"I Vant to Be a Star" on p. 315), we probably never would have
heard of him. It was the 1931 Universal film, starring Bela
Lugosi, that finally made him a household name.

THE SILVER SCREEN

In 1930, impressed by the success of the Dracula stage play, Universal Pictures decided to buy it. They paid $40,000 for all rights to the novel *and* the stage plays, so they would have the exclusive film rights to the Dracula character. Unfortunately, none of the play manuscripts proved to be suitable as a movie screenplay. So Universal brought it to Pulitzer Prize-winning novelist Louis Bromfield. And when the lavish sets and scenes called for in his ambitious screenplay threatened to bust the film's budget, two more writers were brought in to "help" him finish the job.

SPLIT PERSONALITY

But before he left Hollywood (never to return), Bromfield made one lasting contribution: he combined the older, nastier Dracula of Bram Stoker's novel with the suave young Count that had become popular on stage. Starved for fresh blood in Transylvania, the old, tired Dracula would regain his youth drinking fresh blood when he arrived in London.

JUNIOR PARTNER

Dracula would be Universal's first horror movie, but it wouldn't come without a fight: Studio head Carl Laemmle, Sr. was vehemently opposed to the idea of making scary movies. "I don't believe in horror pictures," he would later tell an interviewer. "It's morbid. None of our officers are for it. People don't want that sort of thing."

So why did he agree to make the film? Two reasons: First, *Dracula* was a hot property and he didn't want it to go to the competition;

Russia's Lake Baikal is deep enough to hold four Empire State Buildings stacked atop each other.

and second because, he explained, "Junior wanted it."

"Junior" was Laemmle's son Julius, who changed his name to Carl Jr. when his father made him head of Universal on his 21st birthday. Junior headed Universal until the studio was put up for sale in 1936, and his years at the helm were rocky ones. "His abilities and achievements are still a matter of debate," David Skal writes in *Hollywood Gothic*, "but he made one indelible contribution to American culture: the Hollywood horror movie, an obsessive new genre revolving around threatening, supernaturally powerful male monstrosities."

CASTING CALL

Once they actually decided to make the film, the search for an actor to play Dracula was on.

Silent film star Lon Chaney, Sr., was the top contender for the part...until he was diagnosed with terminal throat cancer. At least five other actors were considered for the part, but none of them panned out.

Meanwhile, Bela Lugosi lobbied hard to win the role, trying to ingratiate himself with Universal by printing up publicity photos showing him posing as Dracula, praising the film in print interviews, and offering unsolicited suggestions on how the script could be improved. When the sale of the film rights was still pending, Lugosi had even tried to intercede with Bram Stoker's widow to get Universal a better price.

Lugosi apparently hoped that bowing and scraping would ingratiate him with the studio, but what it really did was make him appear desperate—which he was. Universal finally did offer him the part, of course, but for only $500 a week. The offer was an insult—David Manners, who received third billing as Jonathan Harker, signed for $2,000 a week. But Lugosi took it anyway. He'd already lost the role once by holding out for too much money (see p. 319), and he wasn't about to let it happen again.

ON THE SCREEN

To direct, Universal picked veteran horror filmaker Ted Browning. Filming *Dracula* took seven weeks. Lugosi delivered a masterful performance, arguably the most memorable and influential ever. It was so convincing that a number of his co-stars wondered if he really was performing…or just being himself. "I never thought he was acting," David Manners remembered, "just being the odd man he was.…I mainly remember Lugosi standing in front of a full-length mirror between scenes, intoning 'I am Dracula.'"

DRACULA MUST DIE!

Dracula is tame by today's standards, but in its day it was a shocker. When it was shown in previews, people actually demanded that it be banned. "I saw the first fifteen minutes of it," wrote the PTA's previewer, "and felt I could stand no more.…It should be withdrawn from public showing, as children, the weak-minded, and all classes attend motion pictures indiscriminately." Even Universal head Carl Laemmle, Jr., was put off by scenes that he found to be suggestively homoerotic. "Dracula should only go for women and not men," he dashed off in an angry memo, and the offending scenes were removed.

IT WAS A GRAVEYARD SMASH

The movie opened on February 12, 1931 and despite *very* mixed reviews, *Dracula* turned out to be a crowd pleaser. The gothic horror film proved to be the kind of escapist fantasy filmgoers were looking for as the country slid deeper into the Great Depression, and the tale of ordinary mortals triumphing over seemingly insurmountable evil must have thrilled a public in the grips of seemingly endless economic troubles.

Dracula went on to be one of the top-grossing films of 1931, and Universal's biggest moneymaker for the year. Thanks to *Dracula*, Universal turned a profit for the first time since 1928, and though its financial problems continued for the rest of the decade, *Dracula* is credited with earning Universal the money it needed to weather the Great Depression.

Just seven weeks after *Dracula* opened in theatres, Universal purchased the film rights to *Frankenstein*, setting it on a course to become Hollywood's reigning horror studio through the 1930s and into the 1940s, thrilling audiences (and its board of directors) with the Werewolf, the Mummy, and other classic Hollywood monsters.

For more, turn to page 408.

Experts say that the most common phobia in the U.S. is *arachnophobia*—fear of spiders.

MYTH-SPOKEN

*We hate to say it (well, actually, we like to say it), but some of
the best-known quotes in history weren't said by the people
they're attributed to...and some weren't even said at all!*

Line: "That government is best which governs least."
Supposedly Said By: Thomas Jefferson (1743–1826)
Actually: William F. Buckley used this quote in a 1987 newspaper column. He probably took it from Henry David Thoreau,
who used it in his 1849 essay "Civil Disobedience." But Thoreau
didn't attribute it to anyone in particular. Why did Buckley attribute it to Jefferson? Who knows. Anyway, it was *first* said by the early American pamphleteer, Thomas Paine.

Line: "Here I stand—warts and all."
Supposedly Said By: Oliver Cromwell (1616-1658)
Actually: Vice President George Bush "quoted" this line in a
1988 campaign speech, but Cromwell never said it. The actual
quote was "Paint me—warts and all". When the *New York Times*
called Bush headquarters to question the reference, one of Bush's
speechwriters claimed to have made up the quote.

Line: "Build a better mousetrap, and the world will beat a path to
your door."
Supposedly Said By: Ralph Waldo Emerson (1803–1882), American essayist, philosopher, and poet.
Actually: Sarah Yule, a writer, took it from an Emerson lecture
and included it in her 1889 book, *Borrowings*, but she got it wrong.
What Emerson actually said: "If a man has good corn, or wood, or
boards, or pigs to sell, or can make better chairs, or knives, cruci-
bles or church organs, than anybody else, you will find a broad,
hard-beaten road to his house, though it be in the woods."

Line: "I can answer you in two words, 'im-possible.'"
Supposedly Said By: Sam Goldwyn (1882–1974), movie mogul
Actually: This is often quoted as one of his famous "Goldwynisms"
(see *Best of Uncle John's Bathroom Reader*, p. 208), but he didn't say
it. Charlie Chaplin did.

Line: "I wish I'd studied Latin at school so I could talk to you in your own language."

Supposedly Said By: Vice President Dan Quayle to a group of schoolchildren, on a tour of Latin American countries

Actually: It was invented by Democratic Congresswoman Pat Schroeder as an attack on Quayle. Even though she publicly apologized to the former VP for the remark, it lives on as a "genuine quote" in popular mythology.

Line: "What we were striving for was a kind of modified form of communism."

Supposedly Said By: Harold Ickes (1874–1952), secretary of the interior under FDR and a strong suppoter of Roosevelt's New Deal

Actually: In 1981, President Ronald Reagan said that Ickes made this statement "in his book," implying that it revealed the true nature of the New Deal. But the White House was "unable to verify the President's reference." Translation: Reagan made it up. Apparently it's just another example of a politician inventing something to make the other side look bad.

Line: "Everyone talks about the weather, but nobody does anything about it."

Supposedly Said By: Mark Twain (1835–1910)

Actually: Twain was so prolific and so clever that a lot of good quotes are mistakenly attributed to him. But journalist Charles Dudley Warner was the real author of this line. To his credit, Twain never claimed it as his own.

Line: "You can't be too rich or too thin."

Supposedly Said By: The Duchess of Windsor, Wallis Simpson (1896–1986)

Actually: Aside from the fact that the king of England abdicated his throne in order to marry her, this is the only thing the duchess is remembered for. Too bad she didn't say it. Truman Capote said it in 1950 on David Susskind's TV talk show.

MOVIE BOMB: *WATERWORLD*

*Some films don't set out to be disaster films, but they still
end up that way. Take this one, for example—it's one
of the most expensive duds in Hollywood history.*

WATERWORLD

In 1986 a recent Harvard graduate named Peter Rader
was working at Venice studios and hoping to get a chance
to direct. One day producer Brad Krevoy called. "Listen," he told
Rader, "I got some South African money, and they want me to
make a *Mad Max* rip-off. If you write one, I'll let you direct it."

Rader had another idea—he wrote a script for a Western set in
the future, when global warming has melted the polar ice caps and
submerged the entire planet under water. Krevoy rejected it out of
hand, "That's ridiculous! That's going to cost us $5 million to
make!" Wishful thinking.

Rader's script was shelved. Then, in 1989, Universal Studios
found it and signed Kevin Costner, who was at the peak of his career, to star in it. All they needed was a director. Universal knew
that shooting a movie on the water would be difficult and expensive, and wanted someone who had experience working on a big-
budget films with lots of special effects. They chose Robert Zemekis,
who'd directed *Forest Gump* and *Who Framed Roger Rabbit?*

But Costner wouldn't hear of it. He insisted that Universal hire
his friend, director Kevin Reynolds, and threatened to quit if they
didn't. Universal caved in and signed him to the film. "We call
Costner 'Buffalo Head,'" said one studio exec. "He's totally stub-
born."

SEASICK

They shot the movie in Hawaii; it was difficult from the beginning.
Seasickness plagued the cast and crew, and every time a ship sailed
by on the horizon, filming had to halt until it sailed out of the shot.
The weather changed from hour to hour, making it nearly impossible to combine footage that had been shot at different times.

But the biggest problem of all was the fact that, as Universal had pointed out from the very beginning, Reynolds and other key players had no experience with a huge and complicated film. They wasted a fortune in some areas, but didn't spend enough in others:

• They built a massive, 1,000-ton floating set, the location of much of the action in the film, using up *all* the available steel in the Hawaiian Islands (they even had to import some from California), but forgot to put any restrooms on the set...or on *any* of the 30 boats used by the 500 members of the cast and crew. Result: Whenever Costner, Reynolds, or any of the other principals had to use the bathroom, filming had to halt while they were ferried all the way back to a port-o-potty barge anchored near the shore.

• Costner, who received $14 million for starring in the film, was put up in a $4,500-a-night oceanfront villa with a butler, a chef, and his own private swimming pool. At the same time, much of the crew was assigned to un-insulated condominiums subject to temperature swings of as much as 50°. "The crew was forced to stay in substandard housing, all in the guise of being economical, which perpetuated hostilities and low morale," one studio executive told reporters,

• The studio didn't spend any money researching weather conditions a quarter-mile off of Hawaii's Kona coast, where the set was anchored. "If they had," Robert Welkos wrote in the *Los Angeles Times*, "they would have learned that the area was subject to sudden 45 mph winds," which repeatedly blew the set out of position, ruining countless shots, and delaying filming for as long as six hours each time as tugboats slowly maneuvered the set back into position.

Thanks to these and other problems, the cost of the film soared from $100 million to $172 million. Costner had personal problems to boot: during filming his 16-year marriage ended in divorce amid tabloid rumors that he was having an affair with a married hula dancer. Costner also had a falling out with Kevin Reynolds over the direction of the film. "Costner should only appear in pictures he directs himself," Reynolds told *Entertainment Weekly* after he quit. "That way he can always be working with his favorite actor and favorite director."

Word of the film's chronic problems (one crewmember called it "a runaway train under water") found its way back to the mainland. The media was calling it a flop even before it was released. Amazingly, despite the bad press, mixed reviews, and disappointing box office sales, *Waterworld* almost broke even.

"If I ever had twins, I'd use one for parts." —Comedian Steven Wright

IRONIC DEATHS

*You can't help laughing at some of life's—and death's—
ironies...as long as they happen to someone else.
These stories speak for themselves.*

FELIX POWELL, *music composer*
Story: Powell, then a British staff sergeant, wrote the music for "Pack Up Your Troubles in Your Old Kit Bag and Smile, Smile, Smile" in 1915 and entered it in a World War I competition for the best morale-building song. The ditty won first prize and has been called "perhaps the most optimistic song ever written."
Final Irony: Powell committed suicide in 1942.

NIC MARCURA, *a Yugoslavian farmer*
Story: Sensing that his end was near, Marcura set to work digging his own grave.
Final Irony: According to news reports, "in a sudden cloudburst, water began to fill up the hole. Marcura tried to bail it out with a bucket, slipped in and drowned."

ALBEN BARKLEY, *former U.S. vice president*
Story: On April 30, 1956, Barkley delivered a speech at a mock political convention at Washington and Lee University.
Final Irony: Moments after declaring to his audience, "I would rather sit at the feet of the Lord than dwell in the house of the mighty," Barkley keeled over and died.

FRIEDRICH RIESFELDT, *a zookeeper in Paderborn, Germany*
Story: When his elephant Stefan became constipated, Riesfeldt fed it 22 doses of animal laxative...and when that didn't work, fed it more than a bushel of high-fiber berries, figs, and prunes. *Still* no luck.
Final Irony: The frustrated zookeeper then gave Stefan an olive-oil enema. That did it. According to one account, the elephant suddenly released approximately 200 pounds of manure, killing Riesfeldt. "The sheer force of the elephant's unexpected defecation knocked Mr. Riesfeldt to the ground, where he struck his head on a rock and

---

In one recent survey, 2.1% of nosepickers said they did so "for enjoyment."

lay unconscious as the elephant continued to evacuate his bowels on top of him," police detective Erik Dern explained. "With no one there to help him, he lay under all that dung for at least an hour and suffocated." (Although this story was widely reported in the press, it may just be an urban legend. What makes it so questionable? Sounds like a lot of dung.)

GEORGE STORY, Life *magazine's "Life Baby"*

Story: In 1936, the premiere issue of *Life* magazine featured a picture of newborn baby George Story. The headline: "Life Begins." Over the years, the magazine periodically updated readers on the progress of Story's life as he married twice, had children, and retired.

Final Irony: Less than a week after *Life* announced it was folding, Story died from heart failure. The final issue of *Life* featured one last article on Story. The headline: "A Life Ends."

MYRA DAVIS, *Janet Leigh's body double in the film* Psycho

Story: Davis was Leigh's stand-in, she was one of several people who provided the voice of Norman Bates's mother, and it was her hand that was seen in the famous shower scene in which Leigh's character is stabbed to death.

Final Irony: On July 3, 1988, Davis was found strangled in her Los Angeles home, murdered by a 31-year-old "caretaker and handyman"…just like the character portrayed by Anthony Perkins in *Psycho*.

BOBBY LEACH, *a professional daredevil*

Story: In 1911, Leach, who made his living risking his life, went over Niagara Falls in a barrel. He survived the attempt.

Final Irony: Fifteen years later, in 1926, Leach slipped on an orange peel…and died from injuries sustained in the fall.

JOHANN UNDERWALD, *a Swiss mathematician*

Story: Underwald, one of the brightest stars in his field, was described by his peers as "the next Albert Einstein."

Final Irony: Underwald died in October 1999. Cause of death: mathematical error—Underwald "made a 250-foot bungee jump with a 300-foot bungee cord, and died immediately on impact."

BOWL, BATH...
AND BEYOND

This article by Patricia Davis first appeared in the Wall St.
Journal *on January 8, 1999, and it's right up our alley.*
"Bathrooms have gotten so big," Davis reports,
"that owners host dinners in the loo."

BEST SEAT IN THE HOUSE
Nancy and Weldon Koenig felt like royalty at the lavish Tuscan theme party given in honor of their son's engagement by some friends last fall. Sunflowers and bunches of grapes were strewn about the Liberty, Texas, house. Italian music wafted through every room. And when dinner was served, the Koenigs had a place of honor: chairs near the tub in the master bathroom.

"We probably had the best seat in the bathroom," says Mrs. Koenig, one of a dozen guests in the sumptuous blush-colored chamber, replete with a fireplace, a glass-enclosed atrium with a goldfish pond, and a large double window overlooking a pond and gazebo. "It is so beautiful you don't even think of it as a bathroom."

COCKTAIL POTTIES?

Forget snack-time at the kitchen counter and cocktail parties in the family den. In a surprising number of American homes, the newest gathering place is the bathroom. After years of expanding to make space for whirlpools, saunas, and multiple shower heads, some bathrooms have become so large and so comfortable that it seems almost wasteful to confine them to their traditional functions. Instead, they are being transformed into de facto living areas, kitchens, gyms, and home offices. Think of this as an outgrowth of the now-familiar magazine rack next to the toilet. If it's socially acceptable to read there, why not squeeze in a movie or a drink with friends?

As a result, televisions, refrigerators, mini-bars, computers, and even antiques are moving into the lavatory. Many designers recommend putting exercise equipment in bathrooms that already look like gyms with their saunas and whirlpools. Some manufacturers offer small refrigerators that fit neatly into bathroom cabinets, as

---

Bad breath caused by onions and garlic originates in the lungs, not the mouth.

well as island sinks that can be used in bathroom mini-kitchens. The result has been a flurry of spending. Last year (1998), home-owners paid about $14 billion on bathroom remodeling, just shy of the 10-year high in 1997.

Drew Bledsoe, quarterback for the New England Patriots, recently finished building a gym-in-a-bathroom for his Medfield, Masschusetts, home. Among its features: treadmills, weight machines, a steambath, sauna, a huge hot tub, and a juice bar. Carol and Joseph Thompson's new bathroom in Ponte Vedra Beach, Florida, has an exercise area, two televisions, a telephone, refrigerator, microwave, and sink. Carol Schmitt of Gibsonia, Pennsylvania, spent over $50,000 building a bathroom with a crystal chandelier lighting and a recessed television wired for high-tech audio.

The best bathrooms are "fully furnished, fully decorated sitting rooms that just happen to have a bathtub, shower, or toilet in the middle," says Manhattan designer Jeffrey Bilhuber. He recently converted a four-bedroom apartment with seven bathrooms into a one-bedroom apartment with four bathrooms.

CHANGING TIMES

Until recently, inviting so much activity in the bathroom would have been not only physically impossible but also culturally unthinkable. Bathrooms were almost taboo parts of the home, where people discreetly closeted themselves and blushed if someone knocked. The very idea of food there was repellent, and appliances, beyond essentials like electric shavers and curling irons, were thought to be electrocution hazards.

But the average bathroom has almost tripled in size in the past decade, designers say, creating plenty of nooks to safely tuck away fine furnishings and electrical equipment. Toilets themselves are quieter because of improved manufacturing and water flow. Meanwhile, the huge proliferation of whirlpool tubs—industry sales have grown about 20% a year since the late 1980s—has transformed bathing from a chore into an experience to be savored.

"You have got to stop thinking of bathrooms in an old-fashioned way," says Washington, D.C., designer Mary Douglas Drysdale, who regularly helps clients with what she calls "bathroom suites" that range in price from $50,000 to $150,000. She suggests installing exercise equipment and at least a mini-kitchen for brewing coffee or making a light breakfast.

When Ms. Drysdale hosts parties, she opens her own master bathroom to guests. She fills one sink with flowers and another with ice to chill champagne, and she uses a nine-foot elliptical cabinet in the dressing area as a dessert buffet. Guests can wander into the main bath area, which has a fireplace, a hidden television, and candles that Ms. Drysdale lights for an air of elegance. The tub rests on a seven-foot marble platform that "almost begs one to sit," says Ms. Drysdale, who boasts that a plumber once called her bathroom the nicest he had ever seen.

SIZE MATTERS

In Linda Paulson's home, the site of the Koenig engagement party, the master bathroom is 28 feet by 35 feet, bigger than the dining room. In addition to the goldfish pond and fireplace, it sports a chaise lounge covered in hand-painted silk, a modest waterfall, and an exercise alcove. Her designer, Barbara Schlattman, put the bathroom television on a rotating pillar so that it can be seen from the tub or the exercise area.

Although she enjoys using her bathroom for parties, Mrs. Paulson says she built it as a retreat. That's a typical rationale, says Geoffrey Godbey, a professor at Penn State University, who specializes in leisure studies. Homeowners are putting more energy into their bathrooms because they are getaways to "hide from work or Monica Lewinsky," he says. But that doesn't mean secluding oneself altogether. "Ironically, if you admire a place because it is private, you may want to celebrate and bring people in," Professor Godbey says.

PRIVACY PROBLEM

Of course, bringing friends into the bathroom raises an awkward question: What if someone has to, actually, um, use it? At her parties, Ms. Drysdale designates another bathroom for that purpose. Many bathrooms have toilets that are closeted off to offer privacy in a crowd. For bathrooms with an outdoor view, Beverly Hills, California, designer Douglas Pierce Hiatt has come up with

---

Things change: Life expectancy of Neanderthal man: 29 years. Cro-Magnon Man: 32.

a contraption that sets off cascades of water down the windows.

Elaborate bathroom products have been increasingly popular, from Japanese-style toilet washlets that spray water on people's bodies to "toe testers" that make it possible to check water temperature before showering. But only recently has such a wide array of other home products moved into the bathroom.

Jacuzzi, Inc. offers a $12,500 unit, the J-Allure that combines a whirlpool bath for two, a built-in curved-glass shower stall, a compact-disc player, four speakers, and a TV. Vicki McCaw of Aiken, South Carolina, recently bought one as an anniversary gift for her husband. It sits directly across from the fireplace and a pair of fish tanks under construction in the couple's bathroom. Mrs. McCaw says she first ordered the J-Allure without a TV, thinking it too small, but later changed her mind. "I thought…'Let's get the whole schmear,' and you know, it's a damn good TV."

BATHING WITH "BARNEY"

Roy Jacuzzi, chief executive of the company that bears his name, says his own children watch "Barney" in the J-Allure while they bathe. He promises more high-tech products for the bathroom, although he won't get specific.

"We've showered people, right?" he says. "What is to stop us from drying them?"

Architects predict the urge to multitask in the bathroom will spread. "People say they read in bed and work in bed. Why not in the bathroom?" asks New York architect Alex Gorlin, who recently designed a bathroom-cum-office for a prominent New York art dealer. When finished, the 600-square-foot lavatory will feature a workspace with built-in pearwood shelving, file cabinets, a writing desk, and computer table. The toilet will be behind a closed door. "That's key," says Mr. Gorlin. "Putting the toilet in its own room opens up the rest of the space for other activities."

All of this can be humbling to people with smaller bathrooms, as the Koenigs can attest. After the engagement celebration at the Paulson home, they surveyed their own bathroom for party potential and found it wanting. The room is big enough for "maybe a card table with four chairs," says Mrs. Koenig. "We just don't have the space."

GROANERS

Faithful BRI members keep sending Uncle John their horrible puns. Of course he loves them—and then insists on "sharing" them with us. So why are we inflicting them on you? Have you ever heard the saying "misery loves company"? Heh, heh. Feel free to groan out loud.

A LITTLE GIRL FELL INTO a well, and although she cried for help, her brother stood by and did nothing. Finally the next-door neighbor came over and pulled the girl up.

"Why didn't you help her?" the neighbor asked the boy.

"How," he replied, "could I be her brother and assist her, too?"

A GUY GOES TO a psychiatrist. "Doc, I keep having these alternating recurring dreams. First, I'm a teepee; then I'm a wigwam; then I'm a teepee; then I'm a wigwam. It's driving me crazy. What's wrong with me?"

The doctor replies: "It's very simple. You're two tents."

A DOCTOR MADE it his regular habit to stop off at a bar for a hazelnut daiquiri on his way home, and the bartender would always have the drink waiting at precisely 5:03 p.m.

One afternoon, as the end of the workday approached, the bartender was dismayed to find that he was out of hazelnuts. Thinking quickly, he threw together a daiquiri made with hickory nuts and set it on the bar. The doctor came in at his regular time, took one sip of the drink and exclaimed, "This isn't a hazelnut daiquiri!"

"No," replied the bartender, "It's a hickory daiquiri, doc."

A PSYCHIATRIST'S RECEPTIONIST alerted the doctor: "A man is out here who says he is invisible."

"Tell him I can't see him right now," said the doctor.

IT IS WELL KNOWN THROUGHOUT Central Europe that members of William Tell's family were early devotees of league bowling. They had sponsors and everything. According to historians, though, the records have been lost, so nobody knows for whom the Tells bowled.

What's the scientific name for the dust we kick up when in motion? The "Pigpen effect."

A GROUP OF CHESS ENTHUSIASTS checked into a hotel and were standing in the lobby discussing their recent tournament victories. After about an hour, the manager came out of the office and asked them to disperse. "But why?" they asked.

"Because," he said, "I can't stand chess nuts boasting in an open foyer."

TRUE STORY: UNCLE JOHN HAD an old telephone booth in his living room. The phone didn't work, but it was quite a conversation piece.

THIS GUY GOES TO A COSTUME party with a girl on his back. "What the heck are you?" asks the host. "I'm a snail," says the guy. "But, you have a girl on your back," replies the host. "Yeah," he says, "that's Michelle."

THERE'S A NUDIST COLONY for communists. Two old men are sitting on the front porch. One turns to the other and says, "I say, old boy, have you read Marx?" And the other says, "Yes...I believe it's these wicker chairs."

THERE WAS THIS HOUSE PAINTER who was always looking for a way to save a buck, so he would often thin his paint to make it go further—and he usually got away with it. When a local church decided to do a big restoration, this fellow put in a bid and because his price was so competitive, he got the job.

One day, just as the job was nearly done, he was up on the scaffold, painting away, when suddenly there was a horrendous clap of thunder. The sky opened and the rain poured down, washing the thin paint off the church and knocking the painter down onto the lawn, surrounded by puddles of the thinned and useless paint.

Fearing this was a judgment from the Almighty, he fell down on his knees and cried, "Oh, God! Forgive me! What should I do?"

And from the thunder, a mighty voice spoke, "Repaint! Repaint and thin no more!"

A FAMOUS VIKING EXPLORER returned home from a voyage and found his name missing from the town register. His wife insisted on complaining to the local civic official who apologized profusely, saying, "I must have taken Leif off my census."

What do your lungs and a tennis court have in common? They have about the same surface area.

FRUIT & VEGGIE QUIZ

*Take this test, and next time you wander through the produce section
of your local grocery store, you may see it in a new light.*

1. According to some estimates, this fruit comprises one-third of *all*
the fruit eaten in the world during the months of July and August.
In China, people believed it grew on the original Tree of Life...so it
was venerated as a symbol of virginity and fertility. What is it?

      a) Peach   *b) Banana*   *c) Apple*

2. Catherine de' Medici, daughter of Lorenzo the Magnificent, left
Florence in 1533 to marry the King of France. Knowing the state of
French cuisine at that time, she brought along an army of chefs to
make the food palatable. She also brought this vegetable, which she
insisted be served at every meal. Result: Now any dish with the
name Florentine contains it. Is it...

      a) Potato   *b) Parsley*   *c) Spinach*

3. Egyptians made a drink from this vegetable. When it was ripe, a
hole was cut at the end. Then a small stick was inserted into the
hole. After much stirring and squashing, the hole was plugged and
the veggie was buried in the ground for a few days. When it was un-
earthed, the fermented pulp inside made for a powerful cocktail.
What veggie are we talking about?

      a) Acorn Squash   *b) Zucchini*   *c) Cucumber*

4. This veggie contains up to 6 times as much vitamin C as oranges
do. Is it...

      a) Pepper   *b) Garlic*   *c) Tomato*

5. Early archeologists found traces of this vegetable in cave dwell-
ings that date back to 9750 B.C. According to Norse legend, it was
given to man by the god Thor, and should be eaten only on his day
(Thursday). It may have been first planted in the New World by
Christopher Columbus himself. Name it.

      a) Cabbage   *b) Peas*   *c) Green Beans*

What do Tom Hanks and Elvis Presley have in common? They're both related to Abe Lincoln.

6. This veggie—called *courgette* by the French and English—is best eaten when immature, because when it's left to grow longer, the seeds suck up most of the flavor.

> a) Okra   b) Zucchini   c) Cucumber

7. Originally came from Africa in the form of a small, bitter-tasting fruit eaten as a kind of salad. The Egyptians cultivated it, then around 5 B.C. brought it across the Mediterranean as a shipboard provision. Italian gardeners then turned it into the sweet fruit it is today.

> a) Watermelon   b) Mango   c) Cantelope

8. Indigenous to India, where it has been grown for more than 4,000 years, it was first brought to the U.S. by Thomas Jefferson.

> a) Strawberry   b) Fig   c) Eggplant

9. The ancient Romans appreciated the healthful properties of this vegetable. In fact, Emperor Augustus put up a statue "praising it for curing him of illness." Are we talking about...

> a) Carrot   b) Lettuce   c) Broccoli

10. A person can do about 18 in a minute, or 8,640 a day; a machine can do 1,800 a minute. What is it?

> a) Picking and sorting grapes   b) Stuffing pimientos in olives
>
> c) Squeezing oranges for orange juice

11. The most popular vegetable in America is...

> a) Carrots   b) Lettuce   c) Potatoes

*   *   *   *

ANSWERS

10-b, 11-c
9-b (Romaine, of course),
5-b, 6-b, 7-a, 8-c,
1-a, 2-c, 3-c, 4-a,

What is Japanese factory worker Kenji Urada's claim to fame? In July 1981 he

PUT A CORK IN IT!

Here's something you may want to remember next time you go to a fancy restaurant (but only if you're over 21).

WHAT DO YOU DO WHEN HANDED THE CORK?

Quiz time: You're in a restaurant. You've studied the wine list and managed to order something without making a fool of yourself. Just when you've relaxed, thinking that your wine ordeal is over, the waiter pulls the cork from the bottle and hands it to you. Conversation stops, and all eyes turn to you expectantly. What do you do now?

a. Sniff the cork.
b. Lick it.
c. Bite lustily into it.
d. Nibble around the edges of it, leaving enough for your friends.
e. Toss it over your left shoulder for luck.
f. Slip it into your pocket or purse for the next time you go to the ol' fishin' hole.
g. Pass it around the table.
h. Fondle it.
i. See if there's something to read on it.
j. Hand it back.
k. Create a diversion and lose it in the confusion.

The correct answers: **h.** and **i.**

FEEL IT

Fondle it, you ask? In a public place? Well, not exactly fondle it. That can be done later in the privacy of your own home. But feel it. Why? To see if it's wet. Why do you care if it's wet? Because a dry cork means that the bottle was not properly stored on its side.

If the cork is dry, can you send the wine back? Well, no, but you can be snotty to the wine steward about it. "Sir," you may say reproachfully, "This bottle has not been properly stored," waving away any apologies and excuses.

became "the first known fatality caused by a robot."

READ IT

Next, you read the cork. You are not looking for messages like "Help, I'm being held prisoner in the wine cellar," although the smart wine drinker will take heed if such a message is found. No, you are making sure the winery information branded on the cork matches what is on the label.

The little ceremony is a throwback to a century ago, when wine fraud was common. It is meant to assure you that the restaurant hasn't tried to rip you off by changing labels on the bottle. Read the cork, compare it with the label, and lay the cork casually on the table. Later, you can nibble it or put it in your pocket for the next time you go fishin', but for now, you must take part in the second part of the ceremony.

SWIRL IT

The waiter pours a splash of wine into your glass and waits expectantly. It's their little trap, just when you think you're out of the woods. DON'T DRINK IT. Instead, swirl the wine around in your glass and take one long, dramatic sniff. Hold your breath for a second in order to build suspense. Unless it smells like vinegar, you exhale, look the server in the eye, and nod once, significantly.

But what if you get that vinegary smell that evokes memories of salad or Easter egg dye? Luckily, being served wine that has turned into vinegar is a pretty rare occurrence, but if that happens, discreetly tell your server, "I believe this wine has passed its peak" or "…turned," or (if you prefer a euphemism) "…gone to meet its maker." The server will whisk it away and bring another bottle, beginning the whole process over.

*　　　*　　　*

BUGS IN THE MOVIES

Scorpions are good for building tense moments on the big screen, but they're much safer than they look. If filmmakers are using a deadly scorpion, its stinger is fixed or covered with wax. And there is a less potent scorpion, called a Desert Hairy scorpion (*Hadrurus arizonensis*). It's larger than the lethal ones. Wranglers trap their scorpions by hunting them at night; if an ultraviolet black light is shined at them, "they glow a bright green."

Q. What sport is played on the largest playing field (300 yards by 200 yards)?　　A. Polo.

THEY WENT THATAWAY

Malcolm Forbes wrote a fascinating book about the deaths of famous people. Here are some of the weirdest stories he found, along with some from the BRI's own files.

YURI GAGARIN

Claim to Fame: The first man ever sent into space

How He Died: Ironically, in a plane crash.

Postmortem: The details of Gagarin's death were kept secret for more than 20 years and revealed only after the fall of the Soviet Union. On March 27, 1968, Gagarin and his copilot were flying at an altitude of 16,000 feet above a thick layer of clouds about 50 miles northeast of Moscow. They were approaching a runway, preparing to land, when another aircraft passed within 2,000 feet of them. The airstream created by the other plane forced Gagarin's plane to dive into the clouds. Gagarin had been told that the clouds were at an altitude of 3,500 feet…but they were actually at less than 2,000, which meant that the ground was 1,500 feet closer than Gagarin thought. By the time he realized what had happened, it was too late to prevent the crash.

HENRY HUDSON

Claim to Fame: A 17th-century navigator and explorer; Hudson Bay and the Hudson River are named after him.

How He Died: Mutiny.

Postmortem: Hudson spent the fall of 1611 exploring Hudson Bay, convinced that he was on the verge of finding the mythical Northwest Passage, a direct route to Asia. But he stayed too long, and when cold weather froze the waters, Hudson and his crew were forced to spend the harsh winter on the southern shore of the bay, 500 miles from the settlement of Toronto.

There wasn't enough food for the crew, a condition Hudson made worse by keeping too much of it for himself. When his top officers protested, he fired them. By the end of the winter, Hudson had made enemies of just about everyone on board. When the ice melted, the crew seized Hudson, his son, and six other crew members and set them adrift in a small sailboat. Hudson was never seen again.

As for the mutineers, they sailed for Canada, where Indians attacked them. The survivors returned to England, where they were put on trial for mutiny, which was be punishable by death. No one knows if they were telling the truth or not, but they blamed the mutiny on the crew members who were killed by natives in Canada. As a result, no one served more than a year in jail.

LOUIS XVII OF FRANCE

Claim to Fame: Son of King Louis XVI and Marie-Antoinette and heir to the throne of France

How He Died: In prison, of tuberculosis.

Postmortem: When the French monarchy was overthrown in 1793, eight-year-old Louis XVII was put into prison. Two years later, the Revolutionary government announced that the boy had died in prison from tuberculosis. He was 10.

That was the official story, but rumor spread that the body of the dead child was too old to have been Louis. A prison guard claimed that he'd heard a boy's muffled screams coming from a covered bathtub as workmen removed it from the prison. Was Louis inside the tub? Did someone sneak him out of jail? For more than 200 years, people have questioned what really happened to Louis XVII.

But we now know for sure what happened to Louis XVII. Why? The doctor who performed the autopsy in 1795 stole the dead boy's heart and preserved it in alcohol. When the French monarchy was restored in 1814, he offered to give it back, but the offer was turned down. The pickled heart was then given to the Spanish branch of the Bourbon dynasty, who held on to it until 1975, when it was returned to the royal crypt in France.

In 1999, French historian Philippe Delorme arranged for the DNA in the heart to be compared with the DNA in some surviving locks of Marie Antoinette's hair. "It was Louis XVII," Delorme says. "It *was* the last little king of France who died in that prison." Will that put an end to the controversy? Not a chance, Delorme says. "There will always be some people who think Louis XVII escaped."

Toughest car ever: A 1966 Volvo P-1800S racked up 1,764,000 *miles* in 34 years.

MORE EXECUTIVE DECISIONS

We don't want to single anyone out—we just want to gloat that even the high and mighty sometimes make embarrassingly bad decisions.

ROSS PEROT

In 1979, Perot employed some of his well-known business acumen and foresaw that Bill Gates was on his way to building Microsoft into a great company. So he offered to buy him out. Gates says Perot offered between $6 million and $15 million; Perot says that Gates wanted $40 million to $60 million. Whatever the numbers were, the two couldn't come to terms, and Perot walked away empty-handed. Today Microsoft is worth hundreds of billions of dollars.

SAN FRANCISCO CHRONICLE

In 1974, the *Washington Post* offered the *Chronicle* the opportunity to syndicate a series of articles that two reporters named Bob Woodward and Carl Bernstein were writing about a break-in at the Democratic headquarters at Washington, D.C.'s, Watergate Hotel. Owner Charles Thieriot said no. "There will be no West Coast interest in the story," he explained. Thus, his rival, the *San Francisco Examiner*, was able to purchase the rights to the hottest news story of the decade for $500.

W.T. GRANT CO.

In the mid-1970s, executives at the W.T. Grant variety store chain, one of the nation's largest retailers, decided that the best way to increase sales was to increase the number of customers...by offering credit. It put tremendous "negative incentive" pressure on store managers to issue credit. Employees who didn't meet their credit quotas risked complete humiliation. They had pies thrown in their faces, were forced to push peanuts across the floor with their noses, and were sent through hotel lobbies wearing only diapers. Eager to avoid such total embarrassment, store managers gave credit "to anyone who breathed," including untold thousands of customers who were bad risks. W.T. Grant racked up $800 million worth of bad debts before it finally collapsed in 1977.

ABC-TV

In 1984, Bill Cosby gave ABC-TV first shot at buying a sitcom he'd created—and would star in—about an upscale black family. But ABC turned him down, apparently "believing the show lacked bite and that viewers wouldn't watch an unrealistic portrayal of blacks as wealthy, well-educated professionals."

So Cosby sold his show to NBC instead. What happened? Nothing much—*The Cosby Show* remained the #1 show for four straight years, was a ratings winner throughout its eight-year run, lifted NBC from its 10-year status as a last-place network to first place, resurrected TV comedy, and became the most profitable series ever broadcast.

DIGITAL RESEARCH

IBM once hired Microsoft founder Bill Gates to come up with the operating software for a new computer that IBM was rushing to market...and Gates turned to a company called Digital Research. He set up a meeting between owner Gary Kildall and IBM...but Kildall couldn't make the meeting and sent his wife, Dorothy McEwen, instead. McEwen, who handled contract negotiations for Digital Research, felt that the contract IBM was offering would allow the company to incorporate features from Digital's software into its own proprietary software—which would then compete against Digital. So she turned the contract down. Bill Gates went elsewhere, eventually coming up with a program called DOS, the software that put Microsoft on the map.

*   *   *

BUGS IN THE MOVIES

You can't train an insect the way you would, say a dog. So how do "insect wranglers" get them to follow a script? "One way," says a wrangler, "is to build the set so it accommodates the natural tendencies of the insects. For example, if an insect is phototropic (goes toward light), you can place the lights where you want the insect to go." Another way: "Have the insect go toward a food source."

What makes January 3rd special? It's the day the Earth is closest to the sun.

POLI-TALKS

More quotes from (and about) our revered politicians.

"I'm not indecisive. Am I indecisive?"
—Jim Scheibel,
mayor of St. Paul, Minn.

"If BS was a dollar a pound, we would have paid off the deficit at about noon."
—Rep. Jim Ross Lightfoot
(R-Iowa)

"Congressmen are so damn dumb they could throw themselves on the ground and miss."
—Rep. James Traficant, Jr.
(D-Ohio)

"I think that's self-evident, but not true."
—Bill Clinton

"It's hard for somebody to hit you when you've got your fist in their face."
—James Carville,
on negative campaigning

"What's the difference between a politician and a catfish? One is a wide-mouthed, bottom-feeding, slime sucker—and the other is a fish."
—Preston Manning,
Reform Party leader

"I'm a politician, and as a politician I have the prerogative to lie whenever I want."
—Charles Peacock,
ex-director of the
Madison Guaranty S&L

"Look, I'm trying to run for president! I can't sit here and debate free trade versus fair trade!"
—Pat Robertson

"The contagious people of Washington have stood firm against diversity during this long period of increment weather."
—Marion Barry,
former mayor of Wash., D.C.

"The senator has got to understand—he can't have it both ways. He can't take the high horse and then claim the low road."
—George W. Bush,
referring to John McCain

"I'm glad I'm not Brezhnev. Being the Russian leader in the Kremlin, you never know if someone's tape-recording what you say."
—Richard Nixon

THE 10 MOST ADMIRED WOMEN IN AMERICA

You may not know it, but since 1948 the Gallup Poll has been asking Americans to name the people they admire the most. At the BRI, we were surprised by a lot of the choices on these lists. Some women we'd never heard of...some we'd forgotten...and some just aren't people we admire anymore. It goes to show how fleeting fame is. Here are a dozen of the lists from the last 50+ years. See what you think.

1986
1. Mother Teresa
2. Margaret Thatcher
3. Nancy Reagan
4. Corazon Aquino
5. Geraldine Ferraro
6. Coretta Scott King
7. Jane Fonda
8. Betty Ford
9. Queen Elizabeth II
10. Jacqueline Onassis

1980
1. Rosalynn Carter
   Mother Teresa (tie)
2. Margaret Thatcher
3. Betty Ford
4. Ella Grasso
5. Barbara Jordan
6. Barbara Walters
7. Indira Gandhi
8. Nancy Reagan
9. Jacqueline Onassis
10. Jane Fonda

1978
1. Betty Ford
2. Rosalynn Carter
3. Golda Meir
4. Patricia Nixon
5. Barbara Walters
6. Jacqueline Onassis
7. Anita Bryant
8. Barbara Jordan
9. Shirley Chisholm
10. Indira Gandhi

1974
1. Golda Meir
2. Betty Ford
3. Patricia Nixon
4. Rose Kennedy
5. Happy Rockefeller
6. Shirley Chisholm/ Indira Gandhi (tie)
7. Coretta Scott King
8. Lady Bird Johnson
9. Jacqueline Onassis
10. Mamie Eisenhower

1970
1. Mamie Eisenhower
2. Patricia Nixon
3. Golda Meir
4. Rose Kennedy
5. Jacqueline Onassis
6. Lady Bird Johnson
7. Ethel Kennedy
8. Indira Gandhi
9. Margaret Chase Smith
10. Coretta Scott King

1966
1. Jacqueline Kennedy
2. Lady Bird Johnson
3. Indira Gandhi
4. Queen Elizabeth II
5. Margaret Chase Smith
6. Lurleen Wallace
7. Mamie Eisenhower
8. Helen Keller
9. Madame Chiang Kai-shek
10. Pearl S. Buck

U.S. Army regulation: A standard sandbag holds 40 lbs. of sand.

1963

1. Jacqueline Kennedy
2. Lady Bird Johnson
3. Queen Elizabeth II
4. Margaret Chase Smith
5. Mamie Eisenhower
6. Clare Boothe Luce
7. Helen Keller
8. Princess Grace of Monaco
9. Madame Ngo Diem Nhu
10. Marian Anderson

1961

1. Eleanor Roosevelt
2. Jacqueline Kennedy
3. Queen Elizabeth II
4. Mamie Eisenhower
5. Clare Boothe Luce
6. Helen Keller
7. Madame Chiang Kai-shek
8. Margaret Chase Smith
9. Pauline Frederick
10. Patricia Nixon

1956

1. Eleanor Roosevelt
2. Clare Boothe Luce
3. Mamie Eisenhower
4. Helen Keller
5. Queen Elizabeth II
6. Helen Hayes
7. Madame Chiang Kai-shek
8. Kate Smith
9. Marian Anderson
10. Princess Grace of Monaco

1955

1. Eleanor Roosevelt
2. Clare Boothe Luce
3. Mamie Eisenhower
4. Helen Keller
5. Queen Elizabeth II
6. Madame Chiang Kai-shek
7. Princess Margaret
8. Madame Vijaya Pandit
9. Margaret Chase Smith
10. Oveta Culp Hobby

1951

1. Sister Kenny
2. Eleanor Roosevelt
3. Kate Smith
4. Queen Elizabeth
5. Princess Elizabeth
6. June Allyson
7. Margaret Chase Smith
8. Clare Boothe Luce
9. Jane Barkley
10. Ethel Barrymore

1948

1. Eleanor Roosevelt
2. Madame Chiang Kai-shek
3. Sister Kenny
4. Clare Boothe Luce
5. Bess Truman
6. Kate Smith
7. Princess Elizabeth
8. Queen Elizabeth
9. Margaret Chase Smith
10. Queen Wilhelmina

WHO ARE THESE WOMEN, ANYWAY?

You get 1,000 points if you can say what each one is famous for. Not even Uncle John has heard of all of them...and we imagine younger readers have a lot of blanks to fill in. So here are thumbnail bios to help identify some of the people your parents and grandparents admired.

Corazon Aquino (1933–). Symbol of democracy. When her husband, Benino Aquino, was assassinated, she took his place in Philippine politics. Became president of the Philippines (1986–1992) restoring democratic rule after the long dictatorship of Ferdinand Marcos.

Chinese chopsticks are about 10" long; Japanese chopsticks are 7" (women's) or 8" (men's).

Ella Grasso (1919–1981). Symbol of female independence in the 1970s. Elected governor of Connecticut, served from 1975 to 1981—the first woman governor who didn't follow her husband into office.

Barbara Jordan (1936–1996). Lawyer, educator, and politician. The first African American congresswoman from the Deep South (Texas, 1972–78). Gained national attention in 1976, when she gave the keynote address at the Democratic National Convention.

Shirley Chisholm (1924–). The first African American woman elected to Congress. The first (and so far, only) African American woman to run for the presidential nomination of a major political party. In 1972, she won 152 Democratic delegates before withdrawing from the race.

Margaret Chase Smith (1897–1995). Senator from Maine. The first woman to serve in both houses of Congress and the first woman to run for the presidential nomination of a major political party when she entered the 1964 Republican race.

Lurleen Wallace (1926–1968). George Wallace's wife. By law, Alabama's fiery segregationist governor George Wallace couldn't run for another term in 1966, so his wife did...and won.

Marian Anderson (1902–1993). American singer, one of the finest contraltos of her time. First African American woman to perform in a lead role at the Metropolitan Opera, in 1955.

Clare Boothe Luce (1903–1987). American playwright, politician, and celebrity, often in the news and gossip columns. A congresswoman from Connecticut noted for her biting humor. Wrote the play *The Women* (rent it at your local video store). Was married to *Time/Life* magazine founder Henry Luce.

Pauline Frederick (1906–1990). Pioneer American female television news correspondent. Reported news for ABC (1946–1953), and NBC (1953-1975).

U.S. straw sizes, in order of increasing diameter: Cocktail, slim, jumbo, super jumbo, and giant.

Helen Hayes (1900–1993). One of the most popular American stage actresses of the 20th century.

Kate Smith (1909–1986). The "First Lady of Radio," a widely popular singer known for her rendition of "God Bless America." (*Note:* She's the "fat lady" referred to in "It ain't over 'til the fat lady sings.")

Madame Vijaya Pandit (1900–1990). Indian political leader, one of the world's leading women diplomats of the 20th century. But we've never heard of her, either.

Oveta Culp Hobby (1905–1995). Director of the U.S. Women's Army Corps (1942–1945), publisher of the *Houston Post* (1952–1953), Secretary of Health, Education, and Welfare under President Eisenhower (1953–1955).

Sister Kenny (1880–1952). Renowned humanitarian. A nurse in the Australian medical corps during World War I, she later began a crusade to help childhood victims of polio. (Before polio could be prevented, it was among the most devastating childhood diseases.) The title of Sister was bestowed as a military rank for nurses in the Australian medical corps. Her invention of a special stretcher for moving patients in shock provided her with the funding to start her own clinic for polio victims, the Kenny Institute.

June Allyson (1917–). One of the most popular actresses of the 1940s and 1950s. She was known for her "husky" singing voice, which caused a sensation during World War II. She starred in 42 films. We have no idea why she's on the list.

Queen Wilhelmina (1880–1962). Queen of the Netherlands from 1890 to 1948. She became the symbol of Dutch resistance to German occupation during World War II with her radio broadcasts from London. (Times change: Uncle John recently had dinner guests from Holland, and they spent part of the evening criticizing Wilhelmina for fleeing to England when the Nazis took over. "It would have been braver to stay," they insisted.)

TECHNO-SLANG

We first found "cyber-definitions" in Gareth Branwyn's Jargon Watch.
Now they're everywhere. Here are a few great ones we found online.

Alpha Geek: The most knowledgeable, technically proficient person in an office or work group. "Ask Larry, he's the alpha geek around here."

Beepilepsy: The brief seizure people sometimes have when their beeper goes off (especially in vibrator mode). Characterized by physical spasms, goofy facial expressions, and interruptions of speech in midsentence.

Betamaxed: When a technology is overtaken by an inferior, but better-marketed, technology. "Apple was Betamaxed out of the market by Microsoft."

Bit Flip: A 180-degree personality change. "Jim did a major bit flip and became a born-again Christian."

Elvis Year: The peak year of something's (or someone's) popularity. "Barney the dinosaur's Elvis year was 1993."

Food coupons: Twenty-dollar bills from an ATM.

Irritainment: Annoying (but riveting) media spectacles. The O. J. trials were a prime example.

Mouse Potato: The online, wired generation's answer to the couch potato.

Ohnosecond: That miniscule fraction of time in which you realize that you've just made a BIG mistake. Seen in Elizabeth P. Crowe's book *The Electronic Traveler*.

SITCOMs: What yuppie parents turn into. Stands for Single Income, Two Children, Oppressive Mortgage.

Swiped Out: Description of an ATM or credit card that has been rendered useless because the magnetic strip is worn away from extensive use.

Xerox Subsidy: Euphemism for swiping free photocopies from a workplace.

YODA (Young Opinionated Directionless Artiste): Person who sits in coffeehouses voicing strong opinions and perennial wisdom while exhibiting little direction or effort to actually make a difference.

Zen Mail: E-mail messages that arrive in one's mailbox with no text in the message body.

404: Someone who's clueless. "Don't bother asking him; he's 404." From the Web error message "404 Not Found," meaning the requested document couldn't be located.

World's largest restaurant: Bangkok's Royal Dragon (serves 5,000; waiters wear roller skates).

KITCHEN SCIENCE

Here are some common questions about food, answered by Howard Hillman in his book Kitchen Science.

A BASIC QUESTION

Q: *What's the difference between a fruit and a vegetable?*

A: Depends on who you ask. "From the botanist's viewpoint, a fruit is the ovary of the plant—that is, the part of the plant that houses the seeds. By that definition, tomatoes, eggplants, cucumbers, and pumpkins are fruits....The other edible parts of the plant are classified as vegetables.

"For cooks, greengrocers, and the U.S. Department of Agriculture, a plant is a vegetable if you usually eat it as part of a meal's main course, and a fruit if it's normally a dessert or a sweet snack. By these guidelines, tomatoes, eggplants, cucumbers, and pumpkins are vegetables."

FAST-FOOD SECRET

Q: *Why are McDonald's and Burger King's french fries so thin?*

A: "More than consumer preference is involved. Since the raw, precut potatoes are shipped and stored frozen, much of the starch in the vegetables converts to sugar. That extra sugar means that the french fries brown faster when cooked. If fast-food [joints] served normal-sized American french fries, their fries would either be too brown on the outside or undercooked on the inside."

FOR CAFFEINE ADDICTS

Q: *Which has more caffeine, tea or coffee?*

A: "A pound of tea—on the average—has twice the caffeine of a pound of roasted coffee. However, since that weight of tea typically yields about 160 cups, whereas the pound of coffee brews about 40 cups, the net result is that the cup of tea has roughly half the caffeine of a cup of coffee.

"The exact amount of caffeine in coffee or tea can vary appreciably [depending on] the bean or leaf type, grind or leaf size, and brewing time and temperature. *Note:* Parents who forbid their young children to drink coffee should be aware that a 12-ounce

---

Advertising success: 1/2 of Americans are self-conscious about dandruff; only 1/3 actually get it.

bottle of a typical cola has approximately one-quarter the caffeine of an average cup of coffee—and many times more of it than found in a cup of decaffeinated coffee."

PRACTICAL TIP

Q: *How do I separate stuck-together glasses?*

A: The trick: "You *contract* the inner glass and you *expand* the outer glass. How? Subjecting them to cold and hot temperatures, respectively. Pour cold water into the inner glass, or use ice. Immediately immerse the outside of the outer glass in hot, but not boiling, water and carefully pull the two apart."

SHELL GAME

Q: *Why does a lobster turn red when cooked?*

A: "Heat liberates a yellowish-red…pigment in the shell. This chemical reaction changes the color of the lobster from (typically) bluish seaweed-green to ruddy red. Cooked shrimp shells also turn red. By the way: Lobsters are cannibals, and unless their claws are disabled, these crustaceans will devour each other while…in lobster tanks or shipping crates. That's why lobsters' claws are always secured with wooden plugs or rubber bands."

GREEN TOMATOES

Q: *Why do most mass-marketed tomatoes seem to have inferior flavor and texture than home-grown ones?*

A: "These tomatoes have a relatively bland flavor and a cottony texture because commercial growers harvest them prematurely. The tomatoes are still very green, immature, and unripe when picked. This practice reduces spoilage losses because the tomatoes are less fragile and are therefore better shippers—and, being less perishable, they are marketable longer.

"The tomatoes are red when they reach the store because the food industry artificially turns them red by gassing them with ethylene. If they had been left on the vine to ripen naturally, they would have generated their own ethylene gas in time enough to trigger the color change. Though both artificially ripened and vine-ripened tomatoes are red, those that are reddened by nature have significantly better flavor, aroma, and texture."

TOY STORIES

Background info about some toys you may have played with.

CLUE

Inventor: A British law clerk named Anthony Pratt

Origin: Pratt invented the game—which is known as Cluedo in England—during World War II to ease the boredom of long hours spent in London bomb shelters. Pratt loved to read murder mysteries and was fond of playing a parlor game called "Murder." "It was a stupid game," he joked years later, "where guests crept up on each other in corridors, and the victim would shriek and fall on the floor." Screaming and falling on the floor was inappropriate in the stressful confines of a bomb shelter, so Pratt decided to create a board game version that could be played more quietly.

The original version had ten characters and nine murder weapons—including an axe, a bomb, and a hypodermic syringe. The original game board, which Pratt's wife Elva drew up on the dining room table, wasn't much different from the one still in use today.

Selling It: Encouraged by a friend, Pratt sold Murder! to the British game company Waddington's in 1945. They reduced the number of characters to six, substituted candlesticks and lead pipes for some of the gorier murder weapons, and began selling it under the name Cluedo in 1945. In 1953 Waddington's advised Pratt that sales were beginning to slow. So he signed away the international rights to the game for a final payment of £5,000—the equivalent of about $100,000 today. Bad move: Cluedo went on to sell more than 150 million sets in 23 countries around the world.

MR. POTATO HEAD

Inventor: A professional toy designer named George Lerner

Origin: In 1951, Lerner paid a visit to the Hassenfeld Brothers Company, a manufacturer of pencils and school supplies that was beginning to dabble in the toy business. He wanted to sell them a toy that consisted of tiny body parts made from plastic—eyes, ears, noses, hair, hats, mustaches, a pipe, etc.—that kids were supposed to stick into fresh vegetables to create funny-faced characters. Any fresh vegetable would do, Lerner told the company's president,

Merrill Hassenfeld, but, he added, "potatoes seemed to work the best."

Selling It: Hassenfeld bought the idea for $500 and a 5% royalty, and made Mr. Potato Head the first toy ever advertised with TV commercials. (That year he also shortened the company's name to Hasbro.) "Whatever Potato Head's secret," G. Wayne Miller writes in *Toy Wars*, "the toy struck a chord, with adults as well as children....Merrill had been optimistic, but he never dreamed of moving a million units the first year." It was Hasbro's first big hit. They followed with Mrs. Potato Head, and the Potato Head Pets. Hasbro, by the way, is now the largest toy company in the world. Coincidence?...Or do vegetables really make you grow?

Going Through Changes: The points on the various pieces had to be sharp for kids to stick into real potatoes, and they were...until the early 1960s. That's when Hasbro started worrying about liability, and decided it would be safer to dull the points and provide a plastic potato to stick the parts into.

• This brought protests: "One of the most wonderful things [was] that a child could place the eyes, ears, nose, and mouth anywhere," philosophy professor Stephen Viccio complained in the *New York Times*, "creating potatoes like Salvador Dali would have made if he were God." Even the natural potato's perishability was a plus, Viccio wrote, because it taught kids an important lesson: "the rotting potato skin began to act as a metaphor for the way of all flesh."

• Remember when Mr. Potato Head smoked a pipe? Not anymore, thanks to U.S. Surgeon General C. Everett Koop, who in 1987 complained that "not only is it dangerous to his health, it gives the message to kids that smoking is not a bad thing to do." So Hasbro pulled the pipe. Their reward: Mr. Potato Head became the "official spokes-spud" for the Great American Smokeout.

*　　　*　　　*

Chutes and Ladders was based on the traditional game, Snakes and Ladders. Milton Bradley simply substituted "a playground setting for the snakes, which were thought to put kids off," says a company spokesperson.

YOU CALL THIS ART?

Have you ever been in an art museum or gallery and seen something that made you wonder: "Is this really art?" Maybe you assumed that there was something you didn't understand. Or maybe you just laughed. Well, we don't know what art is...but we know what sounds ridiculous.

ARTIST: Zhang Huan, a San Francisco performance artist
BACKGROUND: Huan's performance, titled "Dream of the Dragon," was part of "Inside Out: New Chinese Art," an exhibition at San Francisco's Asian Art Museum in 1999. Purpose of the art: "To explore the physical and psychological effects of human violence in modern society."

THIS IS ART? Zhang took off his clothes and lay face down on a tree branch; then an assistant smeared him head-to-toe with pureed hot dogs and sprinkled him with flour. Then, as the grand finale, eight dogs were brought in to take a look. Seven of the dogs were only mildly interested. But one, an Akita named Hercules, mistook the art for food. He took a bite out of Zhang's butt—even drawing a little blood.

Afterthought: "I'm pretty embarrassed," said Lee McCoy, who was dog-sitting Hercules for a friend. "I was afraid Hercules might pee on the tree, but he bit him in the behind instead. Wait until my friend finds out I didn't take the dog to the beach."

ARTIST: Cosimo Cavallore
BACKGROUND: His mother once owned a deli in Canada, and family members made their own cheese to sell there. Cavallore got the idea for using cheese as art one day when he came back from lunch...and noticed his father's old armchair in a way that he'd never noticed it before. So he covered it in melted mozzarella cheese. "It was a childish act," Cavallore says. "I was allowing myself to dirty his chair. I guess I finally stood up to him." Then Cavallore got the urge to drape an entire hotel room in melted cheese.

THIS IS ART? He probably wouldn't have been able to live out his fantasy...but he crossed paths with Jules Feiler, a gallery owner. Feiler helped him find a hotel that was willing to do it. The

Washington Jefferson was undergoing renovation anyway and was looking for "something to draw new customers."

In exchange for the standard rate of $100 a night, the hotel let him coat Room 114 and everything in it with more than 1,000 pounds of melted Gruyere, Swiss and other cheeses. He coated the walls, ceiling and floor with the stuff; he smeared it all over the furniture; he even draped it over the ceiling fan and overhead lights in long ropes that reached to the floor.

Afterthought: When the exhibition ended on June 20, Feiler arranged for a comic to live in the room for a month, telling jokes to anyone who knocked on the door. He insists that he and Cavallore are serious. "When I first talked to Cavallore," Feiler says, "I thought he was just another in a series of nuts that have entered my life, but that's not the case. I really believe his work is genuine."

AND MORE "ART"?

Pachyderm Paintings. In March 2000, Christie's Auction House in New York City held an auction for more than 60 "paintings" created by elephants, presumably by holding some kind of paint brush in their trunks. Yale art historian Mia Fineman, who is writing a book about three different styles of Thai elephant art, compared their work to that of Paul Gauguin for its "broad, gentle, curvy brush strokes," and "a depth and maturity."

Garbage Art. Tom Deininger of Providence, Rhode Island creates sculptures from trash. A network of friends make his work easier by feeding him tips on which dumpsters to raid. At last report he was working on a self-portrait out of cardboard boxes, "with cheeks made of wads of Pokemon wrappers, teeth of Styrofoam, and a toy soldier forming a nostril."

Celebrity Lint Portraits. Bill Gardner of Calgary, Canada, produces his portraits by placing stencils in his dryer's lint screen. He'll use one stencil and a load of dark laundry to get the darker shades of color; then he'll switch stencils and throw in a load of whites to get the lighter colors he needs. Then he peels the lint off the screen and presses it in between two panes of glass. His portraits of public figures such as O.J. Simpson and the Queen of England have sold for as much as $500. Wow.

Got insomnia? Some experts suggest wearing mittens and socks to bed.

WHY DIDN'T *WE* THINK OF THAT?

Ever see a brilliantly conceived product or service, then slapped your head while you grumbled, "Why didn't I think of that?!!?" Well, relax—you don't have to do that with these product ideas.

Entrepreneur: David Anderson, a Minneapolis lawyer
Idea: The Tonya Tapper
Description: A steel club for self-protection. "Named in honor of ice skating's notorious Tonya Harding." Anderson "came up with the idea after hearing about the steel club Harding's henchman whacked rival skater Nancy Kerrigan with." Suggested retail price: $39.95. Anderson dreamed that it might be the start of a whole line of "similar personal security products…a whole line of batons, with different colors, holsters, and grips—even one of key chain size."

Entrepreneur: Jun Sato, a 25-year-old man who lost his job in the recession that plagued Japan in the late 1990s
Idea: The Three-minute Beating
Description: Frustrated by his inability to find another job and figuring others were as exasperated by the economic downturn as he was, Sato made up his own job: He dresses up in protective padding, and lets passersby beat him (with boxing gloves) for three minutes at a time. Price: $1,000 yen, or about $10. "I enjoy being used as a punching bag," he told the Reuters news service, "It's another way to experience life."

Entrepreneurs: Three English advertising executives and a photographer, in the 1960s
Idea: The Really Ugly Modeling Agency
Description: The partners had a hunch that ugly faces would sell products better than pretty faces and perfect profiles. "For example, in the advertisements for second-hand cars," explained one, "we want the salesman to be believable as a second-hand car salesman." They put an ad in the *Times of London* asking, "Are you ugly?"

The Loch Ness monster is a $50 million-a-year business in Scotland.

That got too many ordinary-looking people, so they placed a second ad: 'Are you *really* ugly?'"

Entrepreneur: A Ukranian tourism company called Liko-L
Idea: A tour of Reactor #4 at Chernobyl
Description: Chernobyl was the site of the worst nuclear accident of the atomic age: On April 25, 1986, Unit #4 suffered a partial meltdown, blowing the roof off of the reactor and releasing several times more radioactivity than the Hiroshima and Nagasaki bombs *combined*. Radiation levels are still more than 1,000 times higher than the accepted safe maximum, and Ukranian citizens are not allowed within a 20-mile radius of the power plant.

But that didn't stop Liko-L. By November 1998, the Ukrainian economy was in such bad shape that the government—hoping to increase tax revenues—granted special permission to the company to begin offering daylong trips to the plant. According to a spokesman, the radiation count around the plant is low and "not dangerous."

OTHER IDEAS

• Hunk Towing. "Dispatches body builders in skimpy 'uniforms' to aid stranded motorists....Sometimes calls are received from motorists who haven't actually broken down."

• Belcher Soda. Contains twice the carbonation of regular soft drinks, for "the most 'explosive' belches you'll ever have."

• "A-Bomb" sandals, handbags and accessories, made and marketed in Japan.

• The Lawn Buddy Message Machine. A 5-inch tall mechanical animal "that arises from a flowerpot placed by the front door, announces that the resident is away, and invites the visitor to leave a message."

• Bathtub Spider Ladder. A ladder that helps spiders climb out of bathtubs. "The spider ladder fits neatly around the bath taps and stretches down to the plughole. It comes complete with a poem about saving spiders and the legend: 'Handmade by a mystified craftsman in China.'"

There are 290,000 different beetle species on earth, the most of any animal.

LADIES, BEHAVE YOURSELVES

Ladies, you can follow these antique rules of etiquette...or just laugh at them.

"Immoderate laughter is exceedingly unbecoming a lady; she may affect the dimple or the smile, but should carefully avoid any approximation to a horse-laugh."
—*The Perfect Gentleman* (1860)

"Sending out a letter with a crooked, mangled or upside-down stamp is akin to letting your lingerie straps show."
—*Good Housekeeping's Book of Today's Etiquette* (1965)

"Fingernails are another source of feminine excess. The woman who goes about her daily avocations with blood-red finger-nails is merely harking back to the days of savagry, when hands smeared with blood were a sign of successful fighting."
—*Things That Are Not Done* (1937)

"It's a great idea to file your fingernails in the street car, bus, or train. It's certainly making the most of your time. The noise of the filing drowns the unpleasant noise of the wheels.

But it is the act of an ill-bred person. Who but an ordinary person would allow her epithelium to fly all over? I think that one might as well scatter ashes after a cremation, around the neighborhood."
—*Manners for Millions* (1932)

"The perfect hostess will see to it that the works of male and female authors be properly separated on her bookshelves. Their proximity, unless they happen to be married, should not be tolerated."
—*Lady Gough's Etiquette* (1863)

"No matter what the fashion may be, the gloves of a well-dressed woman are never so tight that her hands have the appearance of sausages."
—*The New Etiquette* (1940)

"[D]on't affect a lisp or talk baby talk. Somebody will probably kill you some time if you do."
—*Compete!* (1935)

State with the most thunderstorms and lightning? The "sunshine state"—Florida.

"A lady-punster is a most unpleasing phenomenon, and we would advise no young woman, however skilled she may be, to cultivate this kind of verbal talent."

—Collier's Cyclopedia of Commercial and Social Information (1882)

"Girls, never, never turn at a whistle, to see if you are wanted. A whistle is usually to call a dog."
—Good Manners (1934)

"A beautiful eyelash is an important adjunct to the eye. The lashes may be lengthened by trimming them occasionally in childhood. Care should be taken that this trimming is done neatly and evenly, and especially that the points of the scissors do not penetrate the eye."
—Our Deportment (1881)

"If a man must be forcibly detained to listen to you, you are as rude in thus detaining him, as if you had put a pistol to his head and threatened to blow his brains out if he stirred."
—The Gentlemen's Book of Etiquette and Manual of Politeness (1860)

"Still less say of anything which you enjoy at table. 'I love melons,' 'I love peaches,' 'I adore grapes'—these are school-girl utterances. We love our friends. Love is an emotion of the heart, but not one of the palate. We like, we appreciate grapes, but we do not love them."
—The American Code of Manners (1880)

"Large hats make little women look like mushrooms."
—Everyday Etiquette (1907)

"Never use your knife to convey your food from your plate to your mouth; besides being decidedly vulgar, you run the imminent danger of enlarging the aperture from ear to ear. A lady of fashion used to say that she never saw a person guilty of this ugly habit without a shudder, as every minute she expected to see the head of the unfortunate severed from the body."
—Etiquette for the Ladies (1849)

"Certain daring necklines have a paralyzing effect on the conversation and even on the appetite of the other dinner party guests, who hope to see a little more than is already revealed and would love to change places with the waiter, who has a particularly stimulating view."
—Accent on Elegance (1970)

UNCLE JOHN'S STALL OF FAME

More memorable bathroom achievements.

Honorees: Don and Penny Karch of Pittsfield, Massachusetts
Notable Achievement: Using toilets—lots of toilets—to make a public statement
True Story: According to news reports, the convenience store next to the Karches' home doesn't have a restroom. So when customers have to answer the call of nature, they do so behind the store, "in full view of the Karches' kitchen window." In September 1998, the Karches decided to fight back—by setting up 28 toilets in their backyard in protest. A local newspaper picked up the story; from there it spread to the wire services, and then to newspapers all over the country. No word on whether the convenience store ever got around to installing a restroom. (Contact us if you know what happened.)

Honoree: Lieutenant Governor Steve Windom of Alabama
Notable Achievement: Strategic use of a chamber pot to wear down his political enemies
True Story: In March 1999, Windom, a Republican, was presiding over the 35-member state legislature composed of 18 Democrats and 17 Republicans. During an important battle over Senate procedures, Windom feared that if he surrendered the gavel and left the chamber for even a minute, the Democrats would take control and his party would lose the fight. So the lieutenant governor decided he wouldn't even to go out to the bathroom until the battle was won.

"Anticipating the worst," one reporter wrote, "he brought a pitcher to the chamber and conducted business—both official and personal—from behind a large podium." Two days and two 15-hour marathon sessions later, the Democrats gave in and Windom won the battle. "It takes guts to be an effective lieutenant governor," he told reporters. "It also takes a bladder of steel."

Country with the longest life expectancy: Japan (76.7 years for men, 82.8 years for women).

Honoree: Delaware Water Gap National Recreation Area

Notable Achievement: Creating America's most expensive publicly funded outhouse

True Story: The Recreation Area, which is administered by the National Park Service, needed a new outhouse. The Park Service assembled more than a dozen designers, architects, and engineers and assigned them to the project—which took two years to complete. The final result: A beautiful "two-holer" (one for men, one for women) with a gabled Vermont slate roof, cottage-style porches with Indiana limestone railings, earthquake-proof cobblestone-and-concrete walls, and custom-built composting toilets that cost $24,000 apiece. Total cost for the two-hole privy: at least $333,000, which comes to $166,500 per hole. Portable outhouses used elsewhere in the park cost $500 each.

"We could have built it cheaper, yes," former park superintendent Roger Rector says, "but we wanted someone coming up the trail to encounter a nice restroom facility."

Honoree: Pat Swisher, head of Swisher International, a nationwide bathroom-cleaning service

Notable Achievement: Turning urinals into public service announcements

True Story: Swisher International makes those little rubbery plastic "urinal screens" that sit at the bottom of urinals. Since 1988—at the instruction of Pat Swisher himself—the screens have been imprinted with the message, "Say No To Drugs."

"It's Pat's way of getting the message out," says company spokesman Milt Goldman, "putting it in a place where every guy looks."

Honorees: Officials at the Amsterdam International Airport in The Netherlands

Notable Achievement: Inventing a new "target game"

True Story: It's a simple but brilliant idea. In 1999, airport officials had workers etch the outline of a housefly into each urinal, near the drain. "Men aim at the fly, which limits splashing," says a spokesman. Since the installation, the flies have been credited with reducing "urinal floor spillage" by 80%.

JUST PLANE WEIRD

Planning a plane trip in the near future? Make copies of this section and pass them out to the people sitting around you. They'll appreciate it.

GOTTA GO

"On a 1999 flight from Sydney to Tokyo, Henry Smithton got so drunk that he thought he was on a bus. Disturbed that he couldn't 'get off at the next stop,' he actually had to be restrained from tugging on the cabin door at 26,000 feet. He was arrested in Tokyo upon landing." (Bizarre News)

DO IT YOURSELF

On August 19, 1980, a Saudi Arabian Airlines flight carrying 285 passengers took off from the capital city of Riyadh. Suddenly the cabin was filled with smoke. The cause: according to *Stuff* magazine, it was a pilgrim on the flight who had "decided to brew his own cup of tea in the aisle...on a kerosene stove." The pilot immediately returned to the airport and landed safely, but did not order an immediate evacuation of the plane. It was a terrible mistake: the fire spread beyond control, and killed everyone on board.

NOT JUST ANOTHER CASE OF AIRSICKNESS

In June 1998 a man in his 60s had a heart attack and died on a United Emirates Airways flight from Dubai. A doctor who happened to be on board examined the man and diplomatically declared him "probably dead." To the dismay of other passengers, however, the flight attendants left him in his seat for the remaining three hours of the flight. 'It was quite distressing,' one passenger told the *South China Morning Post.* 'A lot of people were put off their food.'"

THE FOOD HERE IS TERRIBLE

In November 1999, Northwest Airlines Captain Floyd Dean got a look at the meals being loaded onto the flight he was supposed to pilot from Detroit to Las Vegas...and decided he wanted something different. So he got off the plane—even though the Boeing 757 was scheduled for takeoff—and looked around the terminal for something better to eat. When he couldn't find anything he liked, he hopped in a cab "and continued his search outside the airport," leaving 150 fuming passengers stranded on the plane for more than 90 minutes until he returned. Northwest fired the 22-year veteran on the spot for "abandoning his plane."

IN THE HOLE

On October 26, 1986, a violent explosion ripped through the rear toilet of Thai Airways flight 602 as it was preparing to land in Osaka, Japan. The plane landed safely…at which point investigators found a Japanese "Yakuza" gangster dangling head-first through a hole ripped in the floor by the explosion—his hindquarters badly injured by shrapnel—while two other Yakuza held on to his legs to keep him from falling onto the tarmac. The explosion is believed to have been caused when the Yakuza threw a hand grenade down the restroom trash chute so that it wouldn't be discovered when he went through customs. (*Stuff* magazine)

THE STING

In December 1999, a man on a Mesaba Airlines flight from Detroit to Allentown, Pennsylvania, felt a twinge on his right hand. He looked down and saw a scorpion…which had just stung him. The pilot diverted the plane to Cleveland, where the man was taken away for medical treatment. The rest of the passengers were put on other flights; the plane was fumigated.

AIR WARS

In October 1996, Air Europa pilot Jose Carlos Tuccio was scheduled to fly a plane from Seville to Palma. As passengers settled in, he walked up to seat 6-D and said loudly to a flight attendant: "We have paying garbage aboard today." He was referring to the passenger sitting in the seat—a pilot with whom he been feuding for years. Moments later, Tuccio went on the loudspeaker and welcomed everyone aboard the flight. "Except for the one in 6-D," he said in both English and Spanish. He was suspended for 7 days; a court later fined him $5,000.

EXECUTIVE DECISION: THE MODEL T

Henry Ford was one of the shrewdest businessmen in American history. But he made one really dumb decision.

S HOULD WE INTRODUCE A NEW CAR?

Executive: Henry Ford, founder of the Ford Motor Company

Background: When Henry Ford first marketed the Model T in 1908, it was a state-of-the-art automobile. "There were cheaper cars on the market," writes Robert Lacey in *Ford: The Men and Their Machine*, "but not one could offer the same combination of innovation and reliability." Over the years, the price went down dramatically…and as the first truly affordable quality automobile, the Model T revolutionized American culture.

Decision: The Model T was the only car that the Ford Motor Co. made. As the auto industry grew and competition got stiffer, everyone in the company—from Ford's employees to his family—pushed him to update the design. Lacy writes:

> The first serious suggestions that the Model T might benefit from some major updating had been made when the car was only four years old. In 1912 Henry Ford had taken [his family] on their first visit to Europe, and on his return he discovered that his [chief aides] had prepared a surprise for him. [They] had labored to produce a new, low-slung version of the Model T, and the prototype stood in the middle of the factory floor, its gleaming red lacquer-work polished to a high sheen.
>
> "He had his hands in his pockets," remembered one eyewitness, "and he walked around the car three or four times, looking at it very closely.…Finally, he got to the left-hand side of the car that was facing me, and he takes his hands out, gets hold of the door, and bang! He ripped the door right off! God! How the man done it, I don't know!"

Ford proceeded to destroy the whole car with his bare hands. It was a message to everyone around him not to mess with his prize creation. Lacey concludes: "The Model T had been the making of Henry Ford, lifting him from being any other Detroit automobile maker to becoming carmaker to the world. It had yielded him untold riches and power and pleasure, and it was scarcely surprising that he should feel attached to it. But as the years went by, it became clear that Henry Ford had developed a fixation with his masterpiece which was almost unhealthy."

Ford had made his choice clear. In 1925, after more than 15 years on the market, the Model T was pretty much the same car it had been when it debuted. It still had the same noisy, underpowered four-cylinder engine, obsolete "planetary" transmission, and horse-buggy suspension that it had in the very beginning. Sure, Ford had made a few concessions to the changing times, such as balloon tires, an electric starter, and a gas pedal on the floor. And by the early 1920s, the Model T was available in a variety of colors beyond Ford black. But the Model T was still…a Model T. "You can paint up a barn," one hurting New York Ford dealer complained, "but it will still be a barn and not a parlor."

IMPACT

While Ford rested on his laurels for a decade and a half, his competitors continued to innovate. Four-cylinder engines gave way to more powerful six-cylinder engines with manual clutch-and-gearshift transmissions. These new cars were powerful enough to travel at the high speeds made possible by the country's new paved highways. Ford's "Tin Lizzie," designed in an era of dirt roads, was not.

Automobile buyers took notice and began trading up; Ford's market share slid from 57% of U.S. automobile sales in 1923 down to 45% in 1925, and to 34% in 1926, as companies like Dodge and General Motors steadily gained ground. By the time Ford finally announced, that a replacement for the Model T was in the works in May 1927, the company had already lost the battle. That year, Chevrolet sold more cars than Ford for the first time. Ford regained first place in 1929 thanks to strong sales of its new Model A, but Chevrolet passed it again the following year and never looked back. "From 1930 onwards," Robert Lacey writes, "the once-proud Ford Motor Company had to be content with second place."

THE CHIMP
THAT SAVED TV

One of the most famous celebrities of TV's early years was a chimp. He single-handedly saved the morning talk show.

BACKGROUND. In 1952, when television was just getting started, few people thought an early morning news/talk program like the "Today Show" could succeed...and it almost didn't. At first hardly anyone watched it. But Pat Weaver, the brains behind the show (and father of Sigourney Weaver), refused to give it up.

In 1953, Weaver added a new cast-member whose popularity literally saved "Today." He was J. Fred Muggs—a chimp. Fred dressed like a human and acted like an ape, sometimes playing peacefully, sometimes running wild on the set as host (and veteran newscaster) Dave Garroway watched in amusement—even though he actually hated sharing the spotlight with an ape. It was an unorthodox way to do a news show, but America loved it. Fred became TV's first animal superstar.

TRICKS AND TRAINING

Owner/trainer Buddy Mennella raised Muggs like a son. As a result, Muggs was toilet-trained and enjoyed wearing clothes.

• Muggs's more popular routines on the "Today Show" included impersonations of celebrities like Jack Benny, Popeye the Sailor, and General George Patton. He also did a perfect imitation of Groucho Marx's walk.

• Muggs's main dislike in clothing: long sleeves, which he voluntarily shed if he had to wear them for too long.

• He was an avid finger-painter, doing over 10,000 paintings in his lifetime. J. Fred's crowning achievement: one of his paintings became a *Mad* magazine cover.

INSIDE FACTS

J. Fred overslept and missed his first scheduled "Today Show" appearance in 1953. When he arrived at NBC, the producers told him

"Forget it." So the chimp and his trainer left the studio. Ten minutes later, they realized they'd made a mistake—the show needed the chimp.

• They ran after J. Fred and found him in a nearby drugstore eating a donut. (Mennella was drinking cofffee.) Pushing aside the young man who was playing with Fred, they grabbed the chimp and trainer and brought them back to NBC. By the end of the day Fred had a five-year contract. (They should have grabbed the young man, too. He was James Dean.)

• According to Weaver, Muggs was directly responsible for over $100 million of NBC's ad revenue.

• Muggs's finest hour came in 1953 during the coronation of England's Queen Elizabeth. Because NBC only had access to a radio broadcast of the event, it embellished its television coverage with photographs of the new queen…and occasional live shots of Muggs playing in the studio. The British were so offended by the NBC coverage that the incident was brought up during a session of the House of Commons, and the London stop in Muggs's 1954 World Tour had to be canceled.

• Muggs left the show in 1957 and went to work in a Florida amusement park. He retired in 1975.

*   *   *

BUGS IN THE MOVIES

You may not realize it, but when you see a butterfly land on someone's shoulder in a movie or TV commerical, you're watching the work of an insect "actor." How do insect wranglers make it happen? Either they drug the insect and throw it toward the actor (on whose shoulder it lands) or—this is cheating—they run the film backward.

"With butterflies or bees," says one wrangler, "at the end of the day's shoot, I take them back and release them. I feel good about that." Where do they come from? "Some I catch, some I raise, some I get from breeders." He adds: "If you don't love doing this, it sounds pretty revolting—but it's actually fun."

WIDE WORLD OF WEIRD SPORTS

Here are some more little-known sports that may tickle your fancy.

CANAL JUMPING

Where They Do It: In the Netherlands, where it's known as "fierljeppen"

How It's Played: "Contestants fling themselves into the middle of a canal on a long aluminum pole, like pole vaulting, shimmy to the top of the poles with the aid of bicycle inner tubes strapped to their feet, and then vault off—hopefully (but not always) landing on the opposite bank.…Victors receive no cash, and no lucrative endorsements. 'But to be a Dutch champion,' says contest organizer Wim Vandermeer, 'is always an honor.'"

TOE WRESTLING

Where They Do It: England. The world championships are held each year in a bar in Derbyshire.

How It's Played: Rules are simple: Sit on the floor, with right foot down and left foot suspended in mid-air. Lock halluces (big toes). "Winner must force the top of the other person's foot down, similar to arm-wrestling." Note: Part of each player's bottom must always be touching the ground. "A player may, if the agony becomes too great, surrender by calling out the words 'Toe Much.'"

AND DON'T FORGET...

• **Grenade Throwing.** "In 1976, 36 million Russians participated in flinging de-activated grenades in a competition which resulted in the nationwide finals in Tashkent. Valentina Bykova, a 39-year-old woman, threw her pineapple 132.8 feet."

• **Fireball Soccer.** According to *Stuff* magazine: "In Java, Indonesia, martial artists douse a soccer ball in gasoline, set it on fire, and then kick it around—with bare feet. They embark on this madness to help them overcome their fear of fire."

How do zookeepers get baby alligators to hatch? Like their mom does: They grunt at the eggs.

THE CURSE OF DRACULA

In every film about Dracula, there's a curse. But did the curse extend beyond the screen…and actually affect the people involved with bringing the character to life? Don't dismiss the idea. Read these stories…and then decide.

Horace Liveright. The stage producer who brought *Dracula*—and later *Frankenstein*—to America made a fortune doing it. But he was a terrible businessman and spent money as fast as it came in. He made more than $2 million on *Dracula* alone, but was so slow to pay author Bram Stoker's widow, Florence, the royalties she was due that he lost control of the stage rights in a dispute over a delinquent payment…of a mere $678.01. He died drunk, broke, and alone in New York in September 1933.

Helen Chandler. She was only 20 when she signed on to play the female lead Mina Murray in the 1931 film version of *Dracula*, but she was already close to the end of her film career. It was tragically shortened by a bad marriage and addictions to alcohol and sleeping pills. By the mid-1930s she was no longer able to find work in Hollywood, and in 1940 she was committed to a sanitarium. Ten years later she was severely burned after smoking and drinking in bed, in what may have been a suicide attempt. She died in 1965.

Dwight Frye. In the 1931 film, Frye played Renfield, the character who goes insane after meeting Dracula and spends the rest of the movie as Dracula's slave. He performed so well in that part that he was offered a similar role in the movie version of *Frankenstein*, as Dr. Frankenstein's hunchbacked assistant, Fritz.

Unfortunately for him, he took it—and was promptly typecast as the monster's/mad scientist's assistant for the rest of his career. He didn't get a chance to play any other type of role until 1944, when he was cast as the secretary of war in the film *Wilson*. Not long after he won the part, Frye had a heart attack on a Los Angeles bus and died before he was able to appear in the film.

Carl Laemmle, Jr. As president of Universal Pictures, he did more than anyone else to establish Universal as the horror movie studio of the 1930s. He left the studio after it was sold in 1936 and tried to establish himself as an independent producer. He never succeeded. A notorious hypochondriac, Laemmle eventually did come down with a debilitating disease—multiple sclerosis—in the early 1960s. He died in 1979—40 years to the day after the death of his father.

Bela Lugosi. Worn out by years of playing *Dracula* in New York and on the road, Lugosi was already sick of the vampire character by the time he began work on the film version; the indignity of being paid less than his supporting cast only made things worse. Reporter Lillian Shirley recounted one incident that took place in Lugosi's dressing room between scenes:

> I was with him when a telegram arrived. It was from Henry Duffy, the Pacific Coast theatre impresario, who wanted Mr. Lugosi to play Dracula for sixteen weeks. "No! Not at any price," he yelled. "When I am through with this picture I hope never to hear of Dracula again. I cannot stand it…I do not intend that it shall possess me. No one knows what I suffer for this role."

But like a real vampire, Lugosi was trapped in his role. *Dracula* was a box-office smash when it premiered in 1931 and Universal, eager to repeat its success, offered Lugosi the part of the monster in *Frankenstein*. It was the first in a series of planned monster movie roles for Lugosi that Universal hoped would turn Lugosi into "the new Lon Chaney," man of a thousand monsters.

Stubborn Kind of Fellow

Foolishly, Lugosi turned down the role of the Frankenstein monster because there was no dialogue—Frankenstein spoke only in grunts—and the makeup would have obscured his features, which he feared would prevent fans from knowing that he was the one under all that makeup.

The role went instead to an unknown actor named William Henry Pratt…who changed his name to Boris Karloff and within a year eclipsed Lugosi to become Hollywood's most famous horror star of the 1930s.

"Thereafter," David Skal writes in *V Is for Vampire*, "Lugosi was never able to negotiate a lucrative Hollywood contract. *Dracula* was the height of his Hollywood career, and also the beginning of its end." His last good role was as the monster keeper Ygor in the

1939 film *Son of Frankenstein*, considered to be the finest performance of his entire career.

Count on Him

Lugosi played Count Dracula for a second and final time in the 1948 Universal film *Abbot and Costello Meet Frankenstein*, his last major-studio film. After that he was reduced to appearing in a string of low-budget films, including the Ed Wood film *Bride of the Monster* (1956). Wood also had cast Lugosi in his film *Plan 9 From Outer Space* (1958), but Lugosi died on August 16, 1956 (and was buried in full Dracula costume, cape, and makeup)...so Wood recycled some old footage of Lugosi and hired a stand-in, who covered his face with his cape so that viewers would think he was Lugosi. When he died, Lugosi left an estate valued at $2,900.

...LAST, BUT NOT LEAST

Florence Stoker. Mrs. Stoker was nearly broke when she sold Universal the movie rights to *Dracula*, a sale that, combined with the royalties from the novel and the London and American plays, enabled her to live in modest comfort for the rest of her life. But she never did get rich off of the property that would bring wealth to so many others. When she died in 1937, she left an estate valued at £6,913.

...Then again, Mrs. Stoker may have been luckier than she knew: After her death it was discovered that when Bram Stoker was issued a copyright for *Dracula* in 1897, he or his agents neglected to turn over two copies of the work to the American copyright office as was required by law; and the Stoker estate failed to do so again in the 1920s when the copyright was renewed in the U.K. Since Stoker failed to comply with the requirements of the law, *Dracula* was technically in the public domain, which meant that anyone in the United States could have published the novel or adapted it into plays, movies or any other form without Mrs. Stoker's permission and without having to pay her a cent in royalties.

For more on Dracula, turn to page 436.

VAMPIRES ON BIKINI BEACH

With the single possible exception of Sherlock Holmes, film historian David Skal writes, "Dracula, has been depicted in film more times than almost any fictional being." Here's a look at some of the more unusual vampire movies that have been made.

Dracula Blows His Cool (1982)
"Three voluptuous models and their photographer restore an ancient castle and open a disco in it. The vampire lurking about the castle welcomes the party with his fangs." (*Video Hound's Golden Movie Retriever 2001*)

Little Red Riding Hood and Tom Thumb vs. the Monsters (1960)
"Little Red Riding Hood and Tom Thumb fight a vampire and a witch in a haunted forest! One of three Hood movies made the same year in Mexico and shipped up here like clockwork in the mid-60s to warp the minds of little kids whose parents wanted to go Christmas shopping." (*The Psychotronic Encyclopedia of Film*)

Planet of the Vampires (1965)
"Some astronauts crash land on a strange planet where the undead kill the living, only to discover that the alien-possessed vampiric survivors are preparing to land on another alien world—Earth!" (*The Essential Monster Movie Guide*)

The Devil Bat (1940)
"Bela Lugosi plays a crazed scientist who trains bats to kill at the scent of a certain perfume." (*Halliwell's Film and Video Guide*)

Haunted Cop Shop (1984)
"When vampires invade a meat-packing plant, the elite Monster Police Squad is brought in to stop them. When the squad botches the job, the Police Commissioner bumps them down to foot patrol until the vampires attack the county hospital. Impressive special effects." (*The Illustrated Vampire Movie Guide*)

According to a Tupperware study: You'll wind up throwing out about 3/4 of your leftovers.

Samson vs. the Vampire Women (1961)

"Sexy vampire women keep muscular male slaves on slabs in their atmospheric crypt. Santo the silver-masked Mexican wrestling hero (called Samson in the dubbed version) defeats them all." (*The Psychotronic Encyclopedia of Film*)

Vampires on Bikini Beach (1988)

"Californians save their beach from undesirable vampires." (Is there some other kind?) (*The Illustrated Vampire Movie Guide*)

Billy the Kid vs. Dracula (1965)

"The title says it all. Dracula travels to the Old West, anxious to put the bite on a pretty lady ranch owner. Her fiancé, the legendary Billy the Kid, steps in to save his girl from becoming a vampire herself. A classic." (*Video Hound's Golden Movie Retriever*)

The Return of the Vampire (1943)

"Bela Lugosi plays Armand Tesla (basically Dracula under another name), who returns to claim a girl after 'marking' her when she was a child. But his assitant, the werewolf-with-a-heart, turns on him and drags him out into the sunlight, where he melts in spectacular fashion." (*Amazon Reviews*)

Atom Age Vampire (1960)

"Badly dubbed Italian timewaster with cheese-ball special effects and a tired premise. A mad professor restores the face of a scarred accident victim." (*Video Movie Guide*)

Haunted Cop Shop II (1986)

"This improved sequel to the 1984 original features non-stop action. The vampire creature is destroyed by the hero relieving himself into a swimming pool and completing an electrical circuit!" (*The Illustrated Vampire Movie Guide*)

Blacula (1972)

"In 1815 in Transylvania, an African prince falls victim to Dracula. A hundred and fifty years later, his body is shipped to L.A. and accidentally revived. Jaded semi-spoof notable chiefly as the first black horror film. The star's performance is as stately as could be wished under the circumstances." (*Halliwell's Film Guide*)

At any given moment, about half of the Earth is covered by clouds.

THE HISTORY OF THE IQ TEST, PART IV

Here's the fourth and final installment of the IQ story.
Part III is on page 270. Our own IQ test is on page 416.

FORGET WHAT I SAID BEFORE

In 1923, Carl Brigham published his book *A Study of Human Intelligence*, an analysis of WWI intelligence test data that laid out his eugenic "race hypothesis," that the assimilation of African Americans and large numbers of eastern and southern European immigrants into the intellectually superior "Nordic" American racial stock would lower the overall intelligence of the American gene pool.

Such racist theories were controversial even in the 1920s, but Brigham was determined to take a public stand. "I am not afraid to say anything that is true," he wrote a friend after finishing the book, "no matter how ugly the facts may be."

It turns out that in spite of all his other faults, Brigham really was committed to speaking what he believed to be the truth. Because when he came to realize just how wrong his loony racial theories were, he set out to correct his mistake and undo all the damage he'd done. In 1928, he publicly recanted his theories at a meeting of eugenicists, and two years later he published a formal retraction of his own book, denouncing it as "pretentious" and "without foundation."

Even that wasn't enough—in 1932 he published an entire book called *A Study of Error* that attacked the findings of *A Study of Human Intelligence*.

TEST ANXIETY

Brigham had not given up on the idea of testing; he'd just come to realize that what IQ tests and the SAT really measured was not inborn intelligence. In 1934 he wrote,

The test movement came to this country some twenty-five or thirty years ago accompanied by one of the most glorious fallacies in the history of science, namely that the tests measured native intelli-

---

Happy landings: Approximately 26,000 meteorites crash to Earth each year.

gence purely and simply without regard to training or schooling. I hope nobody believes this now. The test scores are very definitely a composite including schooling, family background, familiarity with English, and everything else, relevant and irrelevant. The "native intelligence" hypothesis is dead.

CHANGING THE SCORE
Brigham continued to believe that tests had merit as predictors of academic performance and, thus, could be useful for determining which students should be admitted to college.

But "he also began trying to put some distance between the SAT and IQ testing," Nicholas Lehman writes in *The Big Test*. "In the beginning, the SAT score had been a single number, like the intelligence quotient, and Brigham had published a crude scale for converting it to an IQ score. He was persuaded by his assistants, however, to divide the SAT score into two parts, one for verbal and one for mathematical ability, and to drop the conversion scale."

As the years went by, acceptance of the SAT test continued to grow. In 1934, Harvard adopted the test as a means of evaluating applicants for its academic merit scholarship; three years later Princeton, Columbia, and Yale adopted the test for their scholarship programs. That same year Harvard president James Bryant Conant proposed establishing a new agency, the Educational Testing Service (ETS), to administer the SAT and other assessment tests that were coming into use, so that they could be administered on a nationwide basis.

FILL IN THE DOTS
Just a few years earlier, the idea of giving a test to hundreds of thousands of students all over the country on the same day would have been unthinkable. As difficult as it would have been to organize and administer such a huge test, correcting that many exams, one by one, in a timely fashion by proctors prone to human error, would have been a nightmare.

In 1933, a Michigan high-school science teacher named Reynold Johnson invented the machine that would make nationwide test-taking and correcting possible. The machine was inspired by a childhood prank—he used to scratch pencil marks on the outside of the spark plugs of Model T Fords. Graphite conducts electricity, so

Johnson's pencil marks drew the spark away from the plug, and the car wouldn't start. Drawing from this experience, Johnson conceived of a machine that could sense pencil marks electrically and detect whether answers were in the right places. He built a prototype and sold it to IBM. The first IBM Markographs went into service in Rhode Island and New York in 1936.

Now that thousands of exams could be graded at once mechanically and without human error, the last barriers to nationwide testing had fallen. Except one: Carl Brigham himself.

JUST SAY NO

Brigham knew firsthand, from his own painful experience advocating and then renouncing his eugenics theories, just how dangerous a diagnostic tool like the SAT test could be in the hands of well-meaning but wrong-headed or misinformed administrators. And he worried that if a national testing agency were established, it would inevitably become more interested in promoting and defending the tests than it would be in questioning whether the test really was as effective as advertised.

As the father of the SAT, Carl Brigham had a great deal of clout in academia and the aptitude-testing community. He vehemently opposed the creation of the Educational Testing Service (ETS), and was against turning the SAT into a nationwide test. His word alone was enough to prevent either from happening.

So how did the ETS, which now develops and administers more than 11 million tests worldwide each year, come to be established? Simple—on January 24, 1943, Brigham died from heart disease at the age of 52.

"The roadblock was removed," Leman writes in *The Big Test*. "On January 1, 1948, the ETS opened for business."

*   *   *

IT'S THE LAW!

Boyle's Other Law: "The pull on the cords ALWAYS sends the drapes in the wrong direction."

The Laws of Assembly: "Interchangeable parts, won't."

Kentucky citizens are required by state law to bathe at least once a year.

UNCLE JOHN'S IQ TEST

Now that the concept of an IQ test has been thoroughly discredited, what better way to pass the time than to take an IQ test? Just because they won't tell you anything about yourself, doesn't make them any less interesting to take. Here are some questions taken from actual IQ tests.

1. Calculate the missing number:

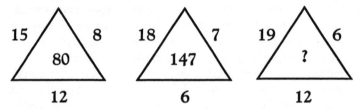

2. Which of the following is not a state?
STAEX
IHGCCOA
GOYIWMN
IMENA

3. Write in the brackets at the end of each line the number that logically should follow in the series:

9, 16, 25, 36, ( )

4. Insert the missing number:

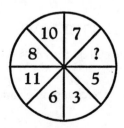

Facts of life: In the next 60 seconds, 101 people will die...and 261 new ones will be born.

5. Choose the two words whose meanings don't belong with the other words in the group:

Cod, halibut, house, flounder, tent

6. Insert the missing number:

19	14	16	32
4	8	2	4
3	3	2	7
5	2	( )	4

7. Write in the brackets one word that means the same in one sense as the word in the left and in another sense the same as the word on the right:

dash (D _ _ T) missile

contest (M _ _ _ H) equal

ignite (F _ _ E) shoot

8. Underline the two words that are most nearly opposite in meaning:

Intense, extensive, majority, extreme, diffuse

9. Which of the two phrases are closest in meaning:

(a) Is the tide turning?

(b) Are you lost for words?

(c) Can an early bird get the worm?

(d) Has the cat got your tongue?

10. Insert the missing number in the blank square:

5	9	17
13	25	49
37	73	?

ANSWERS

1. 57. Multiply the left number in each triangle by the square of the right number, then divide by the bottom number.

2. TEXAS, <u>CHICAGO</u>, WYOMING, MAINE

3. 49. The numbers are squares of 3, 4, 5, 6 and 7

4. 2. (Opposite numbers, when added together, equal 13)

5. House and tent

6. 7. In each column, subtract the second number from the first (top) number, and divide the result to get the bottom number: 16-2=14; 14÷2=7

7. Dart, match, fire

8. Intense, diffuse

9. b and d

10. 145. (After subtracting one from each number, multiply by 3 going down and two going across.)

Q. What is something blue, that's red when it's green? A. A blueberry.

THE 10 MOST ADMIRED MEN IN AMERICA

We've scoured these annual Gallup polls, but can't find Uncle John's name in any of them. Go figure. The "10 Most Admired Women" are on page 384. Here are some of the lists that Gallup has been gathering since 1948. Bet you haven't heard some of these names lately (or maybe ever).

1986
1. Ronald Reagan
2. Lee Iacocca
3. Pope John Paul II
4. Jesse Jackson
5. Rev. Billy Graham
6. Jimmy Carter
7. Desmond Tutu
8. Edward Kennedy
9. George Bush
10. Terry Waite

1979
1. Jimmy Carter
2. Pope John Paul II
3. Edward Kennedy
4. Anwar Sadat
5. Ronald Reagan
6. Rev. Billy Graham
7. Gerald Ford
8. Henry Kissinger
9. Richard Nixon
10. Menachem Begin

1974
1. Henry Kissinger
2. Rev. Billy Graham
3. Gerald Ford

4. Edward Kennedy
5. George Wallace
6. Nelson Rockefeller
7. Richard Nixon
8. Barry Goldwater
9. Ronald Reagan
10. Henry Jackson

1970
1. Richard Nixon
2. Rev. Billy Graham
3. Edward Kennedy
4. Spiro Agnew
5. Pope Paul VI
6. Edward Muskie
7. Lyndon B. Johnson
8. Ronald Reagan
9. Hubert Humphrey
10. Harry Truman

1966
1. Lyndon B. Johnson
2. Dwight Eisenhower
3. Robert Kennedy
4. Rev. Billy Graham
5. Pope Paul VI
6. U Thant
7. Everett Dirksen

8. George Romney
9. Richard Nixon
10. Ronald Reagan

1961
1. John Kennedy
2. Dwight Eisenhower
3. Winston Churchill
4. Adlai Stevenson
5. Albert Schweitzer
6. Harry Truman
7. Rev. Billy Graham
8. Richard Nixon
9. Pope John XXIII
10. Douglas MacArthur

1958
1. Dwight Eisenhower
2. Winston Churchill
3. Albert Schweitzer
4. Rev. Billy Graham
5. Harry Truman
6. Douglas MacArthur
7. Richard Nixon
8. Dr. Jonas Salk
9. Bernard Baruch
10. Orval Faubus

What's the difference between a bay and a gulf? Bays are smaller.

1956
1. Dwight Eisenhower
2. Winston Churchill
3. Bishop Fulton Sheen
4. Albert Schweitzer
5. Adlai Stevenson
6. Douglas MacArthur
7. Pope Pius XII
8. Dag Hammarskjöld
9. Rev. Billy Graham
10. Dr. Jonas Salk

1954
1. Dwight Eisenhower
2. Winston Churchill
3. Adlai Stevenson

4. Joseph McCarthy
5. Harry Truman
6. Douglas MacArthur
7. Pope Pius XII
8. Bishop Fulton Sheen
9. Herbert Hoover
10. Albert Schweitzer

1949
1. Harry Truman
2. Dwight Eisenhower
3. Winston Churchill
4. Douglas MacArthur
5. Herbert Hoover
6. Pope Pius XII

7. Robert Taft
8. Bernard Baruch
9. Alben Barkley
10. Thomas Dewey

1948
1. Harry Truman
2. Dwight Eisenhower
3. Douglas MacArthur
4. Winston Churchill
5. George Marshall
6. Herbert Hoover
7. Thomas Dewey
8. Pope Pius XII
9. Harold Stassen
10. Albert Einstein

WHO ARE THESE GUYS, ANYWAY?

We're offering 1,000 points if you know what each one is famous for. Here are thumbnail bios to help identify some of the people whose names aren't that familiar.

Terry Waite (1939–). British church official who was in the news when he successfully negotiated the release of British hostages in Iran and Libya. Then, while trying to arrange the release of U.S. hostages in Beirut in 1987, he was kidnapped by Shiite Muslims and held until 1991.

Menachem Begin (1913–1992). Prime minister of Israel from 1977 to 1983. Was co-recipient, with Egyptian president Anwar Sadat, of the 1978 Nobel Peace Prize for their amazing achievement—negotiating a peace treaty between Israel and Egypt.

Hubert Humphrey (1911–1978). Senator from Minnesota, 38th vice president of the United States (1965–1969), and Democratic presidential candidate in 1968 (lost to Nixon). Called "The Happy

---

If a volcano has erupted at any time within the last 10,000 years, it's considered "active."

Warrior," his signature phrase was: "I'm pleased as punch to be here."

Edmund Muskie (1914–1996). Senator from Maine, gained national attention as Humphrey's running mate in 1968. Seemed likely Democratic presidential nominee in 1972, but his campaign self-destructed when he seemed to be crying during a press conference. Later, he was secretary of state under Carter.

U Thant (1909–1974). In the 1960s, the United Nations was widely seen as a vital link to peace. Thant, a Burmese educator and civil servant, was the third U.N. secretary general (1962–1971). Often made news because he criticized both West and East for actions he considered threatening to world peace. Americans were fascinated that someone could have a first name like "U."

Everett Dirksen (1896–1969). Republican Senator from Illinois. With wavy white hair and a mellifluous voice, he was perfectly cast as the Senate minority leader during the Kennedy and Johnson administrations. He even had a hit spoken-word record called *Gallant Men*.

George Romney (1907–1995). Chairman of American Motors Corp., who saved AMC from the brink of collapse in the late 1950's by concentrating exclusively on small Ramblers—the first successful "compact" cars in U.S. auto industry history. Elected governor of Michigan, prime contender for the 1968 Republican presidential nomination until he claimed he'd been "brainwashed" by South Vietnamese officials. Secretary of Housing and Urban Development under President Nixon.

Adlai Stevenson (1900–1965). U.S. political leader and diplomat who helped found the United Nations. Mainly remembered as the eloquent, witty Democratic presidential candidate who was crushed in 1952 and 1956 by Dwight Eisenhower. In 1961, he was JFK's ambassador to the United Nations.

Albert Schweitzer (1875–1965). Picture a white-haired caucasian doctor living in a hut in Africa, wearing a white coat and a big, bushy mustache. That's Schweitzer's image. Alsatian-German theologian, philosopher, and mission doctor in equatorial Africa, he received the 1952 Nobel Peace Prize.

Bernard Baruch (1870–1965). America's "elder statesman"—the "go-to" guy for many presidents. Financier who amassed a fortune in the stock market. Never held public office, but served as an adviser to U.S. presidents Wilson, Harding, Coolidge, Hoover, Roosevelt, and Truman.

Orval Faubus (1910–1994). Governor of Arkansas (1954–1967), symbol of white defiance to integration—or, depending on your point of view, to "federal interference." Became famous when he defied a 1957 federal court order to desegregate schools and called out the Arkansas National Guard to "prevent violence" by blocking the entrance to Little Rock Central High School, preventing nine African American students from entering. In response, President Eisenhower mobilized 1,200 U.S. Army paratroopers to escort the students into the school. After leaving office in 1967, Faubus worked as a bank clerk.

Bishop Fulton Sheen (1895–1979). Roman Catholic bishop best known for his inspiring talks on radio and television. Began broadcasting on March 2, 1930, to a 17-station network. By 1950 he was reaching 118 stations, with around-the-world coverage on shortwave. He became so much a part of pop culture that at the peak of his popularity he appeared on prime time TV, opposite the top-rated comedian Milton Berle. Berle, known as "Uncle Miltie," referred to Bishop Sheen as "Uncle Fultie."

Dag Hammarskjöld (1905–1961). Swedish economist and statesman who became the second secretary general of the United Nations (1953–1961). In one of the most dangerous periods in world history—with A-bomb scares, emerging third-world nations, Cold War tensions—he effectively used the United Nations to mitigate crises. Killed in a plane crash while on a peace mission in the Congo in 1961 (during a civil war there) and was awarded the Nobel Peace Prize posthumously that same year.

Robert Taft (1889–1953) "Mr. Republican." Son of William Howard Taft, 27th U.S. president. U.S. senator from Ohio for 14 years (1939–1953). America's most prominent conservative for many years. Narrowly missed the Republican presidential nomination in 1952, losing to "internationalist" Dwight Eisenhower—interpreted as the defeat of isolationism within the party.

The first watches (portable clocks) were known as "Nürnberg eggs."

Alben Barkley (1877–1956). Served as one of the chief builders of FDR's New Deal in the 1930s and as a member of Congress for almost 40 years. The thirty-fifth vice president of the United States (1949-1953), under Harry Truman.

Thomas Dewey (1902–1971). Had a great look—slicked-back hair, pencil-thin mustache. Looked like a New York district attorney, which he was. His successful racket-busting career won him three terms as governor of New York (1943–1955). A long-time Republican leader, he was his party's presidential nominee in 1944 and 1948. You may have seen the famous picture of Truman holding a newspaper that says: "Dewey Defeats Truman." He wasn't, but he was so far ahead that the public assumed he would be. His loss in 1948 is considered the classic "don't count your chickens before they hatch" presidential campaign.

George Marshall (1880–1959). Army chief of staff during World War II and later U.S. secretary of state (1947-1949). His 1947 European Recovery Program became known as the "Marshall Plan" and is credited with saving post-World War II Europe. He received the Nobel Peace Prize in 1953.

Harold Stassen (1907–). Our favorite guy on these lists. The wonder boy of the Republican Party in the 1940s, he became Minnesota's youngest governor and served three terms. He was Dewey's chief rival for the Republican nomination in 1948, but narrowly lost it. (Ironically, if he'd actually been nominated, he might well have been elected president, since Truman was considered extremely vulnerable.) Stassen never got over the loss. He became obsessed with the presidency and ran nine increasingly bizarre campaigns for it over the next 36 years.

*   *   *

IT'S A WEIRD, WEIRD WORLD

"John O'Neill, 73, was recently rescued by firefighters in Huntington, N.Y., after he stumbled out of a bar late at night and somehow got himself wedged between two buildings. He was stuck so tight he had to be pulled out from above."

—**Universal Press Syndicate**

What's another word for the crater caused by a meteor? An "astrobleme."

THE BIRTH OF THE SUBMARINE, PART IV

Believe it or not, it was the invention of the torpedo that transformed the submarine from an underwater deathtrap into a safe, effective killing machine. Here's the last part of our submarine story.

PUSHING AND PULLING

In the final analysis, the main reason governments were interested in developing the submarine was that it had the potential to be an effective instrument of war. If a sub could sneak up on an enemy ship undetected underwater and blow it up, it would be a valuable weapon—but it had to have an effective bomb.

Some early subs mounted a keg of gunpowder on a long pole and tried to ram enemy ships with it. Others dragged barrels of gunpowder behind them until the powder keg (hopefully) bumped into the enemy ship's hull and exploded. Neither method was effective; the kegs seldom hit the target and the attacking submarine was at greater risk than the enemy was.

ABANDON SHIP

In 1867, Captain Giovanni Luppis of the Austrian navy came up with a new, safer method of attacking enemy vessels: Rather than improve the sub, Luppis simply eliminated the crew. He tied long ropes to the boat's steering mechanism and controlled it by pulling the ropes from the shore. An explosive charge mounted to the front of the boat was designed to detonate upon impact when it hit an enemy ship. It didn't matter if the attacking boat was destroyed or not—it was empty.

Today, historians consider Luppis's invention the world's first self-propelled torpedo, but in 1867, the Austrian navy rejected it out of hand, correctly pointing out that the weapon's range was limited to the length of the ropes. So, working with an English engineer named Robert Whitehead, Luppis spent the next three years working on a new design. By 1870 he'd perfected a 16-foot-long torpedo that was powered by compressed air. Boasting a

---

76-pound explosive charge and a top speed of more than 9 mph, the Luppis-Whitehead torpedo could sink an enemy warship from more than 400 yards away.

The One that Got Away

Rather than keep their awesome new weapon a secret, Austria invited other navies to witness a demonstration. Backfire: The British were so impressed that they talked Whitehead into coming back to England...*with* his torpedo. After more than 100 test firings from the deck of a Royal Navy warship, they were convinced that the invention was a winner. "The government, acting with most unusual promptitude, at once came to terms with Mr. Whitehead, and bought the rights of manufacture for £15,000," one naval historian recounted years later. And Whitehead torpedoes were soon adopted by the world's leading navies.

CONTEST

With the invention of the torpedo, submarines became an integral part of naval warfare and France, the United States, and several other countries were in a race to build the best one. To speed the pace of development, in 1888 the U.S. Navy held a design competition for a submarine that could travel 8 mph under water, 15 mph on the surface, and fire torpedoes at enemy ships. The best design would win a $200,000 contract to build it.

There were three entries in the competition. George Baker of the Chicago-Detroit Dry Dock Company designed a 40-foot-long egg-shaped sub, made of wood covered with waterproof cloth. His design was rejected because it couldn't maintain an even depth when traveling underwater. Simon Lake, a Connecticut inventor, submitted a sub which, like an underwater car, had wheels and was designed to be driven along the ocean floor. But Lake must have forgotten that there are no roads on the bottom of the ocean. "The fact that the floor of the ocean might be littered with rocks, that there might be hills and crevices, does not seem to have occurred to him," Richard Garret writes in *Submarines*. "The Navy rejected his submission."

MR. HOLLAND'S OPUS

The third submission came from John P. Holland, an Irish immi-

---

How did fire beetles get their name? They fly into forest fires to lay their eggs.

grant schoolteacher from Paterson, New Jersey. Not long after arriving in America in 1873, Holland had approached the U.S. Navy with his ideas for a submarine. "The Navy," Roy Davies writes in *Nautilus*, "told him he would do well to drop the matter."

Rejected by the United States, Holland built a submarine, called the *Fenian Ram*, for a group of Irish republicans. They planned to smuggle Holland's sub back to England aboard merchant ships and then use it to attack British warships. But when Holland and his Irish backers had a falling out over money, the backers stole the sub from dry dock in New Jersey and ran it aground in New Haven, Connecticut. Holland refused to have anything more to do with them, but with no further financial backing, he was forced to take a job as a draftsman…until the U.S. Navy announced the competition.

Holland had so much experience building subs that he won the competition easily. He based his design "on the model of the Whitehead torpedo," he wrote in the competition notes, "subject to none of its limitations, improving on all of its special qualities, except speed for which it substitutes incomparably greater endurance. It is not, like other small vessels, compelled to select for its antagonist a vessel of about its own or inferior power; the larger and more powerful its mark, the better its opportunity."

DIVE!

Holland began work in 1894 and spent the next three years building the revolutionary porpoise-shaped submarine, which he named the *Plunger*. Holland developed a simpler way to make his *Plunger* dive rapidly, while previous subs had descended slowly by a complicated system of ballasting (making the sub heavy enough to sink by letting sea water enter special compartments in the sub). To comply with the Navy's speed requirements, he had to have two huge steam engines for surface travel, and another innovation—a battery-powered electric motor—for underwater propulsion. But the steam boilers made the inside hull unbearably hot. Holland couldn't fix the problem, so had to scrap the entire design.

By now Holland was short of cash. To raise enough money to build a submarine that would meet the Navy's specifications, he sold his patent rights to the Electric Storage Battery Company (renamed the Electric Boat Company). The next sub he built, the *Holland IV*, was a success. In addition to Holland's previous innovations, he gave the boat a compressed air system that extended the time it could stay under water to nine weeks. It was also the first submarine capable of recharging its batteries and refilling its compressed air tanks at sea. And it could fire *three* torpedoes.

The *Holland IV* was submitted to extensive sea trials in 1899 and passed with flying colors. "I report my belief that the *Holland* is a successful and veritable submarine torpedo-boat, capable of making an attack on an enemy unseen and undetectable," the Navy's observer wrote in his report, "and that, therefore, she is an Engine of Warfare of terrible potency which the Government must necessarily adopt in its service."

The Navy followed the advice, paying Electric Boat $120,000 for the sub and ordering five more subs the following year.

SHIPPING OUT

Holland had spent more than 25 years designing and building submarines and had finally designed a sub that, with a few additional improvements, would serve as the model for virtually all submarines manufactured over the next 50 years. But he would not enjoy his success: In 1900 the Electric Boat Company, which had purchased Holland's submarine patents just a few years earlier, forced him out of the company altogether.

Holland's health failed him and he abandoned submarine building. He died in Newark, New Jersey, on August 12, 1914, five days after the start of World War I, the first war in which submarines would play a major role. Electric Boat became the principal supplier of submarines to the U.S. Navy and is still building them today.

* * *

IT'S THE LAW!

Hartley's First Law: "The probability of someone watching you is proportional to the stupidity of your action."

Maier's Law: "If the facts do not conform to the theory, they must be disposed of."

FINAL THOUGHTS

If you had to pick some last words, what would they be?
Here are a dozen that people are still quoting.

"Don't worry—it's not loaded."
—**Terry Kath,** *leader of the*
band Chicago, playing
Russian roulette

"I should never have switched
from Scotch to Martinis."
—**Humphrey Bogart**

"How about this for a headline
for tomorrow's paper? French
fries."
—**James French,** *executed*
in the Oklahoma
electric chair, 1966

"I'll take a wee drop of that. I
don't think there's much fear
of me learning to drink now."
—**Dr. James Cross,**
Scottish physicist and
lifelong teetotaler

"Am I dying, or is this my
birthday?"
—**Lady Astor,**
awaking to find her relatives
gathered around her bedside

"And now, I am officially
dead."
—**Abram S. Hewitt,**
industrialist, after removing the
oxygen tube from his mouth

"That was a great game of golf,
fellers."
—**Bing Crosby**

"I've had 18 straight whiskeys.
I think that's the record!"
—**Dylan Thomas,** *poet*

On being told that God would
forgive his sins:
"Why, of course....That's His
line of work."
—**Heinrich Heine,**
German poet

"So little done. So much to
do!"
—**Alexander Graham Bell**

"I desire to go to hell and not
to heaven. In the former place
I shall enjoy the company of
popes, kings and princes, while
the latter are only beggars,
monks and apostles."
—**Niccolo Machiavelli**

"Waiting, are they? Waiting,
are they? Well, let 'em wait."
—**General Ethan Allen,**
Revolutionary War hero, on
being told that "the Angels
are waiting for you."

THE
"EXTENDED SITTING" SECTION

A Special Section of Longer Pieces

Over the years, we've gotten
numerous requests from BRI members
to include a batch of long articles—
for those times when you know
you're going to be sitting for a while.
Well, the BRI aims to please…
So here's another great way
to pass the uh…time.

TARZAN OF THE MOVIES, PART I

Elsewhere in this book, we tell the story of Dracula, the creature who couldn't die. In a way, that's Tarzan's story, too. Nothing could kill him—not inept filmmaking...or bad scripts...or terrible acting. No matter how poor the movie, he kept getting more popular. And ultimately, it was his success in these films that turned him into a pop icon. Here are highlights of his career as a star of the silent screen.

ON SCREEN

At about the same time he signed his first Tarzan book deal, Edgar Rice Burroughs became fascinated with the idea of putting Tarzan on the silver screen, too. He hired an agent and tried to sell the idea to several different film studios, but nobody was interested. "The problem with *Tarzan of the Apes* was that it was considered too difficult to film," John Taliaferro writes in *Tarzan Forever*, "No one had ever made a successful movie featuring wild animals. And how to depict a nearly naked man? Even more problematic, how to depict a nearly naked man wrestling and killing a lion? The task was daunting."

LARGER THAN LIFE

Back then, the film industry was brand new, wide open and full of fly-by-night operators out to make a quick buck. When Burroughs finally sold the film rights to *Tarzan of the Apes* in 1916, it was to a Chicago insurance salesman named Bill Parsons...who didn't even have a movie company yet. Parsons scraped together the money to form National Pictures, and then hired an actor to play Tarzan. His choice: a hulk named Elmo Lincoln, a former train engineer whose biggest film attribute (some said it was his only attribute) was his massive barrel chest. He was "everything Burroughs had wished Tarzan *wouldn't* be....His beefy build belied the grace, suppleness, and refinement of the literary Tarzan."

Burroughs was so furious with the choice that he sent a letter to his agent instructing him not to sell the film rights to any more books. In fact, Burroughs was so upset that he boycotted the film's opening at the Broadway Theater on January 27, 1918. He even tried to have his name—and Tarzan's—taken off the film.

SUCCESS!
But even though the first movie Tarzan was little more than a caveman who lived in a tree, audiences loved him. In fact, so many people turned out to see the film that many theaters had to schedule additional screenings, some starting as early as 9:00 a.m.

Film critics were impressed, too. "Remember how you sat up most of the night to finish your first adventure story?" The *Chicago Tribune* asked its readers. "Well, it's better than that! And do you remember your first love story? Well, it's better than that!"

Tarzan of the Apes went on to become one of the most popular movies of the year and one of the first silent movies to gross more than $1 million. The film's popularity introduced the Tarzan character to legions of new fans, and helped drive book and magazine sales to new heights. Burroughs, who was on his way to becoming a national figure, earned a fortune. But success had come at a huge price, Taliferro writes: "In expanding his domain from printed page to motion picture, Burroughs lost custody of Tarzan....He could do little more than sit by as the image of Tarzan was appropriated by directors, actors, and the public imagination. In fact as well as fiction, Tarzan was on his own."

THE NEXT FILM
Money notwithstanding, Burroughs hated the film. But at least, he figured, he wouldn't have to deal with Parsons again.

Wrong. One day, Burroughs happened to read in a newspaper gossip column that Parsons was already at work on a sequel—*The Romance of Tarzan*. Burroughs angrily called his lawyer...and found out that while he'd sold Parsons the film rights to only one Tarzan novel, there was nothing in the contract that limited Parsons to making only one film.

This time, Parsons expected to really cash in. While *Tarzan of the Apes* cost him $300,000 to make, he spent less than $25,000 on *The Romance of Tarzan*. And it showed. A lot of the "action" took place in California, not in the jungles of Africa. And Elmo Lincoln wore a

tuxedo in much of the film. *Romance* premiered at the Strand Theater on October 14, 1918, and ran for only seven days. Nobody went
to see it. Parsons took a financial bath...but it didn't hurt Tarzan.

CHANGE OF HEART

Once again, Burroughs swore he'd never sell the film rights to another story...and then a few months later, changed his mind. And
who did he choose to pilot Tarzan's comeback? Numa Pictures, a
New York film company with a reputation for "shoddy and cheap
products."

For *The Return of Tarzan* (later changed to *Revenge of Tarzan*),
Numa needed a new star. The smart thing would have been to audition actors. But for some reason, the company's execs decided to visit local firehouses instead.

A 25-year-old fireman named Gene Pollar happened to be working that day. "I slid down the pole," he recounted years later, "and I
heard one of the men say, 'That's our man.'" Numa hired him...but
Pollar simply could not act.

Numa pictures lived up to its reputation for cheesiness in *Revenge
of Tarzan*, but the film still did a decent box office business. If nothing else, this proved that Tarzan would bring in audiences, no matter
what the vehicle. Pollar, on the other hand, went back to his old
firefighting job and never made another film.

SON OF TARZAN

In September 1919, Burroughs tried again. He sold the film rights to
his new book, *The Son of Tarzan*, to the new owners of National Pictures. They turned the novel in to a movie serial with 15 chapters,
starring P. Dempsey Tabler as Tarzan. Never heard of him? Of course
not. Tabler was a 41-year-old has been and hoped the serial would
revive his career. It didn't. So he gave up acting, moved to San Francisco, and went into the advertising business.

Meanwhile...Numa Pictures had the right to make one more film
based on *The Return of Tarzan*. When they saw how profitable *Son of
Tarzan* was, they decided to create a 15-part serial called *The Adventures of Tarzan*. They began looking for someone to play the apeman.

Numa may not have made good films, but they knew how to make
money. In the three years since his last Tarzan film in 1918, Elmo

Lincoln had become a genuine box office star on the strength of two of his own serials, *Elmo the Mighty* and *Elmo the Fearless*. So when Numa learned he was available again, they signed him up.

Everyone benefitted. Lincoln's final appearance as Tarzan in *Adventures* breathed new life into the franchise, not just in the U.S. but all over the world. "Within three months," Gabe Essoe writes in *Tarzan of the Movies*, "*Adventures* was completely sold out in the United States, Canada, Australia, Central and Western Europe, Asia, South America, Central America, Mexico, the Indies, Pacific islands and the Philippines."

SON-IN-LAW OF TARZAN

Tarzan's movie career hit a lull, and then in the summer of 1926 Burroughs had a chance to prove that *he* didn't know to pick the right Tarzan, either. One night he threw a party at his Tarzana ranch. One of the people invited was a former all-American center for Indiana University named Jack "Big Jim" Pierce, who was now coaching high school sports, trying to break into the movie business. As Pierce recalls it, he was minding his own business at the party when he heard a man's voice yell, "There's Tarzan!"

"And then he proceeded to talk me into playing the Apeman," Pierce recalled later. "He said I looked just like what he had always had in mind."

Pierce was already signed to appear as an aviator in the Howard Hughes film *Wings*, but Burroughs talked him out of the role...so Paramount gave it to a young actor named Gary Cooper instead, and Pierce signed to star in *Tarzan and the Golden Lion*. During filming Pierce also fell in love with Burroughs' only daughter Joan Burroughs, and they later married.

Tarzan and the Golden Lion premiered in February 1927. It was a moderate success, but it was mauled by the critics. "This wins the hand-embroidered toothpick as being the worst picture of the month,'" *Photoplay* Magazine wrote. Pierce himself became quickly disillusioned. "Because of poor direction, terrible story treatment and putrid acting, the opus was a stinkeroo," he admitted. He went back to coaching high school sports while taking whatever acting jobs he could find. *Wings*, the film he'd backed out of, won the first-ever Academy Award for Best Picture.

TARZAN THE MIGHTY

Burroughs sold *Jungle Tales of Tarzan*, to Universal Studios, the first major motion picture studio to make a Tarzan film. They turned it into a 12-chapter serial called *Tarzan the Mighty*.

Universal cast a 30-year-old stuntman and weightlifter named Frank Merrill as Tarzan. A former national gymnastic champ, he had the slender, muscular physique that was perfect for Tarzan...plus, he had the gymnastic skills that made jungle stunts like climbing ropes, swinging through trees, and climbing out of pits and tiger traps a snap. "Wearing an over-the-shoulder leopard skin outfit [and matching headband], he took vine swinging and climbing to a level that shamed all of his predecessors," John Taliaferro writes. "Future Tarzans would scrap Merrill's corny costume, but hereafter each would be expected to live up to his acrobatic standard."

AIII-AHHH---OWWWW

Tarzan the Mighty was a hit (though, as usual, Burroughs hated it), so Universal quickly signed Merrill to a second serial, titled *Tarzan the Tiger*. The last of the silent Tarzan films, it was also the first attempt at making a Tarzan "talkie." Universal distributed a version of the film with a phonograph record, a "soundtrack" that, when played simultaneously with the film, provided a crude musical score and some sound effects that (hopefully) corresponded to the action on the screen. The record also contained the first snippets of lip-synchronized dialog and the very first Tarzan yell ever heard by movie audiences. What did it sound like? As David Fury writes in *Kings of the Jungle*, Merrill's yell "sounded like a man's response to pounding his thumb with a hammer."

As the 1920s ended, Tarzan was stronger than ever. But once again it was the character, not the actor who played him, who survived. After making a few non-Tarzan films, Merrill gave up acting forever and got a job with the City of Los Angeles teaching athletics to kids. He worked with children for the rest of his life.

Part II of Tarzan of the Movies is on page 475.

Finland is the only nation on Earth that has more cell phones than regular phones.

THE LOST MASTERPIECE

A few years ago one of our B.R.I. writers saw the classic 1931 horror film Dracula *for the first time...and thought it was terrible. He never knew there was a story behind why the film had so many problems— or even that other people agreed with him that this Hollywood classic was flawed—until he came across this story in a book called* Hollywood Gothic *by David J. Skal, a leading authority on the history of monster movies.*

UNIVERSAL LANGUAGE

One of the nice things about silent films is that everyone can understand them, regardless of what language they speak. Of course they needed title cards to help explain the plot, but it was easy—and cheap—to write new cards for each foreign market.

As a result American films found their way into countries all over the world, and silent films became a truly universal art form: American studios made half of their revenues from foreign film sales; silent screen stars like Charlie Chaplin and Jackie Coogan became the most recognized human beings on the face of the Earth.

SILENT TREATMENT

But the advent of talking pictures changed everything—and not just for silent-screen stars whose thick accents or funny-sounding voices quickly consigned them to the Hollywood scrap heap. Suddenly, American films became incomprehensible to anyone who didn't speak English. American film studios faced the prospect of losing up to half of their business overnight.

Foreign countries that had become used to a steady stream of Hollywood films found themselves left out in the cold; some threatened to retaliate by slapping tariffs on films with dialogue in English, or by boycotting American films entirely.

Making matters worse, sound recording and synchronization technology was still very primitive, and dubbing foreign-language dialogue onto English-language films was all but impossible. Besides, one of the things that attracted audiences to the first "talkies" was the thrill of hearing their favorite actors speak for the very first time. Even if dubbing had been practical, it might not have been popular.

There was no easy solution to the problem, and as a result many foreign language markets were left out of the early years of the talkie era—except for the Spanish-language market. Spanish was too popular, and Mexico, Central, and South America were too close for Hollywood to ignore.

THE DOPPELGÄNGER ERA

No film crew works 24 hours a day. At some point everyone goes home, leaving the soundstage and the expensive sets unused until morning. So, reasoned Hollywood studios, why not bring in a second cast and crew at night to film foreign-language versions of the same films that were being made in English during the day?

Because the sets had already been constructed and second-string actors and crews could be hired for much less money than Hollywood stars, a film like *Dracula* that had cost nearly $450,000 to film in English during the day could be remade in Spanish at night for as little as $40,000. By 1930, nearly all of the major studios had begun filming Spanish "doppelgänger" films at night.

GRAVEYARD SHIFT

Universal Pictures was one of the last major studios to adopt the idea, when it filmed Spanish and English versions of the film *The Cat Creeps* in 1930. *Dracula* was slated to be only the studio's second Spanish-language film.

Paul Kohner, Universal's head of foreign production, hired director George Melford, who'd worked with Rudolph Valentino in *The Sheik*, and Cinematographer George Robinson. A 38-year-old Spanish stage actor named Carlos Villarias was cast as Dracula, and a multilingual actor named Barry Norton was hired to play the part of "Juan Harker." A 17-year-old Mexican actress named Lupita Tovar was hired to play Harker's fianceé Eva, who was known as Mina in the English version. ·

"The American crew left at 6:00 p.m. and we were ready," Tovar recalled. "We started shooting at eight. At midnight, they would call for dinner....They didn't pay us much, but we didn't complain. We were happy to have some money—most actors were starving. "

FIRST RATE

Since they were using a second-rate cast and crew after Hollywood's finest had gone home for the day, the assumption was that a film made at night would be inferior to the original. That may have been true in most cases…but not in the case of *Dracula*.

For all of its popularity and accomplishments as Hollywood's first vampire film, on a technical level, the English-language *Dracula* is considered a very poorly made film. A lot of the blame for this goes to director Tod Browning, a hard-drinking recluse with a reputation as a troublemaker. Browning had been fired from at least one studio for his drinking, and was blacklisted by the entire industry for two years in the early 1920s. Making matters worse, Browning had direct-ed nine films starring horror superstar Lon Chaney, Sr., when both men had worked at MGM, and he was still reeling from Chaney's recent death from throat cancer.

Browning's myriad personal problems found their way into the finished film. "In scene after scene," Skal writes, "the script demon-strates just how much Browning cut, trimmed, ignored, and generally sabotaged the screenplay's visual potentials, insisting on static came-ra setups, eliminating reaction shots and special effects, and general-ly taking the lazy way out at every opportunity." In one scene, a piece of cardboard the crew used to reduce the glare of a lamp takes up nearly a quarter of the entire screen, and in the film's climax, Dracula's death isn't even shown on film; moviegoers had to settle for the sound of Lugosi groaning offscreen.

ON PURPOSE
Legend has it that cinematographer Karl Freund got so exasperated with Browning's slipshod style that he just turned the camera on and let it run unattended, Skal writes:

> Indeed, there is one endless take in the finished film featuring Man-ners (who played Jonathan Harker), Chandler (Mina Murray), and Van Sloan (Dr. Van Helsing) that runs 251 feet, nearly three minutes without a cut that was clearly meant to be broken up with close-ups and reaction shots. At one point Chandler tells Manners, "Oh, no—don't look at me like that," in an apparent reference to a dramatic change in his expression. The two-shot, however, shows Manners as motionless as a wax dummy—as if oblivious that the camera is even catching his face.

As if that isn't sloppy enough, in the final credits, Universal Presi-dent Carl Laemmle's title is misspelled as "Presient."

¡EL VAMPIRO!

The film crew on the Spanish *Dracula* was another story.

Kohner, who had produced the Spanish version of *The Cat Creeps*, was headstrong and ambitious—and not above second-guessing the English-language unit, trying to improve upon their work. On *The Cat Creeps*, he watched the daily footage produced by Rupert Julian, the director of the English version, and found the scenes to be poorly lit and uninspiring. So when filming the same scenes for the Spanish film, Kohner relit every set and filled them with atmosphere-creating candles, cobwebs, and shadows that had been missing in the English version. Universal Pictures head Carl Laemmle, Jr. was so impressed with Kohner's work that he ordered Julian to refilm his own footage, this time using Kohner as his artistic advisor.

Kohner did the same thing during the making of the Spanish version of *Dracula*. Using a movieola machine that was kept on the set, they watched the daily footage or "dailies" that had been shot for the English-language version, made note of the sloppiness and mistakes, and then made sure that their own scenes were better.

One thing they didn't try to improve on was Bela Lugosi's masterful performance as Count Dracula. Instead, Kohner insisted that Carlos Villarias imitate Lugosi as closely as possible, and he alone among the actors was allowed to watch the English-language dailies to make sure he got it right. They even let him wear Lugosi's hairpiece, though it's unclear whether Lugosi ever knew about it.

Now You See Him, Now You Don't

Perhaps the most noticeable difference between the two films is in their use—or lack thereof—of special effects. In scenes showing Dracula climbing out of his coffin, for example, the Spanish version uses a double exposure to show a cloud of mist rising out of the coffin and turning into Dracula.

In the English version, the coffin lid starts to tremble, the camera turns away from the coffin and points at a wall...and by the time it returns Bela Lugosi is already out of the coffin.

NUMERO UNO

When completed, the Spanish version of *Dracula* cost just over $66,000 to make and took only 22 nights to film, compared to the

Does anyone know why? For every 100 girls born, there are 105 boys born.

seven weeks and $450,000 it took to film the English version. In fact, the Spanish crew shot the film so fast that they ended up shooting some of their scenes on sets that weren't completely finished. Rather than wait for them to be finished, the filmmakers compensated for the empty sets with the clever lighting.

The first preview was held in early 1931, before the original *Dracula* was even finished, and the reviewers who saw the Spanish version were impressed. "If the English version of *Dracula*, directed by Tod Browning, is as good as the Spanish version," *Hollywood Filmograph* magazine wrote, "why, the Big U (Universal) hasn't a thing in the world to worry about."

The only problem, of course, was that the English version wasn't as good, as *Filmograph* reported a few weeks later. The first few minutes of the film were enthralling, the magazine wrote, but quickly deteriorated after that. "Tod Browning directed, although we cannot believe that the same man was responsible for both the first and latter parts of the picture. Had the rest of the picture lived up to the first sequence in the ruined castle Transylvania, *Dracula* would have been a horror and thrill classic long remembered."

INTO THIN AIR

Dracula was one of the last foreign-language films produced in Hollywood. By 1931 the Great Depression was in full swing, and the American film studios, desperate to cut costs wherever possible, abandoned Spanish-language markets almost entirely. Universal never even bothered to register the copyright on the film and never had preservation copies made so that new prints could be made when the originals wore out.

The Spanish *Dracula* made the rounds of Spanish-language countries into the 1950s, then gradually disappeared.

Life after Death

It was thought to be lost entirely until the late 1970s, when an incomplete negative was found in a warehouse in New Jersey. Then, in 1989, a complete version of the film was found in the Cuban Film Archives in Havana. In the late 1990s, Universal and the UCLA Film Archives restored the film and released it to cable and video markets, where it is developing a new following and has finally received the recognition it deserves.

THE 13TH GUEST

On page 213, we wrote about fear of the #13. In the course of researching that page, we stumbled across the story that is widely regarded as the origin of that superstition—this Norse tale about the death of the god Baldur, who symbolized beauty and good in the world. What's the connection? The murderer, Loki, was the 13th guest at a dinner honoring Baldur's memory. The idea that #13 symbolized evil took hold in Norse culture, and spread to the rest of Europe. Here's the tale, from Myths & Legends of the Ages.

"Baldur was the son of Frigga, the Queen of the Norse gods. Baldur was the most beautiful of the gods, and he was also gentle, fair and wise. Wherever he went, people were happy just at the sight of him. He was not only the favorite of his mother, but the favorite of all the other gods.

"One night, Baldur dreamed three dreams. Each dream was more terrible than the one before it. In the third dream, he found himself in a dark, lonely place. He heard a sad voice cry, 'The sun is gone! The spring is gone! Joy is gone! For Baldur, the beautiful, is dead!'

"The young god was very much upset. He told his lovely young wife, Nanna, about these sad and terrifying dreams. Nanna ran weeping to Queen Frigga saying, 'Oh, mother, this must not come true!' Queen Frigga was deeply frightened. But she spoke soothingly and said, 'Do not fear, Nanna. Bal-dur is so dear to all the world, how could anything in the world want to hurt him?'

"But Queen Frigga was frightened. She thought of a plan. 'I will travel all over the heavens and all over the earth,' she said. 'I will make all things promise not to hurt my boy.'

"First, she went to the gods themselves. She told them of Baldur's dreams. She implored them to promise that none of them would ever harm Baldur. They all promised gladly.

"Then Frigga traveled all over the world step by step. From all things, she got the same promise. From the trees and the plants; from the stones and the metals; from earth, air, fire and water; from sun, snow, wind and rain; and from all the diseases that men know—every creature and every thing promised not to harm Baldur.

"At last, the weary but joyful Queen returned to As-

Q. When did the last Roman aqueduct fall into disuse? **A.** It didn't—some are still in use today.

gard, home of the gods. Frigga brought happy news: there was nothing in the world that would hurt Baldur. And there was great rejoicing in Asgard. All the gods felt relieved. When someone suggested that they play a game which would prove how wrong the dream was, everyone agreed.

"They placed Baldur at one end of the field. He stood there in all his golden beauty, his face glowing with a bright light like that of the sun. And as he stood there unarmed and smiling, the other gods took turns shooting arrows at him, hurling their spears against him, throwing sticks and stones, and every stone fell harmless at Baldur's feet; each arrow and spear turned aside as it reached his body. Baldur stood serene and smiling. Nothing would hurt him.

"But among the crowd, there was one who did not smile. Loki the crafty one, Loki the evil one, did not laugh and cheer like the others. Loki was filled with jealous anger and malice. Baldur had never done him any harm, yet Loki hated him; for Loki knew full well that no one in the world loved him in the same way they loved Baldur. An evil plan took shape in Loki's mind.

While the others were engaged in the happy game, Loki disguised himself as an old woman, and made his way to Queen Frigga.

"'Good day, my lady,' he said. 'What is all that noise and excitement over in the field?'

"'Don't you know?' answered Queen Frigga in surprise. 'They are shooting at my son, Baldur. They are proving the promise that every creature and every thing has made, not to injure him. You see, the promise is being kept.'

"The old woman pretended to be surprised. 'Really!' she cried. 'Do you mean to say that every single thing in the whole world has promised not to hurt Baldur? It is true that he is a fine fellow, but still that is a remarkable thing. Have you gotten such a promise from absolutely everything in the world?'

"'Oh, yes,' said Queen Frigga, 'everything has promised. Of course, there is one tiny little plant so small and unimportant that I did not even bother to ask.'

"'And what little plant is that?' said the old woman.

"'It is the mistletoe that grows nearby. It is really too harmless to bother with,' said Frigga.

"Loki hobbled away, but as soon as he saw that no one was noticing him, he picked up his gown and ran as fast as he could to the spot where the little mistletoe grew. With his knife, Loki cut off a piece of mistletoe, whittled it and shaped it until it was a slender arrow. Then he hobbled back to the field where the merry game was still going on. In one corner of the field stood Hod, the blind brother of Baldur. Loki, still in the guise of an old woman, tapped his arm.

"'Why are you not taking part in the merry game?' she asked. 'They all do honor to your brother. Surely you ought to do so, too.'

"Then Hod touched his sightless eyes. 'Ah,' he said, 'I am blind. How I would rejoice to give honor to my dear brother but I cannot see to aim a weapon.'

"'You ought to at least throw a little stick,' said the old woman. 'Here is a little green twig that you can use as a dart. I will guide your arm while you throw it.'

"Hod smiled and stretched forth his arm eagerly. Then Loki placed the arrow of mistletoe in Hod's hand and taking careful aim, hurled it straight at Baldur's heart. With a cry, Baldur fell forward on the grass. Everyone rushed forward. They could not understand what had happened. When they saw that Baldur was dead, they knew that it was the end of sunshine and spring and joy in Asgard. The terrible dream had come true!

"They turned upon Hod ready to tear him to pieces. 'What is it! What have I done?' asked the poor blind brother.

"'What have you done? You have slain Baldur!' they cried.

"'No! No!' cried Hod. 'I could never have done such a thing. It was the old woman who stood at my elbow and gave me a little twig to throw. She must be a witch.'

"The gods scattered all over the field to look for the old woman, but she had mysteriously disappeared. Then they noticed that Loki was not amongst them 'It must have been Loki!' they said.

"The heartbroken gods placed Baldur on a beautiful ship to send him to Queen Hela, the queen of Death. And weeping and wailing, they sent him on his way. But Queen Frigga sent a message to Hela to find out if there was some way to win back Baldur from the kingdom of Death.

"'I would let him go if I might,' Queen Hela said, 'but a queen cannot always do as she likes. There is only one way that you can bring Baldur back to life. If everything upon Earth will weep for Baldur's death, then he may return. But should even one creature fail to weep, Baldur must remain with me.'

"The gods sent messages all over the world bidding every creature to weep for Baldur's death. There seemed to be little need for such a message, for already there was weeping and mourning in every part of the world. Even the giants, who were enemies of the gods, wept for Baldur. It began to look as though Baldur might be ransomed from Death.

"But when all the messengers returned to Asgard, one of them told of an ugly old giantess in a deep, black cave who refused to weep for Baldur. The messenger had begged her to weep but the giantess had answered, 'Baldur is nothing to me. I care not whether he lives or dies.' So all the tears of the sorrowing world were useless, and Baldur would not return because one creature would not weep.

"To divert their sadness at the loss of their beloved Baldur and to make them forget Loki's treachery, Aegir, the god of the sea, invited the twelve remaining gods to a banquet.

"The twelve gladly accepted the invitation—none refused. But in the middle of the feast, evil Loki, the thirteenth god, appeared, uninvited. When they told him to leave, he cursed them and in a rage of jealousy, he slew Aegir's servant. Angered at the senseless murder, the gods drove Loki from the banquet.

"Scarcely had they recovered from this terrible interruption to their feast, when Loki appeared once more, slandering the gods, taunting them with their weaknesses and imperfections, deriding them for their mistakes. Gathered as a group, the gods were forbidden violence, yet Loki's voice grew louder and louder until Thor could bear it no more.

"'Loki has done his last evil deed,' shouted Thor the Thunderer, as he lifted his mighty hammer. 'Come, my brothers,' Thor cried, 'we have wept long enough. It is now time to punish!'

"Loki tried to escape by changing himself into a fish, hiding in a deep river. 'They'll never be able to find me here,' he said.

"But although Odin, the All-

What's a hooker? An Irish fishing boat with a single mast.

Father, had only one eye, he could see everything in the world. He could see through thick mountains and down into the deepest sea. Odin took a net and scooped Loki out of the river. When he grasped Loki's slippery fish body, Loki was changed back into his own shape. There he stood, surrounded by the wrathful gods.

"'Kill him! Kill him!' they shouted, as Odin pushed him along the road to Asgard. And on the way to the rainbow bridge which led from Asgard to Midgard, the land of the humans, thousands of men lined the road shouting, 'Kill him! Kill him!'

"From their caverns in the mountains came the dwarfs. They stood shaking their fists at Loki. The beasts growled and bared their fangs as if they wished to tear Loki into pieces; the birds flew at him trying to peck out his eyes; insects came in clouds to sting him, and serpents darted their fangs at him, ready to poison him with their deadly bite. But Odin decided on an even worse punishment than death. He led Loki down into a damp, dark cave under the ground where sunlight never shone. The cave was full of ugly toads and snakes. In this terrible prison chamber, Loki was placed upon three sharp stones. He was bound with iron bands, so that no one could ever loosen them. The bands cut into Loki as he lay.

"Over his head was hung a venomous serpent. From its mouth, poison which burned and stung like fire, dropped into Loki's face.

"Everybody in the world hated Loki except one. In spite of all his wickedness, Loki' s wife, Sigyn, remained faithful to him. She stood by his head and held a bowl to catch the poison which dropped from the serpent's jaw, so that it would not reach Loki's face. But whenever the bowl became full, Sigyn had to take it away to empty it and then the burning, horrible drops of poison fell on Loki's face.

"Under the caverns, Loki still lies, struggling to be free. When the poison falls upon his face, he shrieks and struggles so violently that the whole earth trembles. Then people cry, 'An earthquake!' and they run away as fast as they can. For Loki, the evil one, though bound, is still dangerous. And bound as he is, Loki will stay imprisoned until the end of the world."

If you're too young to be a Baby Boomer and too old to be a Generation Xer, you're a "Cusper."

THE MILLION-DOLLAR NICKEL

A few years ago the government announced there was a nationwide copper shortage. One reason…people were hoarding pennies, then sifting through them hoping to find a rare one. You probably have a jar full of change on your dresser. If you're looking for "treasure" in it, you should know how hard it is to find. Check out these stories of the most valuable U.S. coins.

RARE COINS

Most Americans believe it's possible to strike it rich by finding one incredibly rare coin. It might be right in our cash registers or our pockets, if we would only take the time to look.

Hunting for these treasures became a part of popular culture during the Depression when coin dealer B. Max Mehl of Fort Worth, Texas, got the idea of promoting his *Star Rare Coin Encyclopedia and Catalog* by offering $50 for the "legendary" 1913 Liberty nickel. Mehl offered huge sums for coin rarities, too, and thousands of ordinary people started looking through their change. At about the same time, Whitman Publishing put out their first *Guide Book of United States Coins*—the "Red Book"—with pictures and values of all U.S. coins and made a fortune by luring tens of thousands of children into collecting with cardboard albums that held the coins.

THE FEW, THE RARE, THE VALUABLE

Oddly, the most legendary rare coins aren't even official U.S. coins; they are counterfeits or reproductions.

Here are the three rarest coins.

The coin: 1913 Liberty Head nickel
Number minted: 5
Value today: $1.48 million at auction in May 1996

The last one was minted in 1912—in 1913 the dazzlingly artistic Buffalo nickel was introduced, so there were no 1913 Liberty Head nickels minted. But rumors surfaced that a very small number of 1913 Liberty nickels had been struck by an unknown employee.

Years passed. Rumors persisted. In 1919, *The Numismatist* ran an ad in which one Samuel W. Brown of North Tonawanda, New York, offered to pay $500 for any 1913 Liberty nickels. The next month his ad hiked the price to $600. That summer, Brown mysteriously appeared at the annual American Numismatic Convention and exhibited five of them.

As it turns out, in 1913 Brown was curator of the U.S. Mint's "Cabinet Collection." Did he secretly strike the coins, then create a market for them with his ads? No one knows.

In 1924, a Philadelphia coin dealer offered the same five coins, the only 1913 Liberty Nickels known to exist, in a tiny ad in *The Numismatist*. Colonel E. H. R. Green, son of the then-notorious millionaire "Witch of Wall Street," Hetty Green, bought them all. They surfaced again in 1942, when the St. Louis Stamp & Coin Company sold them individually, breaking up the set. Thereafter, the coins were known by numbers 1 through 5.

Where Are They Now?

• **#1** Was purchased by King Farouk of Egypt from Abe Kosoff, the "dean of American numismatics." Later purchased by another numismatist, R. Henry Norweb, whose widow donated it to the Smithsonian.

• **#2** Was part of the fabulously valuable collection of Louis Eliasberg (considered the most complete and highest-grade collection of U.S. coins in existence). The coin brought $1.48 million in 1996.

• **#3** Was "dull, scratched, uncirculated." It was also sold to Farouk, resold in 1972 for $100,000 and again, a few years later, for the then record-setting price of $385,000.

• **#4** Was "uncirculated, but nicked." It has vanished. It was last seen in the possession of George O. Walton, who was killed in a car crash en route to a coin show in North Carolina in the mid-1960s. The American Numismatic Association has a standing $5,000 reward for information on its whereabouts.

• **#5** Was called "uncirculated, but partly rough." When it sold for $46,000 in 1967, this coin had seen a lot of handling. It once belonged to a J. V. McDermott, who would pass it around in his favorite tavern and allow people to admire it, figuring it could never be stolen. Why? No one would be able to sell it. It was too rare.

THE KING

The coin: 1804 Silver Dollar
Number minted: 15
Value today: $4.14 million, which set a record at a 1999 auction

No coin has a more fascinating past than the "King of U.S. Coins." And it's not even an official coin.

This story starts in 1834. To get favorable trade agreements in the Mideast and Far East, the U. S. State Department ordered the Mint to make two cased sets of all domestic coins currently in use—"gifts" for the King of Siam and the Sultan of Muscat (now Oman). But the sets seemed scanty without a silver dollar or gold eagle ($10 gold piece), both of which were discontinued 30 years earlier because bullion dealers were melting them down. What to do? They simply found some old dies in the vault and struck four proof dollars and four proof eagles. And although only four were needed, the Mint struck four more—to trade with serious collectors for rarities missing from the Mint Cabinet Collection. These are the *only* silver dollars with the 1804 date.

Anna

The Sultan of Muscat's set, in a crimson morocco case, was delivered in 1835. Coins from that set eventually reached a British collector in 1917. The other set, in a yellow morocco case, went to the King of Siam in 1836. The king passed it to his successors, who in turn passed it to the granddaughters of Anna Leon-Owens, known to history as "Anna of Siam," whose exploits as tutor to the royal family were the basis of the hit musical "The King and I."

Two other sets, destined for the Emperor of Cochin-China and the Mikado of Japan, were returned to the Mint when the courier died of dysentery en route.

American collectors knew nothing of the 1804 *dollar* until 1842, when *A Manual of Gold and Silver Coinage of All Nations* showed an illustration of the coin. Numismatists from all over the country contacted the Mint to find out about it. In 1843, one collector, Matthew Stickney offered his one-of-a-kind gold colonial 1785

"Immune Columbia" coin and the Mint traded an 1804 dollar for it.

Where are they now?

The eight 1804 dollars, according to the September 20, 1998, *Coin World* magazine:

• **#1** From the Mint Collection, now in the Smithsonian.

• **#2** The Stickney dollar, first shown in the 1842 book. It sold in April 1997 for $1.8 million.

• **#3** The King of Siam dollar, a brilliant proof—never scratched, never dropped, never polished—the finest known. Sold in 1979 for $1 million, then in 1993 for $1.81 million. Now on display at Mandalay Bay Resort and Museum, Las Vegas.

• **#4** The Sultan of Muscat dollar, a blue-toned choice proof. Acquired in 1945 and held in a personal collection for 54 years. It brought $4.14 million at auction in 1999.

• **#5** The Dexter Dollar, so named because one of its many owners, James V. Dexter, stamped his initial "D" on it. It sold in 1989 for $990,000.

• **#6** Bought from the Mint by an "unknown lady" in 1845, this brilliant proof was named the Parmalee Dollar after the Boston baked-bean mogul who bought it in 1874. Now on display at the Durham Western Heritage Museum in Omaha, Nebraska.

• **#7** The Mickley Dollar, graded "almost uncirculated." A bank teller found it in a deposit in 1850. It was acquired by prestigious collector Joseph J. Mickley in 1859. Stack's Auction House sold it for $475,000 in 1993.

• **#8** The Cohen Dollar was received "over the counter" by Edward Cohen of Richmond, Virginia, at his exchange office in 1865. The DuPont family owned it and then lost it in an October 1967 robbery of its Florida estate. It was recovered in Switzerland in 1982 and is now in the museum of the American Numismatic Society in Colorado Springs, Colorado.

A Phony Counterfeit

By 1858, the 1804 dollars had become so famous and valuable that a Mint worker dug up the old 1804 dies and minted some more. Mint nightwatchman Theodore Eckfield fenced these restrikes through a Philadelphia store for $75 each, but the scandal became public and the Mint demanded their return. (Only one survives, identifiable because it was struck over an 1857 shooting medal from Bern, Switzerland, and parts of the "host coin" are visible.)

In 1859, Eckfield was at it again, this time fencing the dollars through European auction houses to give them a credible pedigree. Only six of these restrikes are known and they sell today in the $200,000 to $400,000 range. Finally, in 1860, the Mint director confiscated the dies and sealed them in a vault. They were destroyed in 1867.

I SCREAM, YOU SCREAM

The coin: the 1894-S dime (the "ice cream dime")
Number minted: 24
Value today: $145,000

In 1894, Mint superintendent J. Daggett struck these proof "Barber dimes" for seven banker friends. He gave them three each and kept three for himself. Since these gems would become incredibly valuable very quickly, it's surprising that Daggett gave his three to his young daughter Hallie. "Put them away safely," he told her, "and when you're as old as I am you can sell them for a 'good price.'" Hallie immediately used one of the dimes to buy a dish of ice cream, inadvertently setting a world record for the amount paid for any dessert. Sixty years later, she sold the other two dimes for large sums.

Where Are They Now?
Today, only 12 of the dimes are accounted for (four are listed below).
• **#1** Passed through seven owners, including Max Mehl, sold in 1980 for $145,000.
• **#6** Was sold by Hallie Daggett in 1954, and later resold for $97,000.
• **#11** Was found in circulation in 1957 in "good" condition, meaning so worn that it is without detail and only the bust is outlined. This one is likely the "ice cream" specimen. Despite the extreme wear or perhaps due to the charming legend around it, the coin sold in 1980 for $31,000.
• **#12** Offered in a 1942 Stack's auction then withdrawn "for personal reasons" and not seen since.

The whereabouts of the other 12 specimens remain a mystery.

"I YAM WHAT I YAM"

What cartoon character was so influential that he convinced kids to eat vegetables? Popeye the Sailor Man...Toot... Toot!! Here's the story of how he was born.

WALK ON

In 1919, the *New York Evening Journal* hired a cartoonist named E. C. "Elzie" Segar and told him to create a comic strip called "Thimble Theater." That's all the guidance he had—the rest was up to him. He came up with a weird bunch of characters: a scrawny, gawky old maid named Olive Oyl; her boyfriend Ham Gravy; her loopy brother Castor Oyl; and her parents Cole and Nana Oyl.

The strip's popularity grew steadily over the next ten years, and as time passed Segar graduated from telling a new joke in each strip to developing story lines that went on for weeks, months—and sometimes even years. In 1929, he came up with a story in which Ham and Castor decide to set sail in search of a legendary lucky creature called the Whiffle Hen.

Neither Ham nor Castor knew anything about sailing, so they went down to the waterfront to hire a sailor to take them on their trip. In the June 17, 1929, strip Castor walks up to a scrappy, one-eyed man with a captain's hat and asks him, "Are you a sailor?"

"Ja think I'm a cowboy?" the sailor replies. Popeye the Sailor Man was born.

Segar never intended for the sailor to become a permanent addition to the strip. When the Whiffle Hen story line ended several months later, he retired the character from Thimble Theater. But so many angry readers wrote their newspapers demanding that Popeye be returned to the strip that Segar decided to comply. A few months later, Olive gave him a kiss (on the cheek), and Popeye instantly fell in love. Segar demoted Ham Gravy to a minor character, and Popeye replaced him as Olive Oyl's main love interest. Segar also renamed the strip "Thimble Theater, Starring Popeye."

SILVER SCREEN

The early 1930s was a period of fierce competition among American

---

cartoon animation studios, which were hard at work building up minor cartoon characters into "stars" with strong popular appeal that could be used to increase theater bookings and fatten studio profits. Walt Disney Studios did it with Mickey Mouse, Donald Duck, and Goofy; and Warner Brothers would do it with Bugs Bunny and Daffy Duck. A company called Fleischer Studios, headed by brothers Max and Dave Fleischer, had a very popular character named Betty Boop (see page 275), and was looking for other characters to develop.

Popeye was Max Fleischer's favorite comic strip, and in November 1932, he approached an executive with King Features Syndicate, the company that owned the Popeye strip. "You know, this is a nutty little creature, but I think I could do something with it," he told them.

"Out of that ugly looking thing?" the executive supposedly replied.

"The funnier he looks," Max Fleischer replied, "the better the cartoon will be."

Fleischer decided to test Popeye's appeal by featuring him in a Betty Boop cartoon. But fearing other studios would steal his idea and create their own sailor characters, he locked animator Roland Crandall in a studio, where Crandall spent the next several months animating the first Popeye cartoon by himself, in secret.

WELL, BLOW ME DOWN!

Betty Boop Presents Popeye the Sailor was a huge hit when it premiered in the summer of 1933 and a succession of Popeye cartoons followed over the next several years. Together, the cartoons and newspaper comic strips launched a huge Popeye fad; by the late 1930s Popeye eclipsed even Disney's Mickey Mouse to become the most popular cartoon character in the United States.

At its peak the Popeye craze was more than just a fad—it was a cultural phenomenon. The comic strip, which appeared in 638 newspapers around the country, was responsible for adding the words "jeep" and "goon" (both characters in the strip) to the English language; and spinach farmers credited Popeye's popularity with causing sales of spinach to rise 33% between 1931 and 1936, saving them from ruin during the Great Depression.

MAN O' WAR

Fighting was a part of Popeye's persona from the very beginning. He was the most violent in the earliest days of the comic strip, when he cussed, started fights, and often hit animals, people and inanimate objects with little or no provocation. The scrappiness of those early cartoons was well suited for the audiences of the 1930s and 1940s. Bud Sagendorf writes in *Popeye: The First 50 Years*: "Though today it may seem brutal, Popeye's outlook was a natural reaction of the times. A population frustrated by the Great Depression liked the idea of one small man fighting back and winning. They, too, wanted to strike out at something they feared and didn't understand."

But as Popeye's popularity with children grew throughout the 1930s, King Features Syndicate owner William Randolph Hearst ordered Segar to tone down the cursing and the violence and make the strip more suitable for children. Popeye stopped cursing, but remained just as violent as ever, only now instead of fighting for no reason, Popeye always fought for what was right—no longer a brawler. Thanks to Hearst, Popeye was now a full-fledged hero.

PUNCH DRUNK

Popeye's intemperate nature served him well during the 1930s and the 1940s, when he and Bluto were given white U.S. Navy uniforms so that they could aid in the war effort. Popeye cartoons were a TV staple in the 1950s and 1960s, but the same thing that had made Popeye popular during the Great Depression and World War II—violence—started to work against him, and his popularity slid in the 1970s and 1980s as parents began to worry about the amount of violence their children were watching on television.

A 1980 feature film starring Robin Williams was an even bigger dud. (Popeye was Williams' first feature film, and was so poorly received that many film critics predicted it would be his last.)

Popeye received a makeover in 1987: He traded in sailing in favor of owning a health club, was married to Olive Oyl, and had a son named Junior (no word on what happened to Swee'Pea). Likewise, Bluto was married to a woman named Lizzie and had a son named Tank. The new series, called "Popeye and Son," was such a ratings disaster that it was pulled off the air after only 13 weeks.

According to one poll taken in 1991, Popeye had slipped to

92nd in a national poll ranking the popularity of cartoon characters.

SIGN O' THE TIMES

The old Fleischer Studios cartoons remain popular on cable television, but all attempts to "freshen up" Popeye have failed.

"Poor Popeye. While other classic characters are going strong, Popeye has missed the boat....The 67-year-old comic strip, once in hundreds of U.S. newspapers, now appears in just seven....These days, even the Popeyes Chicken & Biscuit chain has erased the Popeye cartoon from signs and packaging in its U.S. restaurants."
—*The Wall St. Journal*, 1996

"There's only so much you can do with a guy in a sailor suit."
—Cathleen Titus, spokesperson King Features

POPEYE FACTS

• The Popeye theme song was written by Sammy Lerner. For years, he refused to admit publicly that he had composed it—though he made a fortune from it, and it was probably his best-known song.

• Segar needed an explanation for Popeye's super-strength. In the late '20s, health specialists were extolling the benefits of spinach as a super-food (erroneously, it turned out—due to a mistake made in calculating the amount of iron spinach contains), so Segar attributed Popeye's power to the vegetable.

•Popeye is known as "Iron Arm" in Italy, and "Skipper Skraek" or "Terror of the Sea" in Denmark.

• **Bluto vs. Brutus.** Popeye's arch-enemy never appeared in "Thimble Theater." Fleischer Studios needed a regular villain to compete with Popeye for Olive Oyl's affections, so they asked Segar to come up with a composite of all of the characters Popeye had ever fought. Segar came up with Bluto. But when King Features ordered a new batch of "made for TV" cartoons in 1960, a dispute arose over whether King Features owned the rights to the Bluto character. Rather than risk a lawsuit, they replaced the character with Brutus, who served as Popeye's enemy until 1978, when the situation was resolved and King Features was free to use Bluto again.

MONKEY SEE, MONKEY DO?

This article first ran in Time *magazine. It was written by Eugene Linden, author of a fabulous book called* The Parrot's Lament.

THE GREAT ESCAPE

The first time Fu Manchu broke out, zookeepers chalked it up to human error. On a balmy day, the orangutans at the Omaha Zoo had been playing in their big outdoor enclosure. Not long thereafter, shocked keepers looked up and saw Fu and his family hanging out in some trees near the elephant barn. Later investigation revealed that the door that connects the furnace room to the orangutan enclosure was open. Head keeper Jerry Stones chewed out his staff, and the incident was forgotten. But the next time the weather was nice, Fu Manchu escaped again. Fuming, Stones recalls, "I was getting ready to fire someone."

The next nice day, alerted by keepers desperate to keep their jobs, Stones finally managed to catch Fu Manchu in the act. First, the young ape climbed down some air-vent louvers into a dry moat. Then, taking hold of the bottom of the furnace door, he used brute force to pull it back just far enough to slide a wire into the gap, slip a latch and pop the door open. The next day, Stones noticed something shiny sticking out of Fu's mouth. It was the wire lock pick, bent to fit between his lip and gum and stowed there between escapes.

MONKEY IN THE MIDDLE?

Fu Manchu's jailbreaks made headlines in 1968, but his clever tricks didn't make a big impression on the scientists who specialize in looking for signs of higher mental processes in animals. At the time, much of the action in animal intelligence was focused on efforts to teach apes to use human languages. No researcher cared much about ape escape artists.

And neither did I. In 1970, I began following studies of animal intelligence, particularly the early reports of chimpanzees who learned how to use human words. The big breakthrough in these experiments came when two psychologists, R. Allen and Beatrice Gardner, realized their chimps were having trouble forming word-like sounds and decided to teach a young female named Washoe sign language instead. Washoe eventually learned more than 130 words from the language of the deaf called American Sign Language.

Washoe's success spurred more language studies and created such ape celebrities as Koko the gorilla and Chantek the orangutan. The work also set off a fierce debate in scientific circles about the nature of animal intelligence—one that continues to this day. Indeed, it has been easier to defeat Communism than to get scientists to agree on what Washoe meant three decades ago when she saw a swan on a pond and made the signs for "water bird." Was she inventing a phrase, to describe waterfowl, or merely generating signs vaguely associated with the scene in front of her?

A NEW APPROACH

Over the years I have witnessed at close range the problems scientists encounter when they try to examine phenomena as elusive as language and idea formation. Do animals really have thoughts, what we call consciousness? The very question offends some philosophers and scientists, since it cuts so close to what separates men from beasts. Yet, notes Harvard's Donald Griffin, to rule out the study of animal consciousness handicaps our understanding of other species.

Frustrated with what seemed like an endless and barren ideological debate, I began to wonder whether there might be better windows on animal minds than experiments designed to teach them human signs and symbols. When I heard about Fu Manchu, I realized what to me now seems obvious: if animals can think, they will probably do their best thinking when it serves their purposes, not when some scientist asks them to.

And so I started exploring the world of animal intelligence from the other side. I started talking to people who deal with animals professionally: veterinarians, animal researchers, zookeepers. Most are not studying animal intelligence per se, but they encounter it, and the lack of it, every day.

AT THE ZOO

Get a bunch of keepers together and they will start telling stories about how their charges try to outsmart, beguile or otherwise astonish humans. They tell stories about animals that hoodwink or manipulate their keepers, stories about wheeling and dealing, stories of understanding and trust across the vast gulf that separates different species. And, if the keepers have had a few drinks, they will tell stories about escape.

Each of these narratives reveals another facet of what I have become convinced is a new window on animal intelligence: the kind of mental feats they perform when dealing with captivity and the dominant species on the planet—humanity.

WHAT DO YOU WANT FOR THAT BANANA?

Captive animals often become students of the humans who control their lives. The great apes in particular are alert to situations that might temporarily give them the upper hand—for example, when something useful or valuable rolls into their exhibit or is left behind. The more worldly animals recognize the concept of value as meaning "something I have that you want," and they are not above exploiting such opportunities for all they are worth.

Consider the time that Charlene Jenciry was in her office at the Columbus Zoo and word came to her that a male gorilla named Cob was clutching a suspicious object. Arriving on the scene, Jenciry offered Cob some peanuts, only to be met with a blank stare. Realizing that they were negotiating, Jenciry upped the ante and offered a piece of pineapple. At this point, without making eye contact with her, Cob opened his hand and revealed that he was holding a key chain, much in the manner that a fence might furtively show a potential customer stolen goods on the street. Relieved that it was not anything dangerous or valuable, Jenciry gave Cob the piece of pineapple. Astute bargainer that he was, Cob then broke the key chain and gave her a link, perhaps figuring, "Why give her the whole thing if I can get a bit of pineapple for each piece?"

TRADING WITH THE ENEMY

If an animal can show some skill in the barter business, why not in handling money? One ape, an orangutan named Chantek, did just that during his years as part of a study of sign language undertaken by psychologist Lyn Miles at the University of Tennessee. Chantek learned more than 150 words, but that wasn't all. He also figured out that if he did chores such as cleaning up his room, he could earn coins that he could later spend on treats and rides in Miles's car.

Chantek's understanding of money seems to have extended far beyond simple transactions to such sophisticated concepts as inflation and counterfeiting. Miles first used poker chips as the coin of the realm, but Chantek decided that he could expand the money supply by breaking the chips in two. When Miles switched to using washers, Chantek found pieces of aluminum foil and tried to make imitation washers that he could pass off as the real thing. Miles also tried to teach Chantek more virtuous habits such as saving, sharing and charity.

Seeing Is Believing
When I caught up with the orangutan at Zoo Atlanta, where he now lives, I did not see evidence of charity, but I did see an example of sharing that a robber baron might envy. When Miles gave Chantek some grapes and asked him to share them with her, Chantek promptly ate all the fruit. Then, seemingly remembering that he'd been asked to share, handed Miles the bare stem.

What does this tell us? We have been equipped by nature for tasks like juggling numbers and assigning value to things, but these signal human abilities may also be present in more limited form in our closest relatives. Chimps engage in sharing, trading and gift giving in the wild, and they more than hold their own in the primitive bazaar of the zoo.

THE KEEPER ALWAYS FALLS FOR THAT ONE
A sad fact of life is that it is easier to spot evidence of intelligence in devious behavior than in acts of cooperation or love. Sophisticated acts of deception involve the conscious planting of false beliefs in others, which in turn implies awareness that others have mental states that can be manipulated. British psychologist Andrew Whiten of the University of St. Andrews in Scotland says this ability is a "mental Rubicon" dividing humans and at least the other great apes from the rest of the animal kingdom.

While psychologists have studied various forms of animal deception, zookeepers are its targets every day. Helen Shewman, of the Woodland Park Zoo in Seattle, Washington, recalls that one day she dropped an orange through a feeding porthole for Meladi, one of the female orangutans. Instead of moving away, Meladi looked Shewman in the eye and held out her hand. Thinking that the orange must have rolled off somewhere inaccessible, Shewman gave her another one. When Meladi shuffled off Shewman noticed that she had hidden the original orange in her other hand.

Tawan, the colony's dominant male, watched this whole charade, and the next day he too looked Shewman in the eye and pretended that he had not yet received an orange. "Are you sure you don't have one?" Shewman asked. He continued to hold her gaze and held out his hand. Relenting, she gave him another, then noticed that he had been hiding his orange under his foot.

WE GOTTA GET OUTTA THIS PLACE

While all sorts of animals have tried to break out of captivity, orangutans are the master escape artists of the menagerie. Besides picking locks, orangs have been known to make insulation mitts out of straw in order to climb over electric fences. Indeed, orangs have become design consultants: some zookeepers have used them to test new enclosures on the theory that if an orang can't find a way out, no other species of ape will. How do the orangs do it? One ingredient of success may be a patient, observing temperament. Zoologist Ben Beck once noted that if you give a screwdriver to a chimpanzee, it will try to use it for everything except its intended purpose. Give one to a gorilla, and it will first rear back in horror—"Oh, my God, it's going to hurt me!"—then try to eat it, and ultimately forget about it. Give it to an orangutan, however, and the ape will first hide it and then, once you have gone, use it to dismantle the cage.

Along with Fu Manchu's crafty getaways, the most memorable orang escapes include a breakout at the Topeka Zoo. Jonathan, a young male, had been temporarily isolated in a holding area and resented it mightily. Keepers were not particularly worried because his cage was secured with an elaborate "guillotine" door that opened vertically and was remotely controlled by pneumatic pressure. When the door was closed, its top fit between two plates. As an extra precaution, a keeper would insert a pin through keyhole-like apertures in the plates and in the top of the door. The five-inch pin would then be flopped over so that it could not be withdrawn without being flipped into the proper position. Taken together, these redundant security systems should have been able to contain most humans, much less an ape.

Nonetheless, a volunteer who regularly came to play with an infant orang in a neighboring cage began reporting that she could see Jonathan fiddling with something at the top of his cage. Geoff Creswell, a keeper, investigated, but when he looked in on the orang, Jonathan was always sitting quietly in a corner. Always, that is, until the day Creswell had a sudden, heart-stopping encounter with the big male outside his cage in a corridor of the holding area. After Jonathan had been put back behind bars, the keepers discovered that he had used a piece of cardboard to flip the pin into position so that it could be pushed out.

INSTINCT VS. REASON

Jonathan's escape offered evidence of a panoply of higher mental abilities. He concealed his efforts from the humans in charge of him (but seemed not to realize that the person visiting the next cage might snitch on him); he figured out the workings of the locking mechanism and then fashioned a tool that enabled him to pick the lock. Perhaps most impressive was the planning and perseverance that went into this feat.

Sally Hoysen, a psychologist at Ohio State University, probed the degree to which a chimp's ability to reason is subservient to the animal's desires. Her experiment involved two female chimps, Sheba and Sarah, and centered on a game in which Sheba would be shown two dishes filled with different amounts of treats. The first dish Sheba pointed to would be given to Sarah, meaning that Sheba had to think smaller to get larger. When she could actually see the treats, Sheba invariably pointed to the larger amount, only to see them given to Sarah. However, when tokens were substituted for real food, Sheba quickly realized that pointing to the smaller amount would get her the larger amount. It would seem that in the presence of real food, Sheba's appetites persistently overcame her ability to reason. When temptation was removed, Sheba could bring her cognitive abilities to bear and achieve her desired, albeit selfish, goal.

JUST LIKE KIDS

The same experiment was conducted with children. Four-year-olds realize that if they point to a smaller amount of food, they will be rewarded with more. Three-year-olds don't. This suggests that sometime during human maturation, children's cognitive abilities develop to the point that they realize they can be rewarded for restraint. The evidence also suggests that Sheba and other chimps are right on the cusp of that threshold.

"In the course of an afternoon, we could toggle between Sheba reacting like a three-year-old and a four-year-old simply by switching what she was looking at," says Hoysen.

Even if intelligence is shackled in animals, we can see it break out in flashes of brilliance. Countless creatures draw on their abilities not only to secure food and compete with their peers, but also to deal with, deceive and beguile the humans they encounter. Every so often, they do something extraordinary, and we gain insight into our own abilities, and what it's like to be an orangutan or an orca.

WE'RE NOT ALONE

What is intelligence anyway? If life is about perpetuation of a species, and intelligence is meant to serve that perpetuation, then we can't hold a candle to pea-brained sea turtles who predated us and survived the asteroid impact that killed off the dinosaurs. As human history has shown, once minds break free of religious, cultural and physical controls, they burn hot and fast, consuming and altering everything around them. Perhaps this is why higher mental abilities, though present in other creatures, are more circumscribed. Still, it is comforting to realize that other species besides our own can stand back and appraise the world around them, even if their horizons are more constrained than the heady, perilous perspective that is our blessing and curse.

*   *   *

IT'S A LAW!

Gunter's Second Law of Air Travel: "The strength of the turbulence is directly proportional to the temperature of your coffee."

Colorful history: Greenland, which is mostly white (snow and ice), was named by Eric the Red.

Tricks of the Trade:
SELLING TO CHILDREN

*Uncle John was trapped in a bathroom recently with nothing to read—
well, nothing he'd normally read, anyway. In desperation he picked up a
copy of* Mothering *magazine, and to his surprise, found this thought-
provoking article on the way kids are targeted by today's marketers.
Here's a condensed version of the piece, by Gary Ruskin.*

N AG, NAG, NAG
Cheryl Idell knows a lot about nagging. She's written reports
for major corporations with such titles as "The Nag Factor"
and "The Art of Fine Whining." She tells her clients that nagging
spurs about a third of a family's trips to a fast-food restaurant, to buy
children's clothing, or to rent a video.

Idell, chief strategic officer for a major market-research firm,
speaks with the cold precision of a physicist. "Nagging falls into two
categories," she explains. "There is 'persistent nagging,' the fall-on-
the-floor kind, and there is 'importance nagging,' where a kid can
talk about it."

[She considers] either a good first step. But alone they're not
enough. Idell advises Chuck E. Cheese and numerous other corporations that getting kids to *whine* is even better. Better yet is to give
them "a specific reason to ask for the product." In other words,
Idell's job is to make your life miserable. She even rates brands according to their "nag factor"—that is, their capacity to make your
children badger you—and companies toil mightily to rate high on
her list. Some of the most successful are McDonald's, Levi's, Discovery Zone, Burger King, Pizza Hut, Disney, and OshKosh. (Like we
couldn't have guessed.)

WANTED: YOUR KID
Now meet George Broussard. He is co-founder of 3D Realms, a company that makes a video game called Duke Nukem. A violent "first-
person shooter" game, Duke Nukem comes complete with strip bars,
porno theaters, and lots of gore. Even with the "mature" rating, and
all the violence and sexual imagery, Broussard wants to sell this

game to your kids. "Duke is a mass-market character that can sell two million games," Broussard says. "It'd be suicide to make the game unplayable by younger people."

Idell and Broussard are typical of something endemic in America today. Thousands of the brightest minds in the country devote their great talent, and use sophisticated psychological techniques, to influence your children to purchase products—or rather, to want products—regardless of whether or not they are good for your kids. Name something you don't want your kids to have, and chances are, people are trying to entice your kids into wanting it.

WHAT ARE CHILDREN, ANYWAY?

James U. McNeal, a professor of marketing at Texas A&M, is perhaps the foremost expert on selling to children. He is the elder statesman advocating a shift in our thinking from viewing children as trusting, impressionable humans to be protected to seeing children "as economic resources to be mined." His emotional response to this contrast isn't the same as yours. McNeal sees the money in your kids and helps corporations get access to it: "Children are the brightest star in the consumer constellation," he writes.

McNeal divides the booming kiddie market into three parts: There's the "primary" market—the $24.4 billion each year that kids directly control and spend. There's the "influence" market, perhaps as high as $300 billion, the amount of parental spending that children can directly or indirectly influence. And there's the "future" market, which is the purchasing that children will do for the rest of their lives.

Buy-Buy Baby

"Virtually every consumer-goods industry, from airlines to zinnia-seed sellers, targets kids," McNeal enthuses. Johann Wachs, the vice president of Saatchi and Saatchi's Kid Connection unit, agrees: "Marketers are just waking up to the enormous possibility of kid-targeted products," he says. "As kids become more powerful as consumers, they are being targeted more directly."

Children aren't hard to take advantage of. They tend to trust adults even when they shouldn't—sometimes especially when they shouldn't. Marketers know this, while most children don't grasp the motives behind advertising or realize that the products advertised may not be good for them.

31% of American adults say they won't watch a film with subtitles "no matter how good it is."

However, none of this is troubling to the new breed of advertisers and marketers. If they have any qualms, they do a good job of repressing them. Like investors in prime real estate, they see children's minds as a kind of cash cow. "If you own this child at an early age, you can own this child for years to come," explained Mike Searles, president of Kids-R-Us, a major children's clothing store. Companies are saying, 'Hey, I want to own the kid younger and younger.'" Wayne Chilicki, a General Mills executive, agrees: "When it comes to targeting kid consumers, we at General Mills follow the Proctor & Gamble model of 'cradle to grave,'" he says. "We believe in getting them early and having them for life."

BE COOL

Advertisers infuse their pitches with messages that target the weaknesses and insecurities of children. "Advertising at its best is making people feel that without their product, you're a loser," explained Nancy Shalek, president of the Shalek Agency. "Kids are very sensitive to that. If you tell them to buy something, they are resistant. But if you tell them that they'll be a dork if they don't, you've got their attention. You open up emotional vulnerabilities, and it's very easy to do with kids because they're the most emotionally vulnerable."

Moreover, some marketers try to sell by tapping into destructive and antisocial urges. According to Rick Litman, a partner at Kid 2 Kid Market Research, the goal is "to use youth rebellion to more effectively target a product and sell a product."

More than anything, they want your children's minds. "Kids marketing in general is becoming more sophisticated," says Julie Halpin, CEO of Gepetto Group, which specializes in marketing to kids. It is a competition for what she calls "share of mind."

Corporations claim this "share of mind" from every possible angle. They seek to engulf your children with ads. "Imagine a child sitting in the middle of a large circle of train tracks," one market researcher explains. "Tracks, like the tentacles of an octopus, radiate to the child from the outside circle of tracks. The child can be reached from every angle. This is how the [corporate] marketing world is connected to the child's world."

MARKETERS GO TO SCHOOL

Marketers are resorting to extreme measures to gain access to our children. They're invading sanctums that were previously off-limits, such as schools. For example, Channel One is a marketing company that uses TV "news" shows as a come-on. Its daily broadcast shows 10 minutes of "news" and 2 minutes of ads to captive audiences of 8 million children in 12,000 schools across the country. While promoted as "education," the real appeal is to advertisers. "The biggest selling point to advertisers," says Joel Babbit, former president of Channel One, lies in "forcing kids to watch two minutes of commercials." The atmosphere of the school is an advertiser's dream, Babbit says. "The advertiser gets a group of kids who can't go to the bathroom, who can't change the station, who can't listen to their mother yell in the background, who can't be playing Nintendo, who can't have their headsets on."

A new company called ZapMe! has extended this strategy to computers. Like Channel One, ZapMe! offers free equipment to schools—computers and Internet browsers. In return, it advertises to kids, plus it gets a market-research gold mine. The company snoops on schoolchildren as they browse the Internet and then delivers the information to advertisers and marketers. According to Associated Press, ZapMe! "breaks down the data by age, sex, Zip Code. It delivers this information to advertisers and marketers, who use it to target students in school with laserlike precision."

THE LESSON IN THE ADS

Kids are eager learners. "Advertising targeted at elementary school children," Professor McNeal says, "on programs just for them works very effectively in the sense of implanting brand names in their minds and creating desires for the products."

Further, it is well known that RJR Nabisco's Joe Camel ads hooked hundreds of thousands of children into smoking. And Anheuser-Busch created Budweiser ads so captivating—with frogs, penguins, and lizards—that they were kids' favorite ads in 1999.

This is great news for ad agencies and for the corporations they work for. Business is booming. Some win kudos from their corporate peers. The owner of McFarlane Toys, Todd McFarlane, was recently given an award by Ernst & Young for creating a bestselling line of grotesque and violent "Spawn" toys and comic books. Would McFarlane let his own daughters have these toys or comic books? "Are you kidding?" he says. "I'm still a dad after five o'clock."

If scientists didn't know a fault was there until an earthquake hit, it's called a "blind" fault.

THE STORY OF LITTLE LEAGUE

*If you're into baseball, chances are you've had something
to do with Little League. It's an American tradition
now, but it started out as one man's obsession.*

ACCIDENT OF FATE

One afternoon in 1938 a man named Carl Stotz went out into his Williamsport, Pennsylvania, yard to play catch with his two nephews. They would have preferred to play baseball, but the yard was too small to use a bat. So they just had a catch.

On one throw, a nephew tossed the ball so far that Stotz "had to move to the neighbors' side of the yard," he recalled years later. "As I stretched to catch the ball, I stepped into the cut off stems of a lilac bush that were projecting several inches above the ground. A sharp stub tore through my sock and scraped my ankle. The pain was intense."

The Good Old Days

As Stotz sat nursing his ankle, he was suddenly reminded that he had played on the same kind of rough turf when he was a kid...and he remembered a promise he'd made to himself when he was a young boy. Back then, equipment was scarce—he and his friends hit balls with sticks when they didn't have any bats, and used baseballs until the threads unraveled and the skins came off. Then they patched them up with tape and used them until there wasn't anything left to tape back together. Some of his friends had even played barefoot because they didn't have any shoes.

"I remembered thinking to myself, 'When I grow up, I'm gonna have a baseball team for boys, complete with uniforms and equipment. They'll play on a real field like the big guys, with cheering crowds at every game.'"

DOWNSIZING

Stotz didn't have any sons of his own, but he decided to fulfill his promise by organizing his nephews and the other neighborhood boys into baseball teams. That way, they could experience the thrill of playing real games on real fields, wearing real uniforms—not just play stickball in open fields and abandoned lots.

He spent the next few months organizing teams and rounding up sponsors to pay for the equipment. At the same time, he set about "shrinking" the game of baseball so 9–12 year-old kids could really play. "When I was nine, nothing was geared to children," Stotz explained in his book *A Promise Kept*. Take bats, for example:

> We'd step up to the plate with a bat that was both too heavy and too long. Choking up on the bat merely changed the problem. The handle would then bang us in the stomach when we lunged at the ball. We didn't have the strength or leverage for a smooth, controlled swing.

TRIAL & ERROR

Stotz finally found child-sized bats and equipment for his teams, and at every team practice he adjusted the distances between the bases and between the pitcher's mound and home plate, trying to find the ideal size for a field.

"I was trying to find out what distance would enable the boys to throw a runner out from third base or shortstop while still giving the batter a fair chance to beat it out, depending on where he hit the ball," he later wrote. "When I finally had what I thought was the ideal distance, I stepped it off and used a yardstick at home to measure my strides. The distance was so close to sixty feet that I set that as the distance we would use thereafter."

About the only thing Stotz didn't change was the size of the baseball itself. He figured it would enable kids to practice with any baseball they already had on hand. "Remember, this was 1938 when I was making these decisions, and the Great Depression was still with many families," he wrote. "I was afraid the expense of buying special-size balls would be too much for some families and might keep boys from becoming Little Leaguers."

SPONSORS

Shrinking the game turned out to be a lot easier than finding sponsors willing to pay for uniforms and equipment for the three teams in the league. "Ten prospects turned me down," Stotz wrote. "Then 20…40…50." Finally, two and a half months after he'd started, Stotz

---

Which Shakespeare play has been made into more films than any other? *Hamlet* (49).

made his 57th sales pitch at the Lycoming Dairy Farms. He landed his first sponsor; they chipped in $30.

A LITTLE PROBLEM

Stotz used the money to buy uniforms at Kresge's 25¢-to-$1 Store, and set the date of the league's first game for June 6, 1939. He paid a visit to the offices of *Grit*, Williamsport's Sunday paper, and asked them to mention the league's first game in the paper.

Bill Kenoe, *Grit's* sports editor, asked Stotz what the league was called, but Stotz didn't know yet. "I'd been thinking of calling it Junior League Baseball," he explained, "until I remembered there's a woman's organization named 'Junior League.'" Because he'd modeled his kids' league after the "big leagues," he'd considered calling it either the Little Boys' League or the Little League. But he couldn't decide between them. He didn't like the sound of "Little Boys' League," but was worried that people would think the "Little League" meant the size of the league, not the size of the boys. In the end, he let Kehoe choose between the two names...and Kehoe picked Little League.

OUT OF THE PARK

Little League grew slowly over the next several years. As late as 1946, there were only 12 local leagues in the entire United States—all in Pennsylvania.

The turning point came in 1947, two years after the end of World War II. America's fighting men were back home, settled into their new lives, and they finally had time to participate with their sons in Little League.

In 1947, Little League, now up to 17 independent leagues, held its first "World Series"—an event that was covered by the Associated Press and other wire services. Stories and photographs appeared in hundreds of newspapers...and soon Little League headquarters was deluged with letters from all over the country, asking how to set up their own leagues.

MAKING NOISE

As Little League grew, it began to experience a problem: adults were taking the competition more seriously than the children did. In

1947, parents and other spectators began routinely booing players and officials during games.

"Some of them seemed unable to see the games as simply little boys having fun in a structured…athletic program," Little League's founder Carl Stotz wrote in *A Promise Kept*. "After all, many of the 8-to-12-year-old boys had played baseball less than a year. There was certainly no valid excuse for such adult criticism. And it was becoming quite discouraging to some of the boys."

Stotz and other Little League officials complained, and newspaper editorials condemned the conduct. "Fortunately," he wrote, "the booing fad of 1947 faded out." It was one of Little League's first brushes with controversy…but certainly not its last.

LITTLE LEAGUE, INC.

By the beginning of 1950 Little League had grown to more than 300 local leagues all over the United States; by the end of the year it had more than doubled in size to 776 leagues. There was even one in British Columbia, the first outside the U.S. The organization had grown so much that it could no longer be managed effectively by part-time volunteers. So in 1950 Little League voted to incorporate itself and began hiring a paid, full-time staff. Carl Stotz was appointed president and commissioner of the League. He didn't realize it, but his Little League days were numbered.

AND NOW A WORD FROM OUR SPONSOR

A year earlier, in 1949, the U.S. Rubber Corporation had become Little League's first national sponsor. In return, they wanted to help determine the direction of the organization—so executives of the company approached Stotz to discuss it. "Essentially," Stotz wrote, U.S. Rubber "proposed a national body that would have total control of the leagues that evolved from it. That body would own every Little League playing field and every Little Leaguer would be a paying member."

U.S. Rubber's plan was exactly the opposite of Stotz's vision; he favored completely autonomous local leagues, joined together in a national organization that would be run by representatives elected from the ranks of the local leagues.

The discussions broke off without any change in the direction of

Little League…yet. "Our discussion ended amicably," Stotz later wrote. "In retrospect, though, I can see that it was the beginning of a deep philosophical conflict."

THE LITTLE SCHISM

By the early 1950s, Little League was doubling in size every couple of years. It was an enormous success, but Stotz wasn't satisfied; he was concerned about the increasing commercialism that accompanied Little League's rise to national prominence.

Another concern was the prominence placed on the Little League World Series, which was played every year in Williamsport, Pennsylvania. U.S. Rubber and the Little League board of directors wanted to maximize the importance and the publicity value of the event; but Stotz wanted to de-emphasize the series. He feared that teams trying to "win their way to Williamsport" would encourage cheating at the expense of good sportsmanship and fair play. The lure of the national spotlight, he worried, would encourage teams to recruit players who were ineligible either because they were too old or lived outside their league's territorial boundaries.

Yet another controversy erupted when Stotz tried to invite legendary pitcher Cy Young, then in his 80s, to come to the 1951 Little League World Series. "Two members of the board sought to veto Carl's suggestion," Kenneth Loss writes in *A Promise Kept*. One director "said Cy Young was an old man who probably couldn't control his bladder, and would embarrass Little League." Stotz invited Young anyway (nothing happened), but his differences with Little League Inc. continued to fester.

YOU'RE OUT!

In 1952, Stotz stepped down as the president of Little League, but remained as commissioner of the league. He was replaced as president by a U.S. Rubber executive named Peter McGovern.

Stotz still retained a great deal of power…but not for long. In 1954 the board of directors adopted a new set of bylaws that effectively stripped the office of commissioner of much of its power and gave it to McGovern. Then, in 1955, McGovern fired Stotz's secretary while Stotz was out of town promoting Little League, and replaced her with one of his own aides.

That was it—a few months later Stotz resigned as commissioner and filed suit against McGovern, alleging that he was ignoring Little League volunteers. When Stotz lost the suit he cut all ties to Little League forever. A few teams left with him to form the unaffiliated Original Little League, which played their games in a field not far from where Stotz had founded Little League in 1939. Stotz boycotted every Little League Inc. World Series game until 1990, when, at age 79, he attended a game to honor the 50th anniversary of the founding of Little League. He died two years later.

*   *   *

LITTLE LEAGUE BASEBALL: GOOD, CLEAN FUN?
Did Stotz's fears come true? These news reports are food for thought.

OUT OF CONTROL
"In June, 1992, the Little League season in Albuquerque, N.M., was cut short because of hostility and fighting among adults. A postgame fight that sent one person to the hospital included a group of parents, a league director, a coach and even the coach's mother.

"That same year, a coach in Whiteville, N.C., used a pocketknife to slash the throat of another coach in front of 100 Little Leaguers, spattering blood on one boy's jersey."

—*Los Angeles Times, 1994*

FAIR PLAY
"Taiwan and the Dominican Republic were disqualified Wednesday from tournaments leading to the Little League World Series because they violated rules involving player eligibility....Taiwan, which reportedly drew its all-star team from a population pool more than twice the legal limit this year, has won 14 Little League World Series titles since 1969. 'This has to taint all the victories they've had the last 20 years,' Little League coach Larry Lewis said."

—*Long Beach Press-Telegram, 1993*

A HARD FALL
"A 46-year-old Federal Way man has died from injuries after being punched and hitting his head on concrete bleachers during a Little League baseball game last week....Ralph Baldwin, the father of a

player on the Federal Way team, died Saturday at Harborview Medical Center....Several witnesses told police Baldwin and his friend were drunk and ill-behaved during the game. After the men ignored requests to be quiet, several fans asked them to leave, the police report said....Baldwin and his friend left but returned a short time later, the report said. An Everett man, who had a son on the opposing team, asked Baldwin to quiet down, and Baldwin started moving toward him, prompting the punch, witnesses told police. Baldwin fell several rows and hit his head."

—*The Seattle Times, 1994*

YOU'RE OUTTA HERE!

"Stories of bizarre parental behavior at Little League games abound. For example, a pitcher's mother was convicted in Texarkana, Ark., of assault, disorderly conduct, resisting arrest and making 'terrorist threats' after she pulled a knife on two women during an argument at a game. The boy's father was found guilty of disorderly conduct. Reportedly, the women who were threatened had made derogatory comments about the pitcher."

—*The Los Angeles Times, 1985*

THE GANG'S ALL HERE

"Two baseball coaches trade insults. Someone throws a punch. Before it's over, five guys pile on in a no-holds-barred brawl....A major league scuffle? No, it happened in Garden Grove on Tuesday night when a meeting of parents who coach 11- and 12-year-old Little League players turned violent in a dispute over whether a hotshot pitcher is too old to play in the league.

"By the time police arrived, one team manager was on his way to the hospital—gouged with a set of keys....And mothers at the league meeting were clutching their children and screaming for their husbands to stop slugging it out."

—*The Los Angeles Times, 1998*

SWINGING FOR THE GRAVEYARD

"A wild brawl after a weekend Little League baseball game in Castro Valley has left a 17-year-old spectator dead, the suspected bat-wielding assailant struggling for consciousness and the umpire the target of a death threat. Joseph Matteucci, 17, of Castro Valley died Monday after being struck with a bat allegedly swung by catcher Antonio John Messina of San Lorenzo during a melee involving players and spectators at Proctor School. Messina, 18, tried to escape but he was felled by a rock thrown by the Castro Valley pitcher, whose identity has not been revealed. The cause of the melee remained unclear yesterday, but it appeared to start as players and spectators were filing away from the field after a tense game. It was the first game-related homicide in the organization's history, according to Dennis Sullivan of the national Little League Inc. office in Williamsport, Pa. There were signs yesterday that tensions continue to run high. The umpire was the target of attempted arson and a death threat early yesterday."

—*The San Francisco Chronicle*, 1993

YOU'RE FIRED!

"Flaming newspapers were tossed through the smashed window of a Little League umpire's home Tuesday in Castro Valley, Calif., igniting a fire apparently connected to a baseball brawl that killed one teenager and put his attacker in the hospital."

"A brick bearing a note reading 'Talk and Your (sic) Dead' was found outside the home of Robert Lloyd, a key witness in weekend violence after a game between 16-to-18-year-olds in the Big League Division of Little League….Lloyd was threatened after identifying a player who threw a rock that struck and seriously hurt another player suspected of killing Joseph Matteucci, 17. Antonio Messina, 18, suspected of swinging the bat, was in 'stable but guarded' condition at Highland Hospital in Oakland."

—*USA Today*, 1993

STOTZ'S REVENGE

"Little League…suffered the most embarrassing moment in its history in September when it…stripped Zamboanga City of the Philippines of its World Championship title….Although 12 is the official age limit, the team from the Philippines used players as old as 15 in its 15-4 victory over Long Beach in the Major Division World Series final."

—*Los Angeles Times*, 1993

Cruising along: In 1904, a cruise from NY to UK was $10 (third class).

EVERYTHING MEN KNOW ABOUT WOMEN

Some excerpts from a book we picked up at our local bookstore:

TARZAN OF THE MOVIES, PART II: HERE'S JOHNNY!

Besides Edgar Rice Burroughs, the person most associated with the character of Tarzan is a swimmer-turned-actor named Johnny Weismuller. In fact, it wasn't until 1932, when Weismuller took on the role, that Tazan developed a stable personality and face the public could get used to. But to Johnny, it was just a job. Here's the story.

AFRICA SPEAKS

In 1927, MGM bought the film rights to *Trader Horn*, the memoirs of an African adventurer, and assigned director W. S. "Woody" Van Dyke to the picture. The studio originally planned to make it as a silent film, but then decided that *Trader Horn* would be their first talkie.

Making the leap from silent films to sound is considered the biggest technological advance in the history of filmmaking. MGM understood the significance of the coming of sound and wanted its first talkie to be larger than life. Money was no object—*Trader Horn* was going to be the best film possible.

On the Road

Van Dyke persuaded the studio that the only way to do the film justice was to film it on location. So in March 1929, Van Dyke—along with 35 cast and crew members, three sound trucks, and 90 tons of equipment—set sail for Africa. Over the next seven months, they (and 200 African natives) traveled more than 10,000 miles through Africa, shooting more than a million feet of film. Needless to say, the production ran over budget.

"The expense was worth it," John Taliaferro writes. "When *Trader Horn* was released in 1931 it was a huge hit and helped rekindle public interest in the continent of Africa. Even Ernest Hemingway credited *Trader Horn* with giving him his Africa 'bug.'"

MGM had more than just a hit film on its hands: It had thousands and thousands of feet of unused African film footage and the studio began looking for ways to put it to good use.

"Inevitably," Taliaferro says, "someone suggested Tarzan."

TOUGH BREAK

By 1931 MGM had bought the rights to *Tarzan the Ape Man* and hired Van Dyke to direct it. For the first time in the history of the Tarzan franchise, a movie studio was simply buying the right to make a movie about Burroughs's character and was free to come up with its own story.

Having Van Dyke direct the film was a good idea from a stylistic point of view: he was considered Hollywood's finest nature filmmaker. But it made casting the film more difficult, because Van Dyke was a perfectionist who wasn't afraid to turn down Tinseltown's biggest stars if he felt they weren't right for the role. Clark Gable was one of the first actors rejected. "He has *no body*," Van Dyke complained. "What I want is a man who is young, strong, well-built, reasonably attractive, but not necessarily handsome, and a competent actor. The most important thing is that he have a good physique. And I can't find him."

STROKE OF LUCK

Meanwhile, screenwriter Cyril Hume was hard at work in his hotel room cranking out the *Tarzan* screenplay. One afternoon he stepped out for a minute and happened to notice a powerfully built young man swimming in the hotel pool. It was 27-year-old Johnny Weissmuller, the greatest amateur swimmer the world had ever seen.

Between 1921 and 1928, Weissmuller had won 52 national titles, held every freestyle record, and broken his own records dozens of times. Weissmuller won three gold medals at the 1924 Olympics and two more at the 1928 games. Not long afterward he gave up his amateur status and signed on as the national spokesman for BVD swimwear and underwear. He was still modelling for BVD when Cyril Hume discovered him.

MR. NATURAL

Hume was so impressed by Weissmuller that he arranged a meeting with Van Dyke. However, rather than give him a formal screen test, they just had him strip to his shorts to get a sense of what he'd look like in a loin cloth. Two things immediately struck them: 1) Weissmuller clearly had the right build for the part, and 2) he seemed perfectly at ease stripping down to his underpants in front of two men he hardly knew. He actually appeared comfortable in his skivvies, something almost unheard of in an age where most men still wore two-piece, shirt-and-shorts bathing suits on the beach. In fact, Weissmuller had spent so many years modeling underwear and wearing skimpy one-piece racing trunks that he was completely uninhibited about appearing semi-nude on film. Even though he was nearly naked, he somehow seemed wholesome.

"Other Tarzan actors, when they wore loincloths and leopard skins, seemed merely undressed," Taliaferro writes. "Weissmuller, by contrast, was clean-limbed in every sense. He gave the impression that he could have sold Bibles door to door wearing nothing but a G-string....There was no hint of either embarrassment or braggadocio in his comportment."

Weissmuller won the part hands (and pants) down...and just in case anyone failed to notice his unique abilities, in the publicity leading up to *Tarzan the Ape Man*'s premiere, MGM's publicity agents billed Weissmuller as "the only man in Hollywood who's natural in the flesh and can act without clothes."

A CHANGED MAN

Weissmuller still didn't have much acting experience, but it didn't really matter—rather than change Weissmuller to make him better fit the role, MGM simply adjusted the Tarzan character to fit Weissmuller's strengths and weaknesses: the Tarzan of the Edgar Rice Burroughs novels was a self-educated, cultured gentleman who spoke several languages; the Tarzan of the Weissmuller films was someone who spoke very little and swam surprisingly often for a guy who lived in the middle of a jungle. "The role was right up my alley—it was just like stealing," Weissmuller recounted years later.

Not much of Burroughs's original Tarzan character had ever made it to the screen. But by the time MGM was through, the few remaining vestiges had been swept away. The screenplay made absolutely no mention of Tarzan's noble origins and didn't even bother to explain how he'd ended up in the jungle. Even the sound of Tarzan's *name* was changed: Burroughs had always pronounced it as TAR-zn, but MGM changed it to TAR-ZAN; and TAR-ZAN it would stay. Burroughs had always resisted changes to his character in the past; this time he just accepted it. "I don't give a damn what they call him," he told a friend, "as long as their checks come regularly."

FINDING HIS VOICE

Because this was the first true Tarzan talkie, the filmmakers had to figure out what Tarzan's jungle yell would sound like. Nobody really knew what to do...until Weissmuller came up with the yell on his own. He recalled:

> When I was a kid, I used to read the Tarzan books, and they had kind of a shrill yell for Tarzan. I never thought I'd ever make Tarzan movies, but when I finally got the part, they were trying to do yells like that. And I remembered when I was a kid I used to yodel at the picnics on Sundays, so I said, "I know a yell!"

Nobody gave Weissmuller's yell much thought until after the film opened and MGM realized just how popular the yell was. They quickly invented a story that it was created by sound engineers who blended Weissmuller's voice "with a hyena's howl played backward, a camel's bleat, the pluck of a violin string, and a soprano's high C."

"It was a commentary on the mystique of talkies and the bizarre singularity of the yell itself," John Taliaferro writes in *Tarzan Forever*, "that the public accepted the studio's fib as fact."

LOVE INTEREST

MGM knew pretty quickly what Jane would look like—they cast a contract actress named Maureen O'Sullivan to play her. But it took a while to decide what she should wear. "First," O'Sullivan recalled, "they had the idea of having Jane wearing no bra—no brassiere at all—and she would always be covered with a branch. They tried that, and it didn't work. So they made a costume and it wasn't that bad at all. There was a little leather bra and a loincloth."

THE FILMING

The stage was set. Filming of *Tarzan the Ape Man* began on October 31, 1931, and finished eight weeks later. Total cost, even with the free leftover jungle footage from *Trader Horn*, was just over

---

Animal kingdom rule of thumb: If it has hair, feathers, or skin, it also has dandruff (dander).

$650,000. The film had not come cheap, but it turned out to be worth every penny: *Tarzan the Ape Man* opened to huge crowds and rave reviews in March 1932 and went on to become one of Top 10 box-office hits of the year. The movie's success helped increase the popularity of the Tarzan novels and comic strips, whose sales had started to suffer in the grip of the Great Depression.

Weissmuller didn't have a lot of dialogue in the film, but his acting was surprisingly authentic. He became the hottest new star of 1932. "However credible or interesting Tarzan may be on the printed page," Thorton Delehanty wrote in the *New York Evening Post*, "I doubt very much if he emerges in such splendor as he does in the person of Johnny Weissmuller....With his flowing hair, magnificently proportioned body, catlike walk, and virtuosity in the water, you could hardly ask anything more in the way of perfection."

Maureen O'Sullivan also won high praise for her performance and, like Weissmuller, set the standard by which all future Janes would be judged; to this day the six movies she made with Weissmuller are considered the best *Tarzan* films ever made.

THE SEQUEL

When *Tarzan the Ape Man* became a runaway hit, MGM paid Burroughs for the right to make a sequel called *Tarzan and His Mate*. They signed Weissmuller and O'Sullivan for an encore. Influenced by the success of *King Kong* the year before, the makers of *Tarzan and His Mate* spent a lot of money on animal and special effects, including a 20-foot-long, steel-and-rubber mechanical crocodile that Weissmuller wrestles and kills in the film, and a live hippopotamus that was imported from a German zoo so that Weissmuller could ride on its back. Even Cheetah the chimp was given an expanded role to take advantage of the public's newfound fascination with primates.

BIG GAMBLE

The film ultimately cost $1.3 million, nearly double what *Tarzan the Apeman* cost and a huge sum for a Depression-era film. But like its predecessor, it played to packed theaters all over the country—and, when it was released to foreign markets, all over the world. It's considered the best of the Weissmuller Tarzan films and probably the best Tarzan film of all time.

It is also famous for another reason: It features the most nudity of any of Weissmuller's Tarzan films. O'Sullivan wears a skimpy leather top and a loincloth comprised of one flap of leather in front and one in back, leaving her thighs and hips fully exposed. It "started such a furor," O'Sullivan remembered years later. "Thousands of women were objecting to my costume." MGM finally caved in and changed O'Sullivan's costume from "something suitable for the jungle" into "something resembling a suburban housedress," a la Wilma Flintstone. Even Weissmuller had to cover up for the next film in the series: he went from a revealing loincloth to what looked like "leather gym shorts."

BIG BUDGET

In July 1935, MGM began work on *The Capture of Tarzan*, its third Tarzan film. They planned to make it the most elaborate, most expensive, and (they hoped) most profitable one yet.

Set designers built a six-room treehouse for Tarzan and Jane that the Flintstones would have envied, complete with running water, an oven for baking, overhead fans operated by Cheetah, and an elevator powered by an elephant.

The Capture of Tarzan was also supposed to be much more graphic than the earlier films. In one scene, a safari party is captured by the Ganeolis tribe of natives and the captives are spread-eagled on the ground "to be butchered in a two-part ritual: a savage cutting with knives followed by a rock-swing to the head, cracking the skull open," but are rescued by Tarzan just in time. In another scene, the party crosses into a foggy marshland where they're attacked by pygmies, giant lizards, and vampire bats.

Unfortunately, when *The Capture of Tarzan* was shown to preview audiences in 1935, it "terrified children and brought outraged complaints from irate mothers and women's organizations," Gabe Essoe writes. "Afraid that *Capture* would alienate more people than it would attract, studio bosses ordered all gruesome scenes cut out and replaced with re-takes." When director Jim McKay objected to the changes, he was fired and replaced with John Farrow, who was himself later fired. (But not before falling in love with Maureen O'Sullivan and eventually marrying her, and fathering seven children—one of whom is actress Mia Farrow.) Next in line for director was Richard Thorpe, who stayed on as director for the rest of the MGM series.

WATCH OUT FOR THAT TREE!

Thorpe spent months shooting new scenes "as necessary" to make the film "appeal" to young and old alike, and changed the name to *Tarzan Escapes*. Thorpe also began the tradition of reusing scenes from older Tarzan films—in this case cutting out the vampire bat attack scene and replacing it with the crocodile fight from *Tarzan and His Mate*—and cheapening what had been considered a top-notch motion picture franchise. "In essence, this film marked a major step in lowering the Tarzan series to the child's level," Essoe writes.

With all of the rewriting, refilming, and reediting, *Tarzan Escapes* took 14 months to finish and cost more than the first two MGM Tarzan films combined. That would have been okay if it was a good film. But when it finally opened in New York in November 1936, it ran into harsh reviews and lousy ticket sales. "The tree-to-tree stuff has worn pretty thin for adult consumption," *Variety* complained, "While at first the sight of Tarzan doing everything but playing pinochle with his beast pals was a novelty, it's all pretty silly now. Derisive laughter greet the picture too often."

JUNGLE FAMILY VALUES

Johnny Weissmuller was content to continue as Tarzan, but Maureen O'Sullivan wasn't. When she learned that a fourth Tarzan film was in the works, she insisted on being written out of it. MGM offered to let her take a leave of absence, but she insisted on leaving permanently. So screenwriter Cyril Hume decided to kill her off with a spear wound at the end of the fourth film.

This created a problem: the female character helped attract women and families to Tarzan pictures, and the studio was afraid that if Tarzan went solo his audience would shrink. So they gave the couple a son—Boy. And to avoid controversy from censorship groups (because MGM's Tarzan and Jane never married), Boy was adopted. Tarzan and Jane find a baby in the jungle following a plane crash and raise him as their own.

MGM ran an ad in the *Hollywood Reporter* asking readers, "Do you have a Tarzan, Jr., in your backyard?" and auditioned more than 300 boys for the part before finally settling on seven-year-old Johnny Sheffield. (Sheffield's stunts were peformed by a 32-year-old midget named Harry Monty, who billed himself as the "Midget Strong Man.")

Boy king: Among the other "treasures" found in King Tut's tomb: several vials of pimple cream.

BACK FROM THE DEAD

Edgar Rice Burroughs was furious when he learned MGM wanted to kill off his second-most important character. "MGM reminded Burroughs that while their contract forbade them to kill, mutilate, or undermine the character of Tarzan, it didn't mention Jane," Essoe writes. "MGM was free to rub her out and Burroughs was powerless to stop them."

In the end, though, MGM didn't "rub Jane out." Preview audiences were so upset at the prospect of Jane dying that the studio felt compelled to re-film the ending so that she survives. Not only that, O'Sullivan went on to play Jane in two more films before finally hanging it up for good.

TRAPPED IN THE JUNGLE

O'Sullivan made an average of three other films for every *Tarzan* she made, but Weissmuller wasn't that lucky. MGM wouldn't let Weissmuller play any other roles, fearing they'd damage his screen image. So although Johnny had been compared to Clark Gable in 1932, by the late 1930s he was hopelessly typecast.

Another thing that irked Weissmuller was that although he'd done so much to bring millions of dollars into MGM's coffers, the studio refused to give him a share of the profits. When MGM used up the last of its Tarzan movie rights making *Tarzan's New York Adventure* (1942) it decided not to buy any more, and let Weissmuller's option expire. Weissmuller moved over to RKO Pictures, the new owner of the Tarzan film rights, and made *Tarzan Triumphs*—the first of six RKO Tarzan films. But his deal there was the same as at MGM: no profit-sharing. Weissmuller earned his salary and nothing more.

LARGER THAN LIFE

In the years that followed, the Tarzan film budgets shrank as RKO relied more and more on reusing footage from earlier Tarzan movies, and the films themselves became shorter as they slipped from top billing to second place in double features. About the only thing that grew during the 1940s was Weissmuller's waistline: Now in his early 40s, his svelte swimmers' build had long since given way to the barrel-chested brawn of a middle-aged man who was having trouble staying in shape. Weissmuller gained as much as 30 pounds between Tarzan films, and he wasn't always able to take it all back off.

In 1948, Weissmuller finished *Tarzan and the Mermaids*, his 12th Tarzan film in 17 years. When talk of a 13th film began, Weissmuller again asked for a percentage of the profits. Rather than give it to him, producer Sol Lesser let Weissmuller go.

It wasn't the end of his career, though. Weissmuller wound up with the lead in a new series—*Jungle Jim*, based on a comic strip by the same name. This time he talked and wore clothes. He made 20 Jungle Jim films between 1948 and 1956, and when he finished he began looking around for new roles to play. But no one would have him—after spending 26 years in the jungle, no one could see him playing any other kind of part. "Casting directors wouldn't even talk to him," Essoe writes. "After kicking around Hollywood for awhile, Weissmuller went into a forced retirement."

After more than a quarter century in the movie business, Weissmuller had only one non-jungle film to his credit: the 1946 film *Swamp Fire*. "I played a Navy lieutenant in that one," he joked later, "I took one look and went back to the jungle."

Weissmuller died on January 20, 1984, at the age of 79. At his request, a tape recording of his famous Tarzan yell was played as his coffin was lowered into the ground.

* * *

MONKEY MISCELLANY

• The chimpanzee is also one of the few animals that uses tools. In the forest a stick is used to extract termites or honey from nests, and in captivity to reach objects which are beyond the reach of its arms.

• According to some reports, chimpanzees have been taught to play tic-tac-toe. In September 1971, it was reported that "Washoe," the most advanced of a group of chimpanzees being taught to communicate by signs at Norman, Oklahoma, knew 200 words and could construct simple sentences.

THE TARZAN AWARDS

Here's a look at some of the more notable—and notorious Tarzan films that have made it onto the big screen:

TARZAN TRIUMPHS (1943)

Claim to Fame: Most political *Tarzan* movie ever.

Details: Johnny Weissmuller never fought in World War II, but he used his star power to contribute to the war effort in a number of ways, including making the anti-Nazi propaganda film *Tarzan Triumphs* in 1943. The film was a commentary on the dangers of isolationism in the face of Nazi agression: When the Germans invade the jungle and enslave the people of the hidden city of Palandria, Tarzan's first impulse—presumably like that of many people in his audience—was not to get involved, as long as the Germans left *him* alone. In one scene, he bellows, "Nazi go away!"...only to change his tune when the Germans kidnap Boy: "Now Tarzan make war!"

The film ends with a scene Cheetah playing with the two way radio while someone is broadcasting from Berlin. "Idiot!" the voice screams, "this is not von Reichart! This is der Fuhrer!"

TARZAN THE APE MAN (1959)

Claim to Fame: Cheesiest Tarzan special effects ever.

Details: Rather than go to the unnecessary trouble and expense of hiring actors and shooting lots of new footage to make his film, producer Al Zimbalist cast Denny Miller, a UCLA basketball star with no acting experience, as Tarzan...then larded the film with as much stock jungle footage from the 1950 film *King Solomon's Mines* as he could. And when that ran out, he used footage from the original 1932 classic *Tarzan the Ape Man* starring Johnny Weissmuller.

Of course, there was the small problem that Zimbalist's film was filmed in color, and Weissmuller's was shot in black and white...but Zimbalist got around this (or so he thought at the time) by having the black-and-white footage tinted to make it appear as if it had been filmed in Technicolor, like the rest of the movie. No dice— the 1932 footage didn't look like Technicolor, and didn't even look like Denny Miller. "In one scene," David Fury writes in *Kings of the*

Jungle, "you can actually see Johnny Weissmuller's face clearly as he fights the crocodile."

What little footage Zimbalist *did* bother to film was awful. In one important action sequence, real footage of an animal trainer dressed as Tarzan wrestling with a live leopard was combined with shots of Miller wrestling with a large stuffed animal. "This was passable," Fury writes, "but the movie then cut to two separate close-ups of the face of the stuffed animal, resplendent with its plastic fangs and button eyes."

TARZAN AND THE GREAT RIVER (1968)

Claim to Fame: *Tarzan* film most likely to have been plagued by some kind of jungle voodoo curse.

Details: *Tarzan and The Great River* was the second Tarzan film to star Mike Henry, star linebacker for the L. A. Rams who signed on as the Ape Man after producer (and Rams fan) Sy Weintraub promised to make Henry "wealthier than the whole backfield."

Shot in the jungles of Brazil, things were troubled from the start: during filming of one scene in a downtown park in Rio de Janeiro, a 500-pound trained lion named Major got loose and wandered the streets of Rio, scattering passersby until the trainer was finally able to get it back under control.

The worst moment came during filming of a scene with Mike Henry and Dinky, the chimpanzee who played Cheetah. "Dinky seemed uneasy in his new environment," Henry recalls. "I was supposed to run over to the chimp and pick him up, but when I did he bit me on the cheek and ripped my jaw open. I was in a 'monkey fever delirium' for three days and nights, and needed twenty stitches to put my face back together. It took me three weeks to recuperate."

And that was only the beginning—Henry later contracted food poisoning and dysentery…and when the months-long jungle shooting schedule was abruptly expanded to squeeze in a second feature film before the start of the rainy season, he came down with a serious ear infection and then a liver virus. After that, there was rain. "It rained torturously for two weeks," Henry recalls. "The Amazon River swelled and overflowed, and then a typhoon struck, bringing the worst floods Rio had experienced in nearly a century." Soon afterwards, a typhoid fever epidemic swept the city.

At that point Henry had spent nearly a year filming in the jungle, and one year was enough. He returned to the United States, where he promptly sued the producers for $875,000 alleging "maltreatment, abuse, and working conditions detrimental to my health and welfare."

TARZAN'S DESERT MYSTERY (1943)

Claim to Fame: Worst of the Johnny Weissmuller *Tarzan* films.

Details: The film featured Tarzan and Boy, but no Jane—Maureen O'Sullivan was pregnant and bowed out of the film to have her child. There was still some hope she would return in a future film, so MGM left the role unfilled. Actually, there isn't a whole lot of Tarzan in the picture, either. Weissmuller spends most of the film locked away, off camera, in a prison cell; and even when he is free the most exciting scene is his battle with a man-eating plant.

Keeping Tarzan off screen may have been a good idea, though: Weissmuller, trapped in the role of Tarzan, was in the middle of one of his periodic career funks, and it shows on film. "Admittedly, Johnny had let himself get out of shape for this picture," David Fury writes. "At age 39, the years and a few too many pounds were starting to show."

THE ADVENTURES OF TURKISH TARZAN (1944)

Claim to Fame: Worst *Tarzan* ripoff ever.

Details: "While in New York on business in 1944, Tarzan producer Sol Lesser was called by a Turkish film distributor who told him that he had a Turkish Tarzan film for sale. Intrigued by the idea, Lesser set up a screening of the film, after which he confiscated it legally. The film was one of Lesser's own productions, *Tarzan's Revenge* (1938). The Turks had dubbed it and ingeniously cut in the face of a Turkish actor whenever there was a closeup." —*Tarzan of the Movies*, by Gabe Essoe

*   *   *

"The most bizarre permutation of the Tarzan character has to be Jungle Heat, an X-rated, interactive CD-ROM, in which, according to those who have viewed it before Burroughs, Inc.'s lawyer had it quashed, Tarzan plays 'the wrong kind of swinger.' "

—*Tarzan Forever*, by John Taliaferro

The
Back Side

You're not done yet:

Here are the answers
to the quizzes found on pages
39, 109, 163, 248, 268, and 308...

...And info about how to be a part
of the Bathroom Readers' Institute

ANSWERS—Presidential Quiz (page 39)

1—a) Franklin Pierce. Pierce had just learned that his own political party, the Whigs, had refused to nominate him for a second term. But there's another meaning implicit in the quote: Pierce is widely regarded by historians as the only U.S. president to be an alcoholic.

2—b) Warren G. Harding. One morning, Harding read a newspaper article about a dog in Pennsylvania that was going to be put to sleep because it had been brought into the country illegally. Harding, who loved dogs, quickly wrote a letter to the governor of Pennsylvania demanding that the termination be terminated. The governor, not wanting to go against an executive order, saw to it that the dog was taken off death row and set free.

3—c) "There they are—See No Evil, Hear No Evil, and Evil."

4—b) Franklin D. Roosevelt. One of the duties of the U.S. president is to greet and make small talk with huge crowds of people in receiving lines. At one such gathering, President Roosevelt became bored with exchanging little pleasantries. He didn't think anyone was paying attention to what he said anyway. So to prove his point, as he took each patron's hand, he said "I murdered my grandmother this morning." Most people smiled and moved on. Only one man actually listened to what Roosevelt was saying and quickly responded, "She certainly had it coming!"

5—b) A pen-and-pencil set decorated with the presidential seal and President Nixon's autograph. Why did the American military decide to drop pen-and-pencil sets over North Vietnam? The sets were originally designed to be given to Nixon's generous political contributors. The ones dropped over North Vietnam were left-overs. This gesture apparently did little to persuade the North Vietnamese to give up Communism and embrace "the American Way."

6—b) Jimmy Carter. In July 1997, a man named Michael Robinson, who worked at a restaurant in Americus, Georgia, got a credit card number from a customer—who happened to be an ex-president with a common name. Robinson went on a brief buying spree. His first stop was a music store where he purchased $45.27 worth of compact discs and charged it to the stolen credit card account. Imagine his surprise when he was arrested soon thereafter by Secret Service agents.

How did the Joseph Family Disease get its name? Only members of the Joseph Family can get it.

7—a) Andrew Jackson. President Jackson was walking down the steps of the U.S. Capitol on January 30, 1835, when suddenly Richard Lawrence, a house painter with a history of mental illness, rushed toward him. Lawrence reached into his waistcoat and pulled out a single-shot derringer. Before the president could react, Lawrence took aim and pulled the trigger. The percussion cap exploded but for some reason the gunpowder in the barrel failed to ignite. Jackson was furious and raised his cane to strike the would-be assassin. Lawrence was quicker than Old Hickory, however, and deftly pulled out another single-shot derringer and fired at the president, now standing less than four feet away. Again, the percussion cap exploded with a pop but the gunpowder failed to ignite. Lawrence was captured and taken to jail. The pistols were examined by weapons experts who concluded that both pistols were in working order—they both should have fired. The odds that two successive malfunctions on pistols of this sort would occur was calculated to be in the range of 125,000 to 1. Jackson lived another 10 years and died quietly in his bed at the Hermitage in Nashville, Tennessee, at age 78.

8—a) George Washington. That's why Washington's last words to his aide were: "I am just going. Have me decently buried and do not let my body be into a vault in less than two days after I am dead. Do you understand me?" His aide answered, "Yes."

"'Tis well," Washington replied, and then passed away.

9—a) Theodore Roosevelt. The legendary bare knuckles champion, John L. Sullivan, was touring the country and stopped in at the White House to meet—and trade punches with—the president of the United States.

10—a) Franklin D. Roosevelt. It was written before he got heavily involved in politics. The subject: the U.S.S. *Constitution*.

11—c) Ronald Reagan. While President Reagan's plane was circling over Forbes Field near Topeka, Kansas, waiting for clearance to land, security officers noticed a potential hazard. Two dogs were mating on the runway. These same two dogs had resisted earlier attempts to uncouple and were now "taxiing down the runway." The officers decided the two canines posed a danger to Reagan's plane and did the only thing they could think of—they shot them.

12—b) Abraham Lincoln. President Bill Clinton was criticized for having a large number of people spend the night in the Lincoln bedroom. But one guest who keeps showing up uninvited is Lincoln himself. There have been a number of "Lincoln sightings" by such distinguished people as Winston Churchill and Theodore Roosevelt. During her visit to the White House, Queen Wilhelmina of the Netherlands told others she had answered a knock at her door, only to find Lincoln standing there. The queen promptly fainted.

*   *   *

ANSWERS—Where'd They Get That Name? (page 109)

1—B. "The English town Boston has a name that is popularly understood to mean 'Botolphs's stone' on the grounds that the town's main church is dedicated to St. Botolph."

—*Place Names of the World*, **Adrian Room**

2—A. "In 1721, French travelers explored a section of the Louisiana Territory along the Arkansas River…searching for legendary treasure. For a long time, the Native Americans had spoken of a 'green rock' that was upstream at the 'point of rocks' along the river. When the French heard about this green rock, they thought it could only mean emeralds, which is why the expedition began.

The explorers found the point of rocks, which they called Grand Rock. Farther down the stream on the south bank, they found a smaller rock, which they named Little Rock. About a hundred years later, a permanent settlement grew up at Little Rock."

—*Why Do They Call It Topeka?*, **John W. Pursell**

3—B. "Idaho is believed to have gotten its name from a Shoshone phrase, *Ee-dah-how*, translated loosely as 'Look, the sun is coming down the mountain.'

"However, some believe the name was coined by lobbyist George M. Willing, who merely claimed it was a Native American word, which he translated as 'gem of the mountains.'"

—*Why Do They Call It Topeka?*, **John W. Pursell**

4—A. Hong Kong comes from the Chinese xianggang—xiang (hong) meaning fragrant, gang (kong) meaning harbor. It probably refers to the smell of ships carrying opium or to the incense trade which was important to the development of the port.

5—B. Kalamazoo derives from the Algonquin word *kee-ke-la-ma-zoo*, which either means "he who smokes," "boiling water," or "beautiful water." It probably refers to the rapids on the Kalamazoo River.

6—B. "French explorer Pierre LeMoyne d'Iberville came upon a red post—a *baton rouge* in his native language—while mapping the Mississppi Valley in 1699. The post marked the boundry between two Indian nations, the Bayogoulas and the Houmas."

—*A Place Called Peculiar*, **Frank K. Gallant**

7—A. "The former island in southern Brooklyn, was known as *Konihn Eiland*, 'rabbit island,' and the present name is a corrupt English form of this."

—*Place Names of the World*, **Adrian Room**

8—A. "Spanish for 'pelican,' the name was given in 1775 because of the number of such birds there."

—*American Place Names*, **John W. Pursell**

9—C. "The state capital of Kansas derives its name from a Sioux word said to mean 'good place to grow potatoes.'"

—*Place Names of the World*, **Adrian Room**

10—B. "Derives from the Spanish for 'rat's mouth,' referring to the sharply pointed rocks off the coast that were a danger to shipping."

—*Place Names of the World*, **Adrian Room**

11—C. "The local Indian tribes took their names from the cascades that ran through their region. They called the rapidly flowing stream, 'Walla Walla,' meaning 'little swift river.'"

—*The Naming of America*, **Allen Wolk**

*   *   *

ANSWERS—BRI Brainteasers (page 163)

1. The four were musicians, hired to play music during dinner.

2. Your name.

3. The French diplomats are husband and wife, both blind from birth.

4. Your right elbow.

5. I-n-c-o-r-r-e-c-t-l-y.

6. A dentist.

7. Nothing!

8. You ask either of them, "If I asked your twin which road to take to get to the hospital, which way would he tell me to go?" And then you would take the other road.

Why? If the truth-telling twin tells you what his twin would say, it would be a lie, so the direction indicated would be wrong. The lying twin would lie about what his twin would say, which would be the truth, so the lying twin would also indicate the wrong path.

9. A coffin.

*　　　*　　　*

ANSWERS—Caffeine Quiz (page 248)

1—b) About 2 cups a day.

2—False. "Decaffeinated" products can still contain small amounts of caffeine. Only beverages labeled "caffeine-free" contain no caffeine.

3—c) When you drink coffee, caffeine can be surging through your system within 5 minutes, but peak amounts are in the blood-stream after about 30 minutes.

4—False. Ounce for ounce, there's more caffeine in espresso than regular brewed coffee. But you drink much less espresso—about an ounce. So you get less caffeine in a serving of espresso than in a mug of brewed coffee.

5—False. The darkness has to do with how the beans are roasted, not how much caffeine is in them.

6—More sensitive. As you grow older, you're more likely to become sensitive to caffeine.

7—True. Only tea is more popular than coffee (not counting water).

This year, Americans will spend more than $540 million on products that control body odor.

8—b) It takes your body 3 to 6 hours to get rid of half the caffeine you've drunk. The remainder is slowly metabolized over a span of several hours. (That's why it can keep you awake at night.)

9—About 50%.

10—Generally speaking, men. And for what it's worth, smokers get rid of it faster than non-smokers.

11—True. Despite commonly held beliefs, studies have *not* linked caffeine with cancer or heart disease. In fact, studies indicate that coffee and tea may have heart-protective and cancer-preventive compounds in them. Researchers are also studying caffeine as an antidepressant and to see if it can help alcoholics.

12—b) Only 5% to 10% of the caffeine in soda is from the kola nuts used to flavor them. The rest is added by manufacturers, from caffeine extracted in decaffeinating coffee. Because kids weigh less, cans of pop can have the same kick for them that a couple of cups of coffee have for adults.

13—When colas were introduced in the 1880s, caffeine was added to provide an extra kick, just like zip from the bubbles. But according to a study released during the summer of 2000, the real reason appears to be to addict people to the drinks.

14—True. Caffeine is a diuretic, which means it pulls water from your body and makes you urinate more.

*   *   *

ANSWERS—Politically Correct Quiz (page 268)

1—a) The conductor offered a compromise: the ending would be changed so that the wolf is released into the wild instead of taken to a zoo, but the cellist refused the offer. "*Peter and the Wolf*, which teaches children to hate and fear wolves and to applaud a hunter who kills wolves, will be performed despite my protest," Conrad-Antoville wrote in a letter explaining her resignation. "I urge parents to boycott this concert."

2—a) Dogs in the park where the statue was schedule to be unveiled are required to be on a leash at all times. "I've always intended to have a leash," the artist explained after the controversy erupted, "because a man wouldn't sit on a park bench with a dog without having a leash on it. The dog wouldn't stay there. He'd probably be off chasing birds."

3—b) No comment.

4—b) What can we say?

5—c) And the opening line of the Lord's Prayer is changed to "Our Father-Mother in Heaven."

6—b) It was "commercially correct." They didn't want to offend florists who might be buying ads. Their rationale, however, was their own brand of political correctness: Please Omit Flowers "urges a boycott, just like 'don't buy grapes,' and we don't permit that," said a spokesman for the *Press*.

7—a) "I don't like that term at all," Franklin told the Johnstown, Pa., *Tribune-Democrat*. I don't consider myself a serial killer. If I'm a serial killer, then King David was a serial killer. So was Samson. I would classify myself as just a killer."

8—a) No details available.

*   *   *

ANSWERS—A Proverb By Any Other Name Quiz (page 308)

1. If you sleep with dogs, you'll wake up with fleas.

2. Live and let live.

3. United we stand, divided we fall.

4. An ounce of prevention equals a pound of cure.

5. Candy is dandy but liquor is quicker.

6. Don't look a gift horse in the mouth.

7. Beauty is skin deep.

8. Beware of Greeks bearing gifts.

9. Practice what you preach.

10. Beggars can't be choosers.

11. You can run, but you can't hide.

12. Physician, heal thyself.

went between floors at Versailles in 1743.

No Bathroom Is Complete Without...

The Best of Uncle John's Bathroom Reader®!

- All of your favorites from Volumes 1–7
- 522 pages, including:

The Birth of Puff the Magic Dragon
The Simpul Spelling Moovment
The Death of Marilyn Monroe
Start Your Own Country
About James Dean
Left-Handed Facts
Origin of Levi's
The Cola Wars
Banned Books
M*A*S*H
Plus much more!

AVAILABLE AT YOUR LOCAL BOOKSTORE!
or from the BRI
(see ordering information on page 502)

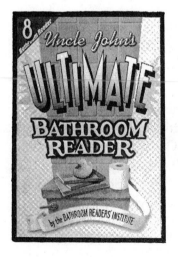

Uncle John's
Absolutely Absorbing
Bathroom Reader®

* Over 500 pages of all-new material

* Read all you would ever want to know about:

The World's Rarest Rock 'n' Roll Record
What Supermarkets Know About You
Famous Unsolved Disappearances
The World's Luckiest Accident
Uncle John's Favorite Monster
The Dark Side of Peter Pan
The Birth of Basketball
Big, Bad Barbie
Dumb Crooks

*...and a host of
other great topics!*

Come on...
TAKE THE PLUNGE!

To read a few sample articles
www.bathroomreader.com

Uncle John's
Bathroom Reader series
—— Order Info ——

Uncle John's **Supremely Satisfying** *Bathroom Reader*,
Copyright © 2001. $16.95

Uncle John's **All-Purpose Extra Strength** *Bathroom Reader*,
Copyright © 2000. $16.95

Uncle John's **Absolutely Absorbing** *Bathroom Reader*,
Copyright © 1999. $16.95

Uncle John's **Great Big** *Bathroom Reader*,
Copyright © 1998. $16.95

Uncle John's **Giant** *10th Anniversary Bathroom Reader*,
Copyright © 1997. $16.95

Uncle John's **Ultimate** *Bathroom Reader (#8)*,
Copyright © 1996. $12.95

The **Best** *of Uncle John's Bathroom Reader*,
Our favorites from *BRs #1 – #7*.
Copyright © 1995. $16.95

Uncle John's **Legendary Lost** *Bathroom Reader*,
BRs #5, #6, & #7 (See page 500)
Copyright © 1999. $18.95

For bulk orders and wholesale prices, call
(541) 488-4642 or fax (541) 482-6159. For credit card orders, visit
www.bathroomreader.com (a membership discount is available), or
simply send a check (including S & H) to the address below
U.S. Shipping & Handling rates:
• 1 book (book rate): add $3.50
• 2 – 3 books: add $4.50 • 4 – 5 books: add $5.50
• 6-10 books: add $1.00 per book

Bathroom Readers' Press
PO Box 1117, Ashland, Oregon 97520
Phone: 541-488-4642 Fax: 541-482-6159
www.bathroomreader.com

If you like reading our books...
try

VISITING THE BRI'S WEBSITE!

www.unclejohn.com
or
www.bathroomreader.com

- Visit "The Throne Room"—a great place to read!
  - Receive our *irregular* newsletters via email
    - Submit your favorite articles and facts
      - Suggest ideas for future editions
        - Order additional BRI books
          - Become a BRI member

Go With the Flow!

THE LAST PAGE

FELLOW BATHROOM READERS:
The fight for good bathroom reading should never be taken loosely—we must sit firmly for what we believe in, even while the rest of the world is taking pot shots at us.

We've proven we're not simply a flush-in-the-pan...writers and publishers will soon find their resistance unrolling.

So we invite you to take the plunge: Sit Down and Be Counted! by joining the Bathroom Readers' Institute. Send a self-addressed, stamped envelope to: BRI, PO Box 1117, Ashland, Oregon 97520. Or contact us through our website at: *www.bathroomreader.com*. You'll receive your attractive free membership card and a copy of the BRI newsletter (sent out irregularly via email), receive discounts when ordering directly through the BRI, and earn a permanent spot on the BRI honor roll!

☞   ☞   ☞

UNCLE JOHN'S NEXT BATHROOM READER IS IN THE WORKS!

Well, we've survived (barely) another year of satisfying your bathroom reading needs, but don't fret—there's more on the way. In fact, there are a few ways *you* can contribute to the next volume:

• Is there a subject you'd like to see us research? Write to us or contact us through our website (*www.bathroomreader.com*) and let us know. We aim to please.

• Have you seen or read an article you'd recommend as quintessential bathroom reading? Or is there a passage in a book or website that you want to share with us and other BRI members? Tell us how to find it. If you're the first to suggest it and we publish it in the next volume, there's a free book in it for you.

Well, we're out of space, and when you've gotta go, you've gotta go. Hope to hear from you soon. Meanwhile, remember:

Go with the flow!